Eric,

My dear friend + colleague, [...] a great blessing to me and one of the gre[...] blessings you have brought to me is knowledge of the R system. Thank you for this and the many other contributions you have made to my life.

Best Regards,
Danny K. How, 17 AUGUST 2010
Psalms 19:1

Statistics and Computing

Series Editors:
J. Chambers
D. Hand
W. Härdle

Statistics and Computing

John M. Chambers

Software for Data Analysis

Programming with R

 Springer

John Chambers
Department of Statistics–Sequoia Hall
390 Serra Mall
Stanford University
Stanford, CA 94305-4065
USA
jmc@r-project.org

Series Editors:

John Chambers	W. Härdle	David Hand
Department of Statistics–Sequoia Hall	Institut für Statistik und Ökonometrie	Department of Mathematics South Kensington Campus
390 Serra Mall	Humboldt-Universität zu Berlin	Imperial College London
Stanford University	Spandauer Str. 1	London, SW7 2AZ
Stanford, CA 94305-4065	D-10178 Berlin	United Kingdom
USA	Germany	

ISBN: 978-0-387-75935-7   e-ISBN: 978-0-387-75936-4
DOI: 10.1007/978-0-387-75936-4

Library of Congress Control Number: 2008922937

Preface

This is a book about *Software for Data Analysis*: using computer software to extract information from some source of data by organizing, visualizing, modeling, or performing any other relevant computation on the data. We all seem to be swimming in oceans of data in the modern world, and tasks ranging from scientific research to managing a business require us to extract meaningful information from the data using computer software.

This book is aimed at those who need to select, modify, and create software to explore data. In a word, programming. Our programming will center on the R system. R is an open-source software project widely used for computing with data and giving users a huge base of techniques. Hence, *Programming with R*.

R provides a general language for interactive computations, supported by techniques for data organization, graphics, numerical computations, model-fitting, simulation, and many other tasks. The core system itself is greatly supplemented and enriched by a huge and rapidly growing collection of software packages built on R and, like R, largely implemented as open-source software. Furthermore, R is designed to encourage learning and developing, with easy starting mechanisms for programming and also techniques to help you move on to more serious applications. The complete picture—the R system, the language, the available packages, and the programming environment—constitutes an unmatched resource for computing with data.

At the same time, the "with" word in *Programming with R* is important. No software system is sufficient for exploring data, and we emphasize interfaces between systems to take advantage of their respective strengths.

Is it worth taking time to develop or extend your skills in such programming? Yes, because the investment can pay off both in the ability to ask questions and in the trust you can have in the answers. Exploring data with the right questions and providing trustworthy answers to them are the key to analyzing data, and the twin principles that will guide us.

What's in the book?

A sequence of chapters in the book takes the reader on successive steps from user to programmer to contributor, in the gradual progress that R encourages. Specifically: using R; simple programming; packages; classes and methods; inter-system interfaces (Chapters 2; 3; 4; 9 and 10; 11 and 12). The order reflects a natural progression, but the chapters are largely independent, with many cross references to encourage browsing.

Other chapters explore computational techniques needed at all stages: basic computations; graphics; computing with text (Chapters 6; 7; 8). Lastly, a chapter (13) discusses how R works and the appendix covers some topics in the history of the language.

Woven throughout are a number of reasonably serious examples, ranging from a few paragraphs to several pages, some of them continued elsewhere as they illustrate different techniques. See "Examples" in the index. I encourage you to explore these as leisurely as time permits, thinking about how the computations evolve, and how you would approach these or similar examples.

The book has a companion R package, SoDA, obtainable from the main CRAN repository, as described in Chapter 4. A number of the functions and classes developed in the book are included in the package. The package also contains code for most of the examples; see the documentation for "Examples" in the package.

Even at five hundred pages, the book can only cover a fraction of the relevant topics, and some of those receive a pretty condensed treatment. Spending time alternately on reading, thinking, and interactive computation will help clarify much of the discussion, I hope. Also, the final word is with the online documentation and especially with the software; a substantial benefit of open-source software is the ability to drill down and see what's really happening.

Who should read this book?

I've written this book with three overlapping groups of readers generally in mind.

First, "data analysts"; that is, anyone with an interest in exploring data, especially in serious scientific studies. This includes statisticians, certainly, but increasingly others in a wide range of disciplines where data-rich studies now require such exploration. Helping to enable exploration is our mission here. I hope and expect that you will find that working with R and related software enhances your ability to learn from the data relevant to your interests.

If you have not used R or S-Plus® before, you should precede this book (or at least supplement it) with a more basic presentation. There are a number of books and an even larger number of Web sites. Try searching with a combination of "introduction" or "introductory" along with "R". Books by W. John Braun and Duncan J. Murdoch [2], Michael Crawley [11], Peter Dalgaard [12], and John Verzani [24], among others, are general introductions (both to R and to statistics). Other books and Web sites are beginning to appear that introduce R or S-Plus with a particular area of application in mind; again, some Web searching with suitable terms may find a presentation attuned to your interests.

A second group of intended readers are people involved in research or teaching related to statistical techniques and theory. R and other modern software systems have become essential in the research itself and in communicating its results to the community at large. Most graduate-level programs in statistics now provide some introduction to R. This book is intended to guide you on the followup, in which your software becomes more important to your research, and often a way to share results and techniques with the community. I encourage you to push forward and organize your software to be reusable and extendible, including the prospect of creating an R package to communicate your work to others. Many of the R packages now available derive from such efforts..

The third target group are those more directly interested in software and programming, particularly software for data analysis. The efforts of the R community have made it an excellent medium for "packaging" software and providing it to a large community of users. R is maintained on all the widely used operating systems for computing with data and is easy for users to install. Its package mechanism is similarly well maintained, both in the central CRAN repository and in other repositories. Chapter 4 covers both using packages and creating your own. R can also incorporate work done in other systems, through a wide range of inter-system interfaces (discussed in Chapters 11 and 12).

Many potential readers in the first and second groups will have some experience with R or other software for statistics, but will view their involvement as doing only what's absolutely necessary to "get the answers". This book will encourage moving on to think of the interaction with the software as an important and valuable part of your activity. You may feel inhibited by not having done much programming before. Don't be. Programming with

R can be approached gradually, moving from easy and informal to more ambitious projects. As you use R, one of its strengths is its flexibility. By making simple changes to the commands you are using, you can customize interactive graphics or analysis to suit your needs. This is the takeoff point for programming: As Chapters 3 and 4 show, you can move from this first personalizing of your computations through increasingly ambitious steps to create your own software. The end result may well be your own contribution to the world of R-based software.

How should you read this book?

Any way that you find helpful or enjoyable, of course. But an author often imagines a conversation with a reader, and it may be useful to share my version of that. In many of the discussions, I imagine a reader pausing to decide how to proceed, whether with a specific technical point or to choose a direction for a new stage in a growing involvement with software for data analysis. Various chapters chart such stages in a voyage that many R users have taken from initial, casual computing to a full role as a contributor to the community. Most topics will also be clearer if you can combine reading with hands-on interaction with R and other software, in particular using the Examples in the SoDA package.

This pausing for reflection and computing admittedly takes a little time. Often, you will just want a "recipe" for a specific task—what is often called the "cookbook" approach. By "cookbook" in software we usually imply that one looks a topic up in the index and finds a corresponding explicit recipe. That should work sometimes with this book, but we concentrate more on general techniques and extended examples, with the hope that these will equip readers to deal with a wider range of tasks. For the reader in a hurry, I try to insert pointers to online documentation and other resources.

As an enthusiastic cook, though, I would point out that the great cookbooks offer a range of approaches, similar to the distinction here. Some, such as the essential *Joy of Cooking* do indeed emphasize brief, explicit recipes. The best of these books are among the cook's most valuable resources. Other books, such as Jacques Pépin's masterful *La Technique*, teach you just that: techniques to be applied. Still others, such as the classic *Mastering the Art of French Cooking* by Julia Child and friends, are about learning and about underlying concepts as much as about specific techniques. It's the latter two approaches that most resemble the goals of the present book. The book presents a number of explicit recipes, but the deeper emphasis is in on concepts and techniques. And behind those in turn, there will be two general principles of good software for data analyis.

Acknowledgments

The ideas discussed in the book, as well as the software itself, are the results of projects involving many people and stretching back more than thirty years (see the appendix for a little history).

Such a scope of participants and time makes identifying all the individuals a hopeless task, so I will take refuge in identifying groups, for the most part. The most recent group, and the largest, consists of the "contributors to R", not easy to delimit but certainly comprising hundreds of people at the least. Centrally, my colleagues in R-core, responsible for the survival, dissemination, and evolution of R itself. These are supplemented by other volunteers providing additional essential support for package management and distribution, both generally and specifically for repositories such as CRAN, BioConductor, omegahat, RForge and others, as well as the maintainers of essential information resources—archives of mailing lists, search engines, and many tutorial documents. Then the authors of the thousands of packages and other software forming an unprecedented base of techniques; finally, the interested users who question and prod through the mailing lists and other communication channels, seeking improvements. This community as a whole is responsible for realizing something we could only hazily articulate thirty-plus years ago, and in a form and at a scale far beyond our imaginings.

More narrowly from the viewpoint of this book, discussions within R-core have been invaluable in teaching me about R, and about the many techniques and facilities described throughout the book. I am only too aware of the many remaining gaps in my knowledge, and of course am responsible for all inaccuracies in the descriptions herein.

Looking back to the earlier evolution of the S language and software, time has brought an increasing appreciation of the contribution of colleagues and management in Bell Labs research in that era, providing a nourishing environment for our efforts, perhaps indeed a unique environment. Rick Becker, Allan Wilks, Trevor Hastie, Daryl Pregibon, Diane Lambert, and W. S. Cleveland, along with many others, made essential contributions.

Since retiring from Bell Labs in 2005, I have had the opportunity to interact with a number of groups, including students and faculty at several universities. Teaching and discussions at Stanford over the last two academic years have been very helpful, as were previous interactions at UCLA and at Auckland University. My thanks to all involved, with special thanks to Trevor Hastie, Mark Hansen, Ross Ihaka and Chris Wild.

A number of the ideas and opinions in the book benefited from collaborations and discussions with Duncan Temple Lang, and from discussions with Robert Gentleman, Luke Tierney, and other experts on R, not that any of them should be considered at all responsible for defects therein.

The late Gene Roddenberry provided us all with some handy terms, and much else to be enjoyed and learned from.

Each of our books since the beginning of S has had the benefit of the editorial guidance of John Kimmel; it has been a true and valuable collaboration, long may it continue.

John Chambers
Palo Alto, California
January, 2008

PS: The Web page `stat.stanford.edu/~jmc4/errata` contains corrections and notes on developments since the initial publication of the book.

Contents

Chapter 1

Introduction: Principles and Concepts

This chapter presents some of the concepts and principles that recur throughout the book. We begin with the two guiding principles: the mission to explore and the responsibility to be trustworthy (Sections 1.1 and 1.2). With these as guidelines, we then introduce some concepts for programming with R (Section 1.3, page 4) and add some justification for our emphasis on that system (Section 1.4, page 9).

1.1 Exploration: The Mission

The first principle I propose is that our *Mission*, as users and creators of software for data analysis, is to enable the best and most thorough exploration of data possible. That means that users of the software must be able to ask the meaningful questions about their applications, quickly and flexibly.

Notice that speed here is human speed, measured in clock time. It's the time that the actual computations take, but usually more importantly, it's also the time required to formulate the question and to organize the data in a way to answer it. This is the exploration, and software for data analysis makes it possible. A wide range of techniques is needed to access and transform data, to make predictions or summaries, to communicate results to others, and to deal with ongoing processes.

Whenever we consider techniques for these and other requirements in the chapters that follow, the first principle we will try to apply is the *Mission*:

1

How can these techniques help people to carry out this specific kind of exploration?

Ensuring that software for data analysis exists for such purposes is an important, exciting, and challenging activity. Later chapters examine how we can select and develop software using R and other systems.

The importance, excitement, and challenge all come from the central role that data and computing have come to play in modern society. Science, business and many other areas of society continually rely on understanding data, and that understanding frequently involves large and complicated data processes.

A few examples current as the book is written can suggest the flavor:

- Many ambitious projects are underway or proposed to deploy *sensor networks*, that is, coordinated networks of devices to record a variety of measurements in an ongoing program. The data resulting is essential to understand environmental quality, the mechanisms of weather and climate, and the future of biodiversity in the earth's ecosystems. In both scale and diversity, the challenge is unprecedented, and will require merging techniques from many disciplines.

- Astronomy and cosmology are undergoing profound changes as a result of large-scale digital mappings enabled by both satellite and ground recording of huge quantities of data. The scale of data collected allows questions to be addressed in an overall sense that before could only be examined in a few, local regions.

- Much business activity is now carried out largely through distributed, computerized processes that both generate large and complex streams of data and also offer through such data an unprecedented opportunity to understand one's business quantitatively. Telecommunications in North America, for example, generates databases with conceptually billions of records. To explore and understand such data has great attraction for the business (and for society), but is enormously challenging.

These and many other possible examples illustrate the importance of what John Tukey long ago characterized as "the peaceful collision of computing and data analysis". Progress on any of these examples will require the ability to explore the data, flexibly and in a reasonable time frame.

1.2   Trustworthy Software: The Prime Directive

Exploration is our mission; we and those who use our software want to find new paths to understand the data and the underlying processes. The mission is, indeed, to boldly go where no one has gone before. But, we need boldness to be balanced by our responsibility. We have a responsibility for the results of data analysis that provides a key compensating principle.

The complexity of the data processes and of the computations applied to them mean that those who receive the results of modern data analysis have limited opportunity to verify the results by direct observation. Users of the analysis have no option but to trust the analysis, and by extension the software that produced it. Both the data analyst and the software provider therefore have a strong responsibility to produce a result that is trustworthy, and, if possible, one that can be *shown* to be trustworthy.

This is the second principle: the computations and the software for data analysis should be trustworthy: they should do what they claim, and be seen to do so. Neither those who view the results of data analysis nor, in many cases, the statisticians performing the analysis can directly validate extensive computations on large and complicated data processes. Ironically, the steadily increasing computer power applied to data analysis often distances the results further from direct checking by the recipient. The many computational steps between original data source and displayed results must all be truthful, or the effect of the analysis may be worthless, if not pernicious. This places an obligation on all creators of software to program in such a way that the computations can be understood and trusted. This obligation I label the *Prime Directive*.

Note that the directive in no sense discourages exploratory or approximate methods. As John Tukey often remarked, better an approximate answer to the right question than an exact answer to the wrong question. We should seek answers boldly, but always explaining the nature of the method applied, in an open and understandable format, supported by as much evidence of its quality as can be produced. As we will see, a number of more technically specific choices can help us satisfy this obligation.

Readers who have seen the *Star Trek*® television series[1] may recognize the term "prime directive". Captains Kirk, Picard, and Janeway and their crews were bound by a directive which (slightly paraphrased) was: Do nothing to interfere with the natural course of a new civilization. Do not distort

---

[1] Actually, at least five series, from "The Original" in 1966 through "Enterprise", not counting the animated version, plus many films. See `startrek.com` and the many reruns if this is a gap in your cultural background.

the development. Our directive is not to distort the message of the data, and to provide computations whose content can be trusted and understood.

The prime directive of the space explorers, notice, was not their *mission* but rather an important safeguard to apply in pursuing that mission. Their mission was to explore, to "boldly go where no one has gone before", and all that. That's really our mission too: to explore how software can add new abilities for data analysis. And our own prime directive, likewise, is an important caution and guiding principle as we create the software to support our mission.

Here, then, are two motivating principles: the mission, which is bold exploration; and the prime directive, trustworthy software. We will examine in the rest of the book how to select and program software for data analysis, with these principles as guides. A few aspects of R will prove to be especially relevant; let's examine those next.

1.3 Concepts for Programming with R

The software and the programming techniques to be discussed in later chapters tend to share some concepts that make them helpful for data analysis. Exploiting these concepts will often benefit both the effectiveness of programming and the quality of the results. Each of the concepts arises naturally in later chapters, but it's worth outlining them together here for an overall picture of our strategy in programming for data analysis.

Functional Programming

Software in R is written in a *functional style* that helps both to understand the intent and to ensure that the implementation corresponds to that intent. Computations are organized around functions, which can encapsulate specific, meaningful computational results, with implementations that can be examined for their correctness. The style derives from a more formal theory of *functional programming* that restricts the computations to obtain well-defined or even formally verifiable results. Clearly, programming in a fully functional manner would contribute to trustworthy software. The S language does not enforce a strict functional programming approach, but does carry over some of the flavor, particularly when you make some effort to emphasize simple functional definitions with minimal use of non-functional computations.

As the scope of the software expands, much of the benefit from functional style can be retained by using *functional methods* to deal with varied types of data, within the general goal defined by the generic function.

Classes and Methods

The natural complement to functional style in programming is the definition of classes of objects. Where functions should clearly encapsulate the actions in our analysis, classes should encapsulate the nature of the objects used and returned by calls to functions. The duality between function calls and objects is a recurrent theme of programming with R. In the design of new classes, we seek to capture an underlying concept of what the objects mean. The relevant techniques combine directly specifying the contents (the slots), relating the new class to existing classes (the inheritance), and expressing how objects should be created and validated (methods for initializing and validating).

Method definitions knit together functions and classes. Well-designed methods extend the generic definition of what a function does to provide a specific computational method when the argument or arguments come from specified classes, or inherit from those classes. In contrast to methods that are solely class-based, as in common object-oriented programming languages such as C++ or Java, methods in R are part of a rich but complex network of functional and object-based computation.

The ability to define classes and methods in fact is itself a major advantage in adhering to the *Prime Directive*. It gives us a way to isolate and define formally what information certain objects should contain and how those objects should behave when functions are applied to them.

Data Frames

Trustworthy data analysis depends first on trust in the data being analyzed. Not so much that the data must be perfect, which is impossible in nearly any application and in any case beyond our control, but rather that trust in the analysis depends on trust in the relation between the data as we use it and the data as it has entered the process and then has been recorded, organized and transformed.

In serious modern applications, the data usually comes from a process external to the analysis, whether generated by scientific observations, commercial transactions or any of many other human activities. To access the data for analysis by well-defined and trustworthy computations, we will benefit from having a description, or model, for the data that corresponds to its natural home (often in DBMS or spreadsheet software), but can also be a meaningful basis for data as used in the analysis. Transformations and restructuring will often be needed, but these should be understandable and defensible.

The model we will emphasize is the *data frame*, essentially a formulation of the traditional view of observations and variables. The data frame has a long history in the S language but modern techniques for classes and methods allow us to extend the use of the concept. Particularly useful techniques arise from using the data frame concept both within R, for model-fitting, data visualization, and other computations, and also for effective communication with other systems. Spreadsheets and relational database software both relate naturally to this model; by using it along with unambiguous mechanisms for interfacing with such software, the meaning and structure of the data can be preserved. Not all applications suit this approach by any means, but the general data frame model provides a valuable basis for trustworthy organization and treatment of many sources of data.

Open Source Software

Turning to the general characteristics of the languages and systems available, note that many of those discussed in this book are *open-source* software systems; for example, R, Perl, Python, many of the database systems, and the Linux operating system. These systems all provide access to source code sufficient to generate a working version of the software. The arrangement is not equivalent to "public-domain" software, by which people usually mean essentially unrestricted use and copying. Instead, most open-source systems come with a copyright, usually held by a related group or foundation, and with a license restricting the use and modification of the software. There are several versions of license, the best known being the Gnu General Public License and its variants (see `gnu.org/copyleft/gpl.html`), the famous GPL. R is distributed under a version of this license (see the `"COPYING"` file in the home directory of R). A variety of other licenses exists; those accepted by the *Open Source Initiative* are described at `opensource.org/licenses`.

Distinctions among open-source licenses generate a good deal of heat in some discussions, often centered on what effect the license has on the usability of the software for commercial purposes. For our focus, particularly for the concern with trustworthy software for data analysis, these issues are not directly relevant. The popularity of open-source systems certainly owes a lot to their being thought of as "free", but for our goal of trustworthy software, this is also not the essential property. Two other characteristics contribute more. First, the simple openness itself allows any sufficiently competent observer to enquire fully about what is actually being computed. There are no intrinsic limitations to the validation of the software, in the sense that it is all there. Admittedly, only a minority of users are likely to delve very far into the details of the software, but some do. The ability to examine and critique every part of the software makes for an open-ended scope for verifying the results.

Second, open-source systems demonstrably generate a spirit of community among contributors and active users. User groups, e-mail lists, chat rooms and other socializing mechanisms abound, with vigorous discussion and controversy, but also with a great deal of effort devoted to testing and extension of the systems. The active and demanding community is a key to trustworthy software, as well as to making useful tools readily available.

Algorithms and Interfaces

R is explicitly seen as built on a set of routines accessed by an interface, in particular by making use of computations in C or Fortran. User-written extensions can make use of such interfaces, but the core of R is itself built on them as well. Aside from routines that implement R-dependent techniques, there are many basic computations for numerical results, data manipulation, simulation, and other specific computational tasks. These implementations we can term *algorithms*. Many of the core computations on which the R software depends are now implemented by collections of such software that are widely used and tested. The algorithm collections have a long history, often predating the larger-scale open-source systems. It's an important concept in programming with R to seek out such algorithms and make them part of a new computation. You should be able to import the trust built up in the non-R implementation to make your own software more trustworthy.

Major collections on a large scale and many smaller, specialized algorithms have been written, generally in the form of subroutines in Fortran, C, and a few other general programming languages. Thirty-plus years ago, when I was writing *Computational Methods for Data Analysis*, those who wanted to do innovative data analysis often had to work directly from such routines for numerical computations or simulation, among other topics. That book expected readers to search out the routines and install them in the readers' own computing environment, with many details left unspecified.

An important and perhaps under-appreciated contribution of R and other systems has been to embed high-quality algorithms for many computations in the system itself, automatically available to users. For example, key parts of the LAPACK collection of computations for numerical linear algebra are included in R, providing a basis for fitting linear models and for other matrix computations. Other routines in the collection may not be included, perhaps because they apply to special datatypes or computations not often encountered. These routines can still be used with R in nearly all cases, by writing an interface to the routine (see Chapter 11).

Similarly, the internal code for pseudo-random number generation includes most of the well-regarded and thoroughly tested algorithms for this purpose. Other tasks, such as sorting and searching, also use quality algorithms. Open-source systems provide an advantage when incorporating such algorithms, because alert users can examine in detail the support for computations. In the case of R, users do indeed question and debate the behavior of the system, sometimes at great length, but overall to the benefit of our trust in programming with R.

The best of the algorithm collections offer another important boost for trustworthy software in that the software may have been used in a wide variety of applications, including some where quality of results is critically important. Collections such as LAPACK are among the best-tested substantial software projects in existence, and not only by users of higher-level systems. Their adaptability to a wide range of situations is also a frequent benefit.

The process of incorporating quality algorithms in a user-oriented system such as R is ongoing. Users can and should seek out the best computations for their needs, and endeavor to make these available for their own use and, through packages, for others as well.

Incorporating algorithms in the sense of subroutines in C or Fortran is a special case of what we call *inter-system interfaces* in this book. The general concept is similar to that for algorithms. Many excellent software systems exist for a variety of purposes, including text-manipulation, spreadsheets, database management, and many others. Our approach to software for data analysis emphasizes R as the central system, for reasons outlined in the next section. In any case, most users will prefer to have a single home system for their data analysis.

That does not mean that we should or can absorb all computations directly into R. This book emphasizes the value of expressing computations in a natural way while making use of high-quality implementations in whatever system is suitable. A variety of techniques, explored in Chapter 12, allows us to retain a consistent approach in programming with R at the same time.

1.4 The **R** System and the **S** Language

This book includes computations in a variety of languages and systems, for tasks ranging from database management to text processing. Not all systems receive equal treatment, however. The central activity is data analysis, and the discussion is from the perspective that our data analysis is mainly expressed in R; when we examine computations, the results are seen from an interactive session with R. This view does not preclude computations done partly or entirely in other systems, and these computations may be complete in themselves. The data analysis that the software serves, however, is nearly always considered to be in R.

Chapter 2 covers the use of R broadly but briefly (if you have no experience with it, you might want to consult one of the introductory books or other sources mentioned on page vii in the preface). The present section give a brief summary of the system and relates it to the philosophy of the book.

R is an open-source software system, supported by a group of volunteers from many countries. The central control is in the hands of a group called R-core, with the active collaboration of a much larger group of contributors. The base system provides an interactive language for numerical computations, data management, graphics and a variety of related calculations. It can be installed on Windows, Mac OS X, and Linux operating systems, with a variety of graphical user interfaces. Most importantly, the base system is supported by well over a thousand packages on the central repository `cran.r-project.org` and in other collections.

R began as a research project of Ross Ihaka and Robert Gentleman in the 1990s, described in a paper in 1996 [17]. It has since expanded into software used to implement and communicate most new statistical techniques. The software in R implements a version of the S language, which was designed much earlier by a group of us at Bell Laboratories, described in a series of books ([1], [6], and [5] in the bibliography).

The S-Plus system also implements the S language. Many of the computations discussed in the book work in S-Plus as well, although there are important differences in the evaluation model, noted in later chapters. For more on the history of S, see Appendix A, page 475.

The majority of the software in R is itself written in the same language used for interacting with the system, a dialect of the S language. The language evolved in essentially its present form during the 1980s, with a generally functional style, in the sense used on page 4: The basic unit of programming is a function. Function calls usually compute an object that is a *function* of the objects passed in as arguments, without side effects to those arguments. Subsequent evolution of the language introduced formal classes and methods, again in the sense discussed in the previous section. Methods are specializations of functions according to the class of one or more of the arguments. Classes define the content of objects, both directly and through inheritance. R has added a number of features to the language, while remaining largely compatible with S. All these topics are discussed in the present book, particularly in Chapters 3 for functions and basic programming, 9 for classes, and 10 for methods.

So why concentrate on R? Clearly, and not at all coincidentally, R reflects the same philosophy that evolved through the S language and the approach to data analysis at Bell Labs, and which largely led me to the concepts I'm proposing in this book. It is relevant that S began as a medium for statistics researchers to express their own computations, in support of research into data analysis and its applications. A direct connection leads from there to the large community that now uses R similarly to implement new ideas in statistics, resulting in the huge resource of R packages.

Added to the characteristics of the language is R's open-source nature, exposing the system to continual scrutiny by users. It includes some algorithms for numerical computations and simulation that likewise reflect modern, open-source computational standards in these fields. The LAPACK software for numerical linear algebra is an example, providing trustworthy computations to support statistical methods that depend on linear algebra.

Although there is plenty of room for improvement and for new ideas, I believe R currently represents the best medium for quality software in support of data analysis, and for the implementation of the principles espoused in the present book. From the perspective of our first development of S some thirty-plus years ago, it's a cause for much gratitude and not a little amazement.

Chapter 2

Using R

This chapter covers the essentials for using R to explore data interactively. Section 2.1 covers basic access to an R session. Users interact with R through a single language for both data analysis and programming (Section 2.3, page 19). The key concepts are function calls in the language and the objects created and used by those calls (2.4, 24), two concepts that recur throughout the book. The huge body of available software is organized around packages that can be attached to the session, once they are installed (2.5, 25). The system itself can be downloaded and installed from repositories on the Web (2.6, 29); there are also a number of resources on the Web for information about R (2.7, 31).

Lastly, we examine aspects of R that may raise difficulties for some new users (2.8, 34).

2.1 Starting R

R runs on the commonly used platforms for personal computing: Windows®, Mac OS X®, Linux, and some versions of UNIX®. In the usual desktop environments for these platforms, users will typically start R as they would most applications, by clicking on the R icon or on the R file in a folder of applications.

An application will then appear looking much like other applications on the platform: for example, a window and associated toolbar. In the

11

standard version, at least on most platforms, the application is called the
"R Console". In Windows recently it looked like this:

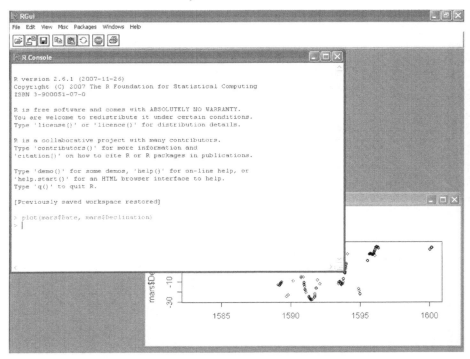

The application has a number of drop-down menus; some are typical of most
applications ("File", "Edit", and "Help"). Others such as "Packages" are
special to R. The real action in running R, however, is not with the menus
but in the console window itself. Here the user is expected to type input to R
in the form of expressions; the program underlying the application responds
by doing some computation and if appropriate by displaying a version of the
results for the user to look at (printed results normally in the same console
window, graphics typically in another window).

    This interaction between user and system continues, and constitutes an
R session. The session is the fundamental user interface to R. The following
section describes the logic behind it. A session has a simple model for
user interaction, but one that is fundamentally different from users' most
common experience with personal computers (in applications such as word
processors, Web browsers, or audio/video systems). First-time users may
feel abandoned, left to flounder on their own with little guidance about what
to do and even less help when they do something wrong. More guidance is
available than may be obvious, but such users are not entirely wrong in their

reaction. After intervening sections present the essential concepts involved in using R, Section 2.8, page 34 revisits this question.

2.2   An Interactive Session

Everything that you do interactively with R happens in a *session*. A session starts when you start up R, typically as described above. A session can also be started from other special interfaces or from a command shell (the original design), without changing the fundamental concept and with the basic appearance remaining as shown in this section and in the rest of the book. Some other interfaces arise in customizing the session, on page 17.

During an R session, you (the user) provide expressions for evaluation by R, for the purpose of doing any sort of computation, displaying results, and creating objects for further use. The session ends when you decide to quit from R.

All the expressions evaluated in the session are just that: general *expressions* in R's version of the S language. Documentation may mention "commands" in R, but the term just refers to a complete expression that you type interactively or otherwise hand to R for evaluation. There's only one language, used for either interactive data analysis or for programming, and described in section 2.3. Later sections in the book come back to examine it in more detail, especially in Chapter 3.

The R evaluator displays a prompt, and the user responds by typing a line of text. Printed output from the evaluation and other messages appear following the input line.

Examples in the book will be displayed in this form, with the default prompts preceding the user's input:

```
> quantile(Declination)
    0%     25%     50%     75%    100%
-27.98 -11.25   8.56   17.46   27.30
```

The "> " at the beginning of the example is the (default) prompt string. In this example the user responded with

```
quantile(Declination)
```

The evaluator will keep prompting until the input can be interpreted as a complete expression; if the user had left off the closing ")", the evaluator would have prompted for more input. Since the input here is a complete expression, the system evaluated it. To be pedantic, it parsed the input text and evaluated the resulting object. The evaluation in this case amounts to calling a function named `quantile`.

The printed output may suggest a table, and that's intentional. But in fact nothing special happened; the standard action by the evaluator is to print the object that is the value of the expression. All evaluated expressions are objects; the printed output corresponds to the object; specifically, the form of printed output is determined by the kind of object, by its *class* (technically, through a method selected for that class). The call to `quantile()` returned a numeric vector, that is, an object of class `"numeric"`. A method was selected based on this class, and the method was called to print the result shown. The `quantile()` function expects a vector of numbers as its argument; with just this one argument it returns a numeric vector containing the minimum, maximum, median and quartiles.

The method for printing numeric vectors prints the values in the vector, five of them in this case. Numeric objects can optionally have a `names` attribute; if they do, the method prints the names as labels above the numbers. So the `"0%"` and so on are part of the object. The designer of the `quantile()` function helpfully chose a names attribute for the result that makes it easier to interpret when printed.

All these details are unimportant if you're just calling `quantile()` to summarize some data, but the important general concept is this: Objects are the center of computations in R, along with the function calls that create and use those objects. The duality of objects and function calls will recur in many of our discussions.

Computing with existing software hinges largely on using and creating objects, via the large number of available functions. Programming, that is, creating *new* software, starts with the simple creation of function objects. More ambitious projects often use a paradigm of creating new classes of objects, along with new or modified functions and methods that link the functions and classes. In all the details of programming, the fundamental duality of objects and functions remains an underlying concept.

Essentially all expressions are evaluated as function calls, but the language includes some forms that don't look like function calls. Included are the usual operators, such as arithmetic, discussed on page 21. Another useful operator is `` `?` ``, which looks up R help for the topic that follows the question mark. To learn about the function `quantile()`:

```
> ?quantile
```

In standard GUI interfaces, the documentation will appear in a separate window, and can be generated from a pull-down menu as well as from the

`?` operator.

Graphical displays provide some of the most powerful techniques in data analysis, and functions for data visualization and other graphics are an essential part of R:

```
> plot(Date, Declination)
```

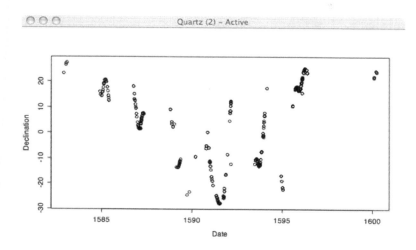

Here the user typed another expression, `plot(Date, Declination)`; in this case producing a scatter plot as a side effect, but no printed output. The graphics during an interactive session typically appear in one or more separate windows created by the GUI, in this example a window using the native `quartz()` graphics device for Mac OS X. Graphic output can also be produced in a form suitable for inclusion in a document, such as output in a general file format (PDF or postscript, for example). Computations for graphics are discussed in more detail in Chapter 7.

The sequence of expression and evaluation shown in the examples is essentially all there is to an interactive session. The user supplies expressions and the system evaluates them, one after another. Expressions that produce simple summaries or plots are usually done to see something, either graphics or printed output. Aside from such immediate gratification, most expressions are there in order to assign objects, which can then be used in later computations:

```
> fitK <- gam(Kyphosis ~ s(Age, 4) + Number, family = binomial)
```

Evaluating this expression calls the function `gam()` and assigns the value of the call, associating that object with the name `fitK`. For the rest of the session, unless some other assignment to this name is carried out, fitK can be used in any expression to refer to that object; for example, coef(fitK) would call a function to extract some coefficients from fitK (which is in this example a fitted model).

Assignments are a powerful and interesting part of the language. The basic idea is all we need for now, and is in any case the key concept: Assignment associates an object with a name. The term "associates" has a specific meaning here. Whenever any expression is evaluated, the context of the evaluation includes a local *environment*, and it is into this environment that the object is assigned, under the corresponding name. The object and name are associated in the environment, by the assignment operation. From then on, the name can be used as a *reference* to the object in the environment. When the assignment takes place at the "top level" (in an input expression in the session), the environment involved is the *global* environment. The global environment is part of the current session, and all objects assigned there remain available for further computations in the session.

Environments are an important part of programming with R. They are also tricky to deal with, because they behave differently from other objects. Discussion of environments continues in Section 2.4, page 24.

A session ends when the user quits from R, either by evaluating the expression q() or by some other mechanism provided by the user interface. Before ending the session, the system offers the user a chance to save all the objects in the global environment at the end of the session:

```
>  q()
Save workspace image? [y/n/c]: y
```

If the user answers yes, then when a new session is started in the same working directory, the global environment will be restored. Technically, the environment is restored, not the session. Some actions you took in the session, such as attaching packages or using options(), may not be restored, if they don't correspond to objects in the global environment.

Unfortunately, your session may end involuntarily: the evaluator may be forced to terminate the session or some outside event may kill the process. R tries to save the workspace even when fatal errors occur in low-level C or Fortran computations, and such disasters should be rare in the core R computations and in well-tested packages. But to be truly safe, you should explicitly back up important results to a file if they will be difficult to recreate. See documentation for functions save() and dump() for suitable techniques.

Customizing the **R** session

As you become a more involved user of R, you may want to customize your interaction with it to suit your personal preferences or the goals motivating your applications. The nature of the system lends itself to a great variety of options from the most general to trivial details.

At the most general is the choice of user interface. So far, we have assumed you will start R as you would start other applications on your computer, say by clicking on the R icon.

A second approach, available on any system providing both R and a command shell, is to invoke R as a shell command. In its early history, S in all its forms was typically started as a program from an interactive shell. Before multi-window user interfaces, the shell would be running on an interactive terminal of some sort, or even on the machine's main console. Nowadays, shells or terminal applications run in their own windows, either supported directly by the platform or indirectly through a client window system, such as those based on X11. Invoking R from a shell allows some flexibility that may not be provided directly by the application (such as running with a C-level debugger). Online documentation from a shell command is printed text by default, which is not as convenient as a browser interface. To initiate a browser interface to the help facility, see the documentation for `help.start()`.

A third approach, somewhat in between the first two, is to use a GUI based on another application or language, potentially one that runs on multiple platforms. The most actively supported example of this approach is ESS, a general set of interface tools in the emacs editor. ESS stands for Emacs Speaks Statistics, and the project supports other statistical systems as well as R; see `ess.r-project.org`. For those who love emacs as a general computational environment, ESS provides a variety of GUI-like features, plus a user-interface programmability characteristic of emacs. The use of a GUI based on a platform-independent user interface has advantages for those who need to work regularly on more than one operating system.

Finally, an R session can be run in a non-interactive form, usually invoked in a batch mode from a command shell, with its input taken from a file or other source. R can also be invoked from within another application, as part of an inter-system interface.

In all these situations, the logic of the R session remains essentially the same as shown earlier (the major exception being a few computations in R that behave differently in a non-interactive session).

Encoding of text

A major advance in R's world view came with the adoption of multiple *locales*, using information available to the R session that defines the user's preferred encoding of text and other options related to the human language and geographic location. R follows some evolving standards in this area. Many of those standards apply to C software, and therefore they fit fairly smoothly into R.

Normally, default locales will have been set when R was installed that reflect local language and other conventions in your area. See Section 8.1, page 293, and ?locales for some concepts and techniques related to locales. The specifications use standard but somewhat unintuitive terminology; unless you have a particular need to alter behavior for parsing text, sorting character data, or other specialized computations, caution suggests sticking with the default behavior.

Options during evaluation

R offers mechanisms to control aspects of evaluation in the session. The function options() is used to share general-purpose values among functions. Typical options include the width of printed output, the prompt string shown by the parser, and the default device for graphics. The options() mechanism maintains a named list of values that persist through the session; functions use those values, by extracting the relevant option via getOption():

```
> getOption("digits")
[1] 7
```

In this case, the value is meant to be used to control the number of digits in printing numerical data. A user, or in fact any function, can change this value, by using the same name as an argument to options():

```
> 1.234567890
[1] 1.234568
> options(digits = 4)
> 1.234567890
[1] 1.235
```

For the standard options, see ?options; however, a call to options() can be used by any computation to set values that are then used by any other computation. Any argument name is legal and will cause the corresponding option to be communicated among functions.

Options can be set from the beginning of the session; see `?Startup`. However, saving a workspace image does not cause the options in effect to be saved and restored. Although the `options()` mechanism does use an R object, `.Options`, the internal C code implementing `options()` takes the object from the base package, not from the usual way of finding objects. The code also enforces some constraints on what's legal for particular options; for example, `"digits"` is interpreted as a single integer, which is not allowed to be too small or too large, according to values compiled into R.

The use of `options()` is convenient and even necessary for the evaluator to behave intelligently and to allow user customization of a session. Writing functions that depend on options, however, reduces our ability to understand these functions' behavior, because they now depend on external, changeable values. The behavior of code that depends on an option may be altered by any other function called at any earlier time during the session, if the other function calls `options()`. Most R programming should be *functional programming*, in the sense that each function call performs a well-defined computation depending only on the arguments to that call. The `options()` mechanism, and other dependencies on external data that can change during the session, compromise functional programming. It may be worth the danger, but think carefully about it. See page 47 for more on the programming implications, and for an example of the dangers.

2.3 The Language

This section and the next describe the interactive language as you need to use it during a session. But as noted on page 13, there is no interactive language, only the one language used for interaction and for programming. To use R interactively, you basically need to understand two things: functions and objects. That same duality, functions and objects, runs through everything in R from an interactive session to designing large-scale software. For interaction, the key concepts are function calls and assignments of objects, dealt with in this section and in section 2.4 respectively. The language also has facilities for iteration and testing (page 22), but you can often avoid interactive use of these, largely because R function calls operate on, and return, whole objects.

Function Calls

As noted in Section 2.2, the essential computation in R is the evaluation of a call to a function. Function calls in their ordinary form consist of the function's name followed by a parenthesized argument list; that is, a sequence of arguments separated by commas.

```
plot(Date, Declination)
glm(Survived ~ .)
```

Arguments in function calls can be any expression. Each function has a set of formal arguments, to which the actual arguments in the call are matched. As far as the language itself is concerned, a call can supply any subset of the complete argument list. For this purpose, argument expressions can optionally be named, to associate them with a particular argument of the function:

```
jitter(y, amount = .1 * rse)
```

The second argument in the call above is explicitly matched to the formal argument named amount. To find the argument names and other information about the function, request the online documentation. A user interface to R or a Web browser gives the most convenient access to documentation, with documentation listed by package and within package by topic, including individual functions by name. Documentation can also be requested in the language, for example:

```
> ?jitter
```

This will produce some display of documentation for the topic "jitter", including in the case of a function an outline of the calling sequence and a discussion of individual arguments. If there is no documentation, or you don't quite believe it, you can find the formal argument names from the function object itself:

```
> formalArgs(jitter)
[1] "x"        "factor" "amount"
```

Behind this, and behind most techniques involving functions, is the simple fact that jitter and all functions are objects in R. The function name is a reference to the corresponding object. So to see what a function does, just type its name with no argument list following.

```
> jitter
function (x, factor = 1, amount = NULL)
{
    if (length(x) == 0)
        return(x)
    if (!is.numeric(x))
        stop("'x' must be numeric")
            etc.
```

The printed version is another R expression, meaning that you can input such an expression to define a function. At which point, you are programming in R. See Chapter 3. The first section of that chapter should get you started.

In principle, the function preceding the parenthesized arguments can be specified by any expression that returns a function object, but in practice functions are nearly always specified by name.

Operators

Function calls can also appear as operator expressions in the usual scientific notation.

```
y - mean(y)
weight > 0
x < 100 | is.na(date)
```

The usual operators are defined for arithmetic, comparisons, and logical operations (see Chapter 6). But operators in R are not built-in; in fact, they are just special syntax for certain function calls. The first line in the example above computes the same result as:

```
`-`(y, mean(y))
```

The notation `-` is an example of what are called *backtick quotes* in R. These quotes make the evaluator treat an arbitrary string of characters as if it was a name in the language. The evaluator responds to the names "y" or "mean" by looking for an object of that name in the current environment. Similarly `-` causes the evaluator to look for an object named "-". Whenever we refer to operators in the book we use backtick quotes to emphasize that this is the name of a function object, not treated as intrinsically different from the name mean.

Functions to extract components or slots from objects are also provided in operator form:

```
mars$Date
classDef@package
```

And the expressions for extracting subsets or elements from objects are also actually just specialized function calls. The expression

```
y[i]
```

is recognized in the language and evaluated as a call to the function `[`, which extracts a subset of the object in its first argument, with the subset defined by the remaining arguments. The expression y[i] is equivalent to:

```
`[`(y, i)
```

You could enter the second form perfectly legally. Similarly, the function `[[` extracts a single element from an object, and is normally presented as an operator expression:

```
mars[["Date"]]
```

You will encounter a few other operators in the language. Frequently useful for elementary data manipulation is the `:` operator, which produces a sequence of integers between its two arguments:

```
1:length(x)
```

Other operators include `~`, used in specifying models, `%%` for modulus, `%*%` for matrix multiplication, and a number of others.

New operators can be created and recognized as infix operators by the parser. The last two operators mentioned above are examples of the general convention in the language that interprets

```
%text%
```

as the name of an operator, for any text string. If it suits the style of computation, you can define any function of two arguments and give it, say, the name `%d%`. Then an expression such as

```
x %d% y
```

will be evaluated as the call:

```
`%d%`(x, y)
```

Iteration: A quick introduction

The language used by R has the iteration and conditional expressions typical of a C-style language, but for the most part you can avoid typing all but the simplest versions interactively. The following is a brief guide to using and avoiding iterative expressions.

The workhorse of iteration is the `for` loop. It has the form:

```
for( var in seq) expr
```

where *var* is a name and *seq* is a vector of values. The loop assigns each element of *seq* to *var* in sequence and then evaluates the arbitrary expression *expr* each time. When you use the loop interactively, you need to either show something each time (printed or graphics) or else assign the result somewhere; otherwise, you won't get any benefit from the computation. For example, the function plot() has several "types" of x-y plots (points, lines, both, etc.). To repeat a plot with different types, one can use a for() loop over the codes for the types:

```
> par(ask=TRUE)
> for(what in c("p","l","b")) plot(Date, Declination, type = what)
```

The call to par() caused the graphics to pause between plots, so we get to see each plot, rather then having the first two flash by. The variables Date and Declination come from some data on the planet Mars, in a data frame object, mars (see Section 6.5, page 176). If we wanted to see the class of each of the 17 variables in that data frame, another for() loop would do it:

```
for(j in names(mars)) print(class(mars[,j]))
```

But this will just print 17 lines of output, which we'll need to relate to the variable names. Not much use.

Here's where an alternative to iteration is usually better. The workhorse of these is the function sapply(). It applies a function to each element of the object it gets as its first argument, so:

```
> sapply(mars,class)
        Year              X         Year.1         Month
   "integer"      "logical"      "integer"      "integer"
         Day       Day..adj.           Hour            Min
  etc.
```

The function tries to simplify the result, and is intelligent enough to include the names as an attribute. See ?sapply for more details, and the "See Also" section of that documentation for other similar functions.

The language has other iteration operators (while() and repeat), and the usual conditional operators (if ... else). These are all useful in programming and discussed in Chapter 3. By the time you need to use them in a non-trivial way interactively, in fact, you should consider turning your computation into a function, so Chapter 3 is indeed the place to look; see Section 3.4, page 58, in particular, for more detail about the language.

2.4   Objects and Names

A motto in discussion of the S language has for many years been: everything is an object. You will have a potentially very large number of objects available in your R session, including functions, datasets, and many other classes of objects. In ordinary computations you will create new objects or modify existing ones.

As in any computing language, the ability to construct and modify objects relies on a way to refer to the objects. In R, the fundamental reference to an object is a *name*. This is an essential concept for programming with R that arises throughout the book and in nearly any serious programming project.

The basic concept is once again the key thing to keep in mind: references to objects are a way for different computations in the language to refer to the same object; in particular, to make changes to that object. In the S language, references to ordinary objects are only through names. And not just names in an abstract, global sense. An object reference must be a name in a particular R environment. Typically, the reference is established initially either by an assignment or as an argument in a function call.

Assignment is the obvious case, as in the example on page 15:

```
> fitK <- gam(Kyphosis ~ s(Age, 4) + Number, family = binomial)
```

Assignment creates a reference, the name "fitK", to some object. That reference is in some environment. For now, just think of environments as tables that R maintains, in which objects can be assigned names. When an assignment takes place in the top-level of the R session, the current environment is what's called the *global* environment. That environment is maintained throughout the current session, and optionally can be saved and restored between sessions.

Assignments appear inside function definitions as well. These assignments take place during a call to the function. They do not use the global environment, fortunately. If they did, every assignment to the name "x" would overwrite the same reference. Instead, assignments during function calls use an environment specially created for that call. So another reason that functions are so central to programming with R is that they protect users from accidentally overwriting objects in the middle of a computation.

The objects available during an interactive R session depend on what packages are attached; technically, they depend on the nested environments through which the evaluator searches, when given a name, to find a corresponding object. See Section 5.3, page 121, for the details of the search.

2.5 Functions and Packages

In addition to the software that comes with any copy of R, there are many thousands of functions available to be used in an R session, along with a correspondingly large amount of other related software. Nearly all of the important R software comes in the form of packages that make the software easily available and usable. This section discusses the implications of using different packages in your R session. For much more detail, see Chapter 4, but that is written more from the view of writing or extending a package. You will get there, I hope, as your own programming efforts take shape. The topic here, though, is how best to use other people's efforts that have been incorporated in packages.

The process leading from needing some computational tool to having it available in your R session has three stages: *finding* the software, typically in a package; *installing* the package; and *attaching* the package to the session.

The last step is the one you will do most often, so let's begin by assuming that you know which package you need and that the required package has been installed with your local copy of R. See the subsection on page 26, for finding and installing the relevant package.

You can tell whether the package is attached by looking for it in the printed result of `search()`; alternatively, you can look for a particular object with the function `find()`, which returns the names of all the attached packages that contain the object. Suppose we want to call the function `dotplot()`, for example.

```
> find("dotplot")
character(0)
```

No attached package has an object of this name. If we happen to know that the function is in the package named `lattice`, we can make that package available for the current session. A call to the function `library()` requests this:

```
library(lattice)
```

The function is `library()` rather than `package()` only because the original S software called them libraries. Notice also that the package name was given without quotes. The `library()` function, and a similar function `require()`, do some nonstandard evaluation that takes unquoted names. That's another historical quirk that saves users from typing a couple of quote characters.

If a package of the name `"lattice"` has been installed for this version of R, the call will attach the package to the session, making its functions and other objects available:

```
> library(lattice)
> find("dotplot")
[1] "package:lattice"
```

By "available", we mean that the evaluator will find an object belonging
to the package when an expression uses the corresponding name. If the
user types dotplot(Declination) now, the evaluator will normally find the
appropriate function. To see why the quibbling "normally" was added, we
need to say more precisely what happens to find a function object.

The evaluator looks first in the global environment for a function of this
name, then in each of the attached packages, in the order shown by search().
The evaluator will generally stop searching when it finds an object of the
desired name, dotplot, Declination, or whatever. If two attached packages
have functions of the same name, one of them will "mask" the object in the
other (the evaluator will warn of such conflicts, usually, when a package is
attached with conflicting names). In this case, the result returned by find()
would show two or more packages.

For example, the function gam() exists in two packages, gam and mgcv. If
both were attached:

```
> find("gam")
[1] "package:gam"   "package:mgcv"
```

A simple call to gam() will get the version in package gam; the version in
package mgcv is now masked.

R has some mechanisms designed to get around such conflicts, at least
as far as possible. The language has an operator, `::`, to specify that an
object should come from a particular package. So mgcv::gam and gam::gam
refer unambiguously to the versions in the two packages. The masked version
of gam() could be called by:

```
> fitK <- mgcv::gam(Kyphosis ~ s(Age, 4) + etc.
```

Clearly one doesn't want to type such expressions very often, and they
only help if one is aware of the ambiguity. For the details and for other
approaches, particularly when you're programming your own packages, see
Section 5.3, page 121.

Finding and installing packages

Finding the right software is usually the hardest part. There are thousands
of packages and smaller collections of R software in the world. Section 2.7,
page 31, discusses ways to search for information; as a start, CRAN, the

central repository for R software, has a large collection of packages itself, plus further links to other sources for R software. Extended browsing is recommended, to develop a general feel for what's available. CRAN supports searching with the Google search engine, as do some of the other major collections.

Use the search engine on the Web site to look for relevant terms. This may take some iteration, particularly if you don't have a good guess for the actual name of the function. Browse through the search output, looking for a relevant entry, and figure out the name of the package that contains the relevant function or other software.

Finding something which is not in these collections may take more ingenuity. General Web search techniques often help: combine the term "R" with whatever words describe your needs in a search query. The e-mail lists associated with R will usually show up in such a search, but you can also browse or search explicitly in the archives of the lists. Start from the R home page, `r-project.org`, and follow the link for "Mailing Lists".

On page 15, we showed a computation using the function `gam()`, which fits a generalized additive model to data. This function is not part of the basic R software. Before being able to do this computation, we need to find and install some software. The search engine at the CRAN site will help out, if given either the function name "gam" or the term "generalized additive models". The search engine on the site tends to give either many hits or no relevant hits; in this case, it turns out there are many hits and in fact two packages with a `gam()` function. As an example, suppose we decide to install the `gam` package.

There are two choices at this point, in order to get and install the package(s) in question: a binary or a source copy of the package. Usually, installing from binary is the easy approach, assuming a binary version is available from the repository. Binary versions are currently available from CRAN only for Windows and Mac OS X platforms, and may or may not be available from other sources. Otherwise, or if you prefer to install from source, the procedure is to download a copy of the source archive for the package and apply the "INSTALL" command. From an R session, the function `install.packages()` can do part or all of the process, again depending on the package, the repository, and your particular platform. The R GUI may also have a menu-driven equivalent for these procedures: Look for an item in the tool bar about installing packages.

First, here is the function `install.packages()`, as applied on a Mac OS X platform. To obtain the `gam` package, for example:

```
install.packages("gam")
```

The function will then invoke software to access a CRAN site, download the packages requested, and attempt to install them on the same R system you are currently using. The actual download is an archive file whose name concatenates the name of the package and its current version; in our example, `"gam_0.98.tgz"`.

Installing from inside a session has the advantage of implicitly specifying some of the information that you might otherwise need to provide, such as the version of R and the platform. Optional arguments control where to put the installed packages, whether to use source or binary and other details.

As another alternative, you can obtain the download file from a Web browser, and run the installation process from the command shell. If you aren't already at the CRAN Web site, select that item in the navigation frame, choose a mirror site near you, and go there.

Select `"Packages"` from the CRAN Web page, and scroll or search in the list of packages to reach a package you want (it's a very long list, so searching for the exact name of the package may be required). Selecting the relevant package takes you to a page with a brief description of the package. For the package gam at the time this is written:

gam: Generalized Additive Models

Functions for fitting and working with generalized additive models, as described in chapter 7 of "Statistical Models in S" (Chambers and Hastie (eds), 1991), and "Generalized Additive Models" (Hastie and Tibshirani, 1990).

Version:	0.98
Depends:	R (>= 2.0), stats, splines
Suggests:	akima
Date:	2006-07-11
Author:	Trevor Hastie
Maintainer:	Trevor Hastie
License:	GPL2.0

Downloads:

Package source:	gam_0.98.tar.gz
MacOS X binary:	gam_0.98.tgz
Windows binary:	gam_0.98.zip
Index of contents:	gam.INDEX
Reference manual:	gam.pdf

At this stage, you can access the documentation or download one of the proffered versions of the package. Or, after studying the information, you could revert to the previous approach and use `install.packages()`. If you do work from one of the source or binary archives, you need to apply the shell-style command to install the package. Having downloaded the source archive for package gam, the command would be:

```
R CMD INSTALL gam_0.98.tar.gz
```

The INSTALL utility is used to install packages that we write ourselves as well, so detailed discussion appears in Chapter 4.

The package for this book

In order to follow the examples and suggested computations in the book, you should install the SoDA package. It is available from CRAN by any of the mechanisms shown above. In addition to the many references to this package in the book itself, it will be a likely source for new ideas, enhancements, and corrections related to the book.

2.6 Getting R

R is an open-source system, in particular a system licensed under the *GNU General Public License.* That license requires that the source code for the system be freely available. The current source implementing R can be obtained over the Web. This open definition of the system is a key support when we are concerned with trustworthy software, as is the case with all similar open-source systems.

Relatively simple use of R, and first steps in programming with R, on the other hand, don't require all the resources that would be needed to create your local version of the system starting from the source. You may already have a version of R on your computer or network. If not, or if you want a more recent version, binary copies of R can be obtained for the commonly used platforms, from the same repository. It's easier to start with binary, although as your own programming becomes more advanced you may need more of the source-related resources anyway.

The starting point for obtaining the software is the central R Web site, r-project.org. You can go there to get the essential information about R. Treat that as the up-to-date authority, not only for the software itself but also for detailed information about R (more on that on page 31).

The main Web site points you to a variety of pages and other sites for various purposes. To obtain R, one goes to the CRAN repository, and from there to either "R Binaries" or "R Sources". Downloading software may involve large transfers over the Web, so you are encouraged to spread the load. In particular, you should select from a list of mirror sites, preferably picking one geographically near your own location. When we talk about the

CRAN site from now on, we mean whichever one of the mirror sites you have chosen.

R is actively maintained for three platforms: Windows, Mac OS X, and Linux. For these platforms, current versions of the system can be obtained from CRAN in a form that can be directly installed, usually by a standard installation process for that platform. For Windows, one obtains an executable setup program (a ".exe" file); for Mac OS X, a disk image (a ".dmg" file) containing the installer for the application. The Linux situation is a little less straightforward, because the different flavors of Linux differ in details when installing R. The Linux branch of "R Binaries" branches again according to the flavors of Linux supported, and sometimes again within these branches according to the version of this flavor. The strategy is to keep drilling down through the directories, selecting at each stage the directory that corresponds to your setup, until you finally arrive at a directory that contains appropriate files (usually ".rpm" files) for the supported versions of R.

Note that for at least one flavor of Linux (Debian), R has been made a part of the platform. You can obtain R directly from the Debian Web site. Look for Debian packages named "r-base", and other names starting with "r-". If you're adept at loading packages into Debian, working from this direction may be the simplest approach. However, if the version of Debian is older than the latest stable version of R, you may miss out on some later improvements and bug fixes unless you get R from CRAN.

For any platform, you will eventually download a file (".exe", "dmg", ".rpm", or other), and then install that file according to the suitable ritual for this platform. Installation may require you to have some administration privileges on the machine, as would be true for most software installations. (If installing software at all is a new experience for you, it may be time to seek out a more experienced friend.) Depending on the platform, you may have a choice of versions of R, but it's unlikely you want anything other than the most recent stable version, the one with the highest version number. The platform's operating system will also have versions, and you generally need to download a file asserted to work with the version of the operating system you are running. (There may not be any such file if you have an old version of the operating system, or else you may have to settle for a comparably ancient version of R.) And just to add further choices, on some platforms you need to choose from different hardware (for example, 32-bit versus 64-bit architecture). If you don't know which choice applies, that may be another indication that you should seek expert advice.

Once the binary distribution has been downloaded and installed, you should have direct access to R in the appropriate mechanism for your platform.

Installing from source

Should you? For most users of R, not if they can avoid it, because they will likely learn more about programming than they need to or want to. For readers of this book, on the other hand, many of these details will be relevant when you start to seriously create or modify software. Getting the source, even if you choose not to install it, may help you to study and understand key computations.

The instructions for getting and for installing R from source are contained in the online manual, *R Installation and Administration*, available from the `Documentation` link at the `r-project.org` Web site.

2.7 Online Information About R

Information for users is in various ways both a strength and a problem with open-source, cooperative enterprises like R. At the bottom, there is always the source, the software itself. By definition, no software that is not open to study of all the source code can be as available for deep study. In this sense, only open-source software can hope to fully satisfy the *Prime Directive* by offering unlimited examination of what is actually being computed.

But on a more mundane level, some open-source systems have a reputation for favoring technical discussions aimed at the insider over user-oriented documentation. Fortunately, as the R community has grown, an increasing effort has gone into producing and organizing information. Users who have puzzled out answers to practical questions have increasingly fed back the results into publicly available information sources.

Most of the important information sources can be tracked down starting at the main R Web page, `r-project.org`. Go there for the latest pointers. Here is a list of some of the key resources, followed by some comments about them.

Manuals: The R distribution comes with a set of manuals, also available at the Web site. There are currently six manuals: *An Introduction to R, Writing R Extensions, R Data Import/Export, The R Language Definition, R Installation and Administration*, and *R Internals*. Each is available in several formats, notably as Web-browsable HTML documents.

Help files: R itself comes with files that document all the functions and other objects intended for public use, as well as documentation files on other topics (for example, ?Startup, discussing how an R session starts).

All contributed packages should likewise come with files documenting their publicly usable functions. The quality control tools in R largely enforce this for packages on CRAN.

Help files form the database used to respond to the help requests from an R session, either in response to the Help menu item or through the `?` operator or help() function typed by the user.

The direct requests in these forms only access terms explicitly labeling the help files; typically, the names of the functions and a few other general terms for documentation (these are called *aliases* in discussions of R documentation). For example, to get help on a function in this way, you must know the name of the function exactly. See the next item for alternatives.

Searching: R has a search mechanism for its help files that generalizes the terms available beyond the aliases somewhat and introduces some additional searching flexibility. See ?help.search for details.

The r-project.org site has a pointer to a general search of the files on the central site, currently using the Google search engine. This produces much more general searches. Documentation files are typically displayed in their raw, LATEX-like form, but once you learn a bit about this, you can usually figure out which topic in which package you need to look at.

And, beyond the official site itself, you can always apply your favorite Web search to files generally. Using "R" as a term in the search pattern will usually generate appropriate entries, but it may be difficult to avoid plenty of inappropriate ones as well.

The Wiki: Another potentially useful source of information about R is the site wiki.r-project.org, where users can contribute documentation. As with other open Wiki sites, this comes with no guarantee of accuracy and is only as good as the contributions the community provides. But it has the key advantage of openness, meaning that in some "statistical" sense it reflects what R users understand, or at least that subset of the users sufficiently vocal and opinionated to submit to the Wiki.

The strength of this information source is that it may include material that users find relevant but that developers ignore for whatever reason (too trivial, something users would never do, etc.). Some Wiki sites have sufficient support from their user community that they can function as the main information source on their topic. As of this writing, the R Wiki has not reached that stage, so it should be used as a supplement to other information sources, and not the primary source, but it's a valuable resource nevertheless.

The mailing lists: There are a number of e-mail lists associated officially with the R project (officially in the sense of having a pointer from the R Web page, `r-project.org`, and being monitored by members of R core). The two most frequently relevant lists for programming with R are `r-help`, which deals with general user questions, and `r-devel`, which deals generally with more "advanced" questions, including future directions for R and programming issues.

As well as a way to ask specific questions, the mailing lists are valuable archives for past discussions. See the various search mechanisms pointed to from the mailing list Web page, itself accessible as the `Mailing lists` pointer on the `r-project.org` site. As usual with technical mailing lists, you may need patience to wade through some long tirades and you should also be careful not to believe all the assertions made by contributors, but often the lists will provide a variety of views and possible approaches.

Journals: The electronic journal *R News* is the newsletter of the R Foundation, and a good source for specific tutorial help on topics related to R, among other R-related information. See the `Newsletter` pointer on the `cran.r-project.org` Web site.

The *Journal of Statistical Software* is also an electronic journal; its coverage is more general as its name suggests, but many of the articles are relevant to programming with R. See the Web site `jstatsoft.org`.

A number of print journals also have occasional articles of direct or indirect relevance, for example, *Journal of Computational and Graphical Statistics* and *Computational Statistics and Data Analysis*.

2.8   What's Hard About Using R?

This chapter has outlined the computations involved in using R. An R session consists of expressions provided by the user, typically typed into an R console window. The system evaluates these expressions, usually either showing the user results (printed or graphic output) or assigning the result as an object. Most expressions take the form of calls to functions, of which there are many thousands available, most of them in R packages available on the Web.

This style of computing combines features found in various other languages and systems, including command shells and programming languages. The combination of a functional style with user-level interaction—expecting the user to supply functional expressions interactively—is less common. Beginning users react in many ways, influenced by their previous experience, their expectations, and the tasks they need to carry out. Most readers of this book have selected themselves for more than a first encounter with the software, and so will mostly not have had an extremely negative reaction. Examining some of the complaints may be useful, however, to understand how the software we create might respond (and the extent to which we can respond). Our mission of supporting effective exploration of data obliges us to try.

The computational style of an R session is extremely general, and other aspects of the system reinforce that generality, as illustrated by many of the topics in this book (the general treatment of objects and the facilities for interacting with other systems, for example). In response to this generality, thousands of functions have been written for many techniques. This diversity has been cited as a strength of the system, as indeed it is. But for some users exactly this computational style and diversity present barriers to using the system.

Requiring the user to compose expressions is very different from the mode of interaction users have with typical applications in current computing. Applications such as searching the Web, viewing documents, or playing audio and video files all present interfaces emphasizing *selection-and-response* rather than composing by the user. The user *selects* each step in the computation, usually from a menu, and then *responds* to the options presented by the software as a result. When the user does have to compose (that is, to type) it is typically to fill in specific information such as a Web site, file or optional feature desired. The eventual action taken, which might be operationally equivalent to evaluating an expression in R, is effectively defined by the user's interactive path through menus, forms and other specialized tools in the interface. Based on the principles espoused in this book, particularly the need for trustworthy software, we might object to a selection-and-response approach to serious analysis, because the ability to justify or reproduce the analysis is much reduced. However, most non-technical computing is done by selection and response.

Even for more technical applications, such as producing documents or using a database system, the user's input tends to be relatively free form. Modern document-generating systems typically format text according to selected styles chosen by the user, rather than requiring the user to express controls explicitly. These differences are accentuated when the expressions required of the R user take the form of a functional, algebraic language rather than free-form input.

This mismatch between requirements for using R and the user's experience with other systems contributes to some common complaints. How does one start, with only a general feeling of the statistical goals or the "results" wanted? The system itself seems quite unhelpful at this stage. Failures are likely, and the response to them also seems unhelpful (being told of a syntax error or some detailed error in a specific function doesn't suggest what to do next). Worse yet, computations that don't fail may not produce any directly useful results, and how can one decide whether this was the "right" computation?

Such disjunctions between user expectations and the way R works become more likely as the use of R spreads. From the most general view, there is no "solution". Computing is being viewed differently by two groups of people, prospective users on one hand, and the people who created the S language, R and the statistical software extending R on the other hand.

The S language was designed by research statisticians, initially to be used primarily by themselves and their colleagues for statistical research and data analysis. (See the Appendix, page 475.) A language suited for this group to communicate their ideas (that is, to "program") is certain to be pitched at a level of abstraction and generality that omits much detail necessary for users with less mathematical backgrounds. The increased use of R and the growth in software written using it bring it to the notice of such potential users far more than was the case in the early history of S.

In addition to questions of expressing the analysis, simply choosing an analysis is often part of the difficulty. Statistical data analysis is far from a routine exercise, and software still does not encapsulate all the expertise needed to choose an appropriate analysis. Creating such expert software has been a recurring goal, pursued most actively perhaps in the 1980s, but it must be said that the goal remains far off.

So to a considerable extent the response to such user difficulties must include the admission that the software implemented in R is not directly suited to all possible users. That said, information resources such as those described earlier in this chapter are making much progress in easing the user's path. And, those who have come far enough into the R world to be reading this book can make substantial contributions to bringing good data analysis tools to such users.

1. Specialized selection-and-response interfaces can be designed when the data analysis techniques can be captured with the limited input provided by menus and forms.

2. Interfaces to R from a system already supporting the application is another way to provide a limited access expressed in a form familiar to the user of that system. We don't describe such interfaces explicitly in this book, but see Chapter 12 for some related discussion.

3. Both educational efforts and better software tools can make the use of R seem more friendly. More assistance is available than users may realize; see for example the suggestions in Section 3.5. And there is room for improvement: providing more information in a readable format for the beginning user would be a valuable contribution.

4. Last but far from least in potential value, those who have reached a certain level of skill in applying data analysis to particular application areas can ease their colleagues' task by documentation and by providing specialized software, usually in the form of an R package. Reading a description in familiar terminology and organized in a natural structure for the application greatly eases the first steps. A number of such packages exist on CRAN and elsewhere.

Chapter 3

Programming with R: The Basics

Nearly everything that happens in R results from a function call. Therefore, basic programming centers on creating and refining functions. Function definition should begin small-scale, directly from interactive use of commands (Section 3.1). The essential concepts apply to all functions, however. This chapter discusses functional programming concepts (Section 3.2, page 43) and the relation between function calls and function objects (3.3, 50). It then covers essential techniques for writing and developing effective functions: details of the language (3.4, 58); techniques for debugging (3.5, 61), including preemptive tracing (3.6, 67); handling of errors and other conditions (3.7, 74); and design of tests for trustworthy software (3.8, 76).

3.1   From Commands to Functions

Writing functions in R is not separate from issuing commands interactively, but grows from using, and reusing, such commands. Starting from basic techniques for reuse, writing functions is the natural way to expand what you can do with the system. Your first steps can be gradual and gentle. At the same time, the functions you create are fully consistent with the rest of the language, so that no limits are placed on how far you can extend the new software.

Exploring data for new insights is a gradual, iterative process. Occasionally we get a sudden insight, but for the most part we try something, look at

37

the results, reflect a bit, and then try something slightly different. In R, that iteration requires entering slightly different expressions as the ideas change. Standard user interfaces help out by allowing you to navigate through the *session history*, that is, the expressions you have previously typed. Hitting the up-arrow key, for example, usually displays the last line typed. With the line displayed, one can navigate back and forth to alter parts of the expression.

Manipulation of the history is a good way to correct simple errors and try out small changes in the computations, particularly when the expressions you have been typing are starting to be longer and more complicated. In the following snippet, we're recreating an ancient example studied in several text books; our version is based on that in *A Handbook of Statistical Analysis Using R* [14, Chapter 9]. This example involves the software for fitting models, but you can imagine this being replaced by whatever software in R is relevant for your applications. Following the reference, we start by constructing a fairly complicated linear model.

```
> formula <- rainfall ~ seeding *
+ (sne + cloudcover + prewetness + echomotion) + time
> model <- lm(fromula, data = clouds)
Error in model.frame(formula = fromula, data = ....:
    object "fromula" not found Oops---back up and edit last input line
> model <- lm(formula, data = clouds)
```

On the first attempt to create a model, we misspelled the name of the formula object, then backed up the history to edit and re-enter the line. The benefits of navigating the history aren't just for errors. Let's pursue this example a bit. It's a small dataset, but we can show the kind of gradual, iterative computing typical of many applications.

The model tries to fit rainfall to some variables related to cloud seeding, arguably with a rather complicated model for 24 poor little observations. So a data analyst might wonder what happens when the model is simplified by dropping some terms. Here is some further analysis in R that drops one of the variables, `sne`. Doing this correctly requires dropping its interaction with `seeding` as well. The user who can work out how to do this needs to have some experience with the model-fitting software. Examining the terms in the model by calling the `anova()` or `terms()` function will show which terms include the variable we want to drop.

A call to the function `update()` updates a model, giving a formula in which "`.`" stands for the previous formula, following by using $\pm$ to add or drop terms (see `?update` for details). In the example below, we generate the updated model and then produce a scatter plot of the two sets of residuals, with the $y = x$ line plotted on it, to see how the residuals have been changed.

```
> model2 <- update(model, ~ . - sne - seeding:sne)
> plot(resid(model), resid(model2))
> abline(0,1)
```

Looking at the plot, it's noticeable that the largest single residual has been made quite a bit larger, so we select this point interactively with identify() to indicate which observation this was.

```
> identify(resid(model), resid(model2))
```

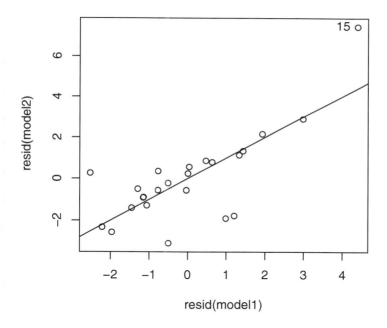

To pursue the data analysis we might ask some questions about run number 15. But our focus is on the computing. Notice that the arguments in the call to identify() are identical to the call to plot(), so once again typing can be saved and errors avoided by backing up the history and editing the line. Keep the session history in mind as a technique for adapting your use of R.

Depending on the interface being used, something more powerful than line-by-line navigation may be available to display or edit the history: The

Mac OS X interface can display the history in a separate panel. The history can also be saved to a file; see `?savehistory`. When portions of the history file have been saved, a text editor or the editor built into the R GUI can facilitate larger changes. The changed code can be returned to R and evaluated by using the `source()` function. Some specialized interfaces, such as ESS, will have short cuts; in ESS for example, there are special key combinations to evaluate whole buffers or regions in emacs.

As soon as you notice that the changes you are making are at all substantial or start to see recurring patterns in them, consider turning the patterns into an R function. A function potentially has several advantages at this stage.

- It helps you to think about the patterns and often to see where they might lead (in my opinion this is the most important advantage).

- You will often have less typing on each call to the function than would be needed to repeatedly edit the lines of history.

- The computations done in the call to the function are local, which can sometimes avoid undesirable side effects.

Even seemingly minor examples can prove interesting, as well as providing practice in designing functions. Continuing the previous example, suppose we decide to delete a different variable from the full model. By bringing back the relevant lines of the history we can construct the same sequence of calls to `update()`, `plot()` and `abline()`. But at this point, and imagining doing the same editing a third or fourth time, the advantages of a function become relevant.

The three commands to update and plot the model are the key; by copying them to an editor and adapting them, we can create a function callable in a variety of ways. Here's a simple version. Let's look at it first, and then explicitly set out the editing techniques to turn history into a function.

```
upd <- function(drop) {
    model2 <- update(model, drop)
    plot(resid(model), resid(model2))
    abline(0,1)
    model2
}
```

The three lines of the history file are in lines 2 to 4. To make it a usable function, the piece that will be different each time—a formula in this case— is replaced by the name of an argument, `drop`. Once we decide to have a function, like all functions in R it will return an object as its value, the last expression computed. That object might as well be the new model.

When converting more than one line from the history into a function, one must enclose all the lines inside braces to make the multiple expressions into a single expression, simply because the *function body* is required in the language to be a single expression. This single expression is turned into a function by preceding it with the keyword `function` followed by a parenthesized list of the arguments.

The expression consisting of the `function` keyword, the argument list, and the body corresponds to a function definition or declaration in many languages. But here is a key concept in programming with R: This is not a declaration but an expression that will be evaluated. Its value is a function object and this object is then assigned, as "`upd`" in the example. The distinction may seem subtle, but it underlies many powerful programming techniques to be discussed in this and later chapters. Whereas in many languages (for example, Perl, C, or Fortran), the function or subroutine name would be part of the definition, in R a function results from evaluating an expression and we choose to assign the function object, for the convenience of referring to it by name. The function is the object, and is therefore as available for computing in R as any other object. Do please reflect on this paragraph; it will be worth the effort. For more details, see Section 3.3, page 50, and Section 13.3, page 460.

From an editor we can save the source in a file. Either the `source()` function or some equivalent technique in the GUI will evaluate the contents of the file. Now `upd()` is a function available in the session. We can create and examine several different models using it.

```
> modelSne <- upd(~. - sne - seeding:sne)
> modelCover <- upd(~. - cloudcover - seeding:cloudcover)
> modelEcho <- upd(~. - echomotion - seeding:echomotion)
```

As often happens, the process of thinking functionally has changed the approach a little in ways that can prove useful. Now that each model is generated by a function call, it's natural to save them as separate objects, which can then be used easily in other comparisons.

What also happens frequently once a function has been written is to ask whether the function might be extended to be useful in other applications. The first version was for immediate use, but what about a few changes? Notice that `upd()` always starts from a fixed object, `model`. This reduced the typing needed to call `upd()`, but it also restricted the function to a special situation. This version of `upd()` only works if we have assigned `model` in the session, that is, in the global environment. That's not only restrictive but dangerous, if `model` existed but was not what we assumed. The function would become generally applicable (our *Mission* of exploring) and also more trustworthy (our *Prime Directive*) if we took that global reference and made it instead an argument:

```
upd <- function(model, drop) {
```

The rest of the function definition stays the same. A little more typing is needed for the examples:

```
> modelSne <- upd(model, ~. - sne - seeding:sne)
> modelCover <- upd(model, ~. - cloudcover - seeding:cloudcover)
> modelEcho <- upd(model, ~. - echomotion - seeding:echomotion)
```

But now `upd()` is a potentially reusable function, and notice that the three calls above have the same first argument, which then only needs to be typed once if we continue to edit the previous call from the session history. The calls themselves are pretty exotic still, in the sense that each takes a formula to define what variable is to be dropped from the model. The example assumed that the original user/programmer was familiar with model-fitting in R, so that a formula in the argument would be acceptable.

Another helpful step in developing functions is often to consider rewriting them for others to use. In this case, one's colleagues might be interested in examining the models, but not prepared to figure out obscure formula arguments. What our function is really doing on each call is to drop all the terms in the model that include a specified variable (`"sne"`, `"cloudcover"` and `"echomotion"` in the example above). The natural functional interface would take a model and the name of a variable as arguments and return the model with all terms involving that variable dropped. An additional computation is required to construct the formulas of the form shown above, starting from the model and the name of the variable.

Going from the variable to the formula is an exercise in computing with text, and is shown as the function `dropFormula()` in Section 8.4, page 304. If we assume that `dropFormula()` is available, we arrive at a "final" version of our function:

```
dropModel <- function(model, drop) {
    model2 <- update(model,
                        dropFormula(model, drop))
    plot(resid(model), resid(model2),
        xlab = "Original Residuals",
        ylab = paste("Residuals after dropping", drop))
```

```
        abline(0,1)
        model2
}
```

The function has also been modified to provide more meaningful labels on the plot.

The `dropModel()` function is now in a form that might be a contribution to one's colleagues (and that will be easier for the author to use as well). The pattern of changes, gradually adding to a simple original idea, is typical of much programming with R. Such incremental expansion is natural and not to be discouraged. However, there should come a time for thinking about the design, as this simple example suggests. Software tends to be written for convenience, initially, but it's important to realize when some design concepts need to be applied. In particular, discussing the concepts behind functions is a good next step for programming with R.

3.2 Functions and Functional Programming

This section examines the underlying concept of a function in R, which in spirit relates to the *functional programming* model for languages. The concept is helpful in designing functions that are useful and trustworthy, even though not everything in R conforms to functional programming.

Creating a function in R is extremely simple. Users of R should quickly get into the habit of creating simple functions, which will make their work more effective (through adaptability to related problems and ease of modification) and also more trustworthy (through a simple interface and freedom from side effects). Extensive use of functions is good from the view of both our fundamental principles, the *Mission* and the *Prime Directive.*

So no one should be embarrassed by creating a function that seems trivial or not ideally designed, if it helps further the analysis. On the other hand, after using and modifying a function, you may realize that it is starting to play a more serious role. Consider at that point an examination of both its meaning and its implementation. The concepts of functions and functional programming in R will help in this examination.

The language we are using, and now contributing to, can be called a *functional language* in two important senses. One is a technical sense, in that the S language shares, although only partially, a model of computation by function evaluation, rather than by procedural computations and changes of state. The other sense derives from the observation that users communicate to R through function calls almost entirely, so that to use R well, the user must understand what particular functions do. Therefore, the *functionality* of an R function, in a non-technical sense, must be clear and well-defined. The version of the S language known later as S3 introduced functions as a central concept.

The function concept

The concept of a function, in a pure form, is intuitively something like this:

> A pure function in R is completely specified by the value returned from a call to that function, for every possible value of the function's arguments.

In other words, whatever objects are chosen to be arguments to the function unambiguously define what object is returned, and no information is needed to define the function other than this relationship between arguments and value. If this relationship can be described meaningfully it defines the function, abstracted away from the issue of what method the implementer of the function uses to achieve the intended result.

If we restrict ourselves temporarily to functions with only one argument, this definition deliberately mimics the mathematical definition of a function: the mapping of any element in the domain (the possible argument objects) into an element of the range (the corresponding value objects). Common R functions correspond to just such familiar mathematical functions, such as numerical transformations (sqrt()) or summaries (mean()). The extension to functions of multiple arguments does not affect the mathematical analogy, because the "domain" could be a mathematical product-space over all the arguments.

In R, as opposed to mathematics, the arguments correspond to objects. Functions following the concept take such objects and return another object as the value of a function call. Well-defined functionality implies a clear relation between the arguments and the value. Such function concepts extend to arguments that can be many kinds of objects. For example, the function lapply() takes another function as one of its arguments and *applies* that function to the elements of a list; that is, it evaluates the supplied function with each of the elements of the list as an argument. The result fits the concept with no difficulty, provided that the function supplied as an argument conforms to the concept.

In R (and perhaps in mathematics as well), it matters very much how the function is "specified". A useful function (for our *Mission*) has a clear, simple, and unambiguous specification for its users. That does not mean that the definition of the function is limited to only certain classes of arguments. Functions can be defined as generic functions, allowing methods for new classes of objects. The complete definition of the function specifies the values returned from all of the current methods. Here especially a clear, consistent definition is needed.

For example, the subset operator, ` [ `, is a generic function with a variety of methods for many classes of objects, with new methods arriving frequently in new packages. The function does have a fairly clear intuitive definition, somewhat along the lines: "Given an object, x, and one or more index objects as arguments, ` [ ` returns an object containing data from x, selected according to the index argument(s)." Whether a new method for the generic function conforms well to the definition cannot be controlled in advance, but writing methods that do so is an important criterion for good software in R.

As a more extended example, the software in R for statistical models (see Section 6.9, page 218) illustrates an application of the function concept. The functions to fit various types of model all take two primary arguments, a formula expressing the structure of the model and a source of data; they then return an object representing the model of this type estimated consistent with the arguments. In principle, the correspondence is clearly defined; for example, the function lm() fits a linear model using least-squares to estimate coefficients for the formula and data supplied. Additional functions then produce auxiliary information such as residuals, with the fitted model now an argument. In particular, the update() function used in Section 3.1, page 39, takes the fitted model and another formula, and returns a new fitted model.

Methods and classes can be understood in a functional language like S largely as a means of maintaining meaningful and well-defined computations while generalizing functionality. The essence of a method is that it provides one definition, that is one implementation, of a function, but only for a restricted range of arguments. The restriction specifies that certain arguments must belong to or inherit from specified classes; the restriction is technically the *signature* of the method. The generic function should specify the value in a meaningful way, but the validity of the computations must be considered separately for each method. A well-designed system of methods and classes allows one to proceed step by step to examine the trustworthiness of the computation. It's a key part of programming with R, examined in detail in Chapters 9 and 10.

Functional programming languages

R shares a number of features with functional programming languages and is sometimes listed among them (currently in Wikipedia, for example). The pure function concept discussed above is in the spirit of functional programming, but proponents of such languages could justifiably object that nothing enforces the concept in programming with R. Languages defined explicitly for functional programming often use forms of computing that are quite different from the explicit, sequential evaluation in R.

Functional programming is a general philosophy and model for how programming languages should work. A general discussion is outside the scope of this book, but our understanding of computing with R will benefit from examining the ways in which R follows this model, and equally the ways in which it may extend or deviate from the model.

A non-technical definition of the functional programming philosophy could expand on the pure function concept on page 44 somewhat as follows.

> A functional programming language provides for the definition of functions. The functions are free of side effects: the value of a function call entirely defines the effect of that call. The function is defined entirely by the value corresponding to all possible arguments, independent of external information. The function defines that value by implicit enumeration over all possible arguments, not by procedural computations that change the value of objects.

The goal of functional programming has much in common with our *Prime Directive*: to provide software that is understandable and as demonstrably correct as possible. Strict versions aim to prove results about functions, including their "correctness".

Most books on functional programming aim their comparisons at traditional procedural languages such as C. For our own purposes, we need to assess the concept against R, or more generally the S language. Functional programming from our view has three main requirements.

1. Freedom from external side effects: calling the function has no effect on any later computation, either in another call to this function or any other function call.

2. Freedom from external influences: the value of a function call depends only on the arguments and the function definitions used.

3. Freedom from assignments: roughly, the function can be defined without repeatedly assigning or modifying internal objects (often called "state variables").

R does not guarantee any of these but many functions satisfy some of the requirements, less so as one goes down the list. Analyzing a function for any of the requirements proceeds top-down, in the sense that one examines the code of the current function; if that code passes, one then examines the functions called by this function for the same requirement.

External side effects are most obviously carried out by non-local assignments, either through the operator `` `<<-` `` or the `assign()` function. There are other forms of side effect, such as writing files, printing or plotting. These can all be fairly easily detected and often are more irrelevant to a functional view rather than seriously damaging to it (see page 48). More insidious are functions, such as `options()`, that create a hidden side effect, usually in C code.

External influences are values that the function uses in its computations. Some of these are part of the installation (such as machine constants or operating system information). These do make the function definition less global, but for most practical purposes software should not ignore them if they are part of the true definition. For example, the value of functions related to numerical computations is, and must be, dependent on the domain of numerical arguments if we use ordinary computer hardware for the computations. Owners of 64-bit machines would not appreciate results computed to 32-bit accuracy to avoid external influences. The dependency does need to be considered in assessing results, as in the discussion of testing in Section 3.8, page 76. Dependencies on software outside of R, such as operating system capabilities, are potentially more disruptive. In R, explicit dependence on these values comes through global objects `.Machine` and `.Platform`. Indirect dependence is more common, and can only be detected from knowledge of the functions called.

More dangerous still are the effects of function `options()` and a few other functions with similar behavior, that preserve user-set values globally. If these options are used in a function, directly or as default values, the value returned by a call to the function can be arbitrarily distorted by undetected computations earlier in the session. A call to `options()` can set named elements in a global object, regardless of where the call originated. So computations inside one function can leave a permanent effect on other functions.

Most of the options relate to values used for graphical and printed output, which are not very testable computations anyway. But a few can be directly damaging to computed results. For example, the option `ts.eps` is used as a default in testing frequencies in the `ts()` function. A call to `options()` that set this option, no matter where it occurred, could alter later results of a call to `ts()`. Here functional programming has a clear message: Avoid dependencies on `options()` if you want functions to have predictable behavior. Use arguments for analogous parameters, and supply those with defaults that are constants or at worst that can be computed from knowing the hardware and operating system context.

The third requirement in the list on page 47, freedom from assignments entirely, aims to avoid analysis of the changing "state" of the local variables, and is the most difficult to follow or even approximate in R (as it is to some extent in all functional languages). Avoiding repeated assignments to state variables is closely related to avoiding iteration. Functional programming languages often advocate extensive use of recursive computations instead of iteration, but traditionally deeply recursive computations are a bad idea in R because of memory growth and computational overhead. The discussion of *vectorizing* (Section 6.4, page 157) is in fact the closest analog in R to the spirit of state-free computing. Good examples of vectorizing often build up computations from other whole-object computations in a way that follows the spirit of functional programming.

Functions with output

Most good functions in R exist for the purpose of creating an object, but some functions legitimately serve other purposes. Displaying printed and graphical output to the user is an important part of data analysis, and some functions exist largely or entirely for display. The `graphics` package is a prime example, with most functions existing to produce graphical output. (It's relevant that the graphics model underlying this software comes from an ancient Fortran graphics library pre-dating S.) More modern graphics software, such as the `grid` and `lattice` packages, conform more closely to a functional view by producing graphics objects. Still, in a system where nearly everything is the result of a function call, some functions must exist to produce output.

The function `plot()` is the best known function in the `graphics` package, so examining it from our conceptual perspective is useful. The R documentation describes the purpose as a "generic function for the plotting of R objects". In this sense, the function can be regarded as one of several functions that provide information about objects based on their class (functions `show()`, `print()`, and `summary()` being others). These functions tend to be attached very closely to single arguments; either they have only one argument, or additional arguments tend to be tuning parameters to control what the function does. Methods corresponding to this argument are often valuable, as discussed in Chapter 10. Given such methods, users can expect the function to be defined for any class of objects, and with luck the designers of the class have taken the trouble to create a suitable method for these objects, unless an inherited method turns out to be adequate. In particular, the functions `plot()` and `print()` can be thought of as the visualization and printed ways of showing the objects; the original intent of `show()` was to produce the best default way to show the object, printed, plotted, or some other medium (in practice, nearly all `show()` methods print).

With this concept, it's not fatal that `plot()` produces no useful value, since its side effect is the purpose. The details of the (default) method are hidden somewhat because the actual graphical output relies on functions that are only interfaces to C code, and so hard to understand.

In terms of a generic function, however, the main difficulty with `plot()` is that the documented purpose of the function does not, in fact, describe all it does. The original `plot()` function in S was for scatter or `x-y` plots, intended to visualize the relation between *two* objects, specifically two numeric vectors. In fact, the `x-y` plot provides a good framework for understanding R graphics generally (see Section 7.2, page 242).

The notion of using `plot()` to visualize a single object was first an option, if the second argument was omitted; later, it became more of a focus particularly when S3 methods were introduced for statistical models. In retrospect, better design might have resulted from introducing a new generic function specifically for visualizing a single object.

Given all the history, it's too late to discourage use of `plot()` or the design of new methods for it. But being relatively clear and explicit about the conceptual intent of an important function should be a goal for future programming with R. Based on the lack of a returned object to analyze, on the obscurity resulting from doing most calculations in C, and on the confusion about its purpose, we can't give the `plot()` function a very high grade on our functional programming criteria.

Later approaches to graphical computing in R, such as that in the `lattice` package, get closer to functional style by producing graphics objects, the actual output being generated by methods (S3 methods for `print()` in most cases).

Functions with external side effects

A second type of function that deviates from the functional concept exists for the effect it has either on an R environment or on the R session, that is on the evaluator itself. Examples of the former are non-local assignment functions (`` `<<-` `` and `assign()`) and the programming tools for methods and classes (as discussed in Chapters 9 and 10). Non-local assignments are encountered in a style of programming known as "closures". The technique is discussed, and commented on, in Section 5.4, page 125; essentially, it involves creating an environment shared by several functions, which then alter non-local objects in the shared environment.

Functions such as `setMethod()` and `setClass()` in the `methods` package are called for their side effect of assigning metadata containing corresponding definitions. They could have been made more functional in appearance by doing ordinary assignments, but the objects created must have special names to trigger the appropriate actions when packages are attached, and also so that classes can have the same name as corresponding functions to generate objects from the class (for example, `matrix()`). The non-functional aspects are fairly harmless as long as other software calls these functions at the top level, preferably in the source defining an R package.

The main function to modify the evaluator is `options()`, which can be used to specify values visible to all computations. Its actions are handled at the C level, and modify a list of values, some known to the base implementation of R and others optionally shared among functions. In either case, code in one function can modify values then seen by any other function, a mechanism strongly at odds with functional programming.

All these programming mechanisms could to some extent be replaced by more functionally oriented alternatives. With `options()` especially, some fairly deep changes would be required, such as making the evaluator itself an object with relevant options as properties.

Most of the existing non-functional features in the core packages are either too entrenched or too useful to be removed. The hope is that future mechanisms will be consistent with functional programming or else will explicitly apply a clear alternative programming model.

3.3   Function Objects and Function Calls

This section looks at function objects as created by evaluating the `function` expression in the language. A function object defines how R evaluates a call to this function. All functions defined in the language share a basic structure that allows us to deal with them consistently and to develop programming tools working directly with function objects.

Function calls are objects also, and the R evaluator uses both objects to evaluate the call. This section concentrates on fairly practical issues, which the object view helps clarify. For a deeper look, see Chapter 13, and particularly Section 13.3, page 460.

Function objects

A function object is created by evaluating an expression of the form:

    function (*formal arguments*) *body*

The object created has object type `"closure"`. Like all object types, closures are defined in the base-level C software. Three essential properties define a closure object: the *formal arguments*, the *body*, and the *environment*. The three properties are available from corresponding functions, `formals()`, `body()`, and `environment()`.

R also has a set of *primitive functions*, implemented directly in C. Primitive functions have either type `"builtin"` or type `"special"`, according to whether they evaluate their arguments. New primitive functions cannot be created by users. We won't consider primitive functions in this chapter except when their behavior requires it, usually because they get in the way of a uniform treatment of functions.

In the grammar of the S language, the formal arguments are a comma-separated list of argument names, each name optionally followed by the corresponding *default expression*, that is, by the syntactic operator `"="` and an arbitrary expression. (The use of `"="` here is related to the assignment operator, but is translated directly into the function object; it does not generate a call to the R operator `` `=` ``.) The function `formals()` returns an ordinary list object, with its names attribute being the formal argument names of the function, and named elements being the unevaluated expressions for the corresponding argument's default value.

The body is any complete expression, but typically a sequence of expressions inside braces. The function `body()` returns the body of the function as an unevaluated expression.

Function objects in R have a third important property, their environment. When a function is created by evaluating the corresponding expression, the current environment is recorded as a property of the function. A function created during an R session at the top level has the global environment as its environment:

```
> f <- function(x)x+1
> environment(f)
<environment: R_GlobalEnv>
> identical(environment(f), .GlobalEnv)
[1] TRUE
```

The environment of a function is important in determining what non-local objects are visible in a call to this function. The global environment is, by definition, the environment in which top-level expressions are evaluated, such as those entered by the user. When an object name appears in a top-level expression, the evaluator looks first in the global environment, then in the environments currently attached to the R session, as suggested by the result of `search()`. (See Section 5.3, page 121 for a discussion.) For a call to a function defined at the top level, the behavior is similar. When a name is to be evaluated inside the call, the evaluator first looks locally for an object, such as an argument, in the call itself. If the name doesn't match, the evaluator looks in the environment of the function, and then through the parent environments as necessary. Thus objects visible in the session will be visible inside the call as well.

In two important cases, functions have environments other than the global environment. If a package is created with a namespace, that namespace is the environment of all functions it contains. And if a function is created dynamically during a call to another function, the current environment of the call becomes the function's environment. We will deal with the implications of both of these later in this chapter. Also, generic functions and methods (Chapter 10) are objects from classes that extend ordinary functions, to add additional information. These objects have special environments to provide that information efficiently.

Function calls

The evaluation of a function call is the most important step in computations using R. It also proceeds quite differently from the behavior of languages such as C or Java®.

The essential communication between the calling and the called function in R, as in any functional language, is via the argument expressions. The call to a function is an object in the language. Technically, a function is not a vector, but its elements are defined and can be used. The first element identifies the function to call, usually by name but potentially as an actual function object. The remaining elements are the unevaluated expressions for each of the actual arguments in the call, which will be matched to the formal arguments of the function definition. Here is a call to the function `mad()`, from the example on page 56.

```
> myCall <- quote(mad(xx[,j], constant = curConst, na.rm = TRUE))
> myCall[[1]]
mad
> myCall[[2]]
xx[, j]
> names(myCall)
[1] ""              ""               "constant" "na.rm"
```

The first actual argument is given without a name, the second and third have names given by the syntactic operator `"="`. As in the function definition, the argument names are transferred directly to the `names` attribute of the call object.

Evaluation of a call proceeds first by matching the actual arguments to the formal arguments, resulting in an object for each formal argument. Details of what "matching" means can be left for Chapter 13, but the rules work as follows. If the function does *not* have `"..."` as one of its arguments, then arguments are matched by three mechanisms, applied in this order:

1. the name in the call matches exactly to the name of the formal argument;

2. the name in the call matches a initial substring of exactly one formal argument (known traditionally as *partial matching*); or,

3. unnamed actual arguments are matched in order to any formal arguments not already matched by the first two steps.

In the example call above, the names `constant` and `na.rm` each match one of the formal arguments exactly. The unnamed argument then matches the first available formal arguments, in this case the first formal argument, `x` (see the example below).

Having `"..."` in the formal arguments changes the matching in two ways. The `"..."` argument itself is matched, not to a single argument, but to a list of all the arguments left unmatched by the process above. This list has no direct equivalent as an R expression, and in fact it is only used to fill in arguments in a subsequent call. You can see the unevaluated matching arguments in a browser, for debugging purposes:

```
substitute(c(...))
```

where `c()` could have been any function. The second effect of "`...`" is that any formal arguments coming after "`...`" in the definition will only be matched by the first mechanism above, exact name matching.

A comment on partial matching: I would recommend avoiding this mechanism in programming. It might have been useful in the old days before interactive user interfaces with name completion, but it's largely an unfortunate relic now, one that is unlikely to disappear, however, for reasons of compatibility. In writing functions, it can lead to confusing code and produce some nasty bugs, in combination with "`...`".

When the arguments have been matched, the evaluator creates an environment in which to evaluate the body of the function. The environment has objects assigned for each of the formal arguments, represented by a special type of objects, known as *promises*, which are essentially only available for computations in C. The promise object contains the expression corresponding to either the matching actual argument or the default expression, a reference to the environment where the expression should be evaluated, and some special structure that ensures the argument will be evaluated only once. Promises corresponding to actual arguments will be evaluated in the environment from which the function was called. Promises for default expressions will be evaluated in the environment created for this call.

Example: A function and calls to it

As an example in this section, let's look at the function `mad()` from the `stats` package in the core R code. This function computes the median absolute deviation of a numeric vector, an estimate of scale for samples from distributions used when greater robustness is desired than provided by the standard deviation.

```
> mad
function (x, center = median(x), constant = 1.4826, na.rm = FALSE,
    low = FALSE, high = FALSE)
{
    if (na.rm)
        x <- x[!is.na(x)]
    n <- length(x)
    constant * if ((low || high) && n%%2 == 0) {
        if (low && high)
            stop("'low' and 'high' cannot be both TRUE")
        n2 <- n%/%2 + as.integer(high)
        sort(abs(x - center), partial = n2)[n2]
    }
```

```
      else median(abs(x - center))
}
<environment: namespace:stats>
```

The function has 6 arguments, with default expressions for all but the first.

```
> dput(formals(mad))
list(x = , center = median(x), constant = 1.4826, na.rm = FALSE,
    low = FALSE, high = FALSE)
```

(Because the elements of the list returned by `formals()` are expressions, it's usually easier to look at the value via `dput()` rather than through the standard printing method for lists.)

One odd detail relates to arguments that do not have a default expression. The element in the formals list corresponding to x appears to be empty, but it must be an object. (Everything is an object.) In fact, it is an anomalous name or symbol object in R, with an empty string as its content. However, you can do almost no computation with this object, because it is interpreted as a missing argument in any other function call, except to `missing()` itself:

```
> xDefault <- formals(mad)$x
> class(xDefault)
Error: argument "xDefault" is missing, with no default
> missing(xDefault)
[1] TRUE
```

The printout for `mad()` ends with `"<environment:  namespace:stats>"`, indicating that the `stats` package has a namespace, and this namespace is the environment for the function. Environments for function objects are important in that they determine what other objects are visible from within a call to the function; most important, they determine what other functions can be called from within this one, and which versions of those functions will be found. As always in evaluation, a name will be looked up first in the current environment. Inside a function call, this environment is a local one created for the call. If the name is not found in the current environment, the evaluator looks next in the parent of that environment, which is the function object's environment. The search continues as necessary through the chain of parent environments.

The package's namespace contains all the objects defined as part of that package. Its parent is a special environment containing all the objects from other packages that the designer of the current package (`stats` in the case of `mad()`) considers relevant, and the parent of that environment in turn is the base package. Thus a namespace allows the package designer to control the external objects visible to the package, with no danger of finding unintended definitions. Without a namespace, the function's environment is the global environment, meaning that objects defined during the session can change the function's behavior–nearly always a bad idea. See page 69 for how to use trace() to deliberately change a function for debugging or development. Details of namespaces in packages are discussed in Section 4.6, page 103.

Next, let's examine how a call to the mad() function would be evaluated.

```
mad(xx[,j],  constant = curConst, na.rm = TRUE)
```

The matching rules match the three actual arguments to x, center, and na.rm, as we can check by using the match.call() function:

```
> match.call(mad,
+       quote(mad(xx[,j], constant = curConst, na.rm = TRUE)))
mad(x = xx[, j], constant = curConst, na.rm = TRUE)
```

The evaluator creates a new environment for the call and initializes promise objects for all six formal arguments. When arguments need to be evaluated, the expressions for the three arguments above will be evaluated in the environment from which the call came. The remaining arguments will be set up to evaluate their default expression in the new environment. Default expressions can involve other arguments; for example, evaluating the default expression for center uses the object x, the first formal argument. Such cross-connections can affect the order in which arguments are evaluated. It is possible to create invalid patterns of default expressions, as in:

```
function(x, y, dx = dy, dy = dx)
```

This fails if both dx and dy are missing. Here the special structure of promises allows the evaluator to detect the recursive use of a default expression.

The six objects corresponding to formal arguments can be re-assigned, as with any other objects (in the example, x may be reassigned to remove NAs). This overwrites the promise object, which may cause the value of missing() to change for this object (be careful to evaluate missing() before any such assignment can occur). Just to re-emphasize a fundamental property: The assignment to x has no effect on the object that supplied the x argument.

Operators

Operators, as objects, are simply functions. Because the S language uses C-style, or "scientific" notation for expressions, the grammar recognizes certain tokens when they appear as prefix (unary) or infix (binary) operators. The definitions of the corresponding names as function objects will have one or two arguments and those arguments will not be supplied by name (at least when the function is used as an operator). In addition, R uses standard notation for subset and element computations, corresponding to the operator functions `` `[` `` and `` `[[` ``. Otherwise, nothing much distinguishes the operators from any other functions.

Operators with specific notation in the language are defined in the base package and should not be redefined. For many of the operators, defining methods involving new classes makes sense, however. Section 2.3, page 21 discusses some of the more frequently used operators. Here are the operators in the base package.

```
"!"      "!="     "$"      "$<-"    "%%"     "%*%"    "%/%"    "%in%"  "%o%"
"%x%"    "&"      "&&"     "("      "*"      "+"      "-"      "/"     ":"
"::"     ":::"    "<"      "<-"     "<<-"    "<="     "="      "=="    ">"
">="     "@"      "["      "[<-"    "[["     "[[<-"   "^"      "{"     "|"
"||"     "~"
```

The object names shown were determined heuristically. The computation that produced them is shown as an example of computing with regular expressions (see Section 8.3, page 303).

Entirely new operators can be written. Any function object with a name having the pattern:

%text%

can be used as an infix or prefix operator. Suppose, for example, we wanted an operator `` `%perp%` `` that returned the component of numerical data y perpendicular to numerical data x. We just define a function with the desired name and the correct definition. The new operator is immediately available.

```
> `%perp%` <- function(y,x)
+        lsfit(x,y, intercept   = FALSE)$residuals
> x <- 1:10
> y <- x + .25 * rnorm(10)
> y %perp% x
 [1] -0.22424843  0.09341398  0.22921013 -0.05308264 -0.05928619
 [6]  0.18727473  0.19218365 -0.11410726 -0.07209999 -0.10486243
```

3.4　The Language

The "programming" language for R is the same language used for interactive computation. In both contexts, function calls are the essence, as discussed in Section 2.3, page 19. The functional programming approach encourages new functions to be built up from calls to existing functions, without introducing complex procedural controls. Initially, new functions will be easier to write and debug if they are simple extensions of interactive computing.

But as you design more extensive functions and other software, you will eventually need some added constructions. This section examines some of the key techniques in the language, most of which have to do with flow of control; that is, deciding what computations to do, returning a value for the function call, and controlling iterations ("looping").

By far the most commonly used looping construct is the `for()` expression, such as:

```
for(i in 1:p)
    value[i,1] <- which.max(x0[,i])
```

(But see Section 6.8, page 212 for this specific loop.) The general syntax is:

```
for(name in range) body
```

where syntactically *name* is a name (or anything in back quotes), and both *range* and *body* are general expressions. The body is evaluated repeatedly with *name* assigned the first element of the evaluated range, then the second, and so on. Let's refer to this object as the index variable. Something like the example, with the index variable being a numeric sequence, is the most common usage. In that example, we're indexing on the columns of v. The evaluated range will typically relate to some sort of vector or array. Quite often, there will be two or more parallel objects (perhaps we're indexing the rows or columns of a matrix or data frame, along with a parallel vector or list, say). Then indexing by a sequence is essential.

The most common error in this most common example is to forget that sometimes the range of the loop may be empty. R is quite prepared to deal with vectors of length 0 or matrices with 0 rows or columns. In programming with R, we should either check or guarantee that the range of the loop is not empty, or else write the code to work if it is. A `for()` loop using the `:` operator is immediately suspect. Two alternatives should be used instead:

```
seq(along = object)
seq(length = number)
```

These both produce a sequence which is empty if the object has length 0 or if the number computes as 0 (beware: in the current implementation, you are responsible for rounding error; any positive fraction is treated as 1). Unless we really knew what we were doing, the example above should have been:

```
for(i in seq(length = p))
    value[i,1] <- which.max(x0[,i])
```

Another detail to note is that, in R, the assignment implied for the index variable is an ordinary assignment in the environment of the computation. For example, if p > 0 in our example, then i will have the value p after the loop is finished, regardless of what if any assignment of i existed before the loop was evaluated. (S-Plus reverts the index variable to its previous value, if any, on exiting the loop.)

Other loops are:

```
while(test) body
repeat   body
```

in which *test* evaluates to test a condition, and *body* is again any expression but typically a braced sequence of expression. (See below for testing a condition, which is a highly special computation in R.)

In any loop, two special reserved words are available:

next: this terminates evaluation of the body of the loop for this iteration;

break: this terminates evaluation of the complete loop expression.

To be useful, either of these control expressions will occur conditionally on some test.

The value of any loop expression is the value of the body, the last time it is evaluated. A loop that is evaluated zero times has value NULL. Programming will usually be clearer if the loop is used to assign or modify local variables, with the value of the loop itself ignored. The value may be unclear if the control expressions are used, because it will depend on where in the loop a break or next occurred. Also, if you're concerned with S-Plus compatibility, be aware that loops there have no useful value.

The conditional test expression has the forms:

```
if(test) expression1
if(test) expression1   else expression2
```

The optional `else` part to the conditional expression can cause problems, particularly when expressions are being typed at the top level. The evaluator will treat the version without `else` as a complete expression, and an expression starting with `else` is a syntax error. When the expressions are inside braces, as is typically the case, then a newline can intervene between *expression1* and `else`.

An important and sometimes tricky aspect of programming in the S language is testing a condition. This arises primarily in `if()` and `while()` expressions. A conditional expression, such as:

```
if(length(x) > 0)
   x <- x - mean(x)
```

looks both innocuous and much like programming in other languages. But it is in fact quite exceptional for an R expression, because the test *must* evaluate to a single `TRUE` or `FALSE` value if the expression as a whole is to work as expected. Similarly, the condition expression in a `while()` loop must evaluate to a single logical value:

```
while( rse > epsilon) {
   wgt <- update(wgt, curModel)
   curModel <- lm(formula, weight = wgt)
   rse <- sqrt(var(resid(curModel)))
}
```

Exceptionally for the S language, the expressions here are required to evaluate to a single value, and in addition to only one of two possible logical values, for the computation to be trustworthy. The code above may look reasonable and may even work for most examples, but it is in fact a potential trap. What if one of the arguments is a vector of length other than 1? Or if one of them evaluates to a non-numeric result, such as `NA`?

Code written for tests and loops should take care to avoid confusing errors and even more to ensure that no invalid results can sneak through. The use of special functions and the avoidance of nice-looking but dangerous expressions (such as the comparison in the loop above) can usually produce trustworthy results. See Section 6.3, page 152 for some techniques.

One more control structure is the function `return()`. As in most languages, this has the effect of ending the current call, with the value of the call being the value of the (single) argument to `return()`.

Functions in R can call themselves recursively, directly or indirectly. No special language mechanism is required, but good programming practice uses a special technique to make sure the recursive call is to the correct function.

A call to `Recall()` finds the function currently being called and calls that function recursively. Why? Because it's the function as an object that must be recalled. Various special circumstances might have changed the reference for the original name. Although not likely to occur often, mistakes of this form could cause very obscure bugs or, worse, subtly incorrect results. A variety of tools in R help to ensure that the correct function object is used. Simple recursion uses `Recall()`; function `local()` controls the context of an expression; functions `callGeneric()` and `callNextMethod()` provide similar facilities for programming with methods.

3.5 Interactive Debugging by Browsing

The term "debugging" has an unpleasant connotation, suggesting software pesticides or other disagreeable treatments. The suggestion is sometimes justified, particularly in dealing with large systems or primitive programming environments. In R, the experience should be more productive and pleasant.

Debugging is not just to recover from bugs, but to study software while it is being developed and tested. Flexible tools that are easy to apply can make the process more effective and much less painful.

In an interactive language such as R, particularly one that can compute with the language itself, debugging should include techniques for browsing interactively in the computation, and for modifying functions interactively to aid in understanding them. These techniques are powerful and often under-utilized by programmers. They do follow a different approach than the debugging used for most programming languages, an approach aimed at building directly on the concepts and techniques in R.

One thing that debugging procedures in any language should *not* be is complicated. There are few things more annoying than having to debug your debugging. Similarly, debugging should not involve learning another language or programming procedure. The main goal of the techniques discussed in this section is to get us back to ordinary interaction with R.

Along these lines, users familiar with more traditional programming languages such as C are often surprised at the absence of a separate debugger program (such as `gdb` for C programming) or a debugging mode (as is used with Perl). In fact, because R is implemented as an application written in C, you can use such an overlaid debugging tool with R, by invoking the application with a debugger argument (see the documentation for R itself on your platform). But debugging at the C level will be irrelevant for most R users. And debuggers of this type, whatever the language being debugged, usually have their own command syntax. The user of the debugger sets break points in the program; when the break point is reached, the user must enter commands in the debugger language to examine or modify variables.

Debugging in this style is unnatural in R. We already have a highly interactive language. What's needed is usually just to interact as we usually do, but at a time and in a context appropriate to the current programming problem. Instead of waiting until the current expression is complete, we either arrange to browse interactively in the middle of the computation, or enter when an error occurs. From either context, the user can examine local variables in the current function calls, using all the same tools that one would normally have at the command prompt, plus some additional functions specifically for debugging.

This section discusses two fundamental mechanisms:

1. Browsing in the context of a particular function call (using the function `browser()`). This involves typing ordinary expressions involving the arguments and other variables visible from the call, in order to examine the current state of computations. Essentially, the standard R interaction with the parser and evaluator is moved into the context of a function call.

2. Navigating a stack of nested function calls, either currently active (using the function `recover()`) or saved from past computation (the function `debugger()`).

In the next section, we discuss a related tool, the `trace()` function, which inserts code dynamically into a function or method, typically to call `browser()` or `recover()`, but in principle for any purpose you like. Combining the two sets of tools gives a powerful environment both for debugging and more generally for studying R software interactively.

After an error: The error option

A user dealing with well-tested software in what's assumed to be a routine way does not expect computations to stop with an error. If they do, the user is unlikely to have the information or the desire to look deeply into what happened where the error was generated. The default R error action is just to print an error message and exit from the top-level expression being evaluated.

As soon as we are involved in programming, the situation changes. We now want to specify a debugging action to take when an error occurs. The action is specified by the value of the global `error` option, specified by a call to the `options()` function as either a function or an unevaluated expression. Once you begin any serious programming, you will benefit from being able to recover information whenever an error occurs. The recommended option during program development is:

```
options(error = recover)
```

If much of your R activity is programming, you may want to have this option specified at session startup, for example by adding it to the `.Rprofile` file (see `?Startup`).

With this option in place, an error during an interactive session will call `recover()` from the lowest relevant function call, usually the call that produced the error. You can browse in this or any of the currently active calls, and recover arbitrary information about the state of computation at the time of the error.

If you don't want to debug interactively at the time of the error, an alternative to `recover()` as an error option is `options(error = dump.frames)`, which will save all the data in the calls that were active when an error occurred. Calling the function `debugger()` later on then produces a similar interaction to `recover()`. Usually, there is no advantage to `dump.frames()`, since `recover()` behaves like `dump.frames()` if the computations are not interactive, allowing the use of `debugger()` later on. Also, some computations don't "save" well, so you may find debugging harder to do later on. For example, interactive graphics and input/output on connections will be easier to study right away, rather than from a dump.

The **browser()** function

The `browser()` function is the basic workhorse of studying computations interactively on the fly. The evaluation of the expression:

```
browser()
```

invokes a parse-and-evaluate interaction at the time and in the context where the call to `browser()` took place. The call to `browser()` is just an ordinary call: It's evaluating the call that does something special. The function invokes some C code that runs an interaction with the user, prompting for R expressions, parsing and evaluating them in approximately the same way as top-level expressions, but as if the expressions occurred in the current context.

A call to `browser()` can appear anywhere a function call is legal:

```
if(min(weights) < 1e-5)
    browser()  ## but don't do this!
```

You should not manually insert calls to `browser()` or other debugging code into your functions. It's all too easy to leave the calls there, particularly if they are only used conditionally on some test, as in the example above. The result will be to plunge you or your users into an unwanted debugging situation sometime later. You might be surprised at how irritated your users may become in such circumstances.

Specifying `recover` as the error option will get you to the browser in any chosen function call active at the time of an error. For all other purposes, use the `trace()` function, as described in Section 3.6, page 67. Simple situations can be handled simply, and the `edit=` argument to `trace()` allows debugging to be inserted anywhere. Any conditional calls or other specialized expressions can then be entered and used, then removed simply by calling `untrace()`.

Browsing in multiple contexts: **recover()**

A call to `browser()` can examine all the information local to a particular function call, but an additional tool is needed to examine interactively the information in a nested sequence of calls. The function `recover()` is designed for this purpose. It essentially manages navigation up and down the calls and invokes `browser()` for interactions in a particular call. The `recover()` function begins the interaction by listing the currently active function calls (the traceback). The user enters the number of the relevant call from the list, or 0 to exit. All other interaction is with the function `browser()` in the usual way. The user can examine any information visible in the chosen context, and then return to `recover()` (by entering an empty line) to select another context. Let's begin with an example.

Suppose the call to `recover()` comes from the function `.Fortran()`, the R interface to Fortran routines. The context here is a call to the `aov()` function, which fits analysis-of-variance models in R by creating linear regression models. There might have been an error in a Fortran computation, but in this case we just wanted to see how the `aov()` function used Fortran subroutines for its numerical work. To do that, we inserted a call to `recover()` using `trace()` (see page 74 for the details). The initial printout is:

```
> aov(yield ~ N + K + Error(block/(N + K)), data=npk)
Tracing .Fortran("dqrls", qr = x, n = n, p = p,   .... on entry
```

```
Enter a frame number, or 0 to exit

1: aov(yield ~ N + K + Error(block/(N + K)), data = npk)
2: eval(ecall, parent.frame())
3: eval(expr, envir, enclos)
4: lm(formula = yield ~ block/(N + K), data = npk, ....
5: lm.fit(x, y, offset = offset, singular.ok = singular.ok, ...)
6: .Fortran("dqrls", qr = x, n = n, p = p, ...

Selection:
```

You may see now why `recover()` was a useful function to call. There are at least three contexts of interest: `aov()` for the original computation, `lm()` for the linear model, and `lm.fit()` for the numerical details. By starting from `recover()`, we can decide to browse in any of these.

The user responds with the number for the call we first want to browse in. If we're interested in the computations that produced the linear model, we want `aov()`, call number 1.

```
Selection: 1
Called from: eval(expr, envir, enclos)
Browse[1]> objects()
 [1] "Call"        "Terms"        "allTerms"    "contrasts"
 [5] "data"        "eTerm"        "ecall"       "errorterm"
 [9] "formula"     "indError"     "intercept"   "lmcall"
[13] "opcons"      "projections"  "qr"
Browse[1]> ecall
lm(formula = yield ~ block/(N + K), data = npk, singular.ok = TRUE,
    method = "qr", qr = TRUE)
Browse[1]>
```

Now we are in the browser, and can do any computations we want; in the example above, we asked for all the local objects in the call, and then looked at a constructed formula used in the call to `lm()`.

If at this point we want to browse in `lm()` instead, we exit the browser (by entering an empty line). That puts us back in the menu from `recover()` and we can enter 4 to examine the call to `lm()`.

Once we're done entirely with the interaction, entering 0 to `recover()` exits that function.

Notice that the `browser()` function would not work conveniently if called directly as an error option or with `trace()` in this example. In a single call to `browser()`, only objects visible from the particular call can be examined. The visible objects will not include the local objects in other calls.

You could call `recover()` interactively from `browser()`, but if you expect to examine more than one currently active function, a simpler choice is to specify `recover` directly, either as the `error` option or in a call to `trace()`.

Browsing on warnings

Warning messages are the grey area of debugging: supposedly not serious enough to interrupt the computation, but worth nagging the user about. These are the buzzing insects of debugging; annoying rather than a direct threat. But even if you are currently convinced the warning messages are harmless, if they persist your users (including yourself when you come back later) may not be so sure.

The simple control over warnings is an argument to `options()`. Unlike the error option, however, the argument `warn=` is just an integer expressing the level of seriousness to give warnings. The default is 0, meaning to collect warnings and report them at the end of the expression. Warnings are often issued in a loop, usually the same warning repeatedly. In this case, the standard action is to save up the warnings (50 maximum), and treat the user to the annoying message:

```
> bar(rnorm(10))
[1] 13
There were 30 warnings (use warnings() to see them)
```

Negative values of the `warn` option say to ignore all warnings. However, this strategy is not a good idea unless you *really* know what warnings can be issued during the enclosed computation. If you or a user of your software did something unanticipated to inspire a warning, that information is now lost.

That leaves us with only one strategy: figure out what caused the warning and if possible avoid it. The simplest mechanism to look deeper is again the warning level option. Setting it to 2 or more converts warnings into errors:

```
> options(warn=2)
> bar(rnorm(10))
Error in foo(x) : (converted from warning) There were missing
values in x
```

At this point, if you have set `options(error=recover)`, you can proceed to debug in the usual way.

The techniques for using `trace()` can also be adapted to deal with warnings, in case you need to keep running after examining the computations interactively. The simple way is:

```
trace(warning, recover)
```

which will let you examine computations from the point where `warning()` was called (but it won't work if the warning is issued from C code, as is often the case). A third approach is to use *condition handlers* (Section 3.7, page 74). These require more programming to set up, but introduce no global changes that need to be undone and are also somewhat more flexible.

3.6 Interactive Tracing and Editing

Waiting for errors to occur before worrying about debugging is not always a good strategy. By the time the error occurs, the relevant information to track down the problem may no longer exist. And the worst problems in computation are not fatal errors at all, but wrong answers from an evaluation that *seems* normal. That's the message of the *Prime Directive*. Even if no mistakes are expected or encountered, we may want to study computations as they take place, for reasons such as performance or just to examine some intermediate results.

For these situations, the `trace()` function is the most useful debugging tool. Its name is too modest; general use of `trace()` doesn't just trace what happens in functions, but can be used to insert interactive debugging of any kind at the start, on exit, or anywhere in the body of a function. The function provides a powerful mechanism to examine the computations during the evaluation of a function or method, whether one you have written or software from an attached package (packages with namespaces included).

Calling `trace()` adds computations to a specified function, `f`. In the simplest use, a function is supplied by name to be called, without arguments, at the start of each call to `f` and/or just before the call returns. The function supplied is usually `browser` or `recover`. For example:

```
trace(f1, recover)
trace(f2, exit = browser)
trace(f3, browser, exit = browser)
```

All future calls to `f1()` will begin with a call to `recover()`; calls to `f2()` will call `browser()` on exit, and calls to `f3()` will call `browser()` on both entry and exit. These are the quick-and-easy forms of interactive tracing, sufficient for many applications.

A second, more powerful use combines `trace()` with interactive editing of the function. Instead of a fixed change, any modification can be made, and the edited version now, temporarily, takes the place of the original. This not only allows arbitrary debugging code, it provides the most convenient way to experiment with changes in a function from a package.

Why use `trace()`?

The mechanism of `trace()` is simple: It constructs a modified version of the function object and re-assigns that in the environment from which the original came. "But, I could do that myself!", you may say. Yes, at least in simple cases, but there are several advantages to letting `trace()` handle the details, some of them important.

There is no need to make changes in a source file, and therefore less chance that you will forget to remove the changes later on. With `trace()` the modified function reverts automatically to the untraced version, either at the end of the session or after the call:

```
untrace(f)
```

The use of `trace()` allows you to examine or even temporarily modify functions or methods in attached packages, including packages using the `namespace` mechanism (even functions not exported from the namespace). For such functions direct editing may not work, for reasons we explore on page 72. If you want to debug or modify code in a loaded namespace, `trace()` may be the only straightforward mechanism.

The option of editing interactively is the most general form of tracing, but also in a sense the most natural. We are back to the intuitive notion of just editing the function, but with the `trace()` mechanism handling the details. In fact, `trace()` with `edit=TRUE` is often a convenient way to try out changes in a function from a package, without having to alter and reinstall the package. The edited changes don't need to be restricted to debugging code.

All the techniques can be applied to any formal method in the same way as to an ordinary function by supplying the method's signature to `trace()` (see page 71).

Tracing and browsing

A simple but effective form of tracing is to invoke `browser()` on entry to a function. The special command `"n"` causes the browser to step through the subexpressions of the function, printing the next subexpression each time before evaluating it. Here is a simple trace-and-browse session with the function `zapsmall()`:

```
> trace(zapsmall, browser)
Tracing function "zapsmall" in package "base"
[1] "zapsmall"
> zapsmall(xx)
Tracing zapsmall(xx) on entry
Called from: eval(expr, envir, enclos)
Browse[1]> n
debug: {
    if (length(digits) == 0)
        stop("invalid 'digits'")
    if (all(ina <- is.na(x)))
        return(x)
    mx <- max(abs(x[!ina]))
    round(x, digits = if (mx > 0)
        max(0, digits - log10(mx))
    else digits)
}
Browse[1]> n
debug: if (length(digits) == 0) stop("invalid 'digits'")
Browse[1]> n
debug: if (all(ina <- is.na(x))) return(x)
Browse[1]> n
debug: mx <- max(abs(x[!ina]))
Browse[1]> any(ina)
[1] FALSE
Browse[1]>
debug: round(x, digits = if (mx > 0) max(0, digits - log10(mx)) else digits)
Browse[1]>      Here the function returns--
   [1] 0.0781455 -1.2417132 0.7709643 1.7353247 1.9750906 -0.7128754
      etc.
```

The first "n" prints the expression to be evaluated, then each subexpression is printed and evaluated *after* the user returns an empty line. Before that, one can evaluate any expression, as we did here with any(ina).

Simple tracing such as this can be useful, but is limited. In this example, the author of zapsmall() was showing off by computing the whole result in one long and rather obscure expression. We can't examine that before the function returns, because it wasn't assigned, leading us to want to edit the function being traced.

Tracing with editing

For completely general tracing, supply the optional argument

```
edit = TRUE
```

in the call to `trace()`. The effect of the `edit` argument is to invoke an editor, initialized with the current definition of the function or method. You can edit the code in any way you like. After you save the result and exit the editor, the modified definition is inserted by `trace()` as a temporary modification of the original. You can cancel tracing by calling `untrace()` as usual.

In the trace of `zapsmall()` above, suppose we call `trace()` again:

```
> trace(zapsmall, edit = TRUE)
```

We then enter an editor (typically the editor associated with the GUI), and can make any changes. Saving and exiting will install the edited function.

In this example, we would edit the last subexpression to:

```
value <- round(x, digits = if (mx > 0)
    max(0, digits - log10(mx))
else digits)
value
```

Now we can examine the value before it's returned. If you try this example yourself, you will notice that the effect of the previous tracing is left in, when `edit=TRUE`; the function begins with the line:

```
.doTrace(browser(), "on entry")
```

The reasoning in `trace()` is that editing will often be iterated, and one does not want to have to retype all the changes.

As a second example, let's trace a function with an internal loop, in particular the function `binaryCount()` discussed in Section 9.7, page 374:

```
binaryCount <- function(nodes, leafValues) {
    nL <- length(leafValues)
    nN <- nrow(nodes)
    left <- nodes[,1]; right <- nodes[, 2]

    left <- ifelse(left<0, -left, left + nL)
    right <- ifelse(right<0, -right , right + nL)

    count <- c(leafValues, rep(NA, nN))

    while(any(is.na(count)))
        count <- c(leafValues, count[left] + count[right])

    count[-seq(length=nL)]
}
```

Never mind what it does in detail; the main interest is in the `while()` loop, which continues as long as there are `NA` values in the vector `count`. Suppose we want to know how many times the code goes through the loop, and perhaps how many `NA` values are left on each iteration. This cannot be done by simple tracing, and if `binaryCount()` is in a package namespace we can't easily change it there by ordinary editing (see page 73). The solution is to use `trace()` with editing:

```
trace(binaryCount, edit = TRUE)
```

In the interactive editor, we edit the loop, to something like:

```
iter <- 1
while (any(is.na(count))) {
    message(iter, ": ", sum(is.na(count)))
    iter <- iter + 1
    count <- c(leafValues, count[left] + count[right])
}
```

Now each call to `binaryCount()`, whether directly or from some other function in the package, prints out information about the iterations; for example:

```
> nodeArea <- binaryCount(usTree@nodes, Area)
1: 49
2: 32
3: 21
4: 15
5: 11
6: 7
7: 4
8: 2
9: 1
```

If you want to change the tracing but start from the current traced version, call `trace()` with `edit=TRUE` again. The version you see in the editor will be whatever is current, either with or without tracing. To delete the edits, call `untrace(binaryCounts)`.

The `edit` version of `trace()` behaves like the `edit()` function in R (for the good reason that it in fact calls `edit()`). By default the call to `trace()` invokes the default editor for the local user interface, or as specified by the `editor` option or a corresponding shell variable setting (see `?options`).

Tracing specific methods

All the techniques for tracing functions apply as well to tracing methods. Supply the `signature=` argument to `trace()` with the same signature that would select the method, and the modified definition will be set to be the corresponding method for that function. Suppose, for example, that we want to trace the method for function `show()` corresponding to class `"GPSTrack"`:

```
trace(show, exit = browser, signature = "GPSTrack")
```

A call to `browser()` will now be inserted into the original method, and the result set as the `"GPSTrack"` method for `show()`.

Because method definition objects belong to a class that extends `"function"`, all the tracing mechanisms extend to methods, in particular the `edit` option.

When `trace()` is applied to a method, it finds the current method definition by a call to `selectMethod()`, which will return either an explicitly defined method or one inherited from another signature. It's not necessary that the signature appeared in an explicit `setMethod()` call for this function. Notice, however, that after specifying the trace, the traced definition will be installed by an explicit call to `setMethod()`. Therefore, subclasses of the classes in the `signature=` argument may select the traced method as well.

How tracing works

The basic idea is entirely simple and epitomizes the S-language style of using dynamically created objects. Evaluating `trace(f, ...)` creates a new version of the function object `f`, containing calls to an interactive browser (or any other computations you like), and assigned in place of the original function or method.

The object created by `trace()` extends both class `"function"` and a virtual class, `"traceable"`. The latter class provides the methods to restore the original version of the function or method, while the new object still behaves like a function or method definition, as the case may be. The mechanism is in fact open-ended in the sense that any class extending `"function"` can have a traceable version. Section 9.4, page 353 discusses the class mechanism used, which illustrates the value of multiple inheritance.

For a plain function, the new object is assigned directly. For a method, the new method is inserted in the appropriate generic function, effectively as if the new definition were assigned via a call to `setMethod()`, but only for the current session. For non-method objects, what happens depends on where the original object came from. An object modified for tracing is always assigned back into the original environment. Emphasis on *always*. For objects from the global environment, an ordinary assignment takes place. Notice that as a result, if you save the image of that environment when you quit, traced versions of these functions will still be traced when you load that data image again. If that's not what you want, you need to `untrace()` the functions before saving.

For objects from other environments, particularly from packages, the situation is different. First, the traced versions of functions in packages are stored in the environment for that package in the current session, and therefore will have no life after the session ends. In particular, they cannot accidentally override the package's version of that function in later sessions, even if you save the global environment when you quit.

Second, the `trace()` mechanism works for objects in namespaces as well, which can be key for debugging. The namespace mechanism is discussed in Section 4.6, page 103, but the aspect relevant to debugging is that when a function in a namespace calls another function, the evaluator looks for the function only in the same namespace and in the objects that namespace imports. It does not look in the global environment. As a result, an attempt to trace computations in a function in a namespace by creating an edited version by hand will usually fail. The edited version is normally saved in the global environment, but other functions in the package's namespace will ignore this version and continue to call the untraced version.

For this reason, `trace()` always assigns the modified function back into the original namespace. It does this even to the extent of overriding locked environments. Normally such overrriding is both antisocial and undesirable, but for the sake of debugging it avoids having to create a whole separate version of the package's software just to trace a single function.

With the same mechanism, you can trace functions in a namespace that are not exported. You might discover such functions by seeing them called from exported functions. These functions will not be visible by name; to trace them, you must use the "triple colon" notation. For example, packages with a namespace may define functions to be automatically called when the namespace is loaded or unloaded (see `?.onLoad`). These functions should not be exported, but it's possible you might want to put a call to the browser in one of them, perhaps to better understand the state of the package when it is loaded or unloaded (admittedly, a highly advanced bit of programming). To call the browser at the end of the unloading of the methods package, for example:

```
> trace(methods:::.onUnload, exit = browser)
Tracing function ".onUnload" in package "methods (not-exported)"
[1] ".onUnload"
```

The comment `"not-exported"` in the printed message confirms that this function is not exported from the package.

R implements some fundamental computations as *primitive* functions. These peculiar objects are not true functions, but essentially an instruction to send the evaluator to a particular C-level computation. Primitives have no formal arguments and no expression as a function body. It barely makes sense to use `trace()` with primitives, because there is nothing to examine inside the call. However, we may want to inspect computations in other functions just before or just after the evaluation of the call to the primitive, which we can do by inserting an entry or exit trace expression in the primitive. The primitive is not actually a function object, so the trace mechanism works by creating an ordinary function containing the tracer expression plus an invocation of the primitive. Here's an example, using the `.Fortran()` function.

```
> trace(.Fortran, recover)
Tracing function ".Fortran" in package "base"
[1] ".Fortran"
```

The use of `recover()` as the trace action suits our need to examine the function that called `.Fortran()`.

3.7 Conditions: Errors and Warnings

The actions taken traditionally on errors and warnings have been folded into a general condition mechanism in more recent versions of R. Similar to mechanisms in other languages such as Java and Lisp, the condition mechanism allows for much more general programming both to generate and to handle conditions that may alter the flow of computations.

In this general formulation `"condition"` is a class of objects[1], with subclasses `"error"`, `"warning"`, `"message"`, and `"interrupt"`. Programmers can introduce new classes of conditions. Corresponding conditions are generated by a call to `signalCondition()` with an object of the corresponding class passed as an argument. See `?signalCondition`.

Two general controlling calls are available for handling conditions:

```
withCallingHandlers(expr, ...)
tryCatch(expr, ...)
```

In both cases `expr` is the expression we want to evaluate (a literal, not an object constructed by `quote()` or other computations). The `"..."` arguments are named by the name of the condition (`error=`, etc.) and supply

---

[1]An S3 class, at the time this is written.

handler functions for the corresponding condition. In addition, `tryCatch()` takes a `finally=` argument. Handler functions are functions that take a single argument, `condition`; when the handler function is called, that argument will be a condition object. Utility functions `conditionMessage()` and `conditionCall()` return the character string message for the condition and the originating function call from which the condition occurred.

The form of the two controlling function calls is similar, but they operate quite differently. Supplying handlers to `withCallingHandlers()` is much like specifying a function as an error option, except for the argument. When the condition occurs, the handler will be called from that context. The usual interactive debugging mechanisms are available. Here is a simple handler function from the SoDA package that prints the message and call, and then starts up the `recover()` function to browse in the current function calls.

```
recoverHandler <- function(condition) {
    string1 <- function(what) if(length(what) > 1)
      paste(what[[1]], "...") else what
    message("A condition of class \"",
          string1(class(condition)),"\" occurred, with message:\n",
          conditionMessage(condition))
    call <- conditionCall(condition)
    if(!is.null(call))
      message(
          "The condition occurred in: ", string1(deparse(call)))
    recover()
}
```

The use of `withCallingHandlers()` requires more specification for each expression, but it provides much greater flexibility than a traditional error option. Any condition can be handled and the specification of handlers is local to this expression evaluation. The following excerpt tracks the occurrence of warnings in multiple calls to `as.numeric()` via `lapply()`.

```
warned <- FALSE
opt <- options(warn= -1); on.exit(options(opt))
nValue <-  withCallingHandlers(lapply(value, as.numeric),
          warning = function(cond) warned <<- TRUE)
```

The handler sets a variable, `warned`, in the calling function. After the `lapply()` call is finished the calling function will decide what to do about the warnings. (The excerpt is from function `splitRepeated()`, for importing data with repeated values; see Section 8.2, page 296 for the rest of the computation.) More than one handler for the same condition can be supplied.

In particular, the standard handlers will be called after handlers specified in the call have returned. That's why the excerpt above used `options()` to turn off printing of warnings during the call to `withCallingHandlers()`.

Note the non-local assignment, `warned <<- TRUE`, in the function passed in as a handler. Because `warned` has previously been assigned locally in the call to `splitRepeated()`, where the handler function was also created, the non-local assignment will also take place there. The rule behind the mechanism is explained in Section 13.5, page 467.

The paradigm for `tryCatch()` is a generalization of the `try()` function. The expression is evaluated; if none of the handled conditions occurs, the value of the expression is returned as the value of `tryCatch()`. If a condition does occur, the corresponding handler is called, and the value of that call is returned from `tryCatch()`. If the `finally=` argument is supplied, that expression is evaluated after the handler returns, but does not affect the value of `tryCatch()`. I have found `withCallingHandlers()` more useful for program development, and `tryCatch()` more appropriate when some value should be returned to signal a condition, overriding the standard behavior.

The use of `tryCatch()` can overcome what Bill Venables calls "design infelicities"; for example, suppose I want to test whether a particular package can be attached, but I only want to test, with no errors or warning messages to confuse my users. The function `require()`, with its `quietly=` argument, might appear to do the trick, but it still generates a warning if the package is not available, and an error if the package exists but cannot be loaded (wrong version of R, perhaps). The computation to silently return `FALSE` in any of these situations is:

```
tryCatch(require(pkg, quietly = TRUE, character.only = TRUE),
    warning = function(w) FALSE,
    error = function(w) FALSE
)
```

Silently ignoring errors is not generally a good idea, but when you're sure you can do so, this is the way.

3.8   Testing R Software

In the spirit of the *Prime Directive*, to provide trustworthy software, we would like to provide assurances that our software does what it aims to do. Programming practices leading to good functional design (Section 3.2, page 43) help, allowing readers to understand what is happening. In addition, some assurances have to be empirical: "See, the software really does what we claim."

Testing R software is particularly important in the context of creating a package, as described in Chapter 4, especially Section 4.5, page 101. In fact, a serious need to test your software is one of the hints that it is time to organize it as a package, so that the tests will be visible and can be run systematically. Even before that stage, when programming primarily to use the results, you need some evidence that your software is trustworthy, in order to present those results with confidence. For this purpose, it's good to accumulate some source files to remind you of tests that were helpful.

Tests can be incorporated most easily if they are *assertion tests*; that is, expressions that are asserted to evaluate to the logical value TRUE. Assertion tests can be automated so human intervention is not required as long as the assertion is in fact valid. R comes with a function designed precisely to run assertion tests, stopifnot(), which takes any number of literal expressions as arguments. As its name suggests, this function generates an error if one of the expressions does not evaluate to TRUE:

```
stopifnot(is(x, "matrix"))
```

In some testing situations, one may want to continue after an assertion failure. One useful general technique is to make the call to stopifnot() itself an argument to try(). The function try() catches any error occurring during the evaluation of its argument; the error message will normally be printed, but evaluation will continue. You don't need to use stopifnot() to generate a warning from try() if a computation fails, but the two functions together are a good way to advertise an assertion that you want to make a warning, or simply to ensure that the software goes on to make further tests.

A different testing situation arises when our software should detect an error either on the user's part or because the input data fails some requirement. The test needed here is to run an example and verify that it does indeed generate an error. The logic is a bit tricky, so package SoDA contains a utility for the purpose, muststop(). This takes a literal expression and catches any error in its evaluation; failure to catch an error causes muststop() itself to generate an error.

The use of stopifnot() and similar tools assumes that we can reliably test an assertion. Important tests may be difficult to make precise, particularly for quantitative applications. The more forward-looking and valuable your software, the harder it may be to specify precise tests.

Tests involving difficult computations often take refuge in the belief that the computation worked once. An object that resulted from a successful run is saved and treated as a standard. The test then compares that object with the result of a current computation asserted to be equivalent to that producing the standard object. Another approach is available if there are two methods that in principle give the same result, allowing the test to compare the two methods. If one method is, say, simple but slow then that can be treated tentatively as the standard.

Either way, the resulting assertion test must compare two objects, often including computed numerical results, and report non-equality, within expected accuracy. One cannot guarantee to distinguish errors in programming from unavoidable differences due to inexact numerical computations, if two expressions are not precisely identical. However, if we believe that likely mistakes will make a substantial change in the numerical result, then a rough test is often the important one. Do, however, use functions such as `all.equal()`, `identical()`, and other tools, rather than computations using the comparison operators. Section 6.7, page 196, deals with numerical comparisons in more detail.

Chapter 4

R Packages

This chapter looks at the organization and construction of R packages. You mainly need this information when you decide to organize your own code into package form, although it's useful to understand packages if you need to modify an existing package or if you have problems installing one.

Section 4.2, page 80, introduces the concept and some basic tools; following sections cover creating the package (4.3, 85); producing documentation (4.4, 95); adding test software (4.5, 101); using the namespace mechanism (4.6, 103); and including other software, whether written in C and related languages (4.7, 108) or from other systems (4.8, 108).

But first, some encouragement.

4.1 Introduction: Why Write a Package?

Unquestionably, one of the great strengths of R is the ability to share software as R packages. For the user, packages provide relatively reliable, convenient, and documented access to a huge variety of techniques, in open-source software. For authors, packages provide both a communication channel for their work and a better way to organize software even for reusing it themselves.

The early position of this chapter in the book reflects some advice: Consider organizing your programming efforts into a package early in the process. You can get along with collections of source files and other miscellany, but the package organization will usually repay some initial bother with easier to use and more trustworthy software.

Admittedly, initial bother does exist: Using the R package tools constrains the organization of your software and requires explicit setup. If you go on to use the `check` command to test your package, the requirements become even more fussy. Isn't this against the spirit of starting small and proceeding through gradual refinement? Why, then, am I encouraging programmers using R to write packages, and earlier rather than later?

The answer largely comes from the *Prime Directive*: making your software trustworthy. As the term "package" suggests, R packages allow you to provide in a single convenient package your functions and other software along with documentation to guide users and with tests that validate important assertions about what the software does. Once you realize that your current programming may be of future value, to you or to others, then good documentation and key tests will likely pay off in fewer future mistakes, in easier reuse of your software, and in increasing the benefits to others from your efforts.

The sooner the software is organized to obtain these benefits, the less will be the initial hurdle, so even the gradual refinement goal benefits, given that you would need to create a package eventually.

The package organization becomes more helpful as the package becomes more ambitious. For example, if you want to include compiled code in C or Fortran, package installation will automatically maintain up-to-date object code, including a dynamically linkable object library.

As for the fuss and occasional bureaucratic intrusions, there are tools to help. R comes with a number of them, and we add some more in this chapter.

4.2 The Package Concept and Tools

An R package is a collection of source code and other files that, when installed by R, allows the user to attach the related software by a call to the `library()` function. During development, the files are organized in a standardized way under a single *source* directory (aka folder). For distribution, the source is organized as a compressed archive file by the *build* tool. The package is not used from the source directory or archive; instead, the source is used to generate an *installed* version of the package in another directory. R itself provides basic tools for installing and testing packages, and for constructing the archives and other files needed to ship and document packages. In this chapter we illustrate the construction of a package using as an example the SoDA package associated with this book.

Packages exist so they can be used during an R session. A package is attached to the session by giving its name as an argument to `library()` or `require()`. The concept behind attaching the package is that the name refers to a subdirectory of that name, underneath a `library` directory. Inside that subdirectory are files and other subdirectories that can be used by the R evaluator and other utilities. In the original, simplest, and still very common situation, the package consists of some R functions and their documentation. As time has passed, the simple original concept has expanded in many directions: R objects in the package can be represented efficiently, enabling packages with many and/or large objects (lazy loading); packages can control what other packages they use and what functions they make public (namespaces); software can be included in the package written in other languages, primarily languages related to C, but in principle any language; documentation can be processed into different forms, suitable for the local environment and supplemented with files to help searching; files will be included that are not directly used in the session but that allow for checking that the package behaves as asserted.

Packages are managed by a set of tools that comes with R itself (you may need to add some support tools; see page 84). The tools are usually accessed from a command shell, in the UNIX/Linux style, although a GUI may hide the shell from the user. The shell commands take the form

    R CMD *operation*

where *operation* is one of the R shell tools. By invoking the tool in this R-dependent way, one ensures that the tool has access to information about the local installation of R. The operation encountered most often in developing your own packages will be installation, taking your source package and making it available as an installed package. As a shell-style command, installation is carried out by:

    $ R CMD INSTALL *packages*

This step works basically the same whether you're writing your own package or downloading a source or binary package from one of the archives. If you are installing packages from a repository, *packages* will typically be one or more files downloaded from the repository. If you are developing packages, the *packages* argument may be the names of source directories. The command also takes a variety of shell-style options to control the installation, such as the option "`-l` *directory*", specifying a library directory under which to install the package.

For example, if SoDA is a directory under the current directory containing the source for that package, we can install it under a library subdirectory, RLibrary, of the login directory by the command:

```
$ R CMD INSTALL -l ~/RLibrary SoDA
```

When you're getting near to distributing your package to other users or even other machines, however, it's better to use the build command (below) first. That way the installation uses the actual archive you will be distributing.

Other tools allow you to check the package and to build archive files so the package can be shipped to other sites. R also provides the function package.skeleton() to create a directory structure and some files suitable for a new package; see Section 4.3.

The shell command

```
$ R CMD build packages
```

will build an archive file for each of the source packages. For example:

```
$ R CMD BUILD SoDA
* checking for file 'SoDA/DESCRIPTION' ... OK
* preparing 'SoDA':
* checking DESCRIPTION meta-information ... OK
* cleaning src
* removing junk files
* checking for LF line-endings in source files
* checking for empty or unneeded directories
* building 'SoDA_1.0.tar.gz'
```

After printing a variety of messages, the command creates a compressed tar archive of the package. The name includes the package name and its current version, SoDA and 1.0 in this case. This is a source archive, essentially like those on the CRAN repository, allowing you to move your package around and distribute it to others.

Once the archive file has been built, it can then be used to drive the installation:

```
$ R CMD INSTALL -l ~/RLibrary SoDA_1.0.tar.gz
```

Besides allowing installation on multiple sites, working from the build has the advantage, for packages that include C or Fortran code, that object code is not left lying around in the source directory.

The build command can be used to build "binary" archives of packages, by using the --binary option to the command:

```
$ R CMD build --binary SoDA
* checking for file 'SoDA/DESCRIPTION' ... OK
* preparing 'SoDA':
*
    Various messages ...

* building binary distribution
* Installing *source* package 'SoDA' ...

  More messages ...

** building package indices ...
packaged installation of 'SoDA' as
            SoDA_1.0_R_i386-apple-darwin8.10.1.tar.gz
* DONE (SoDA)
```

The build is always done from a source directory, regardless of whether you are building a source or binary version. The name of the binary archive file created includes both the version number of the package, taken from the "DESCRIPTION" file, and also a code for the platform, taken from the environment variable R_PLATFORM. Source archives are potentially platform-independent, even when they contain saved images of data files, but binary archives will frequently be platform-dependent, as the name indicates. They could also be dependent on the current version of R, but this information is not currently included in an already very long file name.

To check the correctness of packages, you can use the shell command:

```
$ R CMD check packages
```

This command will attempt to install the package, will check for appropriate documentation, will run any tests supplied with the package, and will apply a variety of specialized checks, such as for consistency of method definitions. Both build and check try to enforce the file and directory structure recommended for R packages.

A package can be uninstalled by the command:

```
$ R CMD REMOVE packages
```

Options will potentially include -l, to specify the library where the package currently resides.

A variety of additional tools are provided, mostly for specialized control of the package definition. Some are discussed in this chapter, others in the *Writing R Extensions* manual.

Some of the tools, particularly `check`, may seem to have an overly fussy definition of what goes into a package, but bear with them. They ensure that your package makes sense to the tools that manage packages, which means that your package is more likely to be valuable to a wider range of potential users. And the pain of dealing with detailed requirements is preferable to distributing a package with avoidable errors. Some additional tools are included with the SoDA package to handle some nonstandard features.

Even more than in other discussions, keep in mind that the final word about R is always with the online documentation and with the system source itself. A chapter of the *Writing R Extensions* manual provides a discussion of writing packages, with pointers to other documentation. That document is precise and the place to go for the latest information, but it is a little terse; in the present chapter, we concentrate as usual on the underlying ideas and how they relate to your likely programming needs.

Setting up the R tools

The R tools for managing packages were largely developed in the UNIX/Linux world. They assume a command shell and various utilities traditionally part of that computing environment. If you're also computing in such an environment, the tools will usually have the resources they need, with little or no intervention on your part, at least until you include software written in other languages, rather than using only R source.

R itself runs on platforms other than Linux or UNIX. On Windows and Mac OS X platforms, R is available bundled into a suitable GUI. Repositories of R packages, notably CRAN, provide binary versions (that is, previously installed versions) of most of the packages on their site. These allow users on Windows and Mac OS X platforms to use R through the GUI and to install binary packages from there.

The situation changes when you need to install a package from source, whether one of your own packages or a package only available in source form. The catch at this point is that the platform does not, by default, contain all the tools required. Open-source, free versions of the necessary tools do exist, but some effort will be required on your part to obtain them.

The following summary should be sufficient for packages using only R code, but for details and more up-to-date information, see the Web pages at CRAN devoted to installing R on Mac OS X and on Windows. The Mac OS X situation is simpler. Although the system does not come with all the needed tools, it is in fact based on the BSD software, a UNIX-like open-source system; therefore, the tools are in fact mostly available in the development environment for the platform. That environment, called *Xcode tools*, is available to anyone with a current version of the operating system. It can usually be installed from the discs supplied with the operating system, or if necessary from the Web. For details and other tools, drill down to the R for Mac tools page at the CRAN Web site.

The Windows situation is more specialized to R, and somewhat more fragmented. A package of shell tools specially chosen for compiling R is available. As this book is written, you need to look first in Appendix E to the online *R Installation and Administration Manual*, at the R or CRAN Web sites. In addition to this toolkit, some other items are currently needed for certain extensions and documentation. However, the Windows tools for R are currently changing (usually for the better), and the specific Web sites for downloading may change also, so I won't try to give more specific advice here.

4.3 Creating a Package

To create a new source package, you must create a directory (usually with the same name you intend to call the package), and put inside that directory some special files and subdirectories containing the source code, documentation and possibly other material from which the installed package can be created. The actual structure can vary in many ways, most of which we discuss in the remainder of the chapter. It's far from free form, however, because the tools that install, check, and build from the source package look for specially formatted information in specifically named files and directories. Your chances of having suitable information available for the tools will be increased by using some special functions to create an initial version of the package itself and initial versions of information about added material later on.

You can create an initial directory for your package with suitable files and subdirectories in one step by calling the function `package.skeleton()`. It's strongly recommended to start this way, so `package.skeleton()` can provide the requirements for a valid R package. The side effect of the call to `package.skeleton()` is to create the directory with the name of your package, and under that to create a number of other directories and files. Specifically, you get source files and documentation files for functions and other objects, based on the arguments in the call to `package.skeleton()`. You also get the essential `"DESCRIPTION"` file for the package as a whole, and a corresponding package documentation file for the package. In this section we cover getting started, filling in general information, and adding new R objects.

The arguments to `package.skeleton()` allow you to start from either files containing R source code or a list of R objects. Either will generate files in the source package. Having initialized the new package, we can add more functions and other objects, again starting from source files or saved data objects. We can also add other material, including code from essentially any programming language.

The package for this book is called `SoDA`, and we start it off with three functions, providing these as objects. We assign the names of those functions to the character vector `SoDAObjects` and call `package.skeleton()` with three arguments: the name of the package (which is also the name of the directory to be created), the object names and the `path`, that is the dircectory in which to create the source code for the new package. In this case the new directory is stored under subdirectory `"RPackages"` of the login directory, denoted by `"~/RPackages"`. It's convenient to keep all source packages under one directory, to simplify installation.

```
> SoDAObjects <- c("geoXY", "geoDist", "packageAdd")
> package.skeleton("SoDA", SoDAObjects, path = "~/RPackages")
Creating directories ...
    and further messages
```

The call to `package.skeleton()` prints a number of messages, but we cover the essentials below rather than try to explain everything here. Let's go next to a command shell to see what we got from the call to `package.skeleton()`[1]. Because of the `path=` argument we supplied to `package.skeleton()`, a directory called `"SoDA"` has been created under the `"RPackages"` directory.

```
$ cd ~/RPackages
$ ls -R SoDA
SoDA:
DESCRIPTION         R                    Read-and-delete-me man
SoDA/R:
geoDist.R  geoXY.R  packageAdd.R

SoDA/man:
geoDist.Rd  geoXY.Rd
 packageAdd.Rd  SoDA.package.Rd
```

Under the `"SoDA"` directory there are two subdiretories, `"R"` and `"man"`, and two additional files, `"DESCRIPTION"` (page 90) and `"Read-and-delete-me"`.

---

[1]The behavior of `package.skeleton()` is still evolving as this is written, so details shown here may change.

The "R" directory is for R source files, and one file has been generated for each of the objects we supplied in the list for `package.skeleton()`. The "man" directory has source for the R online documentation; see Section 4.4, page 95. There are files for each of the objects we supplied, and a further file for the overall package documentation. Some other subdirectories are meaningful for packages, but are not created automatically, or only if the arguments to `package.skeleton()` require them. The "src" directory is meant for source code in the C language, and in related languages such as Fortran or C++ (see Section 4.7, page 108). Files in a directory "data" create data objects in the installed package, handled differently from source code. Files in a directory "inst" are copied without change into the installation directory for the package (giving a convenient way to refer to arbitrary files, including software from other languages; see Section 4.8, page 108). A directory "tests" is used to provide files of R code to test the correctness of the package (Section 4.5, page 101 discusses testing). For more details on these directories, see Section 4.3, page 92.

The "Read-and-delete-me" file contains instructions for you, the programmer, about what to do next to make your package legitimate. You should, as suggested by the name of the file, read it and follow the instructions. You can then throw the file away. The rest of the files constructed will generally become part of your package, although you may want to combine documentation for related functions, rather than keep the separate documentation file for each object.

The directory created is the *source* directory for your package, but you and other users cannot yet use this package. To attach the objects in the new package in the same way one uses the packages supplied with R, the new package must be *installed* as shown on page 81.

Data objects in packages

Packages provide a simple way to supply data objects as examples or references. Many packages in various archives exist mainly for this purpose and even in a package more centered on methodology, you will often want to include relevant data. Data objects differ from functions and other software objects in several ways. They are usually larger, sometimes much so; they frequently were created either outside R or by an extended sequence of computations; and documentation for them follows a different natural pattern than that for functions. For all these reasons, installing and distributing data objects presented some problems in the early development of R. Several approaches evolved, and remain. However, the "LazyData" mechanism shown below works conveniently for nearly all purposes, so you can largely ignore discussions of earlier techniques.

Data objects in source packages may need to be represented by files that are not simply R source. Even if we didn't mind the inefficiency of generating a large data frame object by parsing and evaluating a `dump()` version of the object on a file, this form of the data would be inconvenient and error-prone. To allow for differing source forms, the package structure provides for a directory `"data"` under the source package directory. Files in this directory will be interpreted as generating data objects in the installed directory. What happens to those objects depends on options in the `"DESCRIPTION"` file. The recommended approach includes in the file a line:

```
LazyData: yes
```

When the package is installed, the data objects will be included in the form of *promises*, essentially indirect references to the actual object that will be expanded the first time the object's name needs to be evaluated. An earlier strategy required the user to call the `data()` function to load the object after the package had been attached; this can now essentially be avoided.

Data objects in the *source* package `"data"` directory can come in several form, including:

binary data objects: Files can be created by calls to the `save()` function that contain binary versions of one or more objects from an environment. The function is essentially the same mechanism used to save the image of objects from an R session. It saves (nearly) any R object. Note that both the object and the associated name in the environment are saved. By convention the files generated have suffix either `".rda"` or `".Rdata"`. File names of this form in the `"data"` directory will be interpreted as saved images. Notice that the name of the file has no effect on the name(s) of the objects installed with the package.

Binary data files are in a sense the most general way to provide data objects and, also, the least self-descriptive. From the view of the *Prime Directive* principle, they would be frowned upon, because the user has no way to look back at their actual construction. Still, for objects whose creation involved some nontrivial computation using external sources the binary object option is by far the easiest, giving it support from the *Mission* principle. A conscientious package provider will include details of the data construction in the corresponding documentation.

comma-separated-values files: This is a format frequently used to export data from spreadsheets and other packages. R reads such files with the function `read.csv()`. Files with the ".csv" suffix will be installed this way. Notice that now the file name does define the object name, after removing the ".csv" suffix.

R assignments: The opposite extreme from binary data objects is a piece of R source code. This could, in fact, have been included in the "R" directory of the source package, but if the computation defines a data object it makes somewhat more sense to include it here. The form is most useful for fairly simple objects that have an explicit definition not depending on outside data. For example, the file "dowNames.R" in the SoDA package defines an object to hold the conventional (English-language) days of the week:

```
dowNames <-
c("Sunday", "Monday", "Tuesday", "Wednesday", "Thursday", "Friday",
"Saturday")
```

Notice that the R expressions have to generate the objects in the target environment, usually by assignment expressions. Now we're back to the file name being irrelevant.

Adding to source packages

Once the package has been initialized, you can add any additional material. To add R source code, copy the source files into the R subdirectory of your package source. If we have a file "binaryRep.R" that we want to add to the SoDA package previously initialized:

```
$ cp  binaryRep.R ~/RPackages/SoDA/R/
```

You should also create some documentation for any added functions and other R objects (Section 4.4, page 95 discusses documentation).

To add new files of R source and generate a single documentation shell for all the functions in each file, use the function `packageAdd()` in the SoDA package

```
packageAdd(pkg, files, path)
```

where `pkg` is the name of the package ("SoDA" in our example), `files` is the vector of one or more file names containing R source, and `path` is the location for the package source (as in `package.skeleton()`. The function is called when the target package has been installed and included in the current session, say by a call to `require()`. To add the objects in file `"triDiagonal.R"` to our SoDA package and to document all of the functions in that file together:

```
> packageAdd("SoDA", "triDiagonal.R", "~/RPackages")
Wrote documentation to "~/RPackages/SoDA/man/triDiagonal.Rd"
Copied file triDiagonal.R to ~/RPackages/SoDA/R/triDiagonal
```

The `"DESCRIPTION"` file

As its name suggests, this file gives general information describing the package in which it appears. The contents and format of the file are a bit of a catch-all, but it has proved to be a flexible way to automate handling of the package, along with providing some overall documentation. Running `package.skeleton()` creates the file, which the author then needs to edit to provide specific information, following the hints in the file itself:

```
Package: SoDA
Type: Package
Title: What the package does (short line)
Version: 1.0
Date: 2007-11-15
Author: Who wrote it
Maintainer: Who to complain to <yourfault@somewhere.net>
Description: More about what it does (maybe more than one line)
License: What license is it under?
```

In addition to the fields created automatically, there are a number of others that guide the installation process. Fields in the file are denoted by names at the start of the line, followed by `":"`. Fields can be continued over multiple lines but to be sure the following lines are not interpreted as a new field, start each line with white space. *Warning*: The field names are case-sensitive. You need to follow the capitalization patterns below (not always obvious).

Important fields include the following:

`Package`: This is the official name of the package, and therefore of the directory created when the package is installed.

`Title, Description`: These go into the online package documentation. The information is likely repeated in the file of package-specific documentation in the `"man"` directory, possibly in an expanded form. (Because both files are created by `package.skeleton()` you need to copy the contents manually when creating the new package.)

Version: The version is a multi-numeric-field identifier. The key requirement is that when interpreted as such, the version increases through time. This is the mechanism used to require a sufficiently modern version of other packages (see the `Depends` field below). Authors show a wonderful variety of styles for this field. If you want to follow the R style, have a major version number (possibly 0) before the first period, a minor version after, and optionally a patch number at the end, separated by a period or a dash. Major versions of R itself conventionally mark serious changes, possibly with major incompatibilities.

Depends: This important optional field states what other packages this package must have available in order to run, and optionally puts constraints on the versions. A particularly common constraint is to require that the version of R itself be sufficiently recent, as in the line:

```
Depends: R(>= 2.4), lattice
```

A package with this line in the `"DESCRIPTION"` file can not be installed in a version of R older than 2.4.0. You don't need to be explicit about depending on R or the packages normally installed with the system, unless the version is required. *Warning*: Although the version requirement looks like R, the tool that actually reads it is none too bright; currently, you must write the expression as shown, including the space after the `` `>=` `` operator. See page 94 for more details on requiring other packages.

License: This identifies the license agreement you want people to accept when they use your package. It only matters if you intend to distribute your package. Vast amounts of time and data transmission have gone into arguments about the merits and meaning of the various licenses, a topic that this book will avoid. Look at the license entries for other packages on CRAN, or take the current R choice (which is printed, with comments, by calling the function `license()`).

LazyLoad, LazyData: These fields are options; normally, the rest of the line just contains `"Yes"` or `"No"` to turn the options on or off. The options are desirable for packages that are large, either in the sense of many objects or of large objects. The `LazyLoad` option provides more efficient attachment of large packages, by using a reference to a binary version of the objects. See page 92.

Files and directories in a source package

The tools for handling R packages have a highly structured view of what directories and files to expect, within the directory that contains a source package. You are not much restricted by this structure; essentially anything can be added to the installed package, although you can't omit certain essential ingredients if you plan to have functions, data, documentation or other specialized material.

Table 4.1 lists special directory names known to the INSTALL command and other package tools. Each of these is located in your source package directory (~/RPackages/SoDA for our example). Adding other files or subdirectories in that directory will do nothing for your installed package—the INSTALL command will simply ignore them. (You can add arbitrary stuff, but put it in the "inst" directory, as noted in the table.) The source directories affect directories in the installed package, as listed in the second column of the table. These are subdirectories of the directory with your package's name, under the "library" directory. So, with our convention of installing into RLibrary under the login directory, the directories for our example package would be ~/RLibrary/SoDA/R, and so on.

In addition to the directories, two files are special: the "DESCRIPTION" file, discussed on page 90; and file "INDEX", which, if it exists, is used to construct the online index to interesting topics in the package. However, the "INDEX" file in the installed package is usually generated automatically from the documentation in the "man" directory, so you would not normally need to provide one.

Precomputing objects

In early versions of R, the effect of library() was essentially to evaluate the corresponding source at the time the package was attached. For large packages, and especially for those including class and method definitions, it is more efficient to prepare the contents of the package at installation time, leaving less to do during the session. The essential mechanism is to evaluate the package source when INSTALL runs and to save the resulting collection of R objects to be attached by library(), with the recommended mechanism being *lazy loading*. Lazy loading uses a mechanism in R called *promises* such that the individual objects in the package's environment are in effect indirect references to the actual objects, promises to produce that object the first time that, for example, the corresponding function is called. If only a few of the functions in the package are used in a particular session, the cost

Source Directory	Installed Directories	What Happens
`"R"`	`"R"`	A concatenated source file is made, plus optional processed objects.
`"data"`	`"data"`	Loadable versions of the data objects are created, plus optional lazy data promises.
`"demo"`	`"demo"`	Demonstrations to be run by the `demo()` function are copied.
`"exec"`	`"exec"`	Executable scripts are copied.
`"inst"`	`"."`	All contents are copied (recursively) to the installed package's directory.
`"man"`	*(various)*	Documentation processing creates versions of the documentation in various formats (depending on the platform and available tools), and also generates the examples as R source (in `"R-ex"`). See page 100.
`"po"`		Translation files are created for base messages in the local language. You're unlikely to be involved with this unless you're a translator.
`"src"`	`"libs"`	A compiled library is created from source code in C, etc., for dynamic linking into R.
`"tests"`	`"tests"`	Files of test code in R will be run by the `check` command (see page 102).

Table 4.1: Source package directories that have special meaning to the R package utilities.

in time and space of accessing the unused functions is mostly avoided. The main advantage, however, is in precomputing the objects during installation, rather than when attaching the package.

The author of the package selects the mechanism by entering information in the `"DESCRIPTION"` file.

```
LazyLoad: yes
LazyData: yes
```

The `"LazyData"` directive applies the same mechanism to objects in the `"data"` directory. See Section 13.2, page 457, for how the mechanism works.

Requiring other packages, in various ways

The R installation procedure allows package authors to declare that their package requires certain other packages, and also that the version of either a package or of R itself must be sufficiently recent. This information is encoded in the "DESCRIPTION" file, usually in the Depends entry. For example:

```
Depends:R(>= 2.3), lattice(>= 0.13),nlme
```

There are in fact three entries of this form, "Depends", "Imports", and "Suggests". The first two are for true requirements, without which the package will not run. The "Depends" entry is used if the other package is expected to be attached by this package's code; the "Imports" entry should be used instead if this package uses the namespace mechanism to import from the other package (Section 4.6, page 103). The "Suggests" entry is typically for packages needed only to run examples.

The version numbers for R and for required packages will be used at installation time, to prevent your package being installed with too old a version of the corresponding software. In choosing what version(s) to require, the cautious approach would be to require the version current when you finish developing the source for your package. You might get by with an earlier version, but assuming so incorrectly can lead to bad problems.

Making changes in an installed package

After you have set up your programming project with an R package, you will usually go on to make further changes and extensions. You will often alternate making changes, trying them out, and then making more changes. For isolated software that you source() into the global environment or load via a GUI, the process is simple: source in the new version and re-run whatever test you're currently using. When the changes are to be made in a package, the pattern has to be a little more extended.

Basically, there are two ways to work. The first is the most general and the safest, but requires three steps. Go back to the source of the package and make your editing changes. Then use INSTALL to copy the changes to the installed version of the package. Finally, unload and re-attach the package in the R session to try your tests again. (For changes in R functions, that's enough; but for the changes involving compiled code in C-level languages or those that depend on initializing the package, you may need to exit R and start a new session.)

An alternative approach is available, and more convenient when it applies. If you're making detailed changes to a function, trying to get something to work, quite a number of steps may be needed. To avoid installation and unloading each time, I suggest using the `edit=` option to the `trace()` function, discussed in Section 3.6, page 69. You can make any changes to the body of a function, save it in the editor, and quit. The `trace()` function will then always save the edited version back in the environment from which it came, so that changes are immediately available for testing. Just remember, when the revised function does work, to save it somewhere else, so you can then copy it to the source for your package. (You can just call `trace()` one last time and do a `"Save As"` or equivalent in the editor.) The same mechanism applies to editing a method, by supplying the appropriate `signature=` argument to `trace()`.

However, using `trace()` is only possible for editing the body of a function, not for changing arguments or default expressions. And it won't help when you want to add or remove objects from the package; in that case, you must go back to the basic approach of re-installing.

Warning: What you should not do is to put an edited version of the function into the top-level environment, simple as that may seem, particularly if your package has a namespace. If the function's behavior depends on the package's environment, that behavior may change, with possibly disastrous results. If you put a revised version of a function in the global environment, and if your package has namespace, other functions in the package will not see the revised version, and your new function may see wrong objects as well. The `trace()` mechanism allows editing objects in namespaces (Section 4.6, page 105).

4.4 Documentation for Packages

Let's face it: Most of us don't enjoy the details of documenting our software, much as we may appreciate the importance of the result. Documenting R packages is not likely to be an exception. The R-specific documentation, which we call `Rd` documentation after the suffix for the files created, is processed into a number of forms by utilities provided, with the result that it is available conveniently in several interactive versions and potentially in printed form as well. Unfortunately, the programmer is responsible for writing text in the appropriate markup language, roughly a dialect of TEX; at present, there are no general tools that eliminate this step. Documentation is needed for functions, classes, methods, and general objects, as well as for miscellaneous topics. `Rd` documentation comes in several types, depending on the type of topic being documented. In this section we look at the process of creating documentation for a package, describing utilities and the main features of the markup language. Some documentation generation tools help, particularly in getting the process underway by creating outlines of the Rd files. The support tools are also strong on checking the adequacy and accuracy of the documentation, to the extent possible.

Documentation you may need to create, and tools to help get started, include the following.

- **Overall description of the package.** A package will usually have one Rd file of documentation of type package, documenting the overall purpose and contents. For the package named SoDA, the documentation is invoked in R as package?SoDA.

  If you called package.skeleton() to create the package, that produces an initial package documentation file. However, there's an advantage to recreating the file with the promptPackage() function after you've installed the package, by which time you should also have filled in the "DESCRIPTION" file. The Rd file has information derived from the current content of the package, which is likely to be more useful after you've reached the installation stage.

  For the SoDA package, package documentation could be initialized by:

  ```
  > promptPackage("SoDA")
  Created file named 'SoDA-package.Rd'.
  Edit the file and move it to the appropriate directory.
  ```

  Further editing will usually be needed. The package need not be attached when promptPackage() is called.

- **Functions.** The Rd documentation for functions has specialized sections for describing the arguments and the value returned by the functions, as shown on page 100. Multiple functions can be described in one file, suitable when several functions are similar. R functions are objects from which the names and default expressions for arguments can be extracted; the utility function prompt() and related tools construct initial outlines of Rd files from the function objects. Similarly, the check command utility complains if documentation and actual functions don't match, or if documentation is missing for some functions.

- **Classes and methods.** Classes, like functions, are represented by objects from which metadata defines properties of the class that should be documented. The utility `promptClass()` generates an outline of the class documentation. Because classes and functions can have the same name, documentation for a class $\mathcal{C}$ is stored as `"`$\mathcal{C}$`-class.Rd"` and displayed by the R expression `class?`$\mathcal{C}$.

Similarly, methods for a generic function are defined by metadata objects. Outline documentation for them is generated by the utility function `promptMethods()`. Documentation of methods tends to be more distributed than for functions or classes, because methods in R are indexed by both the generic function and the argument classes in the method signatures. Commonly used functions (arithmetic and other operators, for example) often have methods in several packages, in separate files. There is a syntax for specifying documentation for a particular method (see page 99).

- **Other objects.** Packages can contain arbitrary objects in addition to the functions, classes and methods providing programming. These should also have `Rd` documentation. Such documentation is suitable for datasets, tables of values needed for computation and in general for information that users may need to consult. The same `prompt()` utility function produces outlines of such documentation. It uses the `str()` function to print out a summary of the structure of the object, but the skeleton documentation tends to be less useful than for functions, whose structure the utility understands better. In principle, methods can be written to customize `prompt()` for any class of objects; currently, this has been done for data frame objects.

R utilities for package management encourage complete documentation of functions and other objects. If you plan to use the `check` command to test your package a stronger verb such as "nag" or "badger" rather than "encourage" would be more accurate. The command expects documentation for all visible objects in the package, principally functions but also classes, methods, and data objects. The `codoc()` function in package `tools` compares function documentation with the function definition and reports inconsistencies, and similarly does some consistency checking for methods and classes. The `check` command runs this function, or you can use it directly, giving it the name of your package as an argument.

With large packages, you may find the documentation requirements time-consuming, but `check` and the other quality-assurance utilities are working for the benefit of users, so try to work with them. The functions `prompt()`, `promptPackage()`, `promptMethods()`, and `promptClass()` help to get started.

We add the function `promptAll()` in the SoDA package, to incorporate all the objects in a file of R source code.

You will generally need to edit the contents of the files created to add some substance to the documentation. The files contain hints about what needs to be added; in simple examples you may be able to get by without much knowledge of the documentation format, perhaps by copying existing files. If you have access to the source version of an existing package, you can also look in the `"man"` subdirectory for existing `".Rd"` files to use as examples. Eventually, however, it will be helpful to actually understand something about the documentation format. A few key points are summarized here.

Documentation format and content

Detailed documentation for R objects is written in a markup system that is based on the TEX markup language. It helps to have some familiarity with TEX or LATEX, but the R markup is more specialized and easier to learn, at least for packages that do not involve mathematical descriptions. While the input is related to TEX, the output of the documentation is in several forms, all produced by R utilities from the single source document.

The original purpose of `Rd` files was to produce online documentation in response to the `help()` function or the `` `?` `` operator, `help("`*topic*`")` or `?`*topic*. Each topic corresponds to an alias command in the documentation,

> `\alias{`*topic*`}`

Some of the aliases will be generated automatically by the `prompt` utilities, but you will need to add others if, for example, you document some additional functions in an existing file (see `promptAll()` in the SoDA package as an alternative).

The syntax for *topic* has been extended to allow for documentation types and for signature information needed when documenting methods. A particular type of documentation allows for documentation based on a package name, on a class name, or on methods associated with a function. For example:

```
> class?ts
> methods?show
> package?Matrix
```

These three expressions display documentation on the class `"ts"`, the methods for function `show()` and the `Matrix` package. The type argument to `` `?` `` allows us to distinguish these requests from possible documentation for functions `ts()`, `show()`, and `Matrix()`. Documentation types are coded into the topic in the alias command by following the topic with a hyphen and the type:

```
\alias{ts-class}
\alias{show-methods}
\alias{Matrix-package}
```

The rule is that the actual topic comes first, and the type comes last, preceded by `"-"`. As a result, all the documentation relating to `"ts"` is sorted alphabetically together, making it easier to find in a typical browser interface, where one might find topics `"ts"`, `"ts-class"` and/or `"ts-methods"`. The `` `?` `` operator knows about documentation types, but most browser interfaces currently don't, so you need to search in an alphabetical list of topics for a particular package. Because the type follows the topic in the alias, all the documentation for `"ts"`, for example, will be adjacent, whether for function, class, or methods.

Documentation is possible for individual methods as well. For individual methods, the syntax for *topic* follows the name of the function with the classes in the method signature, separated by commas, then a hyphen and the type, `method`. So the alias command documenting the method for function `show()` for class `"traceable"` would be:

```
\alias{show,traceable-method}
```

and for function `Arith()` with signature `c("dMatrix", "numeric")`:

```
\alias{Arith,dMatrix,numeric-method}
```

The syntax for topics is not the most flexible; in particular, white space is not ignored. Fortunately, most of the time the utilities will generate the alias commands for you. The `promptMethods()` utility will produce aliases from all the methods defined for a given function in a package. If you want to split the documentation, you can move some of the alias lines to other files.

The various `prompt` utilities all have as their objective to use as much information as possible from the R object to initialize a corresponding documentation file, along with hints to the human about the information needed to complete the file. The file consists of various sections, delimited in the style of TEX commands, that is, a command name preceded by a backslash and followed by one or more arguments. TEX arguments are each enclosed in braces and follow one another with no separating commas or blanks. The section of the documentation file giving the calls to functions is the

\usage command, with one argument in braces, typically extending over several lines. This section can be generated automatically by prompt() from the function object. As an example, consider the function packageAdd() in package SoDA. We can create a skeleton of documentation for it:

```
> prompt(packageAdd)
Created file named 'packageAdd.Rd'.
Edit the file and move it to the appropriate directory.
```

The resulting file will contain a usage section:

```
\usage{
packageAdd(pkg, files, path = ".")
}
```

In addition to the usage section, the documentation requires separate descriptions of each of the arguments; here, prompt() can create a skeleton of the required list, but can only prompt the human to fill in a meaningful description:

```
\arguments{
  \item{pkg}{ ~~Describe \code{pkg} here~~ }
  \item{files}{ ~~Describe \code{files} here~~ }
  \item{path}{ ~~Describe \code{path} here~~ }
}
```

Other aspects of function documentation are handled similarly. Try out prompt() on a function and look at the results, which are largely self-explanatory.

Although prompt() creates one documentation file per object, there are advantages to documenting closely related functions together. Such functions often share arguments. Documenting the common arguments in one place is both easier and less likely to produce inconsistencies later on. Clarifying which of the functions should be used or how the functions work together is also easier if they are documented together. Package SoDA includes a function promptAll() that generates a single outline documentation file for all the functions in a single file of source.

Installing documentation

The documentation files in a source package must be stored in directory man under the main directory for the package. All files with the ".Rd" suffix in that directory will be processed when the INSTALL command is executed for the package. Installing the documentation creates several forms of output documentation; for example, building the SoDA package gives the message:

```
>>> Building/Updating help pages for package 'SoDA'
    Formats: text html latex example
```

followed by a list of the documentation generated. If the same package was previously installed in the same place, only the modified documentation files will actually be processed. Of the four formats mentioned in the message, the first three are alternative translations of the ".Rd" files. The fourth is a directory of R source corresponding to the Examples section of each ".Rd" file. These are run when the user invokes the example() function in R with the topic name documented in that file. The example files are also run by the check command, and so form part of the testing facilities for the package, as discussed in the next section.

4.5 Testing Packages

As you program using R, I encourage you to grow a set of tests that help to define what your new software is intended to do. Section 3.8, page 76 provides some suggestions and techniques for testing R software. These can be used at any stage, but as your projects grow and become more ambitious, having good tests becomes that much more important.

The organization of R packages provides a place to put tests (two places, actually) and a shell level command to run these tests, along with a range of other checks on the package. The command is:

```
$ R CMD check packages
```

where *packages* gives the names of one or more source packages or package archive files. Think of the check command as parallel to the INSTALL command. It is run in the same place and on the same source directory or archive file.

The check command does much more than just run some tests. It first checks that the source package can in fact be installed, then checks for a variety of requirements that are imposed on packages submitted to the central CRAN archive.

This section is mainly concerned with testing the software; after discussing that aspect, we look at some of the other checks. The documentation for the package will normally have a number of examples; the organization of the documentation files includes an Examples section, encouraging programmers to provide expressions that can be executed to show the behavior of the documented software. Installation of the package creates files of R source corresponding to each of the example sections in the package's documentation. The `check` command runs all the examples for this package.

In addition, a source package can optionally contain a subdirectory named `tests`. The `check` command examines this directory if it exists and takes two possible actions:

1. Any file whose name ends in ".R" is treated as an R source file and is evaluated, roughly as if the contents were entered as user input, with the package attached.

2. A file with a corresponding name, but ending in ".Rout.save", is assumed to be the intended output of evaluating the ".R" file. The actual output is compared to this file, and any differences are reported.

The `tests` directory and the `Examples` sections offer plenty of scope for installing test code. The question we want to address here is: How best to use them to improve the quality of the packages while not giving the package writer unnecessary problems?

The two locations for test code have grown up with the increasing attention to quality assurance in the central R archive. They have different goals and advantages. The `Examples` sections are primarily to show users how functions in the package behave. The user types, say, `example(lm)` to see the examples from the corresponding documentation page, `?lm`. The printed output (and optionally graphics) can be voluminous, and is in this case. Here's part of it:

```
> example(lm)

lm> ctl <- c(4.17, 5.58, 5.18, 6.11, 4.5, 4.61, 5.17,
    4.53, 5.33, 5.14)

lm> trt <- c(4.81, 4.17, 4.41, 3.59, 5.87, 3.83, 6.03,
    4.89, 4.32, 4.69)
    .......

lm> anova(lm.D9 <- lm(weight ~ group))
Analysis of Variance Table

Response: weight
          Df Sum Sq Mean Sq F value Pr(>F)
group      1 0.6882  0.6882  1.4191  0.249
Residuals 18 8.7293  0.4850
```

. . . . .

```
lm> plot(lm.D9, las = 1)

lm> par(opar)

lm> stopifnot(identical(lm(weight ~ group, method = "model.frame"),
    model.frame(lm.D9)))
```

The last line uses a utility for testing, the `stopifnot()` function (see Section 3.8, page 76), and is clearly there only for testing purposes.

Results of running tests in the `"tests"` directory, on the other hand, are not visible to users except when the `check` command is run. Usually, that's the more natural place to put code that is not informative for users but tests important assertions about the functions in the package. It's possible to hide code in the `Examples` section, and you may prefer to put tests closely related to documented features there to keep the association clear.

In any case, it is much better to have tests than not. The maintainers of the core R code try to keep test code from important bug fixes, in the form of expressions that didn't work until the bug was fixed, but now are asserted to succeed. This is the essence of "regression testing" in the software sense, and it's a very good habit to get into for your packages.

As Section 3.8 suggests, it helps to organize test computations in terms of assertions about what your software should do. Tools such as `stopifnot()`, `identical()`, and `all.equal()` will help; some other common techniques are to be avoided, notably using comparison operators. Relying on the exact form of output is not a good idea, unless that output was in fact the purpose of the function. For this reason, I would discourage use of the `".Rout.save"` mechanism for most purposes; it's difficult to avoid spurious differences that then burn up the programmer's time looking for possible bugs. But, to repeat: better to have plenty of tests than none or too few, even if the tests are not ideal.

4.6 Package Namespaces

For trustworthy computation, the software we write and use, such as the software in an R package, should be well defined: The essential concept of functional programming in the S language and in R is precisely that one should be able to read the definition of a function and figure out from that what the function does. Because nearly all functions call other functions, these must also be well defined, even when they come from other packages. That has always been a potential catch with the S language. Because of dynamic searching, a function I intended my package to use might be hidden by some other package, potentially with disastrous consequences (see the example below).

To avoid such problems and to allow R software to be better defined, the *namespace* mechanism has been added. This allows an R package to define what external software it uses (what objects from what other packages it *imports*), and also what software it wishes to make public (what objects it *exports*). The result is a clearer and more reliable definition of the package's behavior; whenever you are concerned with quality code, use of a namespace is recommended. The ability to define exports helps prevent confusion from multiple objects with the same name. Namespaces also allow somewhat more efficient loading of the software in most cases. But in the spirit of our *Prime Directive* the increase in trust is the key property.

Why and when to give your package a namespace

The need for namespaces in R comes from the traditional S language evaluation model, and in particular from the way functions are found. Each attached package appears on the search list, `search()`:

```
> search()
 [1] ".GlobalEnv"        "tools:quartz"        "package:methods"
 [4] "package:stats"     "package:graphics"    "package:grDevices"
 [7] "package:utils"     "package:datasets"    "Autoloads"
[10] "package:base"
```

In traditional evaluation, when a function in one of these packages calls another function, `f()` say, the evaluator looks for a function object named `"f"` in the same package or in one of the packages following on the search list (in R, the environment of the package and the enclosing environments).

The dynamic search for each function presents a danger when functions in a package rely on calling functions in a different package. Suppose, for example, a package is written that uses the function `gam()` from the package of the same name. In fact, there are two packages in the CRAN repository with a function named `"gam"`, `gam` and `mgcv`. The functions are similar but not identical. If both packages were attached in a session using the new package, the wrong function might be called. Although this situation may not seem very likely, the result could be potentially disastrous if the unintended function returned a wrong answer that was not detected. Even aside from errors, the writer of the new package should have the ability to state precisely what other software the new package uses. One would like a mechanism to declare and enforce such dependencies.

The namespace mechanism provides R programmers that ability. The programmer includes a file called NAMESPACE in the top level of the source package. That file consists of directives, looking like expressions in the R language, that specify both what the package *imports* and what it *exports*. The imports can be either entire packages or specified objects, classes, or methods from a package. The exports are always explicit lists of objects, classes or methods.

Nearly any mature package doing important tasks will benefit from using the namespace mechanism. There are some cautionary points, however, which may suggest holding off until the initial development of a package has stabilized somewhat.

- A namespace requires being explicit, particularly about what is exported. If the contents of the package are changing, revising the namespace for every new function or change in function name can be a burden. Exports can be defined as regular expression patterns, which can circumvent explicit exports (see the example below), but this means that you must tailor the names of functions you do not want to export, somewhat defeating the namespace idea.

- Namespaces are *sealed*; that is, once installed and attached to the session, no changes can normally be made. This means that revising a function by changing the underlying source code requires reinstalling the package, a considerable overhead. The trace() function, called with the argument edit=TRUE, is deliberately designed to allow modification of objects in namespaces, because otherwise debugging would be very difficult. See page 94. The same mechanism can be used to edit non-exported functions, but these must be addressed by the `:::` operator.

  The trace-and-edit mechanism works quite well for trying out changes quickly, but does require you to then save the modified version back in the package's source files. Otherwise the changes will be lost when you quit the current session.

- Packages with namespaces use a different mechanism when the package is attached to the R session. In particular, the mechanism for having an action take place when the package is attached, .First.lib(), must be replaced, usually by the function .onLoad(), called when the package

is loaded, but possibly also by the function `.onAttach()`, called when
the previously loaded package is attached.

A reasonable rule of thumb is that a package sufficiently mature and important to be offered beyond the friendly-user level is ready for a namespace.
Packages with particularly sensitive dependencies on other packages may
need the mechanism well before that stage.

The `NAMESPACE` file and its effect

To apply the namespace mechanism to your package, you must write a sequence of namespace directives in a file called `"NAMESPACE"` that resides in the
top-level directory of your package's source. The directives look roughly like
R expressions, but they are not evaluated by the R evaluator. Instead, the
file is processed specially to define the objects that our package sees and the
objects in our package that are seen by other software. The namespace directives define two collections of objects referenced by names; specifically, two
R environments, one for the objects that perform the computations inside
the package and the other for the objects that users see when the package
is attached in an R session. The first of these is referred to as the package's
namespace. The second, the result of the export directives in the `NAMESPACE`
file, is the environment attached in the search list. When you access the
two environments explicitly, they will print symbolically in a special form.
For package SoDA, the environments would be `<environment:namespace:SoDA>`
and `<environment:package:SoDA>`, respectively.

   The package's namespace contains all the objects generated by installing
the package, that is, all the objects created by evaluating the R source in
the package's R subdirectory. The same objects would have been generated
without a `NAMESPACE` file. The difference comes if we ask about the parent
environment of the namespace; that is, what objects other than local objects
are visible. Without a `NAMESPACE` file, the sequence of parent environments is
defined by the search list when this package is attached during the session.
The resulting uncertainty is just what the `NAMESPACE` file avoids.

1. The parent of the namespace is an environment containing all the
   objects defined by the import commands in the `NAMESPACE` file.

2. The parent of *that* environment is the namespace of R's `base` package.

In other words, computations in the package will see the explicitly imported
objects and the base package, in that order, regardless of what other packages are attached in the session.

Here are some examples. To import all the exported objects from package `methods` include the directive:

```
import(methods)
```

To import only the functions `prompt()` and `recover()` from package `utilities`, include:

```
importFrom(utilities, prompt, recover)
```

For stable packages, importing the whole package is simple and reasonably safe, particularly if the package is part of R's core code or is a widely used package; it's pretty unlikely that a change in the exports will cause problems. Importing large packages as a whole does involve some increased work at install time and a larger environment to be attached, but neither of these is likely to be a serious consideration. On the other hand, if most of the imported package is irrelevant, importing an explicit list of functions makes the relation between the packages clear.

The contents of the package's exports have to be stated explicitly and positively. There is no current way to say that particular objects are private.

```
export(promptAll, packageAdd)
```

The traditional UNIX-inspired convention is to treat function names beginning with a dot as private. This is not always safe in R, because the system itself uses such names for some special purposes. But if you wanted to say that all objects whose names start with a letter are exported:

```
exportPattern("^[a-zA-Z]")
```

Classes and methods require special consideration. Classes defined in the package require a special `exportClass()` directive to be exported:

```
exportClass(GPSTrack)
```

Currently, methods need to be exported explicitly if they are defined for a generic function in another package:

```
exportMethods(show)
```

However, if the generic function is itself an exported function in the package, methods are included automatically.

4.7   Including C Software in Packages

We have emphasized creating a package as a natural step in your programming with R. It's likely then that your first efforts will emphasize functions written in R, perhaps along with some other R software or data. R objects that can be created by sourcing in R code are the easiest software to include in your package, as discussed in section 4.3. Basically, just put the source files in the directory R of your package source and the INSTALL command will include the objects.

But R code is not the only code you can include in a package. Basically, any software that can be invoked from R can be included. Packages are generally the best way, in fact, to "package" any software to be called from R.

Software written in nearly any computer language can be usefully packaged for use with R, but some languages are treated specially. Basically, C and C-related languages (including Fortran) have a reserved place in the package's directory structure, in the directory src. The INSTALL command will automatically compile such source code and collect it into a suitable library file to be linked dynamically with R when first needed.

Techniques for incorporating C and Fortran software into R are discussed in Chapter 11. See that chapter for how to adapt the code and invoke it from R. Once the source files are stored in the src subdirectory of your source package, running the INSTALL command will automatically compile a version of the code that is linked dynamically to the R session when the package is loaded or attached. The details vary slightly depending on the operating system, but basically the install procedure creates an archive library file, for example SoDA.so, containing all the object code for the software in the src directory.

The library file must be loaded into the R application, either by the "useDynLib" directive in the namespace or by the library.dynam() function if there is no namespace. You should also add code to *register* the interfaced routines. Registering routines adds an important check that the interface from R is calling the routine correctly. See Section 11.5, page 426, for both loading and registering.

4.8   Interfaces to Other Software

Software from essentially arbitrary languages, as well as arbitrary data files, can be included in the installed package, by putting it into a directory inst under the package source directory. Installation will copy this material into the installed package, but the programmer is largely left to turn the software into a form that can be called from R.

Usually, the software will be run from within an R function. The two main issues to resolve are finding the relevant command file and communicating data to and from the command. If the software is in the form of a file that could be run as a shell command, the `system()` function in R will invoke the command. Chapter 12 discusses how to make use of such software; in this section, we discuss how to organize the required source files.

Files are usually made accessible by including them in the source for a package. Files that are placed in the `inst` subdirectory of the package's source directory will be copied to the top-level directory of the installed package. To execute or open those files, you must address them relative to that directory. The path of that directory can be found by calling the function `system.file()`. For example, if there is a package called `"P1"` installed, its installed directory is obtained by:

```
> system.file(package = "P1")
[1] "/Users/jmc/RLibrary/P1"
```

A call to `system.file()` can return one or more file names in any subdirectory of the installed package's directory. Suppose we had some Perl code in files `"findDateForm.perl"`, `"hashWords.perl"`, and `"perlMonths.perl"` in the source directory for package `"P1"`; specifically, in a directory `"inst/perl/"` under the source directory for this package.

Files under directory `"inst"` will all be copied to the installed package's top directory, preserving directory structure. Therefore, the files in this case will be in subdirectory `"perl"`, and the three file names, with the complete path, can be obtained from `system.file()`. The arguments to that function give each level of subdirectory. Multiple strings produce multiple file names.

```
> system.file("perl",
+ c("findDateForm.perl", "hashWords.perl", "perlMonths.perl"),
+ package = "P1")
[1] "/Users/jmc/RLibrary/P1/perl/findDateForm.perl"
[2] "/Users/jmc/RLibrary/P1/perl/hashWords.perl"
[3] "/Users/jmc/RLibrary/P1/perl/perlMonths.perl"
```

Empty strings are returned for files that do not exist. If you want to construct a file name to create a new file, call `system.file()` with only the `package=` argument and paste onto that the necessary file and directory names. Windows users should note that R generates strings for file locations using the forward slash, not the Windows backslash (to ensure that software generating file paths is platform-independent).

To avoid conflicts, you should usually organize the `inst` directory into subdirectories, as we did above with a subdirectory `"perl"`. There is a convention that subdirectory `exec` is for executable scripts. You can choose other subdirectory names as you wish, but remember that installation already generates a number of files and directories in the installed package, some of which you won't likely be expecting. To be safe, check the existing contents of the package's installed directory before creating a new file or subdirectory in the source directory `inst`:

```
> list.files(system.file(package="P1"))
 [1] "CONTENTS"    "DESCRIPTION" "INDEX"      "Meta"
 [5] "NAMESPACE"   "R"           "R-ex"       "data"
 [9] "help"        "html"        "latex"      "man"
[13] "perl"
```

Other than the `"perl"` directory, the package `"P1"` has no special files, so the above is about the minimum you can expect in the installation directory.

Chapter 5

Objects

Everything in R is an object; that is, a dynamically created, self-describing container for data. This chapter presents techniques for managing objects. Section 5.1 introduces the fundamental reference technique: assigning a name in an environment. Section 5.2, page 115, discusses the replacement operation, by which assigned objects are modified. Section 5.3, page 119, discusses the environments, in which objects are assigned. R allows assignments to nonlocal environments, discussed in Section 5.4, page 125, and including the technique known as *closures*. The final two sections discuss the transfer of R data and objects to and from external media: Section 5.5, page 131, describes connections, the R technique for dealing with an external medium; Section 5.6, page 135, covers the techniques for transferring data and objects.

5.1 Objects, Names, and References

The central computation in R is a function call, defined by the function object itself and the objects that are supplied as the arguments. In the functional programming model, the result is defined by another object, the value of the call. Hence the traditional motto of the S language: *everything is an object*—the arguments, the value, and in fact the function and the call itself: All of these are defined as objects.

Think of objects as collections of data of all kinds. The data contained and the way the data is organized depend on the class from which the object was generated. R provides many classes, both in the basic system and in

111

various packages. Defining new classes is an important part of programming with R. Chapter 6 discusses existing classes and the functions that compute on them. Chapters 9 and 10 discuss new classes and new functional computational methods. The present chapter explores computations to create and organize objects, regardless of their class or contents. The fundamental dualism in all aspects of R and the S language, the dualism between function calls and objects, is reflected in all these discussions.

As in any programming language, it's essential to be able to refer to objects, in a particular context, in a way that is consistent and clear. In the S language, there is one and only one way to refer to objects: by name. More precisely, the combination of a name (that is, a non-empty character string) and an environment (or context) in which the name is evaluated is the fundamental reference to an object in R. So, the value of the expressions `pi` or `lm` in the global environment, or the value of `x` inside a particular function call, will refer to a specific object (or generate an error, if no corresponding object can be found). The next section elaborates on environments and related ideas: basically, any computation in R takes place in an environment that defines how the evaluator will search for an object by name.

Whenever we talk about a reference to an object, in any language, the key is that we expect to use that reference repeatedly, in the confidence that it continues to refer to the same object. References do usually include the ability to change the object, what is sometimes called a *mutable object reference*, but which in R we can reduce to an assignment. Unless some explicit assignment has occurred, using an object reference means we can be confident that successive computations will see consistent data in the object. It's essentially a sanity requirement for computing: otherwise, there is no way to understand what our computations mean.

A name, with an associated environment, provides a reference in exactly this sense in R, for normal objects and programming style. As for that qualification, "normal", it excludes two kinds of abnormality. R permits some non-standard functions that explicitly reach out to perform non-local assignments. They have their place, and are discussed in section 5.4, but we'll exclude them from the current discussion. In addition, there are some non-standard classes of objects whose behavior also breaks the general model, as discussed beginning on page 114. These too are excluded by the term "normal". (Notice again the duality of functions and objects in the exceptions to normal behavior.)

The reference of a name to an object is made by an assignment, for example:

```
lmFit <- lm(survival ~  ., study2004)
```

This expression creates an object named `lmFit` in the current environment. Having created the object, we can now use it, perhaps to generate some printed or plotted summaries, or to create some further named objects:

```
lmResid <- lmFit$residuals
```

As long as no second assignment for the name `lmFit` took place in the same context, we can be confident that the new object was computed from the `lmFit` object created above—the same object in all respects, regardless of what other computations took place involving `lmFit`.

The assurance of consistency is key for providing clear and valid software. Suppose, between the two assignments you saw an expression such as

```
verySubtleAnalysis(lmFit)
```

Suppose you had no clue what this function was doing internally, except that all its computations are normal in our current sense, and that `lmFit` is a normal object. You can then be quite confident that the intermediate computations will not have modified `lmFit`. Such confidence allows a top-down analysis of the computations, contributing directly to trustworthy software and to our *Prime Directive*.

We said that names are the only general form of reference in R, and that statement is important to understand. In the second assignment above, `lmFit$residuals` extracts a component of the `lmFit` object. To emphasize, the computation extracts the information, as a new object, rather than creating a reference to the portion of `lmFit` that contains this information. If a following computation changes `lmFit`, there will be no change in `lmResid`.

The statement that nearly all object references in R start from assignments needs some elaboration, too. As later sections in this chapter discuss, there are many ways to get access to objects in R: from packages, saved images, and other files. However, these objects were nearly always created by assignments, and then saved in other forms.

The most important objects not created by an assignment are the arguments in a function call. The R evaluator creates an association between the name of the argument and the expression supplied in the actual call. If you are writing a function with an argument named x, then inside the function definition, you can use the name x and be confident that it refers to the corresponding argument in the call. The mechanism involved is extremely important in the way R works, and is somewhat different from an assignment. Section 13.3, page 460, discusses the details. For the most part, however, you just use the argument names in the body of the function in the same way as any other names.

Exceptions to the object model

Most classes of objects in R behave according to the model described in this section, but a few do not. You need to be careful in using such objects, because they do not give you the usual safety of knowing that local changes really are local. Three classes of such exceptional objects are connections, environments, and external pointers. The discussion here summarizes how and why these objects are exceptions to the normal object behavior.

Connections: The class of connection objects represents streams of bytes (characters, usually). Files on disc and other data streams that behave similarly can be used in R by creating a connection object that refers to the data stream. See Section 5.5, page 131, for a general discussion of connections.

The connection refers to a data stream that often has some sort of physical reality in the computer; as a result, any computation that uses the connection object will deal with the same data stream. Reading from a connection in one function call will alter the state of the stream (for example, the current position for reading from a file). As a result, computations in other functions will be affected. Connection objects in a function call are not local. Ignoring the non-local aspect of a connection object leads to obvious, but easy-to-make, errors such as the following.

```
wRead <- function (con) {
  w <- scan(con, numeric(), n=1)
  if(w > 0)
    w * scan(con, numeric(), n=1)
  else
    NA
}
```

The function wRead() is intended to read a weight w from connection con and then to return either the weight times the following data value on the connection, if the weight is positive, or NA otherwise. The danger is that wRead sometimes reads one field from the connection, and sometimes two. If connections were ordinary objects (if, say, we were just picking items from a list), the difference would not matter because the effect would be local to the single call to wRead. But con is a connection. If it contained pairs of numbers, as it likely would, then the first non-positive value of w will cause wRead to leave the following field on the connection. From then on, disaster is likely.

The recommended fix, here and in general, is that all computations on a connection should leave the connection in a well-defined, consistent state. Usually that means reading (or writing) a specific sequence of fields. Each function's specification should include a description of what it does to the connection. Unfortunately, most of the base functions dealing with connections are implemented as internal C code. Their definition is not easily understood, and different functions can behave inconsistently.

Environments: As discussed in section 5.3, one can access a reference to the environment containing objects as if it were itself an object. In detailed programming tasks, you may need to pass such objects to other functions, so they can search in the right place for a particular name, for example. But environments are not copied or made local to a particular function. Any changes made to the environment will be seen by all software using that environment from now on.

Given that environment objects have this highly non-standard behavior, it might have been better if standard R computations were not allowed for them. Unfortunately a number of basic functions do appear to work normally with environments, including replacement functions for components ("$") and attributes (attr). Don't be fooled: the effects are very different. Avoid using these replacement functions with environments.

External pointers: These are a much more specialized kind of object, so the temptation to misuse them arises less often. As the name suggests, they point to something external to R, or at least something that the R evaluator treats that way. As a result, the evaluator does none of the automatic copying or other safeguards applied to normal objects. External pointers are usually supplied from some code, typically written in C, and then passed along to other such code. Stick to such passive use of the objects.

For all such non-standard objects, one important current restriction in programming is that they should not be extended by new class definitions. They can, with care, be used as slots in class definitions.

5.2 Replacement Expressions

In discussing names as references, we stated that an object assigned in an environment would only be changed by another assignment. But R computations frequently have replacement expressions such as:

```
diag(x) <- diag(x) + epsilon
```

```
z[[i]] <- lowerBound
lmFit$resid[large] <- maxR
```

Don't these modify the objects referred to by x, z and lmFit? No, technically they do not: A replacement creates a new assignment of an object to the current name. The distinction usually makes little difference to a user, but it is the basis for a powerful programming technique and affects computational efficiency, so we should examine it here.

The expressions above are examples of a *replacement expression* in the S language; that is, an assignment where the left side is not a name but an expression, identifying some aspect of the object we want to change. By definition, any replacement expression is evaluated as a simple assignment (or several such assignments, for complex replacement expressions), with the right side of the assignment being a call to a *replacement function* corresponding to the expression. The first example above is equivalent to:

```
x <- `diag<-`(x, value = diag(x) + epsilon)
```

The mechanism is completely general, applying to any function on the left side of the assignment defined to return the modified object. The implication is that a new complete object replaces the existing object each time a replacement expression is evaluated.

It may be important to remember how replacements work when replacing portions of large objects. Each replacement expression evaluates to a new assignment of the complete object, regardless of how small a portion of the object has changed. Sometimes, this matters for efficiency, but as with most such issues, it's wise not to worry prematurely, until you know that the computation in question is important enough for its efficiency to matter. The classic "culprit" is an expression of the form:

```
for(i in undefinedElements(z))
    z[[i]] <- lowerBound
```

The loop in the example will call the function for replacing a single element some number of times, possibly many times, and on each call a new version of z will be assigned, or at least that is the model. In this example, there is no doubt that the programmer should have used a computation that is both simpler and more efficient:

```
z[undefinedElements(z)] <- lowerBound
```

In the jargon that has grown up around S-language programming the distinction is often referred to as "vectorizing": the second computation deals with the whole object (in this case, a vector). Some suggestions and examples are provided in Section 6.4, page 157.

However, as is often the case, predicting the actual effect on efficiency requires considerable knowledge of the details, another reason to delay such considerations in many applications. The example above, in fact, will usually prove to be little more efficient in the vectorized form. The replacement function `[[<-` is one of a number of basic replacements that are defined as primitives; these can, sometimes, perform a replacement in place. The distinction is relevant for efficiency but does not contradict the general model. Primitive replacement functions generally will modify the object in place, without duplication, if it is local. If so, then no difference to the overall result will occur from modification in place.

As a result, a simple loop over primitive replacements will at most tend to produce one duplicate copy of the object. Even if the object is not local, the first copy made and assigned will be, so later iterations will omit the duplication.

The argument for this particular vectorizing is still convincing, but because the revised code is a clearer statement of the computation. It's also likely to be slightly faster, because it eliminates the setup and execution of some number of function calls. Even this distinction is not likely to be very noticeable because the replacement function is a primitive.

Replacement functions

The ability to write new replacement functions provides an important programming tool. Suppose you want to define an entirely new form of replacement expression, say:

```
undefined(z) <- lowerBound
```

No problem: just define a function named `undefined<-`. For an existing replacement function, you may often want to define a new replacement method to replace parts of objects from a class you are designing; for example, methods for replacements using `[` or `[[` on the left of the assignment. Again, no special mechanism is needed: just define methods for the corresponding replacement function, `[<-` or `[[<-`.

To work correctly, replacement functions have two requirements. They must always return the complete object with suitable changes made, and the final argument of the function, corresponding to the replacement data on the right of the assignment, must be named "value".

The second requirement comes because the evaluator always turns a replacement into a call with the right-hand side supplied by name, `value=`, and that convention is used so that replacement functions can have optional arguments. The right-hand side value is never optional, and needs to be supplied by name if other arguments are missing.

Let's define a replacement function for `undefined()`, assuming it wants to replace missing values with the data on the right-hand side. As an extra feature, it takes an optional argument `codes` that can be supplied as one or more numerical values to be interpreted as undefined.

```
`undefined<-` <- function(x, codes = numeric(), value) {
    if(length(codes) > 0)
      x[ x %in% codes] <- NA
    x[is.na(x)] <- value
    x
}
```

If the optional `codes` are supplied, the `` `%in%` `` operator will set all the elements that match any of the codes to `NA`.

Notice that one implication of the mechanism for evaluating replacement expressions is that replacement functions can be defined whether or not the ordinary function of the same name exists. We have not shown a function `undefined()` and no such function exists in the core packages for R. The validity of the replacement function is not affected in any case. However, in a nested replacement, where the first argument is not a simple name, both functions must exist; see Section 13.5, page 466.

Replacement methods

Methods can be written for replacement functions, both for existing functions and for new generic functions. When a class naturally has methods for functions that describe its conceptual structure, it usually should have corresponding methods for replacing the same structure. Methods for `` `[` ``, `` `[[` ``, `length()`, `dim()`, and many other similar functions suggest methods for `` `[<-` ``, `` `[[<-` ``, etc.

New replacement functions can also be made generic. To create a generic function similar to the `` `undefined<-` `` example:

```
setGeneric("undefined<-",
    function(x, ..., value) standardGeneric("undefined<-"),
    useAsDefault = FALSE)
```

The argument, `code`, in the original function was specific to the particular method that function implemented. When turning a function into a generic, it often pays to generalize such arguments into "`...`".

We chose not to use the previous function as the default method. The original function above was fine for casual use, but the operator `` `%in%` `` calls the `match()` function, which is only defined for vectors. So a slightly better view of the function is as a method when both `x` and `value` inherit from class `"vector"`. A default value of `NULL` for `code` is more natural when we don't assume that `x` contains numeric data.

```
setMethod("undefined<-",
          signature(x="vector", value = "vector"),
          function(x, codes = NULL, value) {
              if(length(codes) > 0)
                  x[x %in% codes] <- NA
              x[is.na(x)] <- value
              x
          })
```

Class `"vector"` is the union of all the vector data types in R: the numeric types plus `"logical"`, `"character"`, `"list"`, and `"raw"`. A method for class `"vector"` needs to be checked against each of these, unless it's obvious that it works for all of them (it was not obvious to me in this case). I leave it as an exercise to verify the answer: it works for all types except `"raw"`, and does work for `"list"`, somewhat surprisingly. A separate method should be defined for class `"raw"`, another exercise.

A convenience function, `setReplaceMethod()`, sets the method from the name of the non-replacement function. It's just a convenience, to hide the addition `"<-"` to the name of the replacement function.

5.3 Environments

An environment consists of two things. First, it is a collection of objects each with an associated name (an arbitrary non-empty character string). Second, an environment contains a reference to another environment, technically called the *enclosure* of that environment, but also referred to as the *parent*, and returned by the function `parent.env()`.

Environments are created by several mechanisms. The global environment contains all the objects assigned there during the session, plus possibly objects created in a few other ways (such as by restoring some saved data).

The environment of a function call contains objects corresponding to the arguments in the function call, plus any objects assigned so far during the evaluation of the call. Environments associated with packages contain the objects exported to the session or, in the package's namespace, the objects visible to functions in the package. Generic functions have environments created specially to store information needed for computations with methods. Environments created explicitly by `new.env()` can contain any objects assigned there by the user.

When the R evaluator looks for an object by name, it looks first in the local environment and then through the successive enclosing environments. The enclosing environment for a function call is the environment of the function. What that is varies with the circumstances (see page 123), but in the ordinary situation of assigning a function definition, it is the environment where the assignment takes place. In particular, for interactive assignments and ordinary source files, it is the global environment.

The chain of enclosing environments for any computation determines what functions and other objects are visible, so you may need to understand how the chaining works, in order to fully understand how computations will work.

In this section we give some details of environments in various contexts, and also discuss some special programming techniques using environments. A general warning applies to these techniques. As mentioned earlier in the chapter, the combination of a name and an environment is the essential object reference in R. But functional programming, which is central to R (section 3.2), generally avoids computing with references. Given that, it's not surprising that computing directly with environments tends to go outside the functional programming model. The techniques may still be useful, but one needs to proceed with caution if the results are to be understandable and trustworthy.

Environments and the R session

An R session always has an associated environment, the *global* environment. An assignment entered by a user in the session creates an object with the corresponding name in the global environment:

```
sAids <- summary(Aids2)
```

Expressions evaluated directly in the session are also evaluated in the global environment. For the expression above, the evaluator needs to find a function named `"summary"` and then, later, an object named `"Aids2"`. As always, the evaluator looks up objects by name first in the current environment (here the global environment) and then successively in the enclosing or parent environments.

The chain of environments for the session depends on what packages and other environments are attached. The function `search()` returns the names of these environments, traditionally called the "search list" in the S language. It's not a list in the usual sense. The best way of thinking of the search list is as a chain of environments (and thus, conceptually a list).

At the start of a session the search list might look as follows:

```
> search()
[1] ".GlobalEnv"          "package:stats"     "package:graphics"
[4] "package:grDevices" "package:utils"     "package:datasets"
[7] "package:methods"    "Autoloads"          "package:base"
```

The global environment comes first. Its enclosing environment is the second environment on the search list, which has the third environment as its parent, and so on. We can see this by calling `parent.env()`:

```
> ev2 <- parent.env(.GlobalEnv); environmentName(ev2)
[1] "package:stats"
> ev3 <- parent.env(ev2); environmentName(ev3)
[1] "package:graphics"
```

(If you wonder why the call to `environmentName()`, it's because the printed version of packages as environments is confusingly messy; `environmentName()` gets us back to the name used by `search()`.)

The arrangement of enclosing environments, whereby each package has the next package in the search list as its parent, exists so that R can follow the original rule of the S language that the evaluator searches for names in the search list elements, in order.

In evaluating `summary(Aids2)`, the evaluator finds the function object `summary` in the `base` package. However, object `"Aids2"` is not found in any of the elements of the search list:

```
> find("summary")
[1] "package:base"
> find("Aids2")
character(0)
```

That object is contained in the package MASS. To obtain it, the package must be attached to the search list, or the object must be explicitly extracted from the package. Attaching the package, say by calling `require()`, alters the search list, and therefore the pattern of enclosing environments.

```
> require(MASS)
Loading required package: MASS
[1] TRUE
> search()
 [1] ".GlobalEnv"        "package:MASS"       "package:stats"
 [4] "package:graphics"  "package:grDevices"  "package:utils"
 [7] "package:datasets"  "package:methods"    "Autoloads"
[10] "package:base"
> ev2 <- parent.env(.GlobalEnv); environmentName(ev2)
[1] "package:MASS"
> ev3 <- parent.env(ev2); environmentName(ev3)
[1] "package:stats"
```

The search by name for objects now looks in the environment for package MASS before the previous environments in the search list. If there happened to be a function summary() in that package, it would be chosen rather than the function in the base package. The function require() would have warned the user if attaching the package introduced any name conflicts.

However, possible conflicts between packages are a worry; with the very large number of packages available, some conflicts are inevitable. Package mgcv and package gam on CRAN both have a function gam(). The two functions are similar in purpose but not identical, so one might want to compare their results. To do so, one needs to be explicit about which function is being called. The `::` operator prepends the name of the package to the function name, so that mgcv::gam() and gam::gam() refer uniquely to the two functions.

For programming rather than interactive analysis, the problem and the approach are slightly different. If your function calls functions from other packages, you would like to be assured that the intended function is called no matter what other packages might be used in some future session. If the function was loaded into the global environment, say by using source(), such assurance is not available. In our previous example, you cannot ensure that a future user has the intended package in the search list, ahead of the unintended one, when you call gam(), and similarly for every other function called from a package. The problem remains when your function is in a simple package, because the original R model for package software is basically that of source-ing the code in the package when the package is attached. In either case, the environment of the function is the global environment. If a name is encountered in a call to any such function, then by the general rule on page 120, the evaluator searches first in the call, then in the global environment, and then in its enclosing environments. So the object found can change depending on what packages are attached.

Using `` `::` `` on every call is clearly unreasonable, so a more general mechanism is needed to clarify what software your software expects. This is one of the main motivations for introducing the NAMESPACE mechanism for R packages. A "NAMESPACE" file in the package source contains explicit directives declaring what other packages are imported, potentially even what individual objects are imported from those packages. The mechanism implementing the imports can be understood in terms of the current discussion of environments. If the package SoDA had no namespace file, then a function from the package, say binaryRep() would have the global environment as its environment. But SoDA does have a namespace file and:

```
> environment(binaryRep)
<environment: namespace:SoDA>
```

The namespace environment constructed for the package restricts the visible objects to those in the namespace itself, those explicitly imported, and the base package. To implement this rule, the parent of the package's namespace is an environment containing all the imports; its parent is the base package's namespace.

In most circumstances, the namespace mechanism makes for more trustworthy code, and should be used in serious programming with R. See Section 4.6, page 103 for the techniques needed.

Environments for functions (continued)

Functions are usually created by evaluating an expression of the form:

```
function ( formal arguments ) body
```

As discussed in Section 3.3, page 50, the evaluation creates a function object, defined by its formal arguments, body, and environment. The function is basically just what you see: the same definition always produces the same object, with one important exception. When it is created, the function object gets a reference to the environment in which the defining expression was evaluated. That reference is a built-in property of the function.

If the expression is evaluated at the command level of the session or in a file sourced in from there, the environment is the global environment. This environment is overridden when packages have a namespace, and replaced by the namespace environment. There are two other common situations in programming that generate function environments other than the global environment.

Function definitions can be evaluated inside a call to another function. The general rule applies: the function is given a reference to the environment created for the evaluation of that call. Ordinarily, the environment of the call disappears after the call is complete, whenever storage is cleaned up by a garbage collection.

However, there is an R programming technique that deliberately creates functions that share a more persistent version of such an environment. The goal is usually to go beyond a purely functional approach to programming by sharing other objects, within the same environment, among several functions. The functions can then update the objects, by using non-local assignments.

For a discussion of programming this way, and of alternatives, see Section 5.4, page 125. Software that is used by calling functions from a list of functions (in the style of `z$f(···)`), or that discusses R closures, likely makes use of this mechanism.

The other commonly encountered exception is in *generic* functions (those for which methods are defined). These mainly exist for the purpose of selecting methods, and are created with a special environment, whose enclosure is then the function's usual environment (typically the namespace of the package where the function is defined). The special environment is used to store some information for rapid selection of methods and for other calculations. A few other objects involved in method dispatch, such as methods including a `callNextMethod()`, also have specialized environments to amortize the cost of searches. Unlike package namespaces, the special environments for method dispatch don't change the fundamental rules for finding names. The specialized environments are an implementation detail, and might in principle disappear in later versions of R.

Computing with environment objects

Environments arise mostly in the background when expressions are evaluated, providing the basic mechanism for storing and finding objects. They can themselves be created (by `new.env()`) and used as objects, however. Doing so carries risks because environments are not standard R objects. An environment is a reference. Every computation that modifies the environment changes the same object, unlike the usual functional model for computing with R.

If you do want to use environments directly, consider using the following basic functions to manipulate them, in order to make your programming intentions clear. The functions actually predate environments and R itself, and form the traditional set of techniques in the S language for manipulating "database" objects. A 1991 Bell Labs technical report [4] proposed them for database classes. Explicit computation with environments often treats them essentially as database objects. For a more modern approach to a database interface to R, see the DBI package, and Section 12.7, page 446.

The five basic computations, in their R form with environments, are:

assign(x, value, envir =) Store the object value in the environment, as the character string name, x.

get(x, envir =) Return the object associated with the name from the environment..

exists(x, envir =) Test whether an object exists associated with the name.

objects(envir =) Return the vector of names for the objects in the environment.

remove(list = , envir =) Remove the objects named as list from the environment.

The five functions are widely used, but are presented here with somewhat specialized arguments, needed in order to use them consistently with environments. In addition, both functions get() and exists() should be called with the optional argument inherits = FALSE, if you want to search only in the specified environment and not in its enclosures.

If your programming includes defining new classes, it's natural to embed computations with environments in a special class, to clarify the intentions and hide confusing details. Be warned however: You cannot make class "environment" a superclass of a new class, such as by contains = "environment" in the call to setClass(). Because environment objects are references, objects from the new class will actually have the same reference, including all slots and other properties.

You can use an environment as a slot in a new class, provided as always that your computations take account of the environment's non-standard behavior.

5.4   Non-local Assignments; Closures

Many computational objects are naturally thought of as being repeatedly updated as relevant changes occur. Whenever an object represents a summary of an ongoing process, it requires computations to change the object when new data arrives in the process. Other objects that represent physical or visual "real things" also lend themselves to updating; for example, an object representing a window or other component of a user interface will be updated when some preference or other internal setting is changed.

The S language provides a very general mechanism for updating a local object, via replacement expressions (Section 5.2, page 115).

R introduces an alternative mechanism, in which functions share a common environment and update non-local objects in that environment. The mechanism is inspired by other languages; in particular, it has something in common with reference-based object-oriented programming systems, but it does not use formal class definitions. As such, it departs significantly from a functional programming style. All the same, it does enable some useful computations, so let's examine it, show an example, along with a more functional alternative, and then assess the pros and cons.

The trick is made possible by two techniques: non-local assignments and the environment created by a function call. Any assignment or replacement with the `<-` or `=` operator can be made non-local by using the operator `<<-` instead. The meaning is quite different, however, and also different from the same operator in S-Plus. Consider the assignment:

```
dataBuf <<- numeric(0)
```

The rule for such assignments in R is to search for the name through all the enclosing environments, starting from the environment of the function in which the assignment is evaluated. If an existing object of this name is found, the assignment takes place there; otherwise, the object is assigned in the global environment. This is an unusual rule and can have strange consequences (for example, if the name is first encountered in one of the attached packages, an attempt is made to assign in that package, usually failing because the package environment is locked). The intended use in most cases is that an object will have been initialized with this name in an enclosing environment; the `<<-` operator then updates this object.

The other part of the trick involves assigning one or more functions inside a function call, by evaluating an ordinary definition, but inside another call. The primitive code that evaluates the `function` expression sets the environment of the function object to the environment where the evaluation takes place, in this case the local environment of the call. Because the assignment is local, both function and environment normally disappear when the call is completed, but not if the function is returned as part of the value of the call. In that case, the object returned preserves both the function and its environment. If several functions are included in the object returned, they all share the same environment. The R programming mechanism referred to as a *closure* uses that environment to keep references to objects that can then be updated by calling functions created and returned from the original function call.

Here is an example that illustrates the idea. Suppose a large quantity of data arrives in a stream over time, and we would like to maintain an estimate of some quantiles of the data stream, without accumulating an arbitrarily large buffer of data. The paper [7] describes a technique, called *Incremental Quantile estimation* (IQ), for doing this: a fixed-size data buffer is used to accumulate data; when the buffer is full, an estimate of the quantiles is made and the data buffer is emptied. When the buffer fills again, the existing quantile estimates are merged with the new data to create a revised estimate. Thus a fixed amount of storage accumulates a running estimate of the quantiles for an arbitrarily large amount of data arriving in batches over time.

Here's an implementation of the updating involved, using closures in R.

```
newIQ <- function(nData = 1000, probs = seq(0, 1, 0.25)) {
    dataBuf <- numeric(0)
    qBuf <- numeric(0)

    addData <- function(newdata) {
        n <- length(newdata);
        if(n + length(dataBuf) > nData)
          recompute(newdata)
        else
          dataBuf <<- c(dataBuf, newdata)
    }

    recompute <- function(newdata = numeric(0)) {
        qBuf <<- doQuantile(qBuf, c(dataBuf, newdata), probs)
        dataBuf <<- numeric(0)
    }

    getQ <- function() {
        if(length(dataBuf) > 0)
          doQuantile(qBuf, dataBuf, probs)
        else
          qBuf
    }
    list(addData = addData, getQ = getQ)
}
```

Our implementation is trivial and doesn't in fact illustrate the only technically interesting part of the computation, the actual combination of the current quantile estimate with new data using a fixed buffer, but that's not our department; see the reference. We're interested in the programming for updating.

For each separate data stream, a user would create an IQ "object":

```
myData <- newIQ()
```

The actual returned object consists of a list of two functions. Every call to newIQ() returns an identical list of functions, except that the environment of the functions is unique to each call, and indeed is the environment created dynamically for that call. The shared environment is the business end of the object. It contains all the local objects, including dataBuf and qBuf, which act as buffers for data and for estimated quantiles respectively, and also three functions. Whenever data arrives on the stream, a call to one of the functions in the list adds that data to the objects in the environment:

```
> myData$addData(newdata)
```

When the amount of data exceeds the pre-specified maximum buffer size, quantiles are estimated and the function recompute(), conveniently stored in the environment, clears the data buffer. Whenever the user wants the current quantile estimate, this is returned by the other function in the list:

```
> quants <- myData$getQ()
```

This returns the internal quantile buffer, first updating that if data is waiting to be included.

Because the computation is characteristic of programming with closures, it is worth examining why it works. The call to newIQ() assigns the two buffers, in the environment of the call. That environment is preserved because the functions in the returned list have a reference to it, and therefore garbage collection can't release it.

When the addData() function does a non-local assignment of dataBuf, it applies the rule on page 126 by looking for an object of that name, and finds one in the function's environment. As a result, it updates dataBuf there; similarly, function recompute() updates both dataBuf and qBuf in the same environment. Notice that recompute() shares the environment even though it is not a user-callable function and so was not returned as part of the list.

It's helpful to compare the closures implementation to one using replacement functions. In the replacement version, the buffers are contained explicitly in the object returned by newIQ() and a replacement function updates

them appropriately, returning the revised object. Here's an implementation
similar to the closure version.

```
newIQ <- function(nData = 1000, probs = seq(0, 1, 0.25))
    list(nData = nData, probs = probs,
         dataBuf = numeric(0), qBuf = numeric(0))


`addData<-` <- function(IQ, update = FALSE, value) {
    n <- length(value);
    if(update || (n + length(IQ$dataBuf) > IQ$nData))
      recompute(IQ, value)
    else {
        IQ$dataBuf <- c(IQ$dataBuf, value)
        IQ
    }
}

recompute  <- function(IQ, newdata = numeric(0)) {
    IQ$qBuf <- doQuantile(qBuf, c(IQ$dataBuf, newdata), IQ$probs)
    IQ$dataBuf <- numeric(0)
    IQ
}

getQ <- function(IQ) {
    if(length(IQ$dataBuf) > 0)
      doQuantile(IQ$qbuf, IQ$dataBuf, IQ$probs)
    else
      IQ$qBuf
}
```

This version of `addData()` is a replacement function, with an option to update the quantile estimates unconditionally. The logic of the computation is
nearly the same, with the relevant objects now extracted from the `IQ` object,
not found in the environment. Typical use would be:

```
> myData <- newIQ()
  . . . . . . .
> addData(myData) <- newdata
> getQ(myData)
```

The user types apparently similar commands in either case, mainly distinguished by using the `$` operator to invoke component functions of the IQ
object in the closure form, versus an explicit replacement expression in the
alternate version. Even the implementations are quite parallel, or at least
can be, as we have shown here.

What happens, however, follows a very different concept. Closures create a number of object references (always the same names, but in unique environments), which allow the component functions to alter the object invisibly. The component functions correspond to methods in languages such as C++, where objects are generally *mutable*, that is, they can be changed by methods via object references.

The replacement function form follows standard S-language behavior. General replacement functions have often perplexed those used to other languages, but as noted in section 5.2, they conform to the concept of local assignments in a functional language.

Are there practical distinctions? Closures and other uses of references can be more efficient in memory allocation, but how much that matters may be hard to predict in examples.

The replacement version requires more decisions about keeping the quantile estimates up to date, because only an assignment can change the object. For example, although getQ() always returns an up-to-date estimate, it cannot modify the non-local object (fortunately for trustworthy software). To avoid extra work in recomputing estimates, the user would need to reassign the object explicitly, for example by:

```
myData <- recompute(myData)
```

Another difference between the versions arises if someone wants to add functionality to the software; say, a summary of the current state of the estimation. The replacement version can be modified in an ordinary way, using the components of any IQ object. But notice that a new function in the closure version must be created by newIQ() for it to have access to the actual objects in the created environment. So any changes can only apply to objects created after the change, in contrast to the usual emphasis on gradual improvement in R programming.

Finally, I think both versions of the software want to evolve towards a class-and-method concept. The IQ objects really ought to belong to a class, so that the data involved is well-defined, trustworthy, and open to extension and inheritance. The replacement version could evolve this way obviously; what are currently components of a list really want to be slots in a class.

The closure version could evolve to a class concept also, but only in a class system where the slots are in fact references; again, this has much of the flavor of languages such as C++ or Java.

5.5   Connections

Connection objects and the functions that create them and manipulate them allow R functions to read and interpret data from outside of R, when the data can come from a variety of sources. When an argument to the R function is interpreted as a connection, the function will work essentially the same way whether the data is coming from a local file, a location on the web, or an R character vector. To some extent, the same flexibility is available when an R function wants to write non-R information to some outside file.

Connections are used as an argument to functions that read or write; the argument is usually the one named `file=` or `connection=`. In most cases, the argument can be a character string that provides the path name for a file.

This section discusses programming with connection objects, in terms of specifying and manipulating them. Section 5.6 discusses the functions most frequently used with connections.

Programming with connections

For programming with R, the most essential fact about connections may be that they are not normal R objects. Treating them in the usual way (for example, saving a connection object somewhere, expecting it to be self-describing, reusable, and independent of other computations) can lead to disaster. The essential concept is that connections are references to a data stream. A paradigm for defensive programming with connections has the form:

```
con <- create(description, open)
## now do whatever input or output is needed using con
close(con)
```

where *create* is one of the functions (`file()`, etc.) that create connections, *description* is the description of the file or command, or the object to be used as a text connection, and *open* is the string defining the mode of the connection, as discussed on page 134.

Two common and related problems when programming with connections arise from not explicitly closing them and not explicitly opening them (when writing). The paradigm shown is not always needed, but is the safest approach, particularly when manipulating connections inside other functions.

Connections opened for reading implement the concept of some entity that can be the source of a stream of bytes. Similarly, connections opened for writing represent the corresponding concept of sending some bytes to the connection. Actually, hardly any R operations on connections work at such a low level. The various functions described in this chapter and elsewhere are expressed in terms of patterns of data coming from or going to the connection. The lower level of serial input/output takes place in the underlying C code that implements operations on connections.

Connections in R implement computations found at a lower level in C. The most useful property of a connection as an object is its (S3) class. There exist S3 methods for connection objects, for functions `print()` and `summary()`, as well as for a collection of functions that are largely meaningful only for connection-like objects (`open()`, `close()`, `seek()`, and others).

However, connections are distinctly nonstandard R objects. As noted on page 114, connections are not just objects, but in fact references to an internal table containing the current state of active connections. Use the reference only with great caution; the connection object is only usable while the connection is in the table, which will not be the case after `close()` is called. Although a connection can be defined without opening it, you have no guarantee that the R object so created continues to refer to the internal connection. If the connection was closed by another function, the reference could be invalid. Worse still, if the connection was closed and another connection opened, the object could silently refer to a connection totally unrelated to the one we expected. From the view of trustworthy software, of the *Prime Directive*, connection objects should be opened, used and closed, with no chance for conflicting use by other software.

Even when open and therefore presumably valid, connections are non-standard objects. For example, the function `seek()` returns a "position" on the connection and for files allows the position to be set. Such position information is a reference, in that all R function calls that make use of the same connection see the same position. It is also not part of the object itself, but only obtained from the internal implementation. If the position is changed, it changes globally, not just in the function calling `seek()`.

Two aspects of connections are relevant in programming with them: what they are and how information is to be transferred. These are, respectively, associated with the *connection class* of the object, an enumeration of the kinds of entities that can act as suitable sources or sinks for input or output; and with what is known as the *connection mode*, as specified by the `open` argument to the functions that create a connection object.

Connection classes

Connections come from the concept of file-like entities, in the C programming tradition and specifically from the Posix standards. Some classes of connections are exactly analogous to corresponding kinds of file structures in the Posix view, other are extensions or analogs specific to R. The first group includes `"file"`, `"fifo"`, `"pipe"`, and `"socket"` connection objects. Files are the most common connections, the others are specialized and likely to be familiar only to those accustomed to programming at the C level in Linux or UNIX. Files are normally either specified by their path in the file system or created as temporary files. Paths are shown UNIX-style, separated by `"/"`, even on Windows. There are no temporary files in the low-level sense that the file disappears when closed; instead, the `tempfile()` function provides paths that can be used with little danger of conflicting with any other use of the same name.

Three classes of connections extend files to include compression on input or output. They differ in the kind of compression done. Classes `"gzfile"` and `"bzfile"` read and write through a compression filter, corresponding to the shell commands `gzip` and `bzip2`. The `"unz"` connections are designed to read a single file from an archive created by the `zip` command. All of these are useful in compressing voluminous output or in reading data previously compressed without explicitly uncompressing it first. But they are not particularly relevant for general programming and we won't look at examples here.

The `"url"` class of connections allow input from locations on the Web (not output, because that would be a violation of security and not allowed). So, for example, the file `"weather1.csv"` in the example on page 169 exists on my Web site, `stat.stanford.edu/~jmc4` at the URL:

    http://www-stat.stanford.edu/~jmc4/Examples/weather1.csv

Software in R can read this remote data directly by using the connection:

    url("http://www-stat.stanford.edu/~jmc4/Examples/weather1.csv")

Text connections (class `"textConnection"`) use character vectors for input or output, treating the elements of the character vector like lines of text. These connections operate somewhat differently from file-like connections. They don't support seeking but do support `pushBack()` (see that function's documentation). When used for output, the connections write into an object whose name is given in creating the connection. So writing to a text connection has a side effect (and what's more, supports the idea of a non-local side effect, via option `local=FALSE`).

Modes and operations on connections

The modes and operations on connections, like the objects themselves, come largely from the C programming world, as implemented in Posix-style software. The operation of opening a connection and the character string arguments to define the mode of the connection when opened were inspired originally by corresponding routines and arguments in C. You don't need to know the C version to use connections in R; indeed, because the R version has evolved considerably, knowing too much about the original might be a disadvantage.

Connections have a state of being *open* or *closed*. While a connection is open, successive input operations start where the previous operation left off. Similarly, successive output operations on an open connection append bytes just after the last byte resulting from the previous operation.

The mode of the connection is specified by a character-string code supplied when the connection is opened. A connection can be opened when it is created, by giving the `open=` argument to the generating function. The connection classes have generating functions of the name of the class (`file()`, `url()`, etc.) A connection can also be opened (if it is not currently open) by a call to the `open()` function, taking an `open=` argument with the same meaning. Connections are closed by a call to `close()` (and not just by running out of input data, for example).

The mode supplied in the `open=` argument is a character string encoding several properties of the connection in one or two characters each. In its most general form, it's rather a mess, and not one of the happier borrowings from the Posix world. The user needs to answer two questions:

- Is the connection to be used for reading or writing, or both? Character `"r"` means open for reading, `"w"` means open for writing (at the beginning) and `"a"` means open for appending (writing after the current contents).

  Confusion increases if you want to open the connection for both reading and writing. The general notion is to add the character `"+"` to one of the previous. Roughly, you end up reading from the file with and without initially truncating it by using `"w+"` and `"a+"`.

- Does the connection contain text or binary data? (Fortunately, if you are not running on Windows you can usually ignore this.) Text is the default, but you can add `"t"` to the mode if you want. For binary input/output append `"b"` to the string you ended up with from the first property.

So, for example, `open="a+b"` opens the connection for both appending and reading, for binary data.

The recommended rules for functions that read or write from connections are:

1. If the connection is initially closed, open it and close it on exiting from the function.

2. If the connection is initially open, leave it open after the input/output operations.

As the paradigm on page 131 stated, you should therefore explicitly open a connection if you hope to operate on it in more than one operation.

Consider the following piece of code, which writes the elements of a character vector `myText`, one element per line, to a file connection, to the file `"myText.txt"` in the local working directory:

```
txt <- file("./myText.txt")
writeLines(myText, txt)
```

The output is written as expected, and the connection is left closed, but with mode `"w"`. As a result, the connection would have to be explicitly re-opened in read mode to read the results back. The default mode for connections is read-only (`"r"`), but `writeLines()` set the mode to `"wt"` and did not revert it; therefore, a call to a read operation or to `open()` with a read mode would fail. Following the paradigm, the first expression should be:

```
txt <- file("./myText.txt", "w+")
```

Now the connection stays open after the call to `writeLines()`, and data can be read from it, before explicitly closing the connection.

5.6 Reading and Writing Objects and Data

R has a number of functions that read from external media to create objects or write data to external media. The external media are often files, specified by a character string representing the file's name. Generally, however, the media can be any connection objects as described in Section 5.5.

In programming with these functions, the first and most essential distinction is between those designed to work with any R object and those designed for specific classes of objects or other restricted kinds of data. The first approach is based on the notion of *serializing*, meaning the conversion of an arbitrary object to and from a stream of bytes. The content of the file is not expected to be meaningful for any purpose other than serializing and unserializing, but the important property for programming is that any object will be serialized. The second type of function usually deals with files that have some particular format, usually text but sometimes binary. Other software, outside of R, may have produced the file or may be suitable to deal with the file.

Serializing: Saving and restoring objects

The serializing functions write and read whole R objects, using an internal coding format. Writing objects this way and then reading them back should produce an object identical to the original, in so far as the objects written behave as normal R objects. The coding format used is platform-independent, for all current implementations of R. So although the data written may be technically "binary", it is suitable for moving objects between machines, even between operating systems. For that reason, files of this form can be used in a source package, for example in the "data" directory (see Section 4.3, page 87).

There are two different approaches currently implemented. One, represented by the save() and load() functions, writes a file containing one or more named objects (save()). Restoring these objects via load() creates objects of the same names in some specified R environment. The data format and functions are essentially those used to save R workspaces. However, the same mechanism can be used to save any collection of named objects from a specified environment.

The lower-level version of the same mechanism is to serialize() a single object, using the same internal coding. To read the corresponding object back use unserialize(). Conceptually, saving and loading are equivalent to serializing and unserializing a named list of objects.

By converting arbitrary R objects, the serialize() function and its relatives become an important resource for trustworthy programming. Not only do they handle arbitrary objects, but they consider special objects that behave differently from standard R objects, such as environments. To the extent reasonable, this means that such objects should be properly preserved and restored; for example, if there are multiple references to a single environment in the object(s) being serialized, these should be restored by unserialize() to refer to one environment, not to several. Functions built on the serializing techniques can largely ignore details needed to handle a variety of objects. For example, the digest package implements a hash-style table indexed by the contents of the objects, not their name. Using `serialize()` is the key to the technique: rather than having to deal with different types of data to create a hash from the object, one uses `serialize()` to convert an object to a string of bytes. (See Section 11.2, page 416, for an example based on `digest`.)

Two caveats are needed. First, references are only preserved uniquely within a single call to one of the serializing functions. Second, some objects are only meaningful within the particular session or context, and no magic on the part of `serialize()` will save all the relevant context. An example is an open connection object: serializing and then unserializing in a later process will not work, because the information in the object will not be valid for the current session.

Reading and writing data

The serializing techniques use an internal coding of R objects to write to a file or connection. The content of the file mattered only in that it had to be consistent between serializing and unserializing. (For this reason, serializing includes version information in the external file.)

A different situation arises when data is being transferred to or from some software outside of R. In the case of reading such data and constructing an R object, the full information about the R object has to be inferred from the form of the data, perhaps helped by other information. General-purpose functions for such tasks use information about the format of character-string data to infer fairly simple object structure (typically vectors, lists, or data-frame-like objects). Many applications can export data in such formats, including spreadsheet programs, database software, and reasonably simple programs written in scripting, text manipulation, or general programming languages. In the other direction, R functions can write text files of a similar form that can be read by these applications or programs.

Functions `scan()` and `read.table()` read fields of text data and interpret them as values to be returned in an R object. Calls to `scan()` typically return either a vector of some basic class (`numeric` or `character` in most cases), or a list whose components are such vectors. A call to `read.table()` expects to read a rectangular table of data, and to return a `data.frame` object, with columns of the object corresponding to columns of the table. Such tables can be generated by the export commands of most spreadsheet and database systems. Section 8.2, page 294, has an example of importing such data.

A variety of functions can reverse the process to write similar files: `cat()` is the low-level correspondence to `scan()`, and `write.table()` corresponds to `read.table()`.

These functions traditionally assume that file arguments are ordinary text files, but they can in fact read or write essentially any connection. Also, functions exist to deal with binary, `raw`, data on the connection rather than text fields. See the documentation for functions `readBin()` and `writeBin()`.

For many applications, these functions can be used with modest human effort. However, there are limitations, particularly if you need an interface to other software that deals with highly structured or very large objects. In principle, specialized inter-system interfaces provide a better way to deal with such data. Some interfaces are simple (but useful) functions that read the specialized files used by other systems to save data. At the other extreme, inter-system interfaces can provide a model in one language or system for computing in another, in a fully general sense. If a suitable general inter-system interface is available and properly installed, some extra work to adapt it to your particular problem can pay off in a more powerful, general, and accurate way of dealing with objects in one system when computing in another. See Chapter 12 for a discussion.

Chapter 6

Basic Data and Computations

This chapter surveys a variety of topics dealing with different kinds of data and the computations provided for them. The topics are "basic" in two senses: they are among those most often covered in introductions to R or S-Plus; and most of them go back to fairly early stages in the long evolution of the S language.

On the data side, we begin with the various ways of organizing data that have evolved in R. Then object types (Section 6.2, page 141), which characterize data internally; vectors and vector structures (6.3, 143); and data frames (6.5, 166). Matrices and their computations are discussed together in Section 6.8, page 200. Other computational topics are: arithmetic and other operators (6.6, 184); general numeric computations (6.7, 191); statistical models (6.9, 218); random generators and simulation (6.10, 221); and the special techniques known as "vectorizing" (6.4, 157).

Many of the topics deserve a whole chapter to themselves, if not a separate book, given their importance to data analysis. The present chapter focuses on some concepts and techniques of importance for integrating the data and computations into programming with R, particularly viewed from our principles of effective exploration and trustworthy software. Further background on the topics is found in many of the introductions to R, as well as in the online R documentation and in some more specific references provided in the individual sections of the chapter.

6.1   The Evolution of Data in the S Language

Since its beginnings in 1976, the S language has gone through an evolution of concepts and techniques for representing data and organizing computations on data structures. Four main epochs can be identified, all of which are still with us, and all of which need to be understood to some extent to make use of existing software, and sometimes for new programming as well. Labeled by the names used for the corresponding mechanisms in R, the main epochs are:

1. *Object types*, a set of internal types defined in the C implementation, and originally called *modes* in S;

2. *Vector structures*, defined by the concept of vectors (indexable objects) with added structure defined by *attributes*;

3. *S3 classes*, that is, objects with class attributes and corresponding one-argument method dispatch, but without class definitions;

4. Formal *classes* with class definitions, and corresponding generic functions and general methods, usually called S4 classes and methods in R.

This section summarizes the relevance of each approach, with pointers to further details in this chapter and elsewhere. The main recommendation is to use formal classes and methods when developing new ideas in data structure, while using the other approaches for specialized areas of computing.

Object types: All implementations of the S language have started from an enumeration of object types or modes, implied by the very first design documents (such as the figure on page 476). In R, this takes the form of a field in the internal C structure, and the corresponding function `typeof()`. You need to deal with object types for some C extensions and when defining classes that extend a specific type. Section 6.2 gives details.

Vectors and vector structures: The concept of objects as dynamically indexable by integer, logical and perhaps character expressions also goes back to the early days. The S3 version of the language around 1988 added the notion of vector structures defined by named attributes, seen as complementary to the vector indexing. Section 6.3, page 143, discusses these concepts, which remain important for computing effectively with the language. The term *vectorizing* has evolved for computations with vectors that avoid indexing, by expressing computations in "whole object" terms. In favorable applications, efficiency and/or clarity benefits; see Section 6.4, page 157.

S3 classes: As part of the software for statistical models, developed around 1990 and after, a `class` attribute was used to dispatch single-argument methods. The attribute contained one or more character strings, providing a form of inheritance. Otherwise, the change to data organization was minimal; in particular, the content of objects with a particular class attribute was not formally defined. S3 classes are needed today to deal with software written for them (for example, the statistical model software (Section 6.9, page 218) and also for incorporating such data into modern classes and methods (see Section 9.6, page 362 for programming with S3 classes).

Formal (S4) classes: The S3 classes and methods gave a useful return on a small investment in changes to the language, but were limited in flexibility (single-argument dispatch) and especially in supporting trustworthy software. Classes with explicit definitions and methods formally incorporated into generic functions have been developed since the late 1990s to provide better support. That is the programming style recommended here for new software—chapters 9 and 10, for classes and methods respectively.

6.2 Object Types

For most purposes, `class(x)` is the way to determine what kind of thing object x really is. Classes are intended to be the official, public view, with as clear and consistent a conceptual base as possible. Deep down, though, objects in R are implemented via data structures in C. By definition, the *object type* corresponds to the set of possible types encoded in those structures. For a complete list of the internal types at the C level, see the *R Internals* manual in the R documentation or at the CRAN Web site. The function `typeof()` returns a character string corresponding to the internal object type of an object.

Table 6.1 lists the object types commonly encountered in R programming. The first column gives the class name for simple objects of the object type named in the second column. The expressions in the third column will evaluate to an object of the corresponding object type.

The classes in the rows down to the first line in the table are the basic vector classes; these correspond to a object type of the same name, except for type `"double"`, indicating the specific C declaration for numeric data. For more discussion of these, see section 6.3. The classes in the second group of rows are the basic classes for dealing with the language itself. The first three object types correspond to function objects in R: `"closure"` for ordinary functions, `"builtin"` and `"special"` for primitive functions. (For details

Class(es)	Object Type(s)	Examples
`"logical"`	`"logical"`	`TRUE; FALSE`
`"numeric"`	`"double"`	`1; 0.5; 1e3`
`"integer"`	`"integer"`	`as.integer(1)`
`"character"`	`"character"`	`"Carpe \n Diem"`
`"list"`	`"list"`	`list(a=1,b=plot)`
`"complex"`	`"complex"`	`1 + .5i`
`"raw"`	`"raw"`	`as.raw(c(1,4,15))`
`"expression"`	`"expression"`	`expression(a,1)`
`"function"`	`"closure"`	`function(x)x+1`
	`"builtin"`	`` `sin` ``
	`"special"`	`` `if` ``
`"call"`	`"language"`	`quote(x+1)`
`"{"`, etc.		`quote({})`
(many)	`"S4"`	`new("track")`
`"name"`	`"symbol"`	`quote(x)`
`"environment"`	`"environment"`	`.GlobalEnv`

Table 6.1: Object Types in R. The types in the first group are vectors, the types in the first and second behave as non-reference objects. See the text for details, and for types generated from C.

on primitive functions, see Section 13.4, page 463.) Primitive functions are an R implementation extension, not part of the S language definition; for this reason, objects of all three object types have class `"function"`. Conversely, one object type, `"language"`, corresponds to essentially all the unevaluated expressions other than constants or names. Function calls, braced subexpressions, assignments, and other control structures have specific classes as objects, but all are in fact implemented by one object type. In effect, R organizes all `"language"` objects as if they were function calls. The last row in the second group, `"S4"`, is used for objects generated from general S4 classes.

All the classes down to the second line in the table behave normally as arguments in calls, and can be used in class definitions. Classes can be defined to extend these classes, an important ability in programming with R. We might want a new class of data with all the properties of character vectors, but with some additional features as well. Similarly, programming techniques using the language might need to define objects that can behave as functions but again have extra features. Examples of such classes are shown in Chapter 9, on pages 370 and 356. Objects from such classes retain the corresponding basic type, so that legacy code for that type works as it should. If x has a class extending `"character"` or `"function"`, then the value of `typeof(x)` will be `"character"` or `"function"` correspondingly. Objects from classes that do *not* extend one of the basic object types have type `"S4"`.

In contrast to the types in the first two groups of the table, the object types in the third group are essentially references. Passing `.GlobalEnv` as an argument to a function does not create a local version of the environment. For this reason, you should not attach attributes to such objects or use them in the `contains=` part of a class definition, although they can be the classes for slots.

Besides the object types in the table, there are a number of others that are unlikely to arise except in very specialized programming, and in the internal C code for R. These include `"pairlist"`, `"promise"`, `"externalptr"`, and `"weakref"`. Except for the first of these, all are reference types. For a complete table of types, see Chapter 2 of the *R Language Definition* manual.

6.3   Vectors and Vector Structures

The earliest classes of objects in the S language, and the most thoroughly "built-in" are vectors of various object types. Essentially, a vector object is defined by the ability to index its elements by position, to either extract or replace a subset of the data. If x is a vector, then

```
x[i]
```

is a vector with the same type of data, whenever i defines a set of indices (in the simplest case, positive integer values). If y is also a vector (in the simplest case, with the same type of data as x), then after evaluating

```
x[i] <- y
```

the object x will be a vector of the same type of data. The range of possibilities for i and y is much more general than the simple cases, but the simple cases define the essence of the `vector` class, and the general cases can be understood in terms of the simplest case, as discussed on page 146.

An early concept for organizing data in the S language was the *vector structure*, which attached *attributes* to vectors in order to imply structure, such as that of a multi-way array. Vector structures were a step on the way to classes of objects, and usually can be subsumed into class definitions. However, there are some objects and computations in R that still work directly on attributes, so an understanding of vector structures is included, starting on page 154.

Basic classes of vectors

Table 6.2 shows the basic classes of vectors built into R. Identically named functions (`numeric()`, `logical()`, etc.) generate vectors from the corresponding classes.

Class	Data Contained
`"logical"`	Logicals: (TRUE, FALSE).
`"numeric"`	Numeric values.
`"character"`	Character strings.
`"list"`	Other R objects.
`"complex"`	Complex numbers.
`"raw"`	Uninterpreted bytes.
`"integer"`	Integer numeric values.
`"single"`	*For C or Fortran only*
`"expression"`	Unevaluated expressions.

Table 6.2: The vector classes in R.

The basic vector classes are the essential bottom layer of data: indexable collections of values. Single individual values do not have a special character in R. There are no scalar objects, either in the sense of separate classes or as an elementary, "sub-class" layer, in contrast to other languages such as C or Java. Computations in the language occasionally may make sense only for single values; for example, an `if()` test can only use one logical value. But these are requirements for the result of a particular computation, not a definition of a different kind of data (for computations that need a single value, see page 152).

For the basic vectors, except for `"list"` and `"expression"`, the individual elements can only be described in terms of the implementation, in C. In terms of that language, the data in each vector class corresponds to an array of some C type. Only when writing code in C to be used with R are you likely to need the explicit type, and even then the best approach is to hide the details in C macros (see Section 11.3, page 420).

Numeric data occasionally involves considering two other classes, `"integer"` and "`single.`" The type for data of class "`numeric`", as returned by `typeof()`, is "`double`", indicating that the internal data is double-precision floating point. There is also a separate class and type for "`integer`" data. You can force data into integer (via function `as.integer()`) and a few functions do return integer results (function `seq()` and operator `` `:` ``), but because R does not do separate integer computations very often, trying to force integer representation explicitly can be tricky and is usually not needed.

Users sometimes try to force integer representation in order to get "exact" numerical results. In fact, the trick required is not integer representation, but integral (i.e., whole number) values. These are exactly represented by type "`double`", as long as the number is not too large, so arithmetic will give exact results. Page 192 shows an example to generate "exact" values for a numeric sequence.

The "`single`" class is still more specialized. Essentially, it exists to notify the interface to C or Fortran to convert the data to single precision when passing the vector as an argument to a routine in those languages. R does not deal with single-precision numeric data itself, so the class has no other useful purpose.

The S language includes a built-in vector type representing points in the complex plane, class "`complex`".[1] See `?complex` for generating complex vectors and for manipulating their various representations. The class has its own methods for arithmetic, trigonometric, and other numerical computations, notably Fourier transforms (see `?fft`). Most functions for numerical computations do accept complex vectors, but check the documentation before assuming they are allowed. Complex data is also suitable for passing to subroutines in Fortran or C. Fortran has a corresponding built-in type, which can be used via the `.Fortran()` interface function. There is a special C structure in R for calls to `.C()`, which also matches the complex type built into modern C compilers on "most" platforms. Section 11.2, page 415 discusses the interfaces to C and Fortran; for the latest details, see section 5.2 of the *Writing R Extensions* manual.

Vectors of type "`raw`" contain, as the name suggests, raw bytes not assumed to represent any specific numeric or other structure. Although such data can be manipulated using `x[i]`-style expressions, its essential advantage is what will *not* be done to it. Aside from explicitly defined computations, raw vectors will not likely be changed, and so can represent information

---

[1]Statistics research at Bell Labs in the 1970s and before included important work in spectral analysis and related areas, relying on computations with complex data. Complex vectors became a built-in object type with S3.

outside standard R types, exactly and without accidental changes. Neither
of these properties applies, for example, if you try to use numeric data to
represent exact values. Even if the initial data is exactly as expected, numeric computations can easily introduce imprecision. On the other hand,
you can generally count on "raw" data remaining exactly as created, unless
explicitly manipulated. For this reason, objects of class "raw" may be used
to pass data from arbitrary C structures through R, for example.

Vectors of type "expression" contain unevaluated expressions in the language. The main advantages of such an object over having a "list" object
with the same contents are the explicit indication that all elements should be
treated as language expressions and the generating function, expression(),
which implicitly quotes all its arguments:

```
> transforms <- expression(sin(x), cos(x), tan(x))
```

You can mix such literal definitions with computed expressions by replacing
elements of the vector:

```
> transforms[[4]] <- substitute(f(x), list(f=as.name(fname)))
```

Indexing into vectors

The most important data manipulation with vectors is done by extracting or
replacing those elements specified by an index expression, using the function
in R represented by a pair of single square brackets:

```
x[i]
x[i] <- y
```

These are the fundamental *extraction* and *replacement* expressions for vectors.

When i is a vector of positive values, these index the data in a vector,
from 1 for the first element to length(x) for the last. Indexing expressions
of type "logical" are also basic, with the obvious interpretation of selecting
those elements for which the index is TRUE. If you have used R or the S
language at all, you have likely used such expressions. It's valuable, however,
to approach them from the general concept involved, and to relate various
possibilities for the objects x, i, and y in the example to the general concept.

In contrast to programming languages of the C/Java family, expressions
like x[i] are not special, but are evaluated by calling a reasonably normal R
function, with the name ` [`. As with any functional computation in the S
language, the value is a new object, defined by the arguments, x and i. The

expression does not "index into" the vector object in the sense of a reference as used in other languages. Instead, evaluating x[i] creates a new object containing the elements of x implied by the values in i. As an example, let's use the sequence function, seq(), to generate a vector, and index it with some positive values.

```
> x <- seq(from=1.1, to=1.7, by=.1)
> x
[1] 1.1 1.2 1.3 1.4 1.5 1.6 1.7
> length(x)
[1] 7
> x[c(1,3,1,5,1,7)]
[1] 1.1 1.3 1.1 1.5 1.1 1.7
```

Repeated values in the positive index are entirely within the standard definition, returning the values selected in the order of the index. Positive index values are silently truncated to integers: x[1.9], x[1.01], and x[1] all return the same subset.

When the index is a logical vector, it arises most naturally as the value of a test applied to x itself and/or to another vector indexed like x.

```
> x[x>1.45]
[1] 1.5 1.6 1.7
```

Logical indexes are applied to the whole vector; in particular, if i has length less than that of x, it is interpreted as if it were replicated enough times to be the same length as x. The logical index c(TRUE, FALSE) extracts the odd-numbered elements of any vector:

```
> x[c(TRUE, FALSE)]
[1] 1.1 1.3 1.5 1.7
```

Note the second special rule below, however, for the case that i is longer than x.

The behavior of the replacement expression, x[i] <- y, is to create and assign a new version of x in the current evaluation environment. In the new version, the values in x indexed by i have been replaced by the corresponding elements of y. Replacement expressions are evaluated by calling the corresponding *replacement function*, as discussed in Section 5.2, page 117. In this case the replacement function is `[<-`, and the expression is equivalent to:

```
x <- `[<-`(x, i, y)
```

The behavior of replacement functions is still within a simple functional model: A replacement function computes and returns a new object, which is then assigned in the current environment, with the same name as before. In this case the new object is a copy of the old, with the indexed values replaced.

Unlike extraction, replacement can change the type of x. There is an implied ordering of basic vector types from less information to more. Logicals have only two values, numerics many, strings can represent numbers, and lists can hold anything. If the type of y is more general than that of x, the replacement will convert x to the type of y. For example:

```
> x[2] <- "XXX"
> x
[1] "1.1" "XXX" "1.3" "1.4" "1.5" "1.6" "1.7"
```

The numeric vector is converted to a character vector, on the reasoning that this would preserve all the information in x and in y. More details on conversions between basic types are given on page 149.

For simple positive or logical indexing expressions, the interpretation follows naturally from the concept of a vector. There are in addition a number of extensions to the indexing argument in the actual implementation. These can be convenient and you need to be aware of the rules. For your own computing, however, I would discourage taking too much advantage of them, at least in their more esoteric forms. They can easily lead to errors or at least to obscure code. With that in mind, here are some extensions, roughly ordered from the innocuous to the seriously confusing.

1. The index can be a vector of negative values. In this case, the interpretation is that the value should be all the elements of x except the elements corresponding to -i.

   ```
   > x[-c(1,7)]
   [1] 1.2 1.3 1.4 1.5 1.6
   ```

   With this interpretation, the order of the negative values is ignored, and so are repeated values. You cannot mix positive and negative values in a single index.

2. An index for extraction or replacement can be longer than the current length of the vector. The interpretation is that the length of x is set to the largest index (implicitly) and the expression is applied to the

"stretched" version. Replacements can change the length of a vector by assigning beyond its current length.

Increasing the length of a vector is interpreted as concatenating the appropriate number of NA items, with NA being interpreted as an undefined value suitable for the type of the vector.

```
> length(x)
[1] 7
> x[c(1,9)]
[1] 1.1  NA
> x[c(1,9)] <- -1
> x
[1] -1.0  1.2  1.3  1.4  1.5  1.6  1.7   NA -1.0
```

Logical, numeric, character and complex object types have a built-in NA form; lists and expressions use NULL for undefined elements; type "raw" uses a zero byte.

3. Integer index arguments can contain 0 values mixed in with either all positive or all negative indices. These are ignored, as if all the 0 values were removed from the index.

4. When the index contains an undefined value, NA, the interpretation for extraction is to insert a suitable NA or undefined value in the corresponding element of the result, with the interpretation of undefined as above for the various types. In replacements, however, NA elements in the index are ignored.

R also has single-element extraction and replacement expressions of the form x[[i]]. The index must be a single positive value. A logical or negative index will generate an error in R, even if it is equivalent to a single element of the vector.

Conversion of vector types

The basic vector types have some partial orderings from more to less "simple", in the sense that one type can represent a simpler type without losing information. One ordering, including the various numeric types, can be written:

```
"logical", "integer", "numeric", "complex", "character", "list"
```

If a simpler vector type (to the left in the ordering) is supplied where a less simple vector type is wanted, an automatic conversion will take place for numeric and comparison operators (see Section 6.6, page 186). The conversion rules are implemented in the internal code and are not part of the inheritance relations used when methods are dispatched. Defining a method corresponding to an argument of class `"numeric"`, for example, does not result in that method being used when the argument is of class `"logical"` or `"integer"`, even though those classes are "simpler" in terms of the listing above. That implementation decision could be argued, but it's perhaps best just to realize that the two parts of the language—basic code for operators and formal class relations—were written at very different times. In the early coding, there was a tendency to make as many cases "work" as possible. In the later, more formal, stages the conclusion was that converting richer types to simpler automatically in all situations would lead to confusing, and therefore untrustworthy, results.

The rules of conversion are basically as follows.

- Logical values are converted to numbers by treating `FALSE` as 0 and `TRUE` as 1.

- All simpler types are converted to `"character"` by converting each element individually (as, for example, in a call to `cat()` or `paste()`).

- All simpler types are converted to `"list"` by making each element into a vector of length 1.

- Numeric values are converted to `"complex"` by taking them to be the real part of the complex number.

Class `"raw"` is not included in the ordering; generally, your best approach is to assume it is not automatically converted to other types. Vectors of type `"raw"` are not numeric, and attempts to use them in numeric expressions will cause an error. They are allowed with comparison operators, however, with other vectors of any of the basic types except `"complex"`. The implementation of the comparisons with types `"logical"`, `"integer"`, and `"numeric"` uses roughly the following logic. Interpret each of the elements (single bytes, remember) in the `"raw"` vector as a corresponding integer value on the range 0 to 255 ($2^8 - 1$), and then use that conversion in the comparison. This should be equivalent to applying the comparison to `as.numeric(x)` where x is the vector of type `"raw"`. Watch out for comparisons with `"character"` vectors however. The rule, natural in itself, is that the comparison should be done as if with `as.character(x)`. But `as.character()` converts `"raw"` vectors by replacing each element by the two hexadecimal characters that represent it, basically because this is how "raw" vectors are printed. As a result, the comparison is not at all the same as if the"raw" vector had first been converted to the numeric vector of its byte code. On the whole, avoid comparisons of "raw" vectors with "character" vectors, because they are only sensible if the character elements are each the print version of byte codes (and in this case they probably should have been converted to "raw" anyway). And just to make things worse, there is another conversion, rawToChar(), which interprets the bytes as character codes, entirely different from as.character(). The situation is further complicated by the existence in modern R of multiple character encodings to deal with international character sets. Read the documentation carefully and proceed with caution.

Besides automatic conversions, explicit coercion can be performed between essentially any of the basic vector classes, using as(). For the general behavior of as(), see Section 9.3, page 348; in the case of basic vector classes the methods used are identical to the corresponding class-specific functions, as.integer(), as.character(), etc. Some additional general rules for coercion include:

- Numeric values are coerced to logical by treating all non-zero values as TRUE.

- General numeric values are converted to integer by truncation towards zero.

- Complex values are converted to numeric by taking their real part.

- Character data is coerced to simpler types roughly as if the individual values were being read, say by scan(), as the simpler type. On elements for which scan would fail, the result is NA, and a warning is issued (but not an error as scan() would produce).

- Lists are converted to simpler types only if each element of the list is a vector of length one, in which case the coercion works one element at a time. (If an element is itself a list of length 1, that produces an NA, perhaps accidentally.)

- Conversion from "raw" to all numeric types generally treats each byte as an integer value; conversion to "raw" generally converts numeric values to integer, uses values that fit into one byte and sets all others to 00 (which is generally used instead of NA with type "raw").

Conversion from "raw" to "character" produces the hexadecimal codes, from "00" to "ff". Unfortunately, conversion from "character" to "raw" first converts to integer, not likely to be what you want. The inverse of the conversion to "character" is scan(x, raw()).

As will perhaps be clear, the wise approach is to look for ambiguous conversions and either deal with them as makes sense for your own application or else generate an error. The rules are pretty reasonable for most cases but should not be taken as universally appropriate.

Single values when you need them

Vectors in the S language play a particularly important role in that there are no scalar object types underlying them, and more fundamentally there is no lower layer beneath the general model for objects in the language. Contrast this with Java, for example. Java has a general model of classes, objects and methods that forms the analogous programming level to programming with R. The implementation of a Java method, however, can contain scalar variables of certain basic types, which are not objects, as well as arrays, which are objects (sort of) but not from a class definition. The situation in R is simpler: everything is an object and anything that looks like a single value of type numeric, logical or character is in fact a vector. The lower layer is provided instead by the inter-system interface to C, as discussed in Chapter 11.

However, some computations really do need single values. To ensure that you get those reliably and that the values make sense for the context may require some extra care.

By far the most common need for single values comes in tests, either conditional computations or iterations.

```
if(min(sdev) > eps)
    Wt <- 1/sdev
```

The condition in the if expression only makes sense if min(sdev) > eps evaluates to a single value, and that value must be unambiguously interpretable as TRUE or FALSE. Similarly, the condition in a while loop must provide a single TRUE or FALSE each time the loop is tested.

So, what's the problem? Often no problem, particularly for early stages of programming. If we know that eps was supplied as a single, positive numeric value and that sdev is a non-empty vector of numbers (none of them missing values and, most likely, none of them negative), then min(sdev) is a single numeric value and the comparison evaluates to a single TRUE or FALSE. The test will either pass or not, but in any case will be computable.

Problems can arise when such a computation occurs inside a function with the objects eps and sdev passed in or computed from arguments. Now we are making assertions about the way in which the function is called. As time goes by, and the function is used in a variety of contexts, these assertions become more likely to fail. For the sake of the *Prime Directive* and trustworthy software, tests of the arguments should be made that ensure validity of the conditional expression. The tests are best if they are made initially, with informative error messages.

As your functions venture forth to be used in unknown circumstances, try to add some tests on entry that verify key requirements, assuming you can do so easily. Don't rely on conditional expressions failing gracefully deep down in the computations. Failure of assumptions may not generate an error, and if it does the error message may be difficult to relate to the assumptions.

Consider two failures of assumptions in our example: first, that sdev was of length zero; second, that it contained NAs. For trustworthy computation we might reasonably want either to be reported as an error to the user. As it happens, the second failure does generate an error, with a reasonable message:

```
> if(min(sdev) > eps) Wt <- 1/sdev
Error in if (min(sdev) > eps) Wt <- 1/sdev :
    missing value where TRUE/FALSE needed
```

With a zero length vector, however, min() returns infinity, the test succeeds and Wt is set to a vector of length zero. (At least there is a warning.)

If the test is computationally simple, we can anticipate the obvious failures. For more elaborate computations, the test may misbehave in unknown ways. Having verified all the obvious requirements, we may still feel nervous about obscure failures. A strategy in such situations is to guarantee that the computation completes and then examine the result for validity.

Evaluating the expression as an argument to the function try() guarantees completion. The try() function, as its name suggests, attempts to evaluate an expression. If an error occurs during the evaluation, the function catches the error and returns an object of class "try-error". See ?try for details and Section 3.7, page 74, for a related programming technique.

Here is an ultra-cautious approach for this example:

```
testSd <- try(min(sdev) > eps)
if(identical(testSd, TRUE))
```

```
  Wt <- 1/sdev
else if(!identical(testSd, FALSE))
   if(is(testSd, "try-error"))
      stop("Encountered error in testing sdev ",
          testSd, "")
   else
      stop("Testing sdev produced an invalid result: ",
          summaryString(testSd))
```

The only legitimate results of the test are TRUE and FALSE. We check for either of these, identically. If neither is the result, then either there was an error, caught by try(), or some other value was computed (for example, NA if there were any missing values in sdev). With try(), we can re-issue an error message identifying it as a problem in the current expression. For more complicated expressions than this one, the message from the actual error may be obscure, so our extra information may be helpful.

In the case of an invalid result but no error, one would like to describe the actual result. In the example, the function summaryString() might include the class and length of the object and, if it is not too large, its actual value, pasted into a string. Writing a suitable summaryString() is left as an exercise. A reasonable choice depends on what you are willing to assume about the possible failures; in the actual example, there are in fact not very many possibilities.

Some situations require single values other than logicals for testing; for example, computing the size of an object to be created. Similar guard computations to those above are possible, with perhaps additional tests for being close enough to a set of permitted values (positive or non-negative integers, in the case of an object's size, for example).

Overall, trustworthy computations to produce single values remain a challenge, with the appropriate techniques dependent on the application. Being aware of the issues is the important step.

Vector structures

The concept of the vector structure is one of the oldest in the S language, and one of the most productive. It predates explicit notions of classes of objects, but is best described using those notions. In this section we describe the general "structure" class, and the behavior you can expect when computing with objects from one of the classes that extend "structure", such as "matrix", "array", or "ts". You should keep the same expectations in mind when writing software for structure classes, either methods for existing classes or the definition of new classes. We use the name of the corresponding formal class, "structure", to mean "vector structure" throughout this section, as is common in discussions of R.

A class of objects can be considered a structure class if it has two properties:

1. Objects from the class contain a data part that can be any type of basic vector.

2. In addition to the data part, the class defines some organizational structure that describes the layout of the data, but is not itself dependent on the individual values or the type of the data part.

For example, a matrix contains some data corresponding to a rectangular two-way layout, defined by the number of rows and columns, and optionally by names for those rows and columns. A time-series object, of class `"ts"`, contains some data corresponding to an equally-spaced sequence of "times".

Matrices and time-series are regular layouts, where the structure information does not grow with the total size of the object, but such regularity is not part of the requirement. An irregular time series, with individual times for the observations, would still satisfy the structure properties.

The importance of the `"structure"` class comes in large part from its implications for methods. Methods for a number of very heavily used functions can be defined for class `"structure"` and then inherited for specific structure classes. In practice, most of these functions are primitives in R, and the base code contains some of the structure concept, by interpreting certain vector objects with attributes as a vector structure. The base code does not always follow the structure model exactly, so the properties described in this section can only be guaranteed for a formal class that contains `"structure"`.

The two properties of vector structures imply consequences for a number of important R functions. For functions that transform vectors element-by-element, such as the `Math()` group of functions (trigonometric and logarithmic functions, `abs()`, etc.), the independence of data and structure implies that the result should be a structure with the data transformed by the function, but with the other slots unchanged. Thus, if x is a matrix, `log(x)` and `floor(x)` are also matrices.

Most of the functions of this form work on numeric data and return numeric data, but this is not required. For example, `format(x)` encodes vectors as strings, element-by-element, so that the data returned is of type `"character"`. If x is a vector structure, the properties imply that `format(x)` should be a structure with the same slots as x; for example, if x is a matrix, then `format(x)` should be a character matrix of the same dimensions.

Binary operators for arithmetic, comparisons, and logical computations are intrinsically more complicated. For vectors themselves, the rules need to consider operands of different lengths or different types. Section 6.6, page 186, gives a summary of the R behavior. What if one or both of the operands is a vector structure? If only one operand is a structure, and the result would have the same length as the structure, the result is a structure with the same slots. If both operands are structures, then in general there will be no rational way to merge the two sets of properties. The current method for binary operators (function `Ops()`) returns just the vector result. In principle, the structure might be retained if the two arguments were identical other than in their data part, but testing this generally is potentially more expensive than the basic computation. Particular structure classes such as `"matrix"` may have methods that check more simply (comparing the dimensions in the `"matrix"` case).

The `base` package implementation has rules for matrices, arrays, and time-series. If one argument is one of these objects and the other is a vector with or without attributes, the result will have the matrix, array, or time-series structure unless it would have length greater than that of the structure, in which case the computation fails. The rule applies to both arithmetic and comparisons. Operations mixing arrays and time-series or arrays with different dimensions produce an error. See Section 6.8, page 200, for more discussion of computations with matrix arguments.

For vectors with arbitrary attributes, the current base code in R for operators and for element-by-element functions is not consistent with treating these as a vector structure. Numeric element-by-element functions usually retain attributes; others, such as `format()` drop them. For arithmetic operators, if one argument has attributes, these are copied to the result. If both arguments have attributes, then if one argument is longer than the other, arithmetic operators use its attributes; if the arguments are of equal length, the result combines all the attributes from either argument, with the left-hand value winning for attributes appearing in both arguments. Comparison operators drop all attributes, except for the `names` attribute.

The overall message is clear: For consistent vector structure behavior, you should create an explicit class, with `"structure"` as a superclass.

To create a vector structure class formally, call `setClass()` with the `contains=` argument specifying either class `"structure"` or some other S4 vector structure class. Class `"structure"` is a virtual class that extends class `"vector"`, which in turn extends all the basic vector object types in R.

For example, here is a class `"irregTS"` for an irregular time-series structure, with an explicit time slot.

```
setClass("irregTS", representation(time = "DateTime"),
    contains = "structure")
```

Objects from this class will inherit the structure methods, providing much of the desired behavior automatically. Methods then need to be added for the particular behavior of the class (at the least, a `show()` method and some methods for ` [`.)

One can program methods for various functions with class `"structure"` in the signature. The methods will be inherited by specific vector structure classes such as `"irregTS"`. In addition, methods are supplied in R itself for the formal `"structure"` class that implement the vector structure view described in this section. For a list of those currently defined:

```
showMethods(classes = "structure")
```

This will list the corresponding signatures; another `showMethods()` call for a particular function with `includeDefs = TRUE` will show the definitions.

An important limitation arises because the informal vector structures such as matrices, arrays, time-series, and S3 classes will not inherit formal methods for class `"structure"`, at least not with the current version of R. Nor does it generally work to have such informal vector structures in the `contains=` argument of a formal class definition, largely for the same reason. So formal and informal treatment of vector structures don't currently benefit each other as much as one would like.

6.4 Vectorizing Computations

Over the history of R and of S, there has been much discussion of what is variously called "avoiding loops", "vectorizing computations", or "whole-object computations", in order to improve the efficiency of computations. The discussion must appear rather weird to outsiders, involving unintuitive tricks and obscure techniques. The importance of vectorizing is sometimes exaggerated, and the gains may depend subtly on the circumstances, but there are examples where computations can be made dramatically faster. Besides, re-thinking computations in these terms can be fun, and occasionally revealing.

The original idea, and the name "vectorizing", come from the contrast between a single expression applied to one or more R vectors, compared to a loop that computes corresponding single values. Simple vector objects in R consist of n elements, typically numbers. The value of n is often the number of observed values in some data, or a similar parameter describing the size of our application. Very important practical problems involve large applications; n may of necessity be large, and in any case we would like our computations to be reasonably open to large-data applications. A computation of interest that takes one or more such vectors and produces a new vector nearly always takes computing time proportional to n, when n is large. (At least proportional: for the moment let's think of computations that are linear in the size of the problem. The interest in vectorizing will only be stronger if the time taken grows faster than linearly with n.)

Vectorizing remains interesting when the parameter n is not the size of a vector, but some other parameter of the problem that is considered large, such as the length of loops over one or more dimensions of a multiway array; then n is the product of the dimensions in the loops. In other examples, the loop is an iteration over some intrinsic aspect of the computation, so that n is not a measure of the size of the data but may still be large enough to worry about. In an example below, n is the number of bits of precision in numeric data, not a variable number but still fairly large.

We're considering linear computations, where elapsed time can be modeled reasonably well, for large n, by $a + bn$, for some values of a and b, based on the assertion that some multiple of n calls to R functions is required. The goal of vectorizing is to find a form for the computation that reduces the proportionality, b. The usual technique is to replace all or part of the looping by a single expression, possibly operating on an expanded version of the data, and consisting of one or more function calls. For the change to be useful, these functions will have to handle the larger expanded version of the data reasonably efficiently. (It won't help to replace a loop by a call to a function that does a similar loop internally.) The usual assumption is that "efficiently" implies a call to functions implemented in C. Notice that the C code will presumably do calculations proportional to n. This is not quantum computing! The hope is that the time taken per data item in C will be small compared to the overhead of n function calls in R.

The fundamental heuristic guideline is then:

> Try to replace loops of a length proportional to n with a smaller number of function calls producing the same result, usually calls not requiring a loop in R of order n in length.

Functions likely to help include the following types.

1. Functions that operate efficiently on whole objects to produce other whole objects, usually of the same size and structure; examples include the arithmetic and other binary operators, numerical transformation, sorting and ordering computations, and some specialized filtering functions, such as `ifelse()`.

2. Operations that extract or replace subsets of objects, using expressions of the form `x[i]`, provided that the indexing is done on a significantly sizable part of `x`.

3. Functions that efficiently transform whole objects by combining individual elements in systematic ways, such as `diff()` and `cumsum()`.

4. Functions to transform vectors into multi-way arrays, and vice versa, such as `outer()` and certain matrix operations;

5. Functions defined for matrix and array computations, such as matrix multiplication, transposition, and subsetting (these are used not just in their standard roles, but as a way to vectorize other computations, as the example below shows).

6. New functions to do specialized computations, implemented specially in C or by using some other non-R tools.

A different approach uses functions that directly replace loops with sequences of computations. These are the `apply()` family of functions. They don't precisely reduce the number of function calls, but have some other advantages in vectorizing. The `apply()` functions are discussed in Section 6.8, page 212.

The craft in designing vectorized computations comes in finding equivalent expressions combining such functions. For instance, it's fairly common to find that a logical operation working on single values can be related to one or more equivalent numerical computations that can apply to multiple values in one call. Other clues may come from observing that a related, vectorized computation contains all the information needed, and can then be trimmed down to only the information needed. None of this is purely mechanical; most applications require some reflection and insight, but this can be part of the fun.

First, a simple example to fix the idea itself. Suppose we want to trim elements of a vector that match some string, `text`, starting from the end of the vector but not trimming the vector shorter than length `nMin` (the computation arises in summarizing available methods by signature). The obvious way in most programming languages would be something such as:

```
n <- length(x)
while(n > nMin && x[[n]] == text)
    n <- n-1
length(x) <- n
```

Quite aside from vectorizing, the use of `==` in tests is a bad idea; it can return NA and break the computation. Instead, use an expression that will always produce TRUE or FALSE.

Back to vectorizing. First, let's think object rather than single number. We're either looking for the new object replacing x, or perhaps the condition for the subset of x we want (the condition is often more flexible). The key in this example is to realize that we're asking for one of two logical conditions to be true. Can we express these in vector form, and eliminate the loop? If you'd like an exercise, stop reading here, go off and think about the example.

The idea is to compute a logical vector, call it ok, with TRUE in the first n elements and FALSE in the remainder. The elements will be TRUE if either they come in the first nMin positions or the element of x does not match text. The two conditions together are:

```
seq(along = x) <= nMin   # c(1,2,...,n) <= nMin;
 | is.na(match(x, text))
```

The use of seq() here handles the extreme case of zero-length x; the function match() returns integer indices or NA if there is no match. See the documentation for either of these if you're not familiar with them.

The vectorized form of the computation is then:

```
ok <- seq(along = x) <= nMin | is.na(match(x, text))
```

Chances are that either ok or x[ok] does what we want, but if we still wanted the single number n, we can use a common trick for counting all the TRUE values:

```
n <- sum(ok)
```

The computations are now a combination of a few basic functions, with no loops and so, we hope, reasonably efficient. Examining is.na(), match(), and sum() shows that all of them go off to C code fairly quickly, so our hopes are reasonable.

If that first example didn't put you off, stay with us. A more extended example will help suggest the process in a more typical situation.

Example: Binary representation of numeric data

Our goal is to generate the internal representation for a vector of numeric data. Numeric data in R is usually floating point, that is, numbers stored internally as a combination of a binary fraction and an integer exponent to approximate a number on the real line. As emphasized in discussing numeric computations (Section 6.7, page 191), it's occasionally important to remember that such numbers are only an approximation and in particular that most numbers displayed with (decimal) fractional parts will not be represented exactly.

Suppose we wanted to look at the binary fractions corresponding to some numbers. How would we program this computation in R?

To simplify the discussion, let's assume the numbers have already been scaled so $.5 <= x < 1.0$ (this is just the computation to remove the sign and the exponent of the numbers; we'll include it in the final form on page 165). Then all the numbers are represented by fractions of the form:

$$b_1 2^{-1} + b_2 2^{-2} + \cdots + b_m 2^{-m}$$

where m is the size of the fractional part of the numerical representation, and b_i are the bits (0 or 1) in the fraction. It's the vector b of those bits we want to compute. (Actually, we know the first bit is 1 so we only need the rest, but let's ignore that for simplicity.)

This is the sort of computation done by a fairly obvious iteration: replace x by $2x$; if $x >= 1$ the current bit is 1 (and we subtract 1 from x); otherwise the current bit is zero. Repeat this operation m times. In a gloriously C-like or Perl-like R computation:

```
b <- logical(m)
for(j in 1:m) {
  x <- x * 2
  b[[j]] <- (x >= 1)
  if(b[[j]])
    x <- x - 1
}
```

We will vectorize this computation in two ways. First, the computation as written only works for x of length 1, because the conditional computation depends on x >= 1 being just one value. We would like x to be a numeric vector of arbitrary length; otherwise we will end up embedding this computation in another loop of length n. Second, we would like to eliminate the loop of length m as well. Admittedly, m is a fixed value. But it can be large enough to be a bother, particularly if we are using 64-bit numbers. The situation of having two parameters, either or both of which can be large, is a common one (think of the number of variables and number of observations).

Eliminating the loop over 1:m can be done by a conversion rather typical of vectorizing computations. Notice that the iterated multiplication of x by 2 could be vectorized as multiplying x by a vector of powers of 2:

```
pwrs <- 2^(1:m)
xpwrs <- x*pwrs
```

Getting from here to the individual bits requires, excuse the expression, a bit of imaginative insight. Multiplying (or dividing) by powers of 2 is like shifting left (or right) in low-level languages. The first clue is that the i-th element of xpwrs has had the first i bits of the representation shifted left of the decimal point. If we truncate xpwrs to integers and shift it back, say as

```
xrep <- trunc(xpwrs)/pwrs
```

the i-th element is the first i bits of the representation: each element of xrep has one more bit (0 or 1) of the representation than the previous element. Let's look at an example, with x <- .54321:

```
> xrep
 [1] 0.5000000 0.5000000 0.5000000 0.5000000 0.5312500 0.5312500
 [7] 0.5390625 0.5429688 0.5429688 0.5429688 0.5429688 0.5429688
[13] 0.5430908 0.5431519 0.5431824 0.5431976 0.5432053 0.5432091
[19] 0.5432091 0.5432091 0.5432096 0.5432098 0.5432099 0.5432100
```

Next, we isolate those individual bits, as powers of two $(b_j 2^{-j})$: the first bit is xrep[[1]], and every other bit j is xrep[[j]] - xrep[[j-1]]. The difference between successive elements of a vector is a common computation, done by a call to the function diff(). Using that function:

```
bits <- c(xrep[[1]], diff(xrep)
```

We would then need to verify that the method used for diff() is reasonably efficient. An alternative is to realize that the $m-1$ differences are the result of subtracting xrep without the first element from xrep without the last element: xrep[-1] - xrep[-m], using only primitive functions. When we account for multiple values in x, however, we will need a third, more general computation.

Assuming we want the individual bits to print as 0 or 1, they have to be shifted back left, which is done just by multiplying by pwrs. Now we have a complete vectorization for a single value. With the same value of x:

```
> pwrs <- 2^(1:m)
> xpwrs <- x*pwrs
> xrep <- trunc(xpwrs)/pwrs
> bits <- c(xrep[[1]], diff(xrep))*pwrs
> bits
 [1] 1 0 0 0 1 0 1 1 0 0 0 0 1 1 1 1 1 1 0 0 1 1 1 1
```

The computations all operate on vectors of length m; in particular, in the second line, the single value in x is replicated in the multiplication.

The remaining task is to generalize the computation to n values in x. We need n instances of each of the length-m computations. As is often the case, we can get the desired result by expanding the objects into matrices, here with n rows and m columns. To begin, we replicate the x into m columns and define pwrs as a matrix with n identical rows. All the computations down to defining xrep expand to compute n*m values at once:

```
n <- length(x)
x <- matrix(x, n, m)
pwrs <- matrix(2^(1:m), n, m, byrow = TRUE)
xpwrs <- x*pwrs
xrep <- trunc(xpwrs)/pwrs
```

What about c(xrep[[1]], diff(xrep))? Now we want this computation to apply to each row of the matrix, indexing on the columns. Remember that diff() was just a function to subtract x[[2]] from x[[1]], etc. We could introduce a loop over rows, or use the apply() function to do the same loop for us.

But in fact such patterned row-and-column combinations can usually be done in one function call. Here we do need a "trick", but fortunately the trick applies very widely in manipulating vectors, so it's worth learning. Differences of columns are simple versions of linear combinations of columns, and all linear combinations of columns can be written as a matrix multiplication.

```
bits <- xrep %*% A
```

with A some chosen m by m matrix. The definition of matrix multiplication is that, in each row of bits, the first element is the linear combination of that row of xrep with the first column of A, and so on for each element.

This trick is useful in many computations, not just in examples similar to the current one. For example, if one wanted to sum the columns of a matrix, rather than doing any looping, one simply multiplies by a matrix with a single column of 1s:

```
x %*% rep(1, ncol(x))
```

The vector on the right of the operator will be coerced into a 1-column matrix.

To see the form of A, consider what we want in elements 1, 2, ... of each row—that determines what columns 1, 2, ... of A should contain. The first element of the answer is the first element of the same row of xrep, meaning that the first column of A has 1 in the first element and 0 afterwards. The second element must be the second element minus the first, equivalent to the second column being -1, 1, 0, 0, ... The form required for A then has just an initial 1 in the first column, and every other column j has 1 in row j and -1 in row $j - 1$:

```
       [,1] [,2] [,3] [,4] [,5] [,6] [,7] [,8] [,9] [,10]
[1,]    1   -1    0    0    0    0    0    0    0    0
[2,]    0    1   -1    0    0    0    0    0    0    0
[3,]    0    0    1   -1    0    0    0    0    0    0
  ...
```

Constructing this sort of matrix is the other part of the trick. We take account of the way R stores a matrix; namely, by columns. If we lay out all the columns one after the other, the data in A starts off with 1 followed by m-1 zeroes, followed by -1, and then followed by the same pattern again. By repeating a pattern of m+1 values, we shift the pattern down by one row each time in the resulting matrix. We can create the matrix by the expression:

```
A <- matrix(c(1, rep(0, m-1), -1), m, m)
```

The general thought process here is very typical for computing patterned combinations of elements in matrices. The example in Section 6.8, page 206, constructs a general function to produce similarly patterned matrices.

This is clearly a computation with enough content to deserve being a function. Here is a functional version. We have also added the promised code to turn an arbitrary x into a sign, an exponent, and a binary fraction on the range $.5 <= x < 1.0$. The complete representation is then made up of three parts: sign, exponent, and the bits corresponding to the fraction.

We express this result in the form of a new class of objects. The three parts of the answer are totally interdependent, and we would be inviting errors on the part of users if we encouraged arbitrary manipulations on them. Having a special class allows us to be specific about what the objects mean and what computations they should support. Some extra work is required to create the class, but the results of the computations will be easier to understand and to work with when their essential structure is captured in a class definition. Our users will benefit in both insightful exploration (the *Mission*) and trustworthy software (the *Prime Directive*) from our extra effort. (The details are explored in Section 9.2, page 343; for now, just consider them part of the background.)

```
binaryRep <-
function(data, m = .Machine$double.digits) {
    x <- data
    n <- length(x)

    xSign <- sign(x)
    x <- xSign * x
    exponent <- ifelse(x > 0, floor(1+log(x, 2)), 0)
    x <- x/2 ^ exponent
    pwrs <- binaryRepPowers(n, m)
    x <- matrix(x, n, m)
    xpwrs <- x * pwrs
    xrep <- trunc(xpwrs)/pwrs
    bits <- (xrep %*% binaryRepA(m)) *pwrs

    bits[] <- as.integer(bits[])
    new("binaryRep", original = data,
        sign = as.integer(xSign),
        exponent = as.integer(exponent),
        bits = binaryRepBits(bits))
}
```

The body of the function is in three parts, separated by empty lines. It's the middle part that we are concerned with here, the rest has to do with the class definition and is discussed on page 343.

The function `sign()` returns ± 1, and multiplying by the sign shifts x to positive only. The next line computes the exponent, specifically the largest integer power of 2 not larger than x (play with the expression `floor(1+log(x, 2))` to convince yourself). Dividing by 2 to this power shifts x to be larger than .5 but not larger than 1. The rest of the computation is just as we outlined it before.

This has been a long example, but in the process we have touched on most of the mechanisms listed on page 158. We have also worked through heuristic thinking typical of that needed in many vectorizing computations.

6.5   Statistical Data: Data Frames

Through most of this book, we use the term *data* in the computational sense, meaning numerical or other information in some form that can be stored and processed. But in statistics, and more generally in science, the term has an older meaning, from the Latin "datum" for a "given", and so for an observed value.[2] We examine in this section one concept central to data in this sense, the *data frame*, and its implementation in a variety of computational contexts.

The topic is large and important, so while this section is not short, we can only cover a few aspects. The plan is as follows. We start with some reflections on the concept (as usual, you can skip this to get on to techniques). Next, we examine how data frames as a concept can be used in several languages and systems: in R (page 168), in Excel and other spreadsheets (page 173), and in relational database systems (page 178). Each of these discussions focuses on aquiring and using data corresponding to data frames in the corresponding system. Finally, on page 181, we consider transferring data frames between systems, mostly meaning between R and other systems.

The data frame concept

The concept of a data frame lies at the very heart of science. Gradually, very long ago, and in more than one place, people began to act on the belief that things could be meaningfully observed, and that taking these observations as given could lead to true, or at least useful, predictions about the future. This is in fact the central notion for our computational discussion: that there are things that can be observed (in data analysis called *variables*), and that it's meaningful to make multiple *observations* of those variables. The computational version of the concept is the *data frame*. This section deals mainly with practical computations that implement the data frame concept.

If we look for early evidence of the underlying concept, we must go back long before science as such existed. Consider, for example, the structures known as "calendar stones" and the like. These are structures created to behave in a particular way at certain times of the year (typically the summer or winter solstice). Stonehenge in England, built some five thousand years ago, is designed so that the rising sun on the winter solstice appears in a

---

[2]The *American Heritage Dictionary* [13] has a nice definition including both senses. It also disposes of the pedantry that "data" is always plural: in modern usage it can be a "singular mass entity like information".

particular arch of the monument. Some modern interpretations suggest that the monument is designed to match several patterns in the sun/earth/moon system (for example, the book by John North [20]). Similar devices existed in the ancient Near East and Central America.

Think of the process of designing such a calendar stone. Someone must observe the positions of the sun as it rises each day. At Stonehenge, this position will appear to move farther south each day as winter approaches, until at the solstice the sun "stands still", and then begins to move back north. If the site is designed also to correspond to changes in the appearance and position of the moon, corresponding observations for its changes had to be made.

The builders of Stonehenge had no written language, so they probably did not record such data numerically. But they must have made systematic observations and then drew inferences from them. From the inferences they designed a huge structure whose orientation came from a fundamentally scientific belief that observing data (in particular, observing variables such as length of day and sunrise position) would lead to a useful prediction. Where the sun stood still last year predicts where it will stand still in the years to come.

We seem to have digressed a long way indeed from software for data analysis, but not really. It can't be stressed too emphatically how fundamental the data frame concept is for scientific thinking or even for more informal empirical behavior. We select observable things, variables, and then make observations on them in the expectation that doing so will lead to understanding and to useful models and prediction.

Two consequences for our needs arise from the fundamental role of data frame concepts. First, the concepts have influenced many areas of computing, scientific and other. Software ranging from spreadsheets to database management to statistical and numerical systems are all, in effect, realizing versions of the data frame concept, different in terminology and organization, but sharing ideas. We will benefit from being able to make use of many such systems to capture and organize data for statistical computation. Second and related, in order to exploit these diverse systems, we need some central framework of our own, some statement of what data frames mean for us. Given that, we can then hope to express our computations once, but have them apply to different realizations of the data frame ideas. From the perspective of R, it is the class definition mechanism that gives us the essential tools for a central description of data frames. Section 9.8, page 375 outlines one such framework.

The `"data.frame"` class in R

The S language has included the specific `"data.frame"` class since the introduction of statistical modeling software (as described in the *Statistical Models in S* book [6]). This is an informal ("S3") class, without an explicit definition, but it is very widely used, so it's well worth describing it here and considering its strengths and limitations. Section 9.8, page 375, discusses formal class definitions that might represent `"data.frame"` objects.

A `"data.frame"` object is essentially a named list, with the elements of the list representing variables, in the sense we're using the term in this section. Therefore, each element of the list should represent the same set of observations. It's also the intent that the object can be thought of as a two-way array, with columns corresponding to variables. The objects print in this form, and S3 methods for operators such as `` `[` `` manipulate the data as if it were a two-way array. The objects have some additional attributes to support this view, for example to define labels for "rows" and "columns". Methods allow functions such as `dim()` and `dimnames()` to work as if the object were a matrix. Other computations treat the objects in terms of the actual implementation, as a named list with attributes. The expression

```
w$Time
```

is a legal way to refer to the variable `Time` in data frame `w`, and less typing than

```
w[, "Time"]
```

However, using replacement functions to alter variables as components of lists would be dangerous, because it could invalidate the data frame by assigning a component that is not a suitable variable. In practice, a large number of S3 methods for data frames prevent most invalid replacements.

Because of the focus on software for statistical models, the variables allowed originally for `"data.frame"` objects were required to be from one of the classes that the models software could handle: numerical vectors, numerical matrices, or categorical data (`"factor"` objects). Nothing exactly enforced the restriction, but other classes for variables were difficult to insert and liable to cause strange behavior. R has relaxed the original restrictions, in particular by providing a mechanism to read in other classes (see the argument `colClasses` in the documentation `?read.table` and in the example below).

As a first example, let's read in some data from a weather-reporting system as a data frame, and then apply some computations to it in R.

Software for a weather station provides for data export in comma-separated value form. Here are the first 10 lines of an exported file:

```
Time,TemperatureF,DewpointF,PressureIn,WindDirection,WindDirectionDegrees,\
WindSpeedMPH,WindSpeedGustMPH,Humidity,HourlyPrecipIn,Conditions,Clouds,\
dailyrainin,SoftwareType
2005-06-28 00:05:22,72.7,70.6,30.13,ESE,110,3,6,93,0.00,,-RA,,VWS V12.07
2005-06-28 00:15:46,72.7,70.6,30.12,ESE,105,2,5,93,0.00,,-RA,,VWS V12.07
2005-06-28 00:35:28,72.7,70.3,30.12,East,100,3,6,92,0.00,,OVC024,,VWS V12.07
2005-06-28 00:45:40,72.5,70.1,30.12,ESE,113,6,6,92,0.00,,OVC024,,VWS V12.07
2005-06-28 01:05:04,72.5,70.1,30.11,ESE,110,0,7,92,0.00,,OVC100,,VWS V12.07
2005-06-28 01:15:34,72.5,70.1,30.10,East,91,1,2,92,0.00,,OVC100,,VWS V12.07
2005-06-28 01:35:09,72.3,70.2,30.10,SE,127,0,5,93,0.02,,OVC009,0.02,VWS V12.07
2005-06-28 01:45:33,72.3,70.5,30.09,ESE,110,2,2,94,0.04,,OVC009,0.04,VWS V12.07
2005-06-28 02:05:21,72.3,70.5,30.09,ESE,110,1,6,94,0.04,,OVC009,0.04,VWS V12.07
```

The first line contains all the variable names; to show it here we have broken it into 3, but in the actual data it must be a single line. R has a function, `read.table()`, to read files that represent `"data.frame"` objects, with one line of text per row of the object, plus an optional first line to give the variable names.

Two file formats are widely used for data that corresponds to data frames: *comma-separated-values files* (as in the example above) and *tab-delimited files*. Two corresponding convenience functions, `read.csv()` and `read.delim()`, correspond to such files. Both functions then call `read.table()`. For the data above:

```
weather1 <- read.csv("weather1.csv")
```

The result has the desired structure of a data frame with the variables named in the first line of the file:

```
> colnames(weather1)
 [1] "Time"                "TemperatureF"
 [3] "DewpointF"           "PressureIn"
 [5] "WindDirection"       "WindDirectionDegrees"
 [7] "WindSpeedMPH"        "WindSpeedGustMPH"
 [9] "Humidity"            "HourlyPrecipIn"
[11] "Conditions"          "Clouds"
[13] "dailyrainin"         "SoftwareType"
> dim(weather1)
[1] 92 14
```

All is not quite well, however. The first column, `Time`, does not fit the originally planned variable classes, not being either numeric or categorical. The entries for the column contain date-times in the international standard format: 2005-06-28 00:05:22, for example. Some R software does understand time formats but they are not automatically converted in `read.table()`. Because the text is not numeric, the default action is to treat the column as a factor, but because each time is distinct, the factor has as many levels as there are observations.

```
>   wTime <- weather1$Time
> class(wTime)
[1] "factor"
> length(levels(wTime))
[1] 92
```

R has an S3 class `"POSIXct"` that corresponds to time represented numerically. S3 methods exist to convert from character data to this class. The function `read.table()` allows variables from this class, and from any class that can be coerced from a character vector, through an optional argument `colClasses`, in which the user specifies the desired class for columns of the data frame. If told that the `Time` column should have class `"POSIXct"`, `read.table()` will make the correct conversion.

So with a slight extension to the previous call, we can set the `Time` variable to an appropriate class:

```
> weather1 <- read.csv("weather1.csv",
+    colClasses = c(Time = "POSIXct"))
```

Now the variable has a sensible internal form, with the advantage that it can be treated as a numeric variable in models and other computations.

The `colClasses` argument is one of several helpful optional arguments to `read.table()` and its friends:

`colClasses`: The `colClasses` argument supplies the classes (the names, as character strings) that you want for particular columns in the data. Thus, for example, `"character"` keeps the column as character strings, where the default is to turn text data into factors, but see `as.is` below. This argument can also be used to skip columns, by supplying `"NULL"` as the class.

`skip`: The number of initial lines to omit.

`header`: Should the first row read in be interpreted as the names for the variables?

`as.is`: Should text be treated as character vectors, rather than the traditional default, which turns them into factors? It can be a per-column vector, but if factors are irrelevant, just supply it as `TRUE`.

There are many other arguments; see `?read.table`. Similar choices arise when importing data into other systems, such as spreadsheet or database programs. The discussion continues on page 182.

Once data frame objects are created, they can be used with a variety of existing R packages, principally for statistical models (see Section 6.9, page 218) and for the trellis/lattice style of plotting (see Section 7.6, page 280). These both use the idea of formula objects to express compactly some intended relation among variables. In the formula, the names of the variables appear without any indication that they belong to a particular data frame (and indeed they don't need to). The association with the data frame is established either by including it as an extra argument to the model-fitting or plotting function, or else by attaching the data frame to make its variables known globally in R expressions. The attachment can be persistent, by using the `attach()` function, or for a single evaluation by using the `with()` function, as shown on page 172.

For example, to plot temperature as a function of time in our example, one could use the `xyplot()` function of the `lattice` package to produce Figure 6.1 on page 172:

```
> xyplot(TemperatureF ~ Time, data = weather1)
```

The labels on the horizontal axis in the plot need some help, but let's concentrate here on the relationship between the data and the computations. The `data` argument to `xyplot()` and to similar plotting and model-fitting functions supplies a context to use in evaluating the relevant expressions inside the call to the function. The details are sometimes important, and are explored in the discussions of model software and `lattice` graphics. The essential concept is that the object in the `data` argument provides references for names in the `formula` argument. Formulas are special in that the explicit operator, `` `~` ``, is symbolic (if you evaluate the formula, it essentially returns itself). In the `xyplot()` call, the left and right expressions in the formula are evaluated to get the vertical and horizontal coordinates for the plot. You could verbalize the call to `xyplot()` as:

Plot: `TemperatureF` ∼ (as related to) `Time`

The data frame concept then comes in via the essential notion that the variables in the data frame do define meaningful objects, namely the observations made on those named variables.

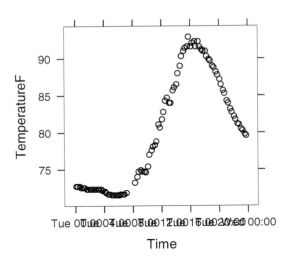

Figure 6.1: Scatter plot of variables from a data frame of weather data.

One can use the same conceptual framework in general computations, either locally by explicitly evaluating an expression using with():

```
> with(weather1, mean(diff(Time)))
Time difference of 15.60678 mins
```

or persistently by attaching the data frame to the session:

```
> attach(weather1)
> mean(diff(Time))
Time difference of 15.60678 mins
```

Using attach() has the advantage that you can type an arbitrary expression involving the variables without wrapping the expression in a call to with(). But the corresponding disadvantage is that the variable names may hide or be hidden by other objects. R will warn you in some cases, but not in all. For this reason, I recommend using a construction such as with() to avoid pitfalls that may seem unlikely, but could be disastrous.

As an example of the dangers, suppose you had earlier been studying a different set of weather data, say weather2, and for convenience "copied" some of the variables to the global environment:

```
> Time <- weather2$Time
```

The global `Time` object hides the one in the attached data frame, and if the `attach()` occurred earlier, no warning is issued. You're supposed to remember the explicit assignment. But if you were, say, to evaluate a model formulated in terms of several variables in the `weather1` data, you could easily forget that just one of those happened to have been hidden. Nothing in the expression itself would reveal that you had just computed an incorrect answer, seriously violating the *Prime Directive*.

Therefore, the general advice is always: if the answer is important, make the computations explicit about what data is used, as the `with()` function did above. The data supplied to `with()` will be searched first, so that other sources of data will not override these. There is still a chance to mistakenly use an object that is *not* in the supplied data (perhaps a mistyped name), because R insists on looking for objects in the chain of parent environments of the `data` object. To be strict about all the available objects in a call to `with()` requires constructing an environment with a suitable parent environment. For example, if `ev` is an environment object:

```
parent.env(ev) <- baseenv()
```

will set the parent environment of `ev` to the environment of the `base` package, essentially the minimum possible. If you're starting with a `"data.frame"` object rather than an environment, the same restriction can be enforced by using the `enclos` argument to `eval()` or `evalq()`. The strict way to evaluate `diff(Time)` as above would be

```
evalq(diff(Time), weather1, baseenv())
```

If the expression requires functions from a package, you need something more generous than `baseenv()`. It's often useful to evaluate an expression using the namespace of a relevant package. For example, to evaluate an expression using the namespace of package `"lattice"`:

```
evalq(xyplot(TemperatureF ~ Time), weather1,
        asNamespace("lattice"))
```

Data frame objects in spreadsheet programs

Because spreadsheets are all about two-way layouts, they have a natural affinity for the data frame concept. In fact, Excel and other spreadsheets are very widely used for computations on data that can be viewed as a data frame. It has been asserted, not always facetiously, that Excel is the world's most widely used statistical software. Spreadsheets include facilities for

summaries and plotting that are applied in many data-intensive activities.
They are less likely to have a wide range of modern data analysis built in,
making R a natural complement for serious applications.

This section will present some techniques for using data frame objects
inside spreadsheet programs. Combined with techniques for exporting data
from R, these will allow the results of analysis to be brought into the spreadsheet. More sophisticated techniques for interfacing to R from a spreadsheet
are possible and desirable, but considerably more challenging to program.
See, for example, RDCOMEvents and related packages at the omegahat Web site;
this approach would in principle allow sufficiently intrepid programmers to
access R functions and objects from the spreadsheet, at least for Windows
applications. The interface in the other direction, for analysis based in R, is
discussed in Chapter 12.

Excel is very widely used, but is not the only spreadsheet program.
Its competitors include several open-source systems, notably OpenOffice.org.
Most of the techniques discussed below are found in OpenOffice.org and other
spreadsheets as well, perhaps with some variation in user interface. In the
discussion below, using "spreadsheet" to describe a system means Excel or
one of its major competitors.

Let's begin by importing into Excel the same csv file shown on page 169.
To import the file, select the menu item for importing external data from a
text file. In the version of Excel I'm using, the import menu selection is:

```
Data > Get External Data > Import Text File...
```

You then interact with an Excel "Wizard" in a sequence of dialogs to identify
the file, choose the delimiter (comma) and specify the format for individual
columns (usually "General", but see below). The text file is then imported
as a worksheet, in Excel terminology. Here's the upper left corner:

◇	A	B	C	D	E
1	Time	TemperatureF	DewpointF	PressureIn	WindDirection
2	6/28/05 0:05	72.7	70.6	30.13	ESE
3	6/28/05 0:15	72.7	70.6	30.12	ESE
4	6/28/05 0:35	72.7	70.3	30.12	East
5	6/28/05 0:45	72.5	70.1	30.12	ESE
6	6/28/05 1:05	72.5	70.1	30.11	ESE
7	6/28/05 1:15	72.5	70.1	30.1	East
8	6/28/05 1:35	72.3	70.2	30.1	SE
9	6/28/05 1:45	72.3	70.5	30.09	ESE
10	6/28/05 2:05	72.3	70.5	30.09	ESE
11	6/28/05 2:15	72.3	70.5	30.08	ESE
12	6/28/05 2:35	72.3	70.5	30.07	SE
13	6/28/05 2:45	72.3	70.5	30.07	ESE
14	6/28/05 3:05	72.3	70.5	30.06	East
15	6/28/05 3:15	72.3	70.5	30.06	SE
16	6/28/05 3:35	72.3	70.5	30.06	ESE

With the spreadsheet, as in the previous section with R, there are a few details to get right, which will also raise some points of general interest.

In an R `"data.frame"` object the variable names are attributes of the data, but in a spreadsheet essentially everything resides in the worksheet itself. Concepts of slots or attributes are uncommon; instead, spreadsheets use individual cells informally to store items other than data values. It's a typical convention to take the first row, or several rows, to include names for the columns and other contextual information. Formally, however, the columns are always `"A"`, `"B"`, `"C"`, etc. and the rows are always `"1"`, `"2"`, `"3"`, etc. The first row happens to contain text items `"Time"`, `"TemperatureF"`, `"DewpointF"`, etc. that we will use to label variables. The remaining rows contain the actual data in the usual sense.

Having a column that contains its name as the first element would pose a problem in R if the data were numeric or any other class than `"character"`. The class of the variable would have to be something able to contain either a string or a number, and computations on the variable would be more complicated. Fortunately, the presence of a name in the first row of every column is less crippling in Excel. For one thing, many computations are defined for a *range* in the worksheet, a rectangular subset of the worksheet defined by its upper-left and lower-right corners cells. So the data-only part of the worksheet starts at the `"$A$2"` cell, in spreadsheet terminology, meaning the first column and the second row.

Names in the first row can cause problems, however, when specifying the format for importing the `csv` file. The Excel wizard allows you to choose a format (`numeric`, `text`, `date`) for each column. Because the variable names are stored in the first row, you cannot choose `numeric` for `TemperatureF` or `date` for `Time`. Instead, Excel allows and suggests choosing format `"General"`, which means that each cell is formatted according to a heuristic interpretation of its contents. Typically, the first cell in each column is text and the rest will be date, number, or text appropriately. If you do this in the present example, however, you will see some strange cells labeled `"Name?"` in the column for the `Clouds` variable. That's because several cells for this column are recorded in the file as `"-RA"` and the Excel heuristic throws up its hands for this entry: it starts out looking like a number but then turns into text. The fix is to specify this column manually as `"Text"` to the wizard, so as not to lose information. The result then looks as it did in the file:

L	
s	Clouds	da
	-RA	
	-RA	
	OVC024	
	OVC024	
	OVC100	
	OVC100	
	OVC009	
	OVC009	
	OVC009	

Take a warning from the example, however. Although the spreadsheet may seem to be dealing with objects in a similar sense to R, that is not really the case. The spreadsheet model for computation is quite different, with an emphasis on cells and ranges of cells as basic concepts. Rather than using class definitions to add extra information, spreadsheet programs tend to differentiate cells within the table.

Nevertheless, there is enough commonality between the systems to allow for exporting and importing data. For the example we've been looking at, the only catch is that dates are by default saved in the local format, not the international standard. Inferring the format of dates is an example in the discussion of computing with text in Chapter 8 (see Section 8.6, page 321).

Worksheets can be exported into the same csv format used to import the data. To illustrate exporting data frames, let's look at a truly classic data set, the observations taken by Tycho Brahe and his colleagues on the declination of Mars (the angle the planet makes with the celestial equator). There are over 900 observations taken in the late 16th century. This fascinating dataset, which inspired Johannes Kepler to his studies of the orbit of Mars, was made available in an Excel spreadsheet by Wayne Pafko at the Web site pafko.com/tycho. Suppose we want to export the data, to be used as a data frame in R. The data may be read into Excel, or into other spreadsheet programs that accept Excel files. A menu selection, typically *Save As*, will give you an option to save as a comma-separated-values, or ".csv" file. The upper-left corner of the worksheet looks like this:

	B	C	D	E	F	G
	Tycho Brahe's Mars Observations					
1						
2	Source: Tychonis Brahe Dani Opera Omnia					
3	Input by: Wayne Pafko (March 24, 2000)					
4	[MS] = Mars Symbol (you know...the "male" sign)					
5						
6	Year	Day	Time	Quote	Volume	Page
7	1582	DIE 12 NOUEMBRIS, MANE.		Declinatio [MS] 23 7 B	10	174
8	1582	DIE 30 DECEMBRIS		AE. R. [MS] 107o 56' Declin. 26o 3	10	197
9	1582	DIE 27 DECEMBRIS		declinatio [MS] 26o 22 1/3' et Absentio	10	200
10	1583	DIE 18 JANUARIJ, VESPERI.		Declinatio 27 18 minus bona	10	244
11	1584	DIE 13 NOUEMBRIS, A.M.	H.13 26 P.M.	Declinatio [MS] B. 15 54	10	321
12	1584	DIE 27 NOUEMBRIS	H.2 15'	Declinatio [MS] 14 42	10	322
13	1584	DIE 20 DECEMBRIS AD VESPERAS.		Decl. [MS] (erat prope horizont.) 14 24	10	322
14	1584	DIE 31 DECEMBRIS AD VESPERAS		Declinatio [MS] 14 31 1/2	10	323

mars.xls

Sheet1 Sheet2 Sheet3 Sheet4 Sheet5 Sheet6 Sheet7 Sheet8

In this example, we use OpenOffice.org rather than Excel to open and then save the spreadsheet. The program provides some useful flexibility, including a simple option to save the data with quoted text fields. The first few lines of the resulting ".csv" file (with lines truncated to fit on the printed page) are:

```
"Tycho Brahe's Mars Observations",,,,,,,,,,,,,,,,,,,
,"Source: Tychonis Brahe Dani Opera Omnia",,,,,,,,,,,,,,,,,,
,"Imput by: Wayne Pafko (March 24, 2000)",,,,,,,"Brahe's Declinati
,"[MS] = Mars Symbol (you know...the ""male"" sign)",,,,,,,"(not a
,,,,,,,,,,,,,,,,,,,,
,"Year","Day","Time","Quote","Volume","Page",,"Year","Month","Day"
,1582,"DIE 12 NOUEMBRIS, MANE.",,"Declinatio [MS]   23   7 B",10,174
,1582,"DIE 30 DECEMBRIS",,"Afc. R. [MS]   107o   56'   Declin. 26o   3
,1582,"DIE 27 DECEMBRIS",,"declinatio [MS] 26o   22 1/3' et Afcenfi
```

The row numbers and the column letters shown in the spreadsheet are not part of the actual data and are not saved.

Then the `read.csv()` function can import the data into R, as in the example on page 169. The first five lines of the file are comments, which we'd like to skip. Also, the text data is just text, so we need to suppress the default computations to turn text into factor variables, by supplying the option `as.is = TRUE`. With two optional arguments then, we can read in the data and examine it:

```
> mars <- read.csv("mars.csv", skip = 5, as.is = TRUE)
> dim(mars)
[1] 923  21
> sapply(mars, class)
            X          Year           Day          Time
    "logical"     "integer"   "character"   "character"
        Quote        Volume          Page           X.1
  "character"     "integer"     "integer"     "logical"
       Year.1         Month         Day.1       Day..adj.
    "integer"     "integer"     "integer"     "integer"
         Hour           Min Days.since.1.AD          Date
    "integer"     "numeric"     "numeric"     "numeric"
          X.2      Dec..deg.      Dec..min.     Dec..sec.
    "numeric"     "integer"     "integer"     "integer"
  Declination
    "numeric"
```

The call to `sapply()` computes and displays the class of each of the variables in the data frame, exploiting its implementation as a list.

In this example, we might have chosen to preprocess the text data to remove uninteresting columns, such as two empty fields, X and X.1. However, these do no particular harm. Cleaning up after reading into R is probably easier in this case. In case you're wondering what the 21 variables are doing: The spreadsheet contains a number of intermediate variables used to arrive at numeric estimates of time and declination, starting from the highly irregular journal entries (in variable Quote). The computation is nontrivial and the data would be fascinating to examine as an example of text analysis.

Data frames in a relational database

From the perspective of statistical computing, the most essential feature of relational databases is that their model for data centers on the *table*, a two-way organization of columns (our variables) by rows (our observations), providing a thoroughly natural analog to a data frame. The analogy is very useful. In this section, we concentrate on using the tools of relational database software directly to store and access data from the data frame perspective. In addition, R packages provide inter-system interfaces to such software, so that SQL queries, such as those illustrated here, can be invoked from R. A discussion of the intersystem interface aspect is provided in Section 12.7, page 446. In addition, database systems usually allow exporting of tables as comma-separated-values files, so that the techniques discussed on page 181 can be used.

Relational databases intersect statistical computing most frequently because such databases are sources of data for analysis. The databases have often been organized and collected for purposes such as business transactions, commercial record keeping, or government information, as well as for scientific data collection. In this context, the data analysis is usually only concerned with extracting data (*queries* in database terminology), possibly also applying some summary calculation at the same time. Frequently these databases are very large, relative to the size of data objects used directly for analysis. In fact, relational databases may also be worth considering for data that is constructed or modified during the analysis (*data manipulation* or *transactions* in database terminology), either because of the software's ability to handle large amounts of data or to interface both read-only and modifiable portions of the data.

Access to data in relational databases other than for whole tables uses queries expressed in SQL, the *S*tructured *Q*uery *L*anguage. SQL is common to essentially all relational database systems, and is in fact an international standard language. In spite of its name, the language includes data manipulation and transaction commands as well as queries.

It's fortunate that SQL is supported by essentially all relational database systems, because there are many of these, and when the database was created for purposes other than data analysis, the analyst usually must use whatever particular system was chosen for this database. Of the many such systems, three will usefully stand in for the range of options.

SQLite: An open-source system implemented as a C library and therefore embeddable in other applications, including R.

MySQL®: Also an open-source system, emphasizing competitive capability for large applications.

Oracle®: One of the most successful commercial systems.

SQLite is usually the easiest to interface to R and to install on a particular platform. All three systems are implemented on a wide range of platforms, however. The other two are more likely to be competitive for large applications, and they do explicitly compete for such applications. In the following discussion we use DBMS to stand for one of these three or some other reasonably compatible relational database system.

SQL's design dates back to the 1970s, when computer languages for business applications often tried to look like human languages, specifically English. "Wouldn't it be nice if you could talk to your computer in English?" Perhaps, and modern technology does make that possible for some purposes, where simple tasks and voice recognition get us close to being able to talk to the machine in more-or-less ordinary English. Unfortunately, that was not what SQL and similar languages provided; instead, they introduced computer languages whose grammar was expressed in terms of English-language keywords and a syntax that combined the keywords into a fixed range of "phrases". English input not matching the grammar would be unintelligible to the parser, however natural to the programmer. In addition, the grammars of such languages tended to enumerate the expected requirements rather than starting with higher-level concepts such as objects, classes, and functional computing. The absence of such concepts makes the use of these languages less convenient for our purposes.

Most of these languages have faded from view, but SQL is definitely still with us. Fortunately, its English-like grammar is fairly simple, particularly if we're concerned largely with extracting data from tables.

Queries are performed by the SELECT command in SQL. (We follow a common convention by showing all command names and other reserved words in SQL in upper case, but beware: SQL is usually case-insensitive, so don't rely on upper case and lower case to distinguish names.)

The SELECT command plays the role of expressions using the operator ` [` in R for extracting subsets from two-way tables. The command takes three "arguments", modifiers that correspond to the table object, the column subset, and the row subset. (There are also a number of optional modifiers.) In the terminology of English or other natural languages, the column subset is given by the direct object of the SELECT verb, the table by a FROM phrase, and the row subset by a WHERE clause. Suppose weather is a table in a DBMS database, with columns including Date, TemperatureF, and Conditions. Then a query that selects TemperatureF and Conditions from the rows for a particular date could be written:

```
SELECT TemperatureF, Conditions
FROM weather
WHERE Date = 2005-06-28 ;
```

Columns are specified by a comma-separated list of names or by "*" to select all columns. The table modifier is usually just a name, but it can also construct a table by combining information from several existing tables (the JOIN operation in SQL).

The WHERE clause is a logical expression involving columns of the table. The rows for which the expression is TRUE will be in the selected data. Simple expressions look familiar to users of R or other C-style languages, as above. To combine simple comparisons, use the AND and OR infix operators.

Notice that only expressions involving data in the columns can be used as row subsets: there are no intrinsic row numbers; unlike "data.frame" objects in R or a worksheet in spreadsheet, tables in SQL are not stored in a specific order by rows. This design decision was made partly for practical reasons, so that storage and updating could be done in a flexible, efficient way. But it makes considerable sense intrinsically as well. If we think of data frames in a general sense, the assumption that the "row numbers" of observations are meaningful is often not correct, and can lead to misleading results. One sometimes thinks of rows as representing the time when the observations are made, but those times may be unknown or meaningless (if observations were made at several recording sites, for example). Better in most cases to require time, place and/or other ordering variables to be included explicitly when they make sense.

Queries in SQL can have additional modifiers to add various features: to order the output, either by grouping together rows having the same value(s) on some column(s) or by sorting according to some column(s) (the GROUP and

ORDER modifiers); to filter the selected data on further criteria (the HAVING
modifier); to direct the output to a file (the INTO modifier); and several
others.

From a modern language perspective, it's easy to deplore the ad hoc
nature of SQL, but its wide availability and efficiency in handling large
amounts of data compensate for programming ugliness. In any case, if your
applications are large, you're unlikely to avoid programming with relational
databases forever. Do be careful, however, if you want to create SQL software
that is portable among database systems. Nearly all major systems extend
the standard SQL language definition, in sometimes inconsistent ways. A
good SQL manual for a particular system should clarify the nonstandard
parts, but don't count on it.

External files for data frames

A "data.frame" object in R or a table in a spreadsheet or relational database
implements a version of the data frame concept. In many applications, you
will need to add such data directly or communicate it between systems.
There are several approaches, but two that work for most applications are
either to enter data from a file of text in a standard format or to use an
inter-system interface in one system to access data managed by another.
Inter-system interfaces are described in Chapter 12. For large or otherwise
computationally intensive applications, they have advantages of efficiency
and flexibility over using files. They do require some initial setup and possibly customization, so it's reasonable to start with external files for less
demanding applications. Files are also needed for getting data into a system or for communicating where an inter-system interface is not available.
We consider here some questions that arise when preparing files to contain
data-frame-style data, and techniques for dealing with the questions.

Once again, the basic data frame concept of observations and variables
is the key: files are simplest when organized as lines of text corresponding
to observations in the data frame, with each line containing values for the
variables, organized as fields by some convention. R, spreadsheets, and most
DBMS can import data from a text file laid out as lines of fields, with the
fields separated by a specified character (with the tab and the comma the
usual choices). Many other software systems also either export or import
data in one of these forms. There are differences in detail among all the
systems, so expect to do some cleaning of the data, particularly if you're
exporting it from a more specialized system.

Text files using tabs or commas are often called "tab delimited files" or "comma-separated-values files" respectively. They work roughly the same way, again up to the inevitable details. Here again is the beginning of the weather-station data introduced on page 169 and used to illustrate input of such data into R:

```
Time,TemperatureF,DewpointF,PressureIn,WindDirection,WindDirectionDegrees,\
WindSpeedMPH,WindSpeedGustMPH,Humidity,HourlyPrecipIn,Conditions,Clouds,\
dailyrainin,SoftwareType
2005-06-28 00:05:22,72.7,70.6,30.13,ESE,110,3,6,93,0.00,,-RA,,VWS V12.07
2005-06-28 00:15:46,72.7,70.6,30.12,ESE,105,2,5,93,0.00,,-RA,,VWS V12.07
2005-06-28 00:35:28,72.7,70.3,30.12,East,100,3,6,92,0.00,,OVC024,,VWS V12.07
2005-06-28 00:45:40,72.5,70.1,30.12,ESE,113,6,6,92,0.00,,OVC024,,VWS V12.07
2005-06-28 01:05:04,72.5,70.1,30.11,ESE,110,0,7,92,0.00,,OVC100,,VWS V12.07
2005-06-28 01:15:34,72.5,70.1,30.10,East,91,1,2,92,0.00,,OVC100,,VWS V12.07
2005-06-28 01:35:09,72.3,70.2,30.10,SE,127,0,5,93,0.02,,OVC009,0.02,VWS V12.07
2005-06-28 01:45:33,72.3,70.5,30.09,ESE,110,2,2,94,0.04,,OVC009,0.04,VWS V12.07
2005-06-28 02:05:21,72.3,70.5,30.09,ESE,110,1,6,94,0.04,,OVC009,0.04,VWS V12.07
```

The basic idea seems trivial, just values separated by a chosen character. Triviality here is a good thing, because the concept may then apply to a wide variety of data sources.

Here is a checklist of some questions you may need to consider in practice.

1. The first line: Variable names or not?

2. One line per observation or free-format values?

3. What are the field types (classes)?

4. What about special values in the fields?

For each question, you need to understand the requirements of the system that will import the data. Options in the system may let you adapt to the details of the file at hand, but expect to do some data cleaning in many cases. Data cleaning in this context requires computing with text, the subject of Chapter 8; that chapter presents some additional techniques related to the questions above.

First, variable names: Are they included in the data; does the target system want them; and do you want them? The answer to the first part depends on where the data came from. Many specialized systems that support data export in one of the data-frame-like formats do generate an initial line of column names. The names will be meaningful to the originating system, so they may not be in the natural vocabulary of the data analysis, but it's a good default to leave them alone, to reduce the chance of confusion when you look back at the documentation of the originating system to understand what some variable means. As for the target system, R's `read.table()` function allows them optionally, spreadsheets have no concept of variable names but an initial row of labels is a common convention, and for a relational database, you can't usually provide variable names in the imported table (and in any case you will have to have defined names and types for the variables before doing the import). Once you have decided what you need to do, removing/adding/changing the first line should be easy, but you may want to check that the line does really look like variable names if it should (and doesn't if it shouldn't).

For the free-format question, we usually need to ensure that lines in the file correspond to rows in the data frame. All three systems we've discussed really believe in importing lines of text. A line with p fields has $p-1$ delimiter characters, as shown in our example where $p == 14$. If the exporting system takes "comma separated values" literally, however, it may include a trailing delimiter at the end of each line or, worse, believe the input can be in free format ignoring the one-line/one-row correspondence. Excel does not mind the trailing comma, but the other systems do; and none of them will accept input in free format.

Turning free form input into regular lines is an exercise in computing with text, and can be handled either in R or in a language such as Perl or Python. The comparison is a good example of the tradeoffs in many applications: R is simpler, partly because it absorbs all the data in free form, and then just recasts it in a fixed number of fields per row. Perl has to do some more complicated book-keeping to read free-form lines and write fixed-form when enough fields have been read. But the extra logic means that the Perl code deals more efficiently with data that is large enough to strain memory limits in R. The details are presented as an example of computing with text in Section 8.6, page 325.

The third question, specifying the types or classes, may require attention to ensure that the contents of each variable conform to what the receiving system expects in that variable. All three systems need some specification of the "class" of data expected, although in both R and spreadsheets the variables can contain arbitrary character strings, so specification is only needed when something more specialized is expected. Standard SQL on the other hand is throughly old-fashioned in requiring declarations for the columns when the table is created (prior to actually filling the table with any data). The declarations even require widths (maximum number of characters) for text fields. A declaration for the table in our example might look something like:

```
CREATE TABLE weather (Time DATETIME, TemperatureF FLOAT, DewpointF FLOAT,
    PressureIn FLOAT, WindDirection VARCHAR(10), WindDirectionDegrees FLOAT,
    WindSpeedMPH FLOAT, WindSpeedGustMPH FLOAT, Humidity FLOAT,
    HourlyPrecipIn FLOAT, Conditions VARCHAR(20), Clouds VARCHAR(20),
    dailyrainin FLOAT, SoftwareType VARCHAR(20)
);
```

The weather data has an initial field giving the date and time, and then a variety of fields containing either numeric values or character strings, the strings usually coding information in a more-or-less standardized way. For all the systems, date/time and numeric fields are common occurrences, but each system has its own view of such data, and the data in the input needs to be checked for conformity.

The fourth question, special values, arises because transferring data from one system to another may require attention to conventions in the two systems about how values are represented. There are many potential issues: different conventions according to locale for dates and even for decimal numbers, techniques for quoting strings and escaping characters, and conventions for missing values. Techniques may be available in the receiving system to adjust for some such questions. Otherwise, we are again into text computations. For example, Section 8.6, page 321, has computations to resolve multiple formats for dates.

6.6   Operators: Arithmetic, Comparison, Logic

The S language has the look of other languages in the C/Java family, including a familiar set of operators for arithmetic, comparisons and logical operations. Table 6.3 lists them. Operators in the S language are more integrated, less specialized, and open to a wider role in programming than in many languages. In C, Java, and similar languages, the operators are nearly always built in. They translate into low-level specialized computations, and often assume that arguments are simple data. In languages that support OOP-style classes and methods, methods are not natural for operators, because method invocation is itself an operator (usually ".").

In R, each operator is a function, with the rights and generality of other functions, for the most part. Operator expressions are evaluated as function calls; all that is fundamentally different is that one can write these function calls in the familiar operator form. In fact

```
x+1
```

could legally be written as `+`(x, 1), and would return the same value.

An operator in R is in fact anything the parser is willing to treat as one. Binary and unary operators (sometimes called infix and prefix operators) are any pattern *op* for which the parser will interpret the forms

```
e1 op e2   # or
op e1
```

as equivalent to the function calls

```
`op`(e1, e2) # or
`op`(e1)
```

Here *e1* and *e2* stand for arbitrary expressions. The "`" quotes mean that the string will be treated as a name, to be looked up as the name of a function object.

It is true that many built-in operators are *primitive* functions, which does occasionally make them special for programming (for the way primitives work, see Section 13.4, page 463). However, this only becomes relevant after finding the particular object corresponding to the operator's name, and does not differ fundamentally from the treatment of any primitive function.

Table 6.3 on page 186 shows operators found in the `base` package of R. This section examines the implementations, particularly of the arithmetic and comparison operators. The implementations handle arguments from commonly occurring classes, such as vectors of the various basic R object types, matrices, arrays and time-series. For more information on the other operators, see the function index of the book and/or the online documentation for the operators.

From a programming view, operators in R are part of its extensible functional model. They can be extended to apply to new classes of objects, by defining methods to use when the arguments come from such classes. Operator methods are discussed in Section 10.3, page 389. If a group name is shown in a row of Table 6.3, methods for all the operators in the group may be provided by defining a method for the corresponding group generic (see Section 10.5, page 404).

New operators can be introduced using a lexical convention that `%text%` can appear as a binary operator. Just define a function of two arguments, assign it a name matching this pattern, and users can insert it as an operator. R has added operators `%in%` and `%x%` to the language, for example, to carry out matching and compute Kronecker products respectively. The grammar only recognizes such operators in binary form; you cannot define a new unary operator.

Operator	Group	Comment
`` `+` ``, `` `-` ``, `` `*` ``, `` `/` ``, `` `^` ``, `` `%%` ``, `` `%/%` ``	`Arith()`	Operations for numerical arithmetic, the last two being modulus and truncated division. The arguments are, or are coerced to, `"numeric"` or `"complex"`.
`` `>` ``, `` `<` ``, `` `>=` ``, `` `<=` ``, `` `==` ``, `` `!=` ``	`Compare()`	Comparison operations, defined for arguments that are, or are coerced to, `"numeric"`, `"character"`, or `"complex"`.
`` `&` ``, `` `|` ``, `` `!` ``	`Logic()`	Logical operations "and", "or", and "not".
`` `&&` ``, `` `||` ``		Control operations, only valid with single logical values as arguments.
`` `%%` ``, `` `%in%` ``, `` `%o%` ``, `` `%*%` ``, `` `%x%` ``		Binary operators using the general convention that `` `%text%` `` is an operator name.
`` `$` ``, `` `?` `` `` `@` ``, `` `~` ``, `` `:` ``, `` `::` ``, `` `:::` ``		Other binary operators.

Table 6.3: Binary and unary operators defined in the `base` package of R.

Table 6.3 is not quite complete. The various assignment operators are all treated as binary operators (with limited programming allowed; for example, methods cannot be defined for them). Among the miscellaneous operators, `` `?` `` and `` `~` `` can also be used as unary operators.

Rules for operator expressions with vector arguments

There are general rules for the arithmetic and comparison operators, specifying the objects returned from calls to the corresponding functions, depending on the class and length of the arguments. The rules date back to the early design of the S language. Restricting our attention to the basic vector object types, the following summarizes the current rules in the `base` package implementation.

1. If the arguments are of the same type and length, the operation is unambiguous. The value returned will be of that length and either of the same type or `"logical"`, depending on the operator.

   Arithmetic operators work on `"logical"`, `"numeric"`, and `"complex"` data, but not on `"raw"`,`"character"`, or `"list"`. Comparison operators work on all types, but not if both arguments are lists.

2. Given two arguments of different type, one will be coerced to the type of the other argument before the operation takes place. Arithmetic operations are limited to the four types mentioned in item 1, but for comparisons nearly anything goes, other than a few comparisons with `"complex"` data. Conversions are made to the less simple type, according to the rules discussed in Section 6.3, page 149.

3. If one argument is shorter than the other, it will be implicitly replicated to the length of the other argument before the operation takes place, except that a zero-length operand always produces zero-length results. A warning is given if the longer length is not an exact multiple of the shorter.

For more details on conversions see Section 6.3, page 149.

As mentioned, most of these rules date back to early in the evolution of the S language, and are unlikely to change. With hindsight though, I'm inclined to think the original design was too eager to produce an answer, for any arguments. Some of the rules, such as those for replicating shorter objects, were heuristics designed to work silently when operating on a matrix and one of its rows or columns.

For important computations, stricter rules that only allow unambiguous mixing of types and lengths would be more trustworthy. The function `withStrictOps()` in the SoDA package allows you to evaluate any expression applying such rules. A call to `withStrictOps()` either returns the value of the expression or generates an error with an explanation of the ambiguities. Mixtures of types are allowed only for numeric types, including complex (no logical/numeric conversion, for example). Unequal lengths are allowed only if one operand is a "scalar", of length 1. I would recommend running examples whose validity is important with these rules in place; in other words, when the *Prime Directive* weighs heavily on you, it pays to check for ambiguous code.

Arithmetic and comparison operators deal with vector structures as well as simple vectors, both in general and specifically for matrices, multi-way arrays, and time-series. Classes can be formally defined to be vector structures (see Section 6.3, page 154), in which case they inherit methods from class `"structure"`. As noted on page 156, the current base package rules do not treat vectors with arbitrary attributes as a vector structure. You should use a formal class definition that extends `"structure"` rather than relying on the base package behavior to obtain trustworthy results for vector structures.

Arithmetic operators

Arithmetic operations with numeric arguments go back to the early history of computing with "floating-point numbers". Down to the 1970s, software for these computations was complicated by a variety of representations and word lengths. An essential step forward was the adoption of the IEEE floating point standard, which mandated aspects of both the representation and the way computations should behave. The standard included a model for the numbers, with parameters expressing the range of numbers and the accuracy. The model also included both Inf, to stand for numbers too large to be represented, and NaN for the result of a computation that was *N*ot *a N*umber; for example,

```
> 0/0
[1] NaN
```

The S language adopted the model, and R includes it. The object .Machine has components for the parameters in the model; see its documentation. We look at some details of numeric computations in Section 6.7, page 191.

For most numeric computations in R, numeric means double-precision, type "double". This is certainly true for arithmetic. The operators will take arguments of type logical or integer as well as numeric, but the results will nearly always be of type "double", aside from a few computations that preserve integers. Logicals are interpreted numerically by the C convention that TRUE is 1 and FALSE is 0. Complex arithmetic accepts "numeric" arguments with the usual convention that these represent the real part of the complex values. Raw and character data are not allowed for arithmetic.

Arithmetic operators allow operands of different lengths, according to the rules described on page 186, calling for replicating the shorter operand. R warns if the two lengths are not exact multiples. The following examples illustrate the rules.

```
> 1:5 + 1
[1] 2 3 4 5 6
> 1:6 + c(-1, 1)
[1] 0 3 2 5 4 7
> 1:5 + c(-1, 1)
[1] 0 3 2 5 4
Warning message:
```

```
longer object length
     is not a multiple of shorter object length in: 1:5 + c(-1, 1)
```

The second and third examples would be errors if the strict rules implemented by the function withStrictOps() were applied.

Comparison and logical operators.

The comparison operators (`>`, `>=`, `<`, `<=`, `==`, and `!=`), when given
two vectors as arguments return a logical vector with elements TRUE, FALSE, or
NA reflecting the result of the element-by-element comparisons. Arguments
will be implicitly replicated to equal length and coerced to a common type,
according to the ordering of types shown in Section 6.3, page 149. So,
for example, comparing numeric and character data implicitly converts the
numbers to character strings first.

Comparison expressions in R look much like those in languages such as
C, Java, or even Perl. But they are designed for different purposes, and need
to be understood on their own. The purpose of a comparison in R is to
produce a vector of logical values, which can then be used in many other
computations. One typical use is to select data. The logical vector can be
used to select those elements of any other object for which the comparison
is TRUE.

```
y[ y > 0 ]; trafficData[ day != "Sunday", ]
```

Comparisons are often combined using the logical operators:

```
weekend <- trafficData[ day == "Sunday" | day == "Saturday", ]
```

Combinations of comparisons and logical operators work in R similarly to
conditions in database selection. If you're familiar with database software
queries, using SQL for example, then consider the comparison and logical
operators as a way to obtain similar data selection in R.

One consequence of the general operator rules on page 186 needs to be
emphasized: The comparison operators are not guaranteed to produce a single logical value, and if they do, that value can be NA. For really trustworthy
programming, try to follow a rule such as this:

> Don't use comparison operators naked for control, as in if()
> expressions, unless you are really sure the result will be a single
> TRUE or FALSE. Clothe them with an expression guaranteed to
> produce such a value, such as a call to identical().

Violations of this rule abound, even in core R software. You may get away
with it for a long time, but often that is the bad news. When the expression
finally causes an error, the original programming experience may be long
gone, possibly along with the programmer responsible.

The most commonly occurring unsafe practice is to use the "==" operator
for control:

```
if(parameters$method == "linear") # Don't do this!
    value <- lm(data)
```

What can go wrong? Presumably `parameters` is meant to be an object with
components corresponding to various names, usually an R list with names.
If one of the names matches `"method"` and the corresponding component is a
single character string or something similar, the computation will proceed.
Someday, though, the assumption may fail. Perhaps the computations that
produced `parameters` changed, and now do not set the `"method"` component.
Then the unfortunate user will see:

```
Error in if (parameters$method == "linear") ... :
        argument is of length zero
```

The `if` expression may have looked reasonable, particularly to someone used
to C-style languages, but it did not actually say what it meant. What we
meant to say was:

```
if(the object  parameters$method  is identical to
    the object "linear" )
```

A function defined to implement this definition would return `TRUE` if the
condition held and `FALSE` in all other circumstances. Not surprisingly, there
is such a function, `identical()`. The condition should have been written:

```
if(identical(parameters$method, "linear"))
    value <- lm(data)
```

For more on techniques to produce such single values, see Section 6.3, page
152.

The two operators `&&` and `||`, however, are specifically designed for
control computations. They differ from `&` and `|` in that they are expected
to produce a single logical value and they will not evaluate the second argument if that argument cannot change the result. For example, in the
expression

```
if(is(x, "vector") && length(x)>0) x[] <- NA
```

the expression `length(x)>0` will not be evaluated if `is(x, "vector")` evaluates to `FALSE`. Here too, however, the evaluation rules of R can be dangerously generous. Arguments to these operators can be of length different from 1. Only the first element will be used, but no warning is issued, and if one argument is of length zero, the result is silently `NA`. Therefore, the arguments to `` `&&` `` and `` `||` `` themselves need to follow the guidelines for computing single logical values.

6.7 Computations on Numeric Data

Numeric data in R can in principle be either `"double"` or `"integer"`, that is, either floating-point or fixed-point in older terminology. In practice, numeric computations nearly always produce `"double"` results, and that's what we mean by the term `"numeric"` in this discussion. Serious modern numeric computation assumes the floating-point standard usually known as "IEEE 574" and R now requires this. The standard enforces a number of important rules about how numeric data is represented and how computations on it behave. Most of those don't need to concern us explicitly, but a brief review of floating-point computation will be useful here.

Standard floating-point numbers have the form $\pm b2^k$ where b, known as the *significand*,[3] is a binary fraction represented by a field of m bits:

$$b_1 2^{-1} + b_2 2^{-2} + \cdots + b_m 2^{-m}$$

and k, the *exponent* is an integer field of fixed width. Given the size of the floating-point representation itself (say, 32 or 64 bits) the standard specifies the width of the fraction and exponent fields. Floating-point numbers are usually *normalized* by choosing the exponent so that the leading bit, b_1, is 1, and does not need to be stored explicitly. The fraction is then stored as a bit field $b_2 \cdots b_m$. The $\pm$ part is conceptually a single sign bit. The exponent represents both positive and negative powers, but not by an internal sign bit; rather, an unsigned integer is interpreted as if a specific number was subtracted from it. All that matters in practice is that the exponent behaves as if it has a finite range $-k_u < k <= k_u$. In the standard, only a few choices are allowed, mainly single and double precision. However, the model is general, and future revisions may add further types.

In addition to the general patterns for floating-point numbers, the standard defines some special patterns that are important for its operations.

---

[3]In my youth, this was called the *mantissa*, but the standard deprecates this term because it has a conflicting usage for logarithms.

Zero, first off, because that cannot be represented as a normalized number; in fact, the standard includes both ±0. Then a pattern to represent "infinity"; that is, numbers too large in absolute value for the representation. This we will write as ±Inf. Finally, a pattern called NaN (*Not a Number*) indicates a result that is undefined as a number. This is related to the long-standing value NA in the S language standing for a *Not Available*, or missing value. The latter is more general and should be used in most R programming; see page 194.

The standard also set down requirements for arithmetic operations and for rounding. If you want to understand more about floating-point computations and the standard, there is a huge literature. One of the best items is an unpublished technical report by one of numerical analysis' great figures and eccentrics, W. Kahan [18].

Details of numerical representation are usually far from your thoughts, and so they should be. A few important consequences of floating-point representation are worth noting, however. The finite set of floating-point numbers represented by the standard, for a given word size, are essentially a model for the mathematical notion of *real* numbers. The standard models all real numbers, even though only a finite subset of real numbers correspond exactly to a particular floating-point representation. The general rule of thumb is that integer values can be represented exactly, unless they are very large. Numbers expressed with *decimal fractions* can be represented exactly only if they happen to be equal to an integer multiplied by a negative power of 2. Otherwise, the stored value is an approximation. The approximation is usually hidden from the R user, because numbers are approximated from decimal input (either parsed or read from a file), and printed results usually round the numbers to look as if they were decimal fractions.

The approximate nature of the floating-point representation sometimes shows up when computations are done to produce numbers that we think should be exactly zero. For example, suppose we want the numbers (-.3, -.15, 0., .15, .3). The function seq() computes this, taking the first element, the last, and the step size as arguments. But not quite:

```
> seq(-.45, .45, .15)
[1] -4.500000e-01 -3.000000e-01 -1.500000e-01 -5.551115e-17
[5]  1.500000e-01  3.000000e-01  4.500000e-01
```

Did something go wrong? (Every so often, someone reports a similar example as a bug to the R mailing lists.)

No, the computation did what it was asked, adding a number to the initial number to produce the intermediate results. Neither number is represented exactly as a binary fraction of a power of 2, as we can see using the `binaryRep()` function developed as an example in Section 6.4, page 161:

```
> binaryRep(c(-.45, .15))
Object of class "binaryRep"
1: -.1110011001100110011001100110011001100110011001101 * 2^-1
    (-0.45)
2:  .100110011001100110011001100110011001100110011001100110011 * 2^-2
    (0.15)
```

In fact, we can see what probably happens in the computation:

```
> binaryRep(c(3 * .15))
Object of class "binaryRep"
1:  .1110011001100110011001100110011001100110011001100 * 2^-1
    (0.45)
```

Notice that the last bit is different from the representation of -.45; the difference is in fact, 2^{-54}, or `5.551115e-17`.

There is nothing numerically incorrect in the computed result, but if you prefer to get an exact zero in such sequences, remember that integer values are likely to be exact. Rescaling an integer sequence would give you the expected result:

```
> seq(-3, 3, 1) * .15
[1] -0.45 -0.30 -0.15  0.00  0.15  0.30  0.45
```

Although `seq()` returns a result of type `"integer"`, that is not the essential point here. Integer values will be represented exactly as `"double"` numbers so long as the absolute value of the integer is less than 2^m, the length of the fractional part of the representation (2^{54} for 32-bit machines).

Numbers that are too large positively or negatively cannot be represented even closely; the floating-point standard models these numbers as `Inf` and `-Inf`. Another range of numbers cannot be represented because they are too close to zero (their exponents are too negative for the model). These numbers are modeled by 0. In terms of arithmetic operations, these two ranges of numbers correspond to *overflow* and *underflow* in older terminology; in R, overflow and underflow just produce the corresponding values in the floating-point standard, with no error or warning.

The standard specifies that arithmetic operations can also produce `NaN`. If either operand is a `NaN`, the result will be also. In addition certain computations, such as 0/0, will generate a `NaN`.

The NaN pattern will immediately remind R users of the NA pattern, which also represents an undefined value, although not just for floating-point numbers. The two patterns arose separately, but R treats NaN in numeric data as implying NA. Therefore, for most purposes you should use the function is.na() to test for undefined values, whether they arose through numerical computations or from other sources. There is also a function is.nan() that in principle detects only values generated from floating-point operations. Much more important in thinking about undefined values than the distinction between NA and NaN is to be careful to treat either as a pattern, not as a value. Always use the functions to detect undefined values rather than testing with identical(), and certainly never use the `==` operator:

```
identical(x, NaN) # Never do this! Use is.nan() instead.
x == NA; x == NaN # Always wrong!
```

The first expression is lethally dangerous. The floating-point standard defines NaN in such a way that there are many distinct NaN patterns. There is no guarantee which pattern an internal computation will produce. Therefore identical(x, NaN) may sometimes be TRUE and at other times FALSE on numerical results for which is.nan(x) is TRUE. The second and third expressions always evaluate to NA and NaN, and so will always be wrong if you meant to test for the corresponding condition.

Having warned against comparisons using the objects NA and NaN, we now have to point out that they are quite sensible in some other computations. For example, if input data used a special value, say 9999 to indicate missing observations, we could convert those values to the standard NA pattern by assigning with the NA object.

```
x[ x == 9999] <- NA
```

Just a moment, however. If you have been reading about the generally inexact numeric representation of decimal numbers, you would be wise to ask whether testing for exact equality is dangerous here. The answer depends on how x arose; see below on page 196 for some discussion.

Similar computations can set elements to the floating-point NaN pattern:

```
x[ x < 0 ] <- NaN
```

When does it make sense to use NaN versus NA? Because the NaN pattern is part of the floating-point standard, it's natural to insert it as part of a numeric calculation to indicate that the numeric value of the result is undefined for some range of inputs. Suppose you wanted a function inv to be 1/x, but only for positive values, with the transform being undefined for negative values.

```
invPos <- function(x) {
    ifelse( x<0, NaN, 1/x)
}
```

Regular missing values (NA) will now be distinguished from numerically undefined elements.

```
> xx <- c(NA, -1, 0, 1, 2)
> invPos(xx)
[1]   NA NaN Inf 1.0 0.5
```

Similar built-in mathematical functions follow the same pattern (for example, log() and sqrt()), but with a warning message when NaN is generated. The use of ifelse() here makes for simple and clear programming, but keep in mind that the function evaluates all its arguments, and then selects according to the first. That's fine here, but you might need to avoid computing the values that will not be used in the result, either because an error might occur or because the computations would be too slow. If so, we would be thrown back on a computation such as:

```
invPos <- function(x) {
    value <- rep(NaN, length(x))
    OK <- x >= 0
    value[OK] <- 1/x[OK]
}
```

As an exercise: This version fails if x has NAs; how would you fix it?

Turning back to general treatment of NA, you may encounter a replacement version of is.na():

```
is.na(x) <- (x == 9999)
```

The right side of the assignment is interpreted as an index into x and internal code sets the specified elements to be undefined. The catch with using the replacement function is interpretation: What is it supposed to do with elements that are already missing? Consider:

```
> x <- c(NA, 0, 1)
> is.na(x) <- c(FALSE, FALSE, TRUE)
```

What should the value of is.na(x) be now? You could expect it to be the pattern on the right of the assignment, but in fact the replacement does not alter existing NA elements. (What value would it use for those elements?)

```
> is.na(x)
[1]  TRUE FALSE  TRUE
```

Given the ambiguity, I suggest using the direct assignment.

Numerical comparisons

Numerical comparisons are generally applied in R for one of two purposes: *filtering* or *testing*. In filtering, a computation is to be applied to a portion of the current data, with a numerical comparison determining that portion:

```
x[ x<0 ] <- NaN
```

In testing, a single logical value will control some step in a calculation, maybe the convergence of an iterative computation:

```
if(abs(xNew - xOld) < xeps)
    break
```

Discussions of numerical accuracy often mix up these situations, but the whole-object computational picture in R makes them quite distinct. Considerations of numerical accuracy and in particular of the effect of numerical error in floating-point representation (so-called "rounding error") have some relevance to both. But it's testing that provides the real challenge, and rounding error is often secondary to other limitations on accuracy.

Having said that, we still need a basic understanding of how numerical comparisons behave in order to produce trustworthy software using them. The six comparison operators will produce logical vectors. The rules for dealing with arguments of different length are those for operators generally (see page 189). As with other operators, the wise design sticks to arguments that are either the same length and structure, or else with one argument a single numeric value.

The elements of the object returned from the comparison will be TRUE, FALSE, or NA, with NA the result if either of the corresponding elements in the arguments is either NA or NaN.

The two equality operators, `==` and `!=`, are dangerous in general situations, because subtle differences in how the two arguments were computed can produce different floating-point values, resulting in FALSE comparisons in cases where the results were effectively equal. Some equality comparisons are safe, if we really understand what's happening; otherwise, we usually need to supply some information about what "approximately equal" means in this particular situation.

Floating-point representation of integer numbers is exact as long as the integers are within the range of the fractional part as an integer (for 64-bit double precision, around 10^{17}). Therefore, provided we know that all the numeric computations for both arguments used only such integer values, equality comparisons are fine.

```
x[ x == 9999 ] <- NA
```

If the data were scanned from decimal text, for example, this test should be valid. A safer approach is to apply the tests to the data as character vectors, before converting to numeric, but this might not be simple if a function such as read.table() was reading a number of variables at once.

As should be obvious, just the appearance of integer values when an object is printed is no guarantee that equality comparisons are safe. The following vector looks like integers, but examining the remainder modulo 1 shows the contrary:

```
> x
 [1] 10  9  8  7  6  5  4  3  2  1  0
> x%%1
 [1] 0.000000e+00 1.776357e-15 0.000000e+00 8.881784e-16
 [5] 0.000000e+00 0.000000e+00 8.881784e-16 0.000000e+00
 [9] 4.440892e-16 8.881784e-16 0.000000e+00
```

No surprise, after we learn that x<-seq(1.5,0,-.15)/.15, given the example on page 192.

Using greater-than or less-than comparisons rather than equality comparisons does not in itself get around problems of inexact computation, but just shifts the problem to considering what happens to values just on one side of the boundary. Consider:

```
x[ x<0 ] <- NaN
```

This converts all negative numbers to numerically undefined; the problem is then whether we are willing to lose elements that came out slightly negative and to retain elements that came out slightly positive. The answer has to depend on the context. Typically, the filtering comparison here is done so we can go on to another step of computation that would be inappropriate or would fail for negative values. If there is reason to retain values that might be incorrectly negative as a result of numerical computations, the only safe way out is to know enough about the computations to adjust small values. It's not just comparison operations that raise this problem, but any computation that does something discontinuous at a boundary. For example,

```
xx <- log(x)
```

has the same effect of inserting NaN in place of negative values. Once again, if we need to retain elements computed to be slightly negative through inexact computation, some adjustment needs to be made and that in turn requires considerable understanding of the context.

When we turn from filtering during the computation to testing for control purposes, we have the additional requirement of choosing a single summary value from the relevant object. R deals with objects, but tests and conditional computations can only use single TRUE or FALSE values. Typical tests discussed in the numerical analysis literature involve comparisons allowing for a moderate difference in the low-order bits of the floating-point representation, plus some allowance for the special case of the value 0. We saw on page 192 that seemingly identical computations can produce small differences in the floating-point representation of the result. For a non-zero correct result, then, the recommendation is to allow for relative error corresponding to a few *ulp*s (*u*nits in the *l*ast *p*lace). A correct value 0 is a special case: If the correct test value is 0 then the computed value has to be tested for sufficiently small absolute value, because relative error is meaningless. There are some good discussions of how to do such comparisons very precisely (reference [18]; also search the Web, for example for "IEEE 754").

The first problem in applying tests in this spirit in practice is to deal with objects, not single values. The function all.equal.numeric() in basic R implements a philosophy designed to treat objects as equal if they differ only in ways that could plausibly reflect inexact floating-point calculations. Given arguments current and target and a suitable small number, tolerance, it tests roughly:

```
mean(abs(current - target))/mean(abs(target)) < tolerance
```

as long as mean(abs(target)) is non-zero, and

```
mean(abs(current - target)) < tolerance
```

otherwise. Tests of this sort are fine as far as they go, but unfortunately only apply to a small minority of practical situations, where there is a clear target value for comparison and usually where deviations from the target can be expected to be small.

We created the all.equal methods originally to test software for statistical models, when it was installed in a new computing environment or after changes to the software itself. The tests compared current results to those obtained earlier, not "exact" but asserted to be correct implementations, run in an environment where the needed numerical libraries also worked correctly for these computations. (This is "regression" testing in the computational, not statistical, sense.) Numerical deviations were only one aspect; `all.equal()` methods also check various structural aspects of the `current` and `target` objects.

The general problem, unfortunately, is much harder and no automatic solution will apply to all cases. Testing numerical results is an important and difficult part of using statistical software. Providing numerical tests is an equally important and difficult part of creating software. Most of the difficulty is intrinsic: It is often harder to test whether a substantial numerical computation has succeeded (or even to define clearly what "succeeded" means) than it is to carry out the computation itself. Computing with R does have the advantage that we can work with whole objects representing the results of the computation, providing more flexibility than computations with single numbers or simple arrays. Also, the interactive context of most R computation provides rich possibilities for choosing from a variety of tests, visualizations, and summaries. It's never wise to base an important conclusion on a single test.

With all these disclaimers firmly in mind, we can still consider a simple style of test, analogous to the `all.equal.numeric()` logic above, to be adapted to specific testing situations. Two relevant considerations correspond to *convergence* and *uncertainty*. In convergence tests, one would like to test how near the iterative computation is to the target, but naturally the target is generally unknown. With luck, some auxiliary criterion should apply at the target. In linear least-squares regression, for example, at the target model the residuals are theoretically orthogonal to the predictor; therefore, comparing the inner products of residuals with columns of X to the value 0 would be a way of testing an iterative computation. Care is still needed in choosing tolerance values for the comparison.

New methods for complicated problems often have no such outside criterion. The natural inclination is then to test the iteration itself. The `target` and `current` objects are taken to be the parameters of the model or some other relevant quantity, from the current and previous iteration. Such a test may work, and in any case may be all you can think of, but it is rarely guaranteed and can be dangerously over-optimistic. Use it by all means, if you must, but try to experiment thoroughly and if possible replace it or calibrate by whatever theory you can manage to produce. Some examples of related test criteria are discussed when we consider software for statistical models in Section 6.9, page 218.

Issues of uncertainty, on the other hand, correspond to questions about the data being used. Limitations in our ability to measure the data used in a model or other statistical computation, or even limitations in our ability to define what is being measured, must naturally translate into uncertainty in any parameters or other summaries computed. Some tests or measures based on these uncertainties are essential as part of reporting a model if we are not to run the risk of implying more accurate knowledge than we really possess. If nothing else, it's a good idea to do some simulations using as plausible assumptions as can be made about the uncertainties in the data, to see how reproducible are the results of the computation.

6.8   Matrices and Matrix Computations

Matrix computations are the implementation for much fundamental statistical analysis, including model-fitting and many other tasks. They also have a central role in a wide variety of scientific and engineering computations and are the basis for several software systems, notably MATLAB®. Matrices play an important role in R as well, but less as the basic objects than as an example of some general approaches to data and computation.

In spite of the conceptual difference, many matrix computations will look similar in R to those in other systems. A matrix object can be indexed by rows and columns. R includes most of the widely used numerical methods for matrices, either in the base package or in add-on packages, notably `Matrix`. The usual search lists and tools will likely find some functions in R to do most common matrix computations.

This single section has no hope of covering matrix computations in detail, but it examines the concept of a matrix in R, its relation to some other concepts, such as general vector structures, and a variety of techniques often found useful in programming with matrix objects. We discuss different techniques for indexing matrices and use these in an extended example of constructing matrices with a particular pattern of elements (page 206). We discuss the `apply()` family of functions (page 212), consider some basic numerical techniques (page 214), and finally look briefly at numerical linear algebra (page 216).

Moving from the inside out, first, the `"matrix"` class extends the `"array"` class: a matrix is a multi-way array in which "multi" happens to be "two". The defining properties of an R matrix, its dimension and optional `dimnames` are simply specializations of the same properties for a general multi-way array. Indexing of elements is also the same operator, specialized to two index expressions.

An array, in turn, is a special case of the classic S language concept of a *vector structure* discussed in Section 6.3, page 154; that is, a vector that has additional properties to augment what one can do, without losing the

built-in vector computations, such as ordinary indexing by a single variable
and the many basic functions defined for vectors.

As a result of what a matrix is in R, there are some important things
it is not; most importantly, it is not itself a basic concept in the system,
contrasting with MATLAB, for example. Neither is the multi-way array a
basic concept, contrasting with the APL language, from which many of the
array ideas in the S language were derived. Arrays never stop being vectors
as well. Many useful computational techniques come from combining vector
and matrix ways of thinking within a single computational task.

To make a vector, x, into a matrix, information is added that defines
`dim(x)`, its dimensions. For a matrix, `dim(x)` is the vector of the number of
rows and columns. The elements of x are then interpreted as a matrix stored
by columns. For general k-way arrays, the same information is added, but
`dim(x)` has length k. As a result, any vector can be made a matrix, not just
a numeric vector. The data part of a matrix can be a vector of any of the
basic types such as `"logical"`, `"character"`, or even `"list"`.

The programming model for matrices, and for arrays in general, includes
the mapping between matrix indexing and vector indexing. That mapping
is defined by saying that the first index of the matrix or array varies most
rapidly. Matrices are stored as columns. Three-way arrays are stored as
matrices with the third index constant, and so on. Fortran prescribed the
same storage mechanism for multi-way arrays (not a coincidence, given the
history of S).

Because matrices in R are an extension of basic vectors rather than a
built-in structure at the lowest level, we might expect more specialized matrix languages, such as MATLAB, to perform more efficiently on large matrix
objects. This is fairly often the case, particularly for computations that in
R are not directly defined in C.

Extracting and Replacing Subsets of a Matrix

To see how matrix and vector ideas work together, let's consider expressions
to manipulate pieces of a matrix. Subsets of a matrix can be extracted or
replaced by calls to the `` `[` `` operator with four different forms for the index
arguments:

1. two index arguments, indexing respectively the rows and columns;

2. a single index argument that is itself a two-column matrix, each row
   specifying the row and column of a single element;

3. a single logical expression involving the matrix and/or some other matrix with the same number of rows and columns;

4. a single numeric index, using the fact that matrices are stored by column to compute vector index positions in the matrix.

All four techniques can be useful, and we will look at examples of each. The first case returns a matrix (but see the discussion of `drop=` on page 203), the other three return a vector. All four can be used on the left side of an assignment to replace the corresponding elements of the matrix.

The third and fourth methods for indexing are not specially restricted to matrices. In fact, we're using some basic properties of any vector structure: logical or arithmetic operations produce a parallel object with the same indexing of elements but with different data. And any structure can be subset by a logical vector of the same size as the object. Because a matrix or other structure is also a vector by inheritance, comparisons and other logical expressions involving the object qualify as indexes. This is the fundamental vector structure concept in R at work.

Similarly, the indexing in the fourth form is matrix-dependent only in that we have to know how the elements of the matrix are laid out. Similarly for time-series or any other structure class, once we use knowledge of the layout, any vector indexing mechanism applies.

Indexing rows and columns

The obvious way to index a matrix, `x[i, j]`, selects the rows defined by index `i` and the columns defined by index `j`. Any kind of indexing can be used, just as if one were indexing vectors of length `nrow(x)` and `ncol(x)`, respectively. Either index can be empty, implying the whole range of rows or columns. Either index can be positive or negative integers, or a logical expression. Consider, for example:

```
x[ 1:r, -1 ]
```

The first index extracts the first `r` rows of the matrix, and in those rows the second index selects all the columns except the first. The result will be an `r` by `ncol(x)-1` matrix. As with vectors, the same indexing expressions can be used on the left of an assignment to replace the selected elements.

The result of selecting on rows and columns is itself a matrix, whose dimensions are the number of rows selected and the number of columns selected. However, watch out for selecting a single row or column. In this case there is some question about whether the user wanted a matrix result or a vector containing the single row or column. Both options are provided, and the choice is controlled by a special argument to the `` `[` `` operator, `drop=`. If this is `TRUE`, single rows and columns have their dimension "dropped", returning a vector; otherwise, a matrix is always returned. The default is, and always has been, `drop=TRUE`; probably an unwise decision on our part long ago, but now one of those back-compatibility burdens that are unlikely to be changed. If you have an application where maintaining matrix subsets is important and single rows or columns are possible, remember to include the `drop=FALSE` argument:

```
model <- myFit(x[whichRows,,drop=FALSE], y[whichRows])
```

Indexing with a row-column matrix

Row and column indices can be supplied to `` `[` `` as a single argument, in the form of a two-column matrix. In this form, the indices are not applied separately; instead, each row i of the index matrix defines a single element to be selected, with $[i, 1]$ and $[i, 2]$ being the row and column of the element to select. For an example, suppose we wanted to examine in a matrix, `x`, the elements that corresponded to the column-wise maxima in another matrix, `x0` (maybe `x0` represents some initial data, and `x` the same process at later stages). Here's a function, `columnMax()`, that returns a matrix to do this indexing.

```
columnMax <- function(x0) {
  p <- ncol(x0)
  value <- matrix(nrow = p, ncol = 2)
  for(i in seq(length = p))
    value[i,1] = which.max(x0[,i])
  value[,2] <- seq(length = p)
  value
}
```

The function `which.max()` returns the first index of the maximum value in its argument. The matrix returned by `columnMax()` has these (row) indices in its first column and the sequence `1:p` in its second column. Then `x[columnMax(x0)]` can be used to extract or replace the corresponding elements of `x`.

```
> x0
      [,1] [,2] [,3]
[1,] 11.4 11.0  9.2
[2,] 10.0 10.1 10.4
```

```
[3,]  9.2  8.9  8.7
[4,] 10.7 11.5 11.2
> columnMax(x0)
     [,1] [,2]
[1,]    1    1
[2,]    4    2
[3,]    4    3
> x
     [,1] [,2] [,3]
[1,] 11.1 11.0  9.0
[2,]  9.6 10.1 10.5
[3,]  9.2  8.7  9.0
[4,] 10.7 11.6 11.0
> x[columnMax(x0)]
[1] 11.1 11.6 11.0
```

It takes a little thought to keep straight the distinction between indexing rows and columns separately, versus indexing individual elements via a matrix of row and column pairs. In the example above, suppose we take the row indices, the first column, from columnMax(x0), and index with that:

```
> rowMax <- unique(columnMax(x0)[,1]); x[rowMax,]
     [,1] [,2] [,3]
[1,] 11.1 11.0    9
[2,] 10.7 11.6   11
```

This does something different: it creates a new matrix by selecting those rows that maximize some column of x0, but keeps all the corresponding columns of x.

Notice the use of unique(), so that we don't get multiple copies of the same row. In indexing any object, R allows a positive integer index to appear any number of times, and then repeats the same selection each time. Your application may or may not want to replicate the selection, so remember to eliminate any duplicates if it does not.

Indexing matrices with logical expressions

Logical index expressions typically involve the matrix whose values we want to select or replace, or perhaps some companion matrix of the same dimensions. For example, the value of a comparison operation on a matrix can be used as a single index to subset that matrix. To set all the negative values in x to NA:

```
x[ x < 0 ] <- NA
```

(When dealing with missing values, watch out for the opposite computation, however. To refer to all the missing values in x, use x[is.na(x)], and never use NA in comparisons; see Section 6.7, page 192.)

Indexing in this form applies to any vector or vector structure, and uses nothing special about matrices. However, two auxiliary functions for matrices can be useful in logical indexing, row() and col(). The value of row(x) is a matrix of the same shape as x whose elements are the index of the rows; similarly, col(x) is a matrix containing the index of the columns of x. The function triDiag() on page 207 shows a typical use of these functions.

Indexing matrices as vectors

The fourth indexing technique for matrices is to use knowledge of how a matrix is laid out as a vector; namely, by columns. Logical indices are in a sense doing this as well, because the logical expression ends up being treated as a vector index. However, when the expression involves the matrix itself or other matrices of related shape, the code you write should not require knowledge of the layout.

In contrast, we now consider numeric index expressions explicitly involving the layout. Using these is somewhat deprecated, because the reliance on the physical storage of matrix elements in R tends to produce more obscure and error-prone software. On the other hand, knowledge of the layout is required if you write C software to deal with matrices (Section 11.3, page 424). And computations for some general indexing are more efficient if done directly. Don't worry that the column-wise layout of matrix elements might change. It goes back to the original desire to make objects in the S language compatible with matrix data in Fortran.

If the matrix x has n rows and p columns, elements 1 through n of x are the first column, elements $n + 1$ through $2n$ the second, and so on. When you are programming in R itself, the arrangement works identically regardless of the type of the matrix: "numeric", "logical", "character", or even "list". Be careful in using non-numeric matrix arguments in the C interface, because the declaration for the argument corresponding to the R matrix must match the correct C type for the particular matrix (Section 11.3, page 424).

From examination of data manipulation functions in R, particularly the seq() function and arithmetic operators, you can construct many special sections of a matrix easily. For example, suppose we wanted to select or replace just the elements of x immediately to the right of the diagonal; that is, elements in row-column positions [1,2], [2,3], and so on. (Sections such

as this arise often in numerical linear algebra.) As vector indices, these are
positions $n + 1$, $2n + 2$, ... A function that returns them is:

```
upper1 <- function(x) {
  n <- nrow(x); p <- ncol(x)
  seq(from = n+1, by = n+1, length = min(p-1, n))
}
```

There is one small subtlety in defining functions of this form: computing
the length of the sequence. Often the length depends on the shape of the
matrix, specifically whether there are more columns or rows. Try out your
computation on matrices that are both short-and-wide and long-and-skinny
to be sure.

```
> xLong <- matrix(1:12, nrow = 4)
> xLong
     [,1] [,2] [,3]
[1,]    1    5    9
[2,]    2    6   10
[3,]    3    7   11
[4,]    4    8   12
> xLong[upper1(xLong)]
[1]  5 10
> xWide <- matrix(1:12, nrow = 2)
> xWide
     [,1] [,2] [,3] [,4] [,5] [,6]
[1,]    1    3    5    7    9   11
[2,]    2    4    6    8   10   12
> xWide[upper1(xWide)]
[1] 3 6
```

Example: Matrix indexing and tridiagonal matrices

To illustrate some additional techniques and to clarify the different mechanisms, we will develop a function that can be implemented in different ways
by three of the four matrix indexing techniques. Let's consider what are
called *banded* matrices, and in particular *tri-diagonal matrices*. A number
of numerical techniques with matrices involve special forms in which all the
elements are zero except for those on the diagonal or next to the diagonal.
In general, this means there are at most 3 nonzero elements in each row or
column, leading to the term tri-diagonal matrix. Multiplication by a banded
matrix applies linear combinations to nearby elements of each column or row
of another matrix. This technique aids in *vectorizing* a computation that
might otherwise involve looping over the rows of the matrix. We used this

technique in the example on computing binary representations (Section 6.4, page 163).

Suppose we wanted a function to construct a general tri-diagonal matrix. The natural way to define the matrix is usually by specifying three vectors of numbers, the diagonal, the values above the diagonal, and the values below the diagonal. For example a 5 by 5 matrix of this form is:

```
      [,1] [,2] [,3] [,4] [,5]
[1,]    2    1    0    0    0
[2,]   -1    2    1    0    0
[3,]    0   -1    2    1    0
[4,]    0    0   -1    2    1
[5,]    0    0    0   -1    2
```

In this case the diagonal is `rep(2, 5)`, the upper off-diagonal elements are `rep(1, 4)`, and the lower off-diagonal elements `rep(-1, 4)`. A nice utility would be a function:

```
triDiag(diagonal, upper, lower, nrow, ncol)
```

If it adopted the usual R convention of replicating single numbers to the length needed, and set `ncol = nrow` by default, we could create the matrix shown by the call:

```
triDiag(2, 1, -1, 5)
```

Three different matrix indexing techniques can be used to implement function `triDiag()`. (All three versions are supplied with the SoDA package, so you can experiment with them.)

An implementation using logical expressions is the most straightforward. The expressions `row(x)` and `col(x)` return matrices of the same shape as x containing the corresponding row and column indices.

```
> row(x)
      [,1] [,2] [,3] [,4] [,5]
[1,]    1    1    1    1    1
[2,]    2    2    2    2    2
[3,]    3    3    3    3    3
[4,]    4    4    4    4    4
[5,]    5    5    5    5    5
```

This immediately tells us how to implement the `triDiag()` function: the upper diagonal elements always have a column index one greater than the row index, and conversely the lower diagonal elements have row index one greater than the column index. The diagonal has equal row and column indices, but another useful auxiliary matrix function, `diag()`, lets us construct the matrix with its diagonal elements already in place, and all other elements set to 0. Here, then, is a definition of `triDiag()`:

```
triDiag <- function(diagonal, upper, lower,
                    nrow = length(diagonal), ncol = nrow) {
    value <- diag(diagonal, nrow, ncol)
    R <- row(value)
    C <- col(value)
    value[C == R + 1] <- upper
    value[C == R - 1] <- lower
    value
}
```

The value is created initially with the specified diagonal elements. Then the upper and lower off-diagonal elements are inserted using logical expressions, on the left of an assignment, to replace the correct elements. The function `diag()` and the two replacements use the standard R rule of replicating single values to the necessary length.

A second version of `tridiag()` can be implemented using a single matrix. The implementation is not as simple, but has some efficiency advantages for large problems that are typical of using explicit indices. Once again we use the fact that the upper diagonal has column indices one greater than row indices, and the lower diagonal has column indices one less than row indices. But in this case we will construct explicitly the two-column matrix with the row and column indices for each of these. For the moment, assume the desired matrix is square, say r by r. Then the upper diagonal is the elements `[1, 2]`, `[2, 3]`, ..., `[r-1, r]`. The matrix index corresponding to the upper diagonal has `1:(r-1)` in its first column and `2:r` in its second column. Given these two expressions as arguments, the function `cbind()` computes just the index required. The whole computation could then be done by:

```
value <- diag(diagonal, nrow = nrow, ncol = ncol)
rseq <- 2:r
value[cbind(rseq-1, rseq)] <- upper
value[cbind(rseq, rseq-1)] <- lower
```

What makes this version more efficient than the logical expressions above for large problems? Only that it does not create extra matrices of the same size as x, as the previous implementation did. Instead it only needs to create two matrices of size 2*r. Don't take such considerations too seriously for most applications, but it's the sort of distinction between "quadratic" and "linear" requirements that can be important in extreme situations.

What makes this version more complicated is that the precise set of elements involved depends on whether there are more rows or columns. The expressions shown above for the case of a square matrix will not work for the non-square case. There will be `nrow` upper-diagonal elements, for example, if `ncol>nrow`, but only ncol-1 otherwise. Conversely, there are `min(ncol, nrow-1)` lower diagonal elements.

```
> triDiag(2, 1, -1, 4, 6)
      [,1] [,2] [,3] [,4] [,5] [,6]
[1,]    2    1    0    0    0    0
[2,]   -1    2    1    0    0    0
[3,]    0   -1    2    1    0    0
[4,]    0    0   -1    2    1    0
> triDiag(2, 1, -1, 6, 4)
      [,1] [,2] [,3] [,4]
[1,]    2    1    0    0
[2,]   -1    2    1    0
[3,]    0   -1    2    1
[4,]    0    0   -1    2
[5,]    0    0    0   -1
[6,]    0    0    0    0
```

The general implementation of `triDiag()` using matrix index arguments then has the following form.

```
triDiag2 <- function(diagonal, upper, lower,
                     nrow = length(diagonal), ncol = nrow) {
    value <- diag(diagonal, nrow = nrow, ncol = ncol)
    n <- min(nrow, ncol-1)
    if(n>0) {
        rseq <- 1:n
        value[cbind(rseq, rseq+1)] <- upper
    }
    n <- min(nrow-1, ncol)
    if(n > 0) {
        rseq <- 1:n
        value[cbind(rseq+1, rseq)] <- lower
    }
    value
}
```

We also needed to look out for "degenerate" cases, where the resulting lower- or upper- diagonal was missing altogether (of length 0). Convince yourself that the logical expressions involving `row(x)` and `col(x)` take care of all these variations.

As a third implementation, let's consider using the explicit layout of a matrix to analyze the index values needed to fill in the data elements, and derive a simple computation to generate them. The implementation will repay presenting in detail (perhaps somewhat more than the actual function deserves) because the process of analysis illustrates a useful approach to many problems. We will derive a pattern for the data needed, and find some R utilities that generate this pattern as an object.

Let's look again at the example of a tridiagonal matrix, but this time thinking about the storage layout.

```
      [,1] [,2] [,3] [,4] [,5]
[1,]    2    1    0    0    0
[2,]   -1    2    1    0    0
[3,]    0   -1    2    1    0
[4,]    0    0   -1    2    1
[5,]    0    0    0   -1    2
```

Starting with the first column, what are the index values for the non-zero elements? The first and second row of the first column are the first two elements; then the first three elements in the second column; then the second through fourth in the third column; and so on, shifting down one index for the three non-zero elements in each successive column. With a matrix having n rows, the non-zero elements appear in positions with the following pattern: $1, 2, n+1, n+2, n+3, 2n+2, 2n+3, 2n+4, 3n+3, 3n+4, 3n+5,$ .... These come in triples, except for the first two. Let's make each triple correspond to the row of a matrix. Notice that the first element of each row is a multiple of $n+1$, the second adds 1 to the first and the third adds 2 to the first.

$$\begin{bmatrix} -- & 1 & 2 \\ (n+1) & (n+1)+1 & (n+1)+2 \\ 2(n+1) & 2(n+1)+1 & 2(n+1)+2 \\ & \cdots & \end{bmatrix}$$

If we fill the empty upper-left element with 0, it becomes obvious that the matrix can be computed by adding $(0, 1, 2)$ for the columns and $(0, (n+1), 2(n+1), \ldots$ for the rows.

The pattern of applying a function to a set of row values and a set of column values occurs in many matrix computations. It is handled by the R function `outer()`, which takes row values, column values, and the applied function as its arguments. The name `outer` refers to the outer product of two vectors, but instead of multiplying elements here, we add them; with $n = 5$,

```
> outer((0:4)*6, 0:2, `+`)
     [,1] [,2] [,3]
[1,]    0    1    2
[2,]    6    7    8
[3,]   12   13   14
[4,]   18   19   20
[5,]   24   25   26
```

Convince yourself that the 3 columns are in fact the positions of the upper-diagonal, diagonal, and lower-diagonal non-zero elements of a 5 by 5 matrix, with the exception that the [1,1] element and the [5,3] element of the index matrix are outside the range, and have to be dropped out by our function. The third argument to outer() uses "backtick" quotes to pass in a name for the operator, `+`.

By extracting the suitable elements of the three columns from the index matrix, we can insert the correct upper, diagonal, and lower values. Here then is a third definition of triDiag():

```
triDiag3 <- function(diagonal, upper, lower,
                  nrow = length(diagonal), ncol = nrow) {
    value <- matrix(0, nrow = nrow, ncol = ncol)
    r <-max(nrow, ncol)
    if(r > 1) {
        nu <- min(nrow, ncol-1)
        nl <- min(nrow-1, ncol)
        index <- outer((0:nu)*(nrow+1), 0:2, `+`)
        value[index[1:min(nrow, ncol), 2]] <- diagonal
        if(nu > 0)
            value[index[-1, 1]] <- upper
        if(nl > 0)
            value[index[1:nl, 3]] <- lower
    }
    value
}
```

As with the second version of triDiag(), the number of lower- and upper-diagonal elements depends on whether there are more rows or columns in the matrix. By experimenting with the function (supplied in package SoDA), you can test whether the range of values inserted is indeed correct for square, wide, and skinny matrices.

In this version, we need to be even more careful about special cases. The compensation is that the call to `outer()` does all the actual index calculations at once. This version also generalizes to an arbitrary "bandwidth", that is to upper- or lower-diagonal elements removed by more than just one place from the diagonal.

The `apply()` functions

One frequently wants to assemble the results of calling a function repeatedly for all of the rows or all of the columns of a matrix. In the `columnMax()` example on page 203, we assembled a vector of all the row indices maximizing the corresponding columns, by iterating calls to the function `which.max()` for each column. The function `apply()` will perform this computation, given three arguments: a matrix, a choice of which dimension to "apply" the function to (1 for rows, 2 for columns), and a function to call. A single call to `apply()` will then produce the concatenated result of all the calls.

In the case of `columnMax()`, using `apply()` allows the function to be rewritten:

```
columnMax <- function(x0) {
  p <- ncol(x0)
  cbind(apply(x0, 2, which.max),
        seq(length = p))
}
```

We showed `apply()` used with a matrix, and this indeed is the most common case. The function is defined, however, to take a general multi-way array as its first argument. It also caters to a wide range of possibilities for details such as the shape of the results from individual function calls and the presence or not of `dimnames` labels for the array. See `?apply` for details.

The `apply()` idea is more general than arrays, and corresponds to the common notion of an *iteration operator* found in many functional languages. The array version came first, and stole the general name `"apply"`, but a number of other functions apply a function in iterated calls over elements from one or more lists: `lapply()`, `mapply()`, `rapply()`, and `sapply()`. The first three differ in the way they iterate over the list object(s), while the last attempts to simplify the result of a call to `lapply()`. For an example of `mapply()`, see Section 8.6, page 319.

There are at least two reasons to prefer using `apply()` and friends to an explicit iteration.

1. The computation becomes more compact and clearer.

2. The computation should run faster.

The first of these is often true, and certainly applies to the `columnMax()` example. The second reason, however, is more problematic, and quite unlikely for `apply()` itself, which is coded in R, though carefully. The other functions do have a chance to improve efficiency, because part of their computation has been implemented in C. However, none of the apply mechanisms changes the number of times the supplied function is called, so serious improvements will be limited to iterating simple calculations many times. Otherwise, the n evaluations of the function can be expected to be the dominant fraction of the computation.

So, by all means use the `apply()` functions to clarify the logic of computations. But a major reprogramming simply to improve the computation speed may not be worth the effort.

One detail of `apply()` that sometimes causes confusion is its behavior when we expect to construct a matrix or array result. The function works by concatenating the results of successive calls, remembering each time the length of the result. If the length is identical each time, the result will be a vector (for results of length 1) or a matrix (for vector results of length greater than 1). But the matrix is defined, naturally enough, by taking the length as the first dimension, because that's the way the values will have been concatenated.

Users may be surprised, then, if they apply a function to the rows that always returns a result that looks like the row (i.e., of length `ncol(x)`). They might expect a matrix of the same shape as x, but instead the result will be the transpose of this shape. For example:

```
> xS
     [,1] [,2] [,3]
[1,]    6    9   12
[2,]    2    3    5
[3,]    8   11   10
[4,]    1    4    7
> apply(xS,1,order)
     [,1] [,2] [,3] [,4]
[1,]    1    1    1    1
[2,]    2    2    3    2
[3,]    3    3    2    3
> apply(xS,2,order)
     [,1] [,2] [,3]
[1,]    4    2    2
[2,]    2    4    4
```

```
[3,]    1    1    3
[4,]    3    3    1
```

Just remember to transpose the result when applying over rows.

Numerical computations with matrices

Numerical matrix computations, including those based on mathematical ideas of linear algebra, are fundamental to many statistical modeling and analysis techniques. Matrix computations are also useful ways to formulate computations that might otherwise be programmed as iterations of elementary arithmetic, with the matrix version being significantly more efficient for large problems.

In fact, some numerical computations with matrices may be measurably more efficient in terms of CPU time than other computations that do the same number of arithmetic operations. Examples include matrix multiplication and other similar operations, usually based on *inner products*, $\sum_{i=1}^{n} x_i y_i$, or *scalar products*, $\{y_i + ax_i, i = 1, \cdots, n\}$. Subprograms for these, usually in Fortran, are known as Basic Linear Algebra Subroutines, or BLAS. The computations done by these subprograms are themselves quite simple and capable of being programmed efficiently. But at the same time a number of higher-level operations can be programmed to do much of their computation through calls to the BLAS routines, leading to efficient implementations, even for quite large problems. Matrix multiplication, for example, is just an iteration of inner products. Many decompositions of numerical linear algebra use BLAS for most of their numerical computation. Linear least-squares fitting, in turn, can be written in terms of numerical decompositions and other efficient matrix operations.

R users don't need to be aware of the underlying operations directly. Functions for numerical linear algebra, statistical models and other applications will make use of the operations through interfaces to compiled code.. If you are installing R from source on a special computing platform, some extra steps may be needed to ensure you get efficient versions of the subprograms. See the installation instructions and related Web pages and FAQ lists for your particular platform.

But when does the speed really matter? Throughout this book, our *Mission* is exploring data—asking questions and trying out new ideas—and the other essential criterion is the *Prime Directive*—providing trustworthy software. Blazingly fast numerical computation does not directly relate to the *Prime Directive* and only serves the *Mission* when it widens the range of potential computations. The CPU unit on your computer is likely to be idle most of the time, and so it should be if you are spending that time constructively thinking about what you want to do or contemplating some interesting data analysis. For many applications the difference between a very fast numerical method and a similar, less optimized computation would be barely noticeable. It would be a mistake to choose a computation because of numerical speed, if an alternative choice would give more informative results. Having said all that, there remain applications that test the speed of even current computers. Knowing about fast methods can occasionally let us ask questions for such applications that would otherwise not be practical. If you think you have computing needs at this level, by all means try to apply the matrix techniques to your application (see, for example, Section 6.4, page 161, where some of these techniques are applied to "vectorize" a computation).

Matrix operations and matrix arithmetic

Matrices in R that contain numerical data can be used with all the standard arithmetic and comparison operators. The computations work element-by-element and generally return a matrix of the same dimension as the arguments. Consider computations such as:

```
x + y; x / y; x ^ y; x %% y; x >= y;
```

When either x or y is a matrix, the correct answer is obvious if the other argument is either another matrix of the same dimensions or a numeric vector of length 1 (a "scalar"). So, if x is an n by p matrix, the result of each of the following expressions is also a matrix of this shape:

```
x ^ 2; x + 1/x; abs(x) >= .01
```

As the third example shows, the various mathematical and other functions that operate elementwise return a matrix with unchanged dimensions when called with a matrix argument.

Operators called with matrix arguments other than the two cases above are always less clearly defined. R allows a few without comment, warns on some, and generates an error on others.

1. An error results if the arguments are two matrices of different dimensions.

2. An error also results if one argument is a vector larger than the matrix (i.e., of length greater than np).

3. If one argument is a vector exactly of length np, the computation completes silently.

4. If one argument is a vector of length less than np, the vector is implicitly repeated to be of length np. If the original vector was the length of a column, n, the computation silent; otherwise, a warning is generated.

Getting the answer you expect from the last two cases depends on knowing the representation of a matrix; namely, as a structure with data stored by columns.

Numerical linear algebra

This section outlines some of the central tools for numerical computations on matrices, the functions implementing key concepts in numerical linear algebra, particularly computations related to statistical computing. Most of the functions interface to implementations in Fortran or C of corresponding algorithms. Many of the algorithms are taken directly or with some modification from LAPACK, a collection of Fortran subroutines well tuned for both accuracy and speed.

Applications of linear algebra in statistical computing largely come from considering linear combinations of quantitative variables. The standard functions for linear models and analysis of variance, as supplied in the stats package, and extended in a number of other R packages, provide users with an interface to the models that largely hides the underlying linear algebra. You should use functions at that higher level unless you really need to work with the fundamental linear algebra relations directly. If you're uncertain, read the documentation for related statistical model software and determine whether it could meet your needs. If so, use it, because many details will be handled that could otherwise compromise the quality of the computed results.

If you really do want to deal with the linear algebra directly, press on, but you may still want to use utilities from the statistical models software to convert from variables such as factors into the matrix arguments used for linear algebra; see, for example, ?data.matrix and ?model.frame.

The fundamental role of linear algebra in statistical computing dates back a couple of centuries, and is based on the ability to solve two related computational problems. The first is to find a vector or matrix β that satisfies a set of linear equations. Using the S language operator, `%*%`, for matrix multiplication:

```
a %*% β = b
```

where `a` is a square, p by p, matrix and `b` is either a vector of length p or a matrix with p rows. The second problem is linear least-squares, finding a vector or matrix β that minimizes the column sums of squares

```
y - x %*% β
```

where `x` is an n by p matrix and `y` is either a vector of length n or a matrix with n rows.

R functions to solve both of these problems are available and apply to most applications. They are `solve()` for linear equations and `lm.fit()` for least squares. If your application seems to be expressed naturally as one or the other of the two numerical problems, you can probably go away now and use the appropriate function. If you think you need to dig deeper, read on.

The main computational tools for these problems use some fundamental *matrix decompositions*, that is, the computation of special matrices and vectors which if combined, usually by matrix multiplication, would closely approximate the original matrix. The special forms of the decomposition allow them to express the solution to the two problems straightforwardly in most cases, and also make them useful tools in other problems. To see how these relate to modern numerical linear algebra, a little history is needed.

Prior to large-scale electronic computing, the linear least-squares problem would be solved by reducing it to a special linear equation. Linear equations, in turn, could be solved for at least single-digit values of p. When computers came along, software to solve linear equations was very high priority, particularly motivated by military applications and problems in physics. From about the 1960's, software based on matrix decompositions was developed for linear equations, for direct solutions to least-squares problems, and for other problems, such as solving differential equations. The program libraries implementing these results have continually improved in accuracy, speed, and reliability. In particular, the LAPACK software for linear algebra is the current reference for numerical linear algebra, and forms the base for these computations in R.

What does this history imply for modern statistical computing? First, that computations expressed in terms of the standard operations of linear algebra can be applied with confidence, even for quite large problems. If the matrices involved are not so large that manipulating them in R at all is impractical, then at least some operations of linear algebra will also likely be practical for them. Second, a fairly wide range of other computations can be usefully solved by reducing them to operations in linear algebra, either directly through some imaginative re-casting (see the discussion of vectorizing in Section 6.4, page 158) or by an iterative computation where each iteration is carried out by linear computations (as is the case for some important statistical models). The speed and accuracy provided by LAPACK and similar software means that iterated linear computations may be competitive with other implementations, even though the amount of "arithmetic" seems to be larger.

In addition to the functions for fitting statistical models and the functions `solve()` and `lm.fit()` to solve equations and least-squares problems, the base code for R provides access to several matrix decompositions. These organize themselves naturally on two dimensions; first, on whether the matrix in question is rectangular or square; and, second, between simple decompositions and those that maximize an approximation for each submatrix. The simple decompositions are mainly the `qr()` function for the QR decomposition, for rectangular matrices; and the `chol()` function for the Choleski decomposition, essentially for cross-products and other matrices with similar form. The maximizing decompositions are function `svd()` for the singular-value decomposition of rectangular matrices and `eigen()` for the eigenvalue decomposition of symmetric square matrices. See the online documentation and the references there for some of the details. To really understand the decomposition will require digging into the numerical analysis background. Try the documentation of LAPACK and good books on the subject, such as *Matrix Algorithms* by G. W. Stewart [22].

Beyond the base code for R, there are now a number of packages that extend the range of numerical linear algebra software available. If you have special needs, such as computations for sparse matrices or other decompositions, browse in the documentation for the Matrix package by Douglas Bates and Martin Maechler.

6.9   Fitting Statistical models

R and S-Plus both contain software for fitting and studying the types of statistical model considered in the book *Statistical Models in S* [6]. Many of the techniques described in the book are supplied in the stats package; a number of other packages fill in the gaps and add other similar types of models or additional techniques. From a programming viewpoint the essential property of the software is that it takes a functional, object-based view of models. For software details, see documentation of the stats package. In addition to the original reference, nearly all the general introductions to statistics using R cover the basics; *Modern Applied Statistics with S* by

Venables and Ripley [23] gives a broad, fairly advanced treatment.

There are many other sources of software for statistical models as well (notably for Bayesian model inference and graph-based model formulations). We will not cover any of these here; in many cases, there are either R implementations or R interfaces to software implemented in other languages. Good starting points for a search are the `"Related Projects"` pointer on the R home page and the usual Web search resources, such as `rseek.org`.

In the *Statistical Models in S* approach, the functions to fit various types of model all take two primary arguments, a formula expressing the structure of the model and a source of data; they then return an object representing a fitted model estimated according to the arguments. The type of model (linear least-squares, etc.) depends on the choice of function and possibly also on other arguments.

The various top-level fitting functions can be viewed as generators for corresponding classes of objects. For example, the function `lm()` fits a linear model using least-squares to estimate coefficients corresponding to the formula and data supplied, and returns an object of (S3) class `"lm"`, whose elements define the fit.

Other functions then take the fitted model object as an argument and produce auxiliary information or display the model in graphical or printed form. Functions specifically related to the model software include `residuals()` and `fitted()`, with the interpretation depending on the type of model. The function `update()` will allow modification of the fitted model for changes in the data or model. These are S3 generic functions, with methods corresponding to the class of the fitted model. General functions such as `plot()`, `print()`, and `summary()` also have S3 methods for most classes of models.

The various model-fitting functions share the same main arguments and, for the most part, similar computational structure. Here are the main steps, using `lm()` as an example. The functions generally have arguments `formula` and `data`, and it is from the combination of these that the model-fitting proceeds:

```
lm(formula, data, ...)
```

Caution: `formula` is always the first argument, but `data` is not always the second: check the arguments for the particular function.

The `formula` argument must be an object of the corresponding `"formula"` class, which is generated by a call to the `` `~` `` operator. That operator returns its call as its value, promoted to the `"formula"` class, meaning that the formula is essentially a symbolic constant describing the structure of the model, with one sometimes crucial addition: It has an attribute with a reference to the environment in which the call took place.

The convention is to read the `~` as "is modeled by", so the left-side argument to the operator is the variable or derived quantity being modeled and the right-side argument is the expression for the predictor. Just how the arguments are interpreted depends on the kind of model. Linear models and their extensions use conventions about the meaning of other operators (`+`, `*`, and `:`) to indicate combinations of terms, along with other functions that are interpreted as they usually would be in R. Other models will use other conventions.

The `data` argument is optional and if supplied is usually an object of S3 class `"data.frame"`, containing named variables, each of which corresponds to values on the same n observations. Some of the names will typically appear in the `formula` object, and if so, those variables will be used in fitting the model.

Section 6.5, page 168 discusses `"data.frame"` objects generally. For model-fitting, some classes of variables that are valid in a data frame may not be valid in a particular type of model. Linear models and their extensions in `glm()` and `gam()` essentially only allow numeric predictors, which can be supplied as `"numeric"`, `"matrix"` or `"factor"` objects. The matrix must be numeric with n rows. A factor is included by being coded numerically using *contrasts* to differentiate observations according to the levels of the factor.

The `formula` and `data` arguments are used to prepare the more explicit data required to fit the model. The form depends on the type of model but again linear models provide an example typical of many types of model.

The preparation of a linear model for actual fitting by `lm.fit()` proceeds in two steps. First, a data frame containing the specific variables implied by the `formula` and `data` arguments is computed by the `model.frame()` function. Then the matrix for the linear model fitting itself is computed from the model frame by the `model.matrix()` function.

The computation of the model frame brings the formula and the supplied data frame together, evaluating expressions derived from the formula by an explicit call to `eval()`. The purpose of the call is to form a data frame containing all the variables appearing in the formula; this is the "model frame" object. The model frame also has a `"terms"` object as an attribute; essentially, this is the formula with some extra attributes. When the `data` argument is supplied and all the variables in the model are found in that object, the result is to select the suitable variables, and all is well. That's the trustworthy approach: Assemble all the relevant variables explicitly in a data frame, and supply that data frame to the model-fitting function (`lm()`, `gam()`, etc.).

Otherwise, the computations for the model frame must look elsewhere for some or all of the variables. The critical fact is that the computations look in the environment of the formula object, stored in the object as the environment where the formula was created.

If the formula was typed by the user interactively, then the call came from the global environment, meaning that variables not found in the data frame, or all variables if the `data` argument was missing, will be looked up in the same way they would in ordinary evaluation. But if the formula object was precomputed somewhere else, then its environment is the environment of the function call that created it. That means that arguments to that call and local assignments in that call will define variables for use in the model fitting. Furthermore, variables not found there will be looked up in the parent (that is, enclosing) environment of the call, which may be a package namespace. These rules are standard for R, at least once one knows that an environment attribute has been assigned to the formula. They are similar to the use of closures described in Section 5.4, page 125.

Where clear and trustworthy software is a priority, I would personally avoid such tricks. Ideally, all the variables in the model frame should come from an explicit, verifiable data source, typically a data frame object that is archived for future inspection (or equivalently, some other equally well-defined source of data, either inside or outside R, that is used explicitly to construct the data for the model).

Once the model formula and (in the case of linear-style models) the model matrix have been constructed, the specific fitting mechanism for this class of models takes over, and returns an object from the corresponding S3 class, such as `"lm"`, `"gam"`, `"nls"` and many more. The mechanisms and the interpretation of the fitted model objects that result vary greatly. Generally, however, you can get a good picture of the programming facilities provided by looking for S3 methods associated with the generic functions for models (`residuals()`, `update()`, etc.) and for printed or graphical summaries (`print()`, `summary()`, `plot()`, etc.).

6.10 Programming Random Simulations

This section considers some programming questions related to the use of pseudo-random generators, or less directly, computations involving the *Monte-Carlo method*.

We begin by summarizing the overall organization of simulation functions in R, with an assessment of the level of trust one can have in their "correctness". A second issue for trustworthy simulation results is that others can reproduce them; on page 226 we discuss techniques for this goal. We then show a related example that examines how robust a simulation is to small failures in reproducibility (page 230). Finally, on page 234, we consider the use of generators in low-level code, such as C or C++, which we may want to use for efficiency.

The starting point for simulating in R is a set of "random generator" functions that return a specified number of values intended to behave like a sample from a particular statistical distribution. Because no common generators in practice use an external source thought to be truly random, we are actually talking about *pseudo-random generators*; that is, an ordinary computation that is meant to simulate randomness. We follow common custom in this section by dropping the "pseudo-" when we talk about random generators; you can mentally put it back in, and prepend it to statements about how "likely" some event is, or to other properties of sequences from pseudo-random generators.

Basic concepts and organization

R provides random generators for a variety of statistical distributions as well as some related generators for events, such as sampling from a finite set. Conceptually, all the generators in the stats package work through the package's uniform generator, either at the R level or the C level. This leads to the key techniques for achieving trustworthy software for simulation, as we explore on page 226, but the concept is worth noting now.

Random generators don't follow the functional programming model, as implemented in R or in most other systems, because they depend on a current global state for the generator. How would we formulate a functional approach to simulation? Given that all generators work through the uniform generator, we could imagine an object that is our personal stream of uniform random numbers. If this stream was an argument to all the actual generators and to any other function for simulation, then all the remaining computations can be defined in terms of the stream. In practice, this would require quite a bit of reorganization, but the essential point is that no other external dependence is required.

In practice, such a stream is represented by a seed for the generator. A combination of techniques in the stats package and some extensions in the SoDA package can get us trustworthy software, essentially by incorporating sufficient state information with the computed results.

Functions for probability distributions in R are organized by a naming tradition in the S language in which the letters "r", "p", "q", and "d" are prepended to a fixed name for a distribution to specify functions for random numbers, cumulative probability, quantiles, and density function values for the distribution. So, "unif" is the code for the uniform distribution, resulting in functions runif(), punif(), qunif(), and dunif() (admittedly, none but the first of these is hard to program). Similar functions are defined for the normal ("norm"), Poisson ("pois"), and a number of others, all on the core package stats; to look for the distribution you need, start with:

```
help.search("distribution", package = "stats")
```

Some distributions may not have all four functions. If no random generator is provided but a quantile function does exist, you can get a random sample by what's known as the *probability integral transformation*, which just says to compute the quantiles corresponding to a sample from the standard uniform distribution. The Studentized range ("tukey") distribution has a quantile version but no random generator, so you could define a rough version for it as:

```
rtukey <- function(n, ...)
    qtukey(runif(n), ...)
```

Where some functions are missing, there may be numerical issues to consider, so it's a good idea to check the documentation before putting too much faith in the results.

Additional random generators are supplied in other packages on CRAN and elsewhere; for these non-stats generators, especially, you should check whether they are integrated with the basic uniform generator if trustworthy results are important.

Are pseudo-random generators trustworthy?

From early days, statistical users of generators have asked: "Can the numbers be treated as if they were really random?". The question is difficult and deep, but also not quite the relevant one in practice. We don't need real randomness; instead, we need to use a computed simulation as the approximate value of an integral (in simple cases) or an object defined as a probabilistic limit (for example, a vector of values from the limiting distribution of a Markov chain). All we ask is that the result returned be as good an approximation to the limit value as probability theory suggests. (We'd even settle for "nearly as good", if "nearly" could be quantified.)

Good current generators justify cautious confidence, with no absolute guarantees, for all reasonably straightforward computations. Popular generators, such as the default choice in R, have some theoretical support (although limited), have performed adequately on standard tests, and are heavily used in an increasingly wide range of applications without known calamitous failures. R's default generator is also blazingly fast, which is an important asset as well, because it allows us to contemplate very extensive simulation techniques.

If this sounds like a lukewarm endorsement, no radically better support is likely in the near future, as we can see if we examine the evidence in a little more detail.

As in the `stats` package, we assume that all simulations derive from a *uniform pseudo-random generator*, that is, a function that simulates the uniform distribution on the interval $0 < x < 1$. Function `runif()` and a corresponding routine, `unif_rand`, at the C level are the source of such numbers in R.

If one completely trusted the uniform generator, then that trust would extend to general simulations, as far as approximating the probabilistic limit was concerned. There would still be questions about the logical correctness of the transformation from uniforms to the target simulation, and possibly issues of numerical accuracy as well. But given reassurances about such questions, the statistical properties of the result could be counted on.

The evidence for or against particular generators is usually a combination of mathematical statements about the complete sequence, over the whole period of the generator, and empirical tests of various kinds. A complete sequence is a sequence from the generator with an arbitrary starting point such that, after this sequence, the output of the generator will then repeat.

Generators going back to the early days provide equidistribution on the complete sequence. That is, if one counts all the values in the sequence that fall into bins corresponding to different bit representations of the fractions, the counts in these bins will be equal over the complete sequence. More recent generators add to this equidistribution in higher dimensions; that is, if we take k successive numbers in the sequence to simulate a point in a k-dimensional unit cube, then the counts in these k-dimensional bins will also be equal over the complete sequence.

Such results are theoretically attractive, but a little reflection may convince you that they give at best indirect practical reassurance. The period of most modern generators is very long. The default generator for R, called the "Mersenne-Twister" has a period a little more than 10^{6000}, effectively infinite. (To get a sense of this number, I would estimate that a computer producing one random uniform per nanosecond would generate about 10^{25} numbers, an infinitesimal fraction of the sequence, before the end of the earth, giving the earth a rather generous 10 billion years to go.)

Sequences of a more reasonable length are not directly predictable, nor would you want them to be. Exact equidistribution over shorter subsequences is likely to bias results.

A more fundamental limitation of equidistribution results, however, is that most use of generators is much less regular than repeated k-dimensional slices. Certainly, if one is simulating a more complex process than a simple sample, the sequence of generated numbers to produce one value in the final set of estimates will be equally complex. Even for samples from distributions, many algorithms involve some sort of "rejection" method, where candidate values may be rejected until some criterion is satisfied. Here too, the number of uniform values needed to generate one derived value will be irregular. Some implications are considered in the example on page 230.

Turning to empirical results, certainly a much wider range of tests is possible. At the least, any problem for which we know the limiting distribution can be compared to long runs of a simulation to test or compare the generators used. Such results are certainly useful, and have in the past shown up some undesirable properties. But it is not easy to devise a clear test that is convincingly similar to complex practical problems for which we don't know the answer. One needs to be somewhat wary of the "standardized test syndrome" also, the tendency to teach students or design algorithms so as to score well against standardized tests rather than to learn the subject or do useful computations, respectively.

The results sound discouraging, but experience suggests that modern generators do quite well. Lots of experience plus specific tests have tended to validate the better-regarded generators. Subjective confidence is justified in part by a feeling that serious undiscovered flaws are fairly unlikely to coincide with the pattern of use in a particular problem; based on something of a paraphrase of Albert Einstein to the effect that God is mysterious but not perverse.

To obtain this degree of confidence does require that our results have some relation to the theoretical and empirical evidence. In particular, it's desirable that the sequence of numbers generated actually does correspond to a contiguous sequence from the chosen generator. Therefore, all the generators for derived distributions should be based in a known way on uniform random numbers or on compatible R generators from the standard packages. New generators implemented at the level of C code should also conform, by using the standard R routines, such as `unif_rand`. One wants above all to avoid a glitch that results in repeating a portion of the generated sequence, as could happen if two computations used the same method but inadvertently initialized the sequence at two points to the same starting value. Taking all the values from a single source of uniforms, initialized once as discussed below, guards against that possibility.

In using packages that produce simulated results, try to verify that they do computations compatible with R. There are packages on CRAN, for example, that do their simulation at the C level using the `rand` routine in the C libraries. You will be unable to coordinate these with other simulations in R or to control the procedures used. If you are anxious to have reliable simulations, and particularly to have simulations that can be defended and reproduced, avoid such software.

Reproducible and repeatable simulations

Ensuring that your simulation results can be verified and reproduced requires extra steps, beyond what you would need for a purely functional computation. Reproducible simulations with R require specifying which generators are used (because R supports several techniques) and documenting the initial state of the generator in a reproducible form. Another computation that uses the same generators and initial state will produce the same result, provided that all the numerical computations are done identically. The extra requirement is not just so that the last few bits of the results will agree; it is possible, although not likely, that numerical differences could change the simulation itself. The possibility comes from the fact we noted earlier: Nearly all simulations involve some conditional computation based on a numerical test. If there are small numeric differences, and if we run a simulation long enough, one of those conditional selections may differ, causing one version to accept a possible value and the other to reject the value. Now the two sequences are out of sync, a condition we discuss as *random slippage* on page 230. To avoid this possibility, the numerical representations, the arithmetic operations, and any computational approximations used in the two runs must be identical.

The possibility of numerical differences that produce random slippage emphasizes the need to verify that we have reproduced the simulation, by checking the state of the generator after the second run. To do so, we need to have saved the final state after the initial run. Verification is done by comparing this to the state after supposedly reproducing the result. Both the two simulation results and the two states should match.

But reproducing a simulation exactly only tests that the asserted computations produced the results claimed, that is, the programming and software questions. For simulations, another relevant question is often, "How do the results vary with repeated runs of this computation?". In other words, what is the statistical variability? Repeated runs involve two or more evaluations of the computation, conceptually using a single stream of random numbers, in the sense introduced on page 222.

> A simulation result is *repeatable* if the information provided allows the same simulation to be repeated, with the same result as running the simulation twice in a single computation.

The technique to assure repeatability is to set the state of the generator at the beginning of the second run to that at the end of the first run. Once more, we see that saving the state of the generator at the end of the simulation is essential.

The SoDA package has a class, `"simulationResult"`, and a related function of the same name that wraps all this up for you. It records the result of an arbitary simulation expression, along with the expression itself and the first and last states of the generator. An example is shown on page 230.

The state, or *seed* as it is usually called, is a vector of numbers used by a particular uniform generator. Intuitively, the generator takes the numbers and scrambles them in its own fashion. The result is both a new state and one or more pseudo-random uniform numbers. The generators are defined so that n requests for uniform variates, starting from a given initial state will produce the same final state, regardless of whether one asks for n variates at once or in several steps, provided no other computations with the generator intervene. The information needed in the state will depend on which generator is used.

The user's control over the generator comes from two steps. First, the generating method should be chosen. R actually has options for two generators, for the uniform and normal distributions. For completeness you need to know both, and either can be specified, via a call to the function `RNGkind()`. The call supplies the uniform and normal generator by name, matched against the set of generators provided. For those currently available, see the documentation `?RNGkind`. If you're happy with the default choices, you should nevertheless say so explicitly:

```
RNGkind("default", "default")
```

Otherwise R will continue to use whatever choice might have been made before. Provided we know the version of R, that specifies the generators unambiguously.

Second, the numerical seed is specified. The simplest approach is to call:

```
set.seed(seed)
```

where `seed` is interpreted as a single integer value. Different values of `seed` give different subsequent values for the generators. For effective use of `set.seed()`, there should be no simple relation of the state to the numerical value of `seed`. So, for example, using `seed+1` should not make a sequence "nearer" to the previous one than using `seed+1000`. On the other hand, calling `set.seed()` with the same argument should produce the same subsequent results if we repeat exactly the same sequence of calls to the same generators.

The use of an actual seed object can extend the control of the generators over more than one session with R. As mentioned before, the generators must save the state after each call. In R, the state is an object assigned in the top-level, global environment of the current session, regardless of where the call to the generator occurred. This is the fundamentally non-functional mechanism. The call to `set.seed()` also creates the state object, `.Random.seed`, in the global environment. After any calls to the uniform generator in R, the state is re-saved, always in the global environment. Note, however, that random number generation in C does not automatically get or save the state; the programmer is responsible for this step. See the discussion and examples on page 234.

When the generator is called at the beginning of a session, it looks for `.Random.seed` in the global environment, and uses it to set the state before generating the next values. If the object is not found, the generator is initialized using the time of day. As you might imagine, the least significant part of the time of day, say in milliseconds, would plausibly not be very reproducible, and might even be considered "random".

To continue the generator sequence consistently over sessions, it is sufficient to save `.Random.seed` at the end of the session, for example by saving the workspace when quitting. The `.Random.seed` object can also be used to rerun the generator from a particular point in the middle of a simulation, as the following example illustrates.

Example: Reproducible computation using simulations for model-fitting

One aspect of the *Prime Directive* is the ability to reproduce the result of a computation: To trust the result from some software, one would at least like to be able to run the computation again and obtain the same result. It's natural to assume that a fitted model is reproducible, given the data and knowledge of all the arguments supplied to the fitting function (and, perhaps, some information about the computing platform on which the computation ran).

For classical statistical models such as linear regression, reproducibility is usually feasible given this information. But a number of more modern techniques for model-fitting, statistical inference, and even general techniques for optimization make use of simulations in one form or another. Modern Bayesian techniques do so extensively. But other techniques often use simulated values internally and here the dependence may be less obvious. A whole range of optimization techniques, for example, use pseudo-random perturbations.

The package `gbm` by Greg Ridgeway fits models by the technique of "gradient boosting". In Section 12.6, page 441, we look at the software as an example of an interface to C++. Examining the code shows that the method uses random numbers, but a casual reader of the literature might easily not discover this fact. If not, the non-reproducibility of the results might be a shock.

Running `example(gbm)` from the package produces `gbm1`, a model fitted to some constructed data, and then continues the iteration on that model to produce a refined fit, `gbm2`. If the results are reproducible, we should be able to redo the second stage and get an object identical to `gbm2`:

```
> gbm2 <- gbm.more(gbm1,100,
+ verbose=FALSE) # stop printing detailed progress

> gbm22 = gbm.more(gbm1,100,verbose=FALSE)
> all.equal(gbm2, gbm22)
 [1] "Component 2: Mean relative  difference: 0.001721101"
 [2] "Component 3: Mean relative  difference: 0.0007394142"
 [3] "Component 4: Mean relative  difference: 0.0004004237"
 [4] "Component 5: Mean relative  difference: 0.4327455"
        And many more lines of output
```

Component 2 is the fitted values. A difference of .1% is not huge, but it's not a reproducible computation, perhaps weakening our trust in the software.

In fact, nothing is wrong except that we don't have control of the state of
the generator.

Examining the implementation shows that the C++ code is importing the R random number generator, but is not providing a mechanism
to set the seed. Once this is seen, a solution is straightforward. The
`simulationResult()` function in the SoDA package wraps the result of an
arbitrary expression to include the starting and ending states of the generator.

```
run2 <- simulationResult(
    gbm.more(gbm1, 100, verbose = FALSE))
```

By making the previous expression the argument to `simulationResult()`, we
can at any time reset the generator to either the first or last state corresponding to the run.

```
> .Random.seed <- run2@firstState
> gbm22 <- gbm.more(gbm1,100,verbose=FALSE)
> all.equal(run2@result, gbm22)
[1] TRUE
```

Remember that the generator looks for the seed only in the global environment; if the computation above were done in a function, the first step would
require:

```
assign(".Random.seed", run2@firstState, envir = .GlobalEnv)
```

Example: Are pseudo-random sequences robust?

Our next example investigates what happens when a sequence of generated
numbers is perturbed "a little bit". As mentioned earlier, such slippage can
occur in an attempt to reproduce a simulation, if small numerical differences
cause a conditional result to be accepted in one case and rejected in the other.
To catch such an event is tricky, but we can emulate it and study the effect.
Does such a small change completely alter the remainder of the simulation
or is there a resynchronization, so that only a limited portion of the results
are changed?

Consider the following experiment. We simulate $n = n_1 + n_2$ values
from the normal distribution, in two versions. In the first version, nothing
else is generated. In the second version, we make the smallest possible
perturbation, namely that after n_1 values are generated, we generate one
uniform variate, then go on to generate n_2 more normals, as before. What

should happen? And how would we examine the results of the two runs to describe the perturbation?

In the simplest concept of a generator, each normal variate is generated from a uniform variate. The obvious method is to compute the quantile corresponding to the generated uniform, in this case `qnorm(runif(1))`. With this computation, the second sample lost out on one normal value, but from then on the samples should match, but just be off by one.

As it happens, the default normal generator in R is indeed defined as this computation, known in Monte-Carlo terminology as the inversion method. We might expect the slippage as described, but in fact that does not happen. All the generated values in the second version are different from those in the first version. Why? Because the inversion code uses two uniforms in order to get a more extended argument for the quantile function. As a result, if the slippage involves an even number, $2k$, of uniforms, then the output will resynchronize after k values, but slippage by an odd number of uniforms will never resynchronize.

The default algorithm for normals shows the fragility, but an alternative algorithm gives a more typical example. Let's set the normal generator technique by:

```
RNGkind(normal.kind = "Ahrens-Dieter")
```

This technique uses some tests to choose among alternative approximations, so that the number of uniform values needed per normal variate is random (well, pseudo-random). To see how slippage affects this algorithm, let's program our experiment. The computation in a general form is done by the function `randomSlippage()` in the SoDA package, which does essentially the following computation.

We carry out the preliminary simulation, and save the state:

```
g1 <- rnorm(n1)
saveSeed <- .Random.seed
```

Now we carry out the second simulation and save the result, twice. The second time we reset the seed, but this time generate some uniforms (1 in the simplest experiment), before the repeated simulation:

```
g21<-rnorm(n2)
assign(".Random.seed",  saveSeed, envir = .GlobalEnv)
u1<-runif(slip)
g22<-rnorm(n2)
```

The next step is to compare the second batch of normal variates, g21 and g22 from the two branches. The question of interest is whether the two sequences resynchronize and if so, where. The generator starts off producing values under the two situations. If at some point the two batches contain exactly the same number, we expect this to have been produced by the same set of uniforms in both cases, given our overall confidence in the uniform generator. From this point on, the two sequences should be exactly identical, after having slipped some amount on each sequence. The two slippage amounts measure how much we have perturbed the simulation.

How to program this? Whenever the word "exactly" comes up in comparisons, it's a clue to use the function match(). We're dealing with numerical values but are uninterested in these as numbers, only in equality of all the bits. Suppose we match the two second-part sequences:

```
m <- match(g21, g22)
```

What do we expect in m? Because the second sequence inserted *slip* uniforms, we expect the first few elements of g21 won't appear in g22. The corresponding elements of m will be NA. If the sequence resynchronizes, some element will match beyond some point, after whihc all the elements of m should be successive positive integers. The two numbers representing the slippage are the index of the first non-NA value in m, and the corresponding element of m. In the following code, we find this index, if it exists, and insert the two numbers into a row of the matrix of slippage values being accumulated.

```
seqn2 <- seq(along = g21)
m <- match(g21, g22)
k <- seqn2[!is.na(m)]
if(length(k) > 0) {
        k <- k[[1]]
        slippage[i,] <- c(k, m[[k]])
}
```

If the normal generator uses just one uniform, then we expect the second item in the unperturbed generator to match the first in the perturbed generator if *slip* is 1. The corresponding row of the test results would be c(2, 1). The Ahrens-Dieter generator uses one value most of the time, and applies various tests using more uniform values to match the generated distribution to the normal. Here is an example, doing 1000 runs, and then making a table of the results:

```
> RNGkind("default", "Ahrens")
```

```
> set.seed(211)
> xx <- randomSlippage(1000, rnorm(10), rnorm(10))
> table(xx[,1], xx[,2])
```

	1	2	3	4	5	6	7	8
2	891	49	5	24	9	2	3	1
3	0	4	1	2	1	1	0	0
4	0	2	1	1	1	0	0	0
5	0	0	1	0	0	0	0	0
6	0	1	0	0	0	0	0	0

As expected, about 90% of the time the generator resynchronizes after missing one of the original values. The remainder of the pattern is more complex, depending on the algorithm's choices of alternative computation in the perturbed or unperturbed sequence.

Notice that the experiment specified both the initial seed and the types of generator to use. The initial value of .Random.seed will contain the internal version of both the seed and the choices of generator. This seed is included as an attribute of the value returned by randomSlippage(), so to redo the computations:

```
.Random.seed <- attr(xx, "seed")
newXX <- randomSlippage(1000, rnorm(10), rnorm(10))
```

The various other arguments could be inferred from the previously returned value as well. When designing simulation experiments for serious applications, try to include such information in the object returned, particularly the initial seed.

A few programming comments on randomSlippage(). It takes two literal expressions as arguments, the computations to be done before and after the slippage, as well as a third argument for the slippage itself, which defaults to runif(1). As often in programming with R, we have turned the specific experiment into a rather general technique with only a little extra work, by computing with the language itself. The expression for the simulation after the slippage can do anything at all, so long as it returns an object for which the matching comparison makes sense. See the listing of the function in the SoDA package for details.

A note on *vectorizing*: Because the result returned uses only the first matching position, on the assumption that the two series are then synchronized, one might object to matching the whole object. However, because match() operates by creating a hash table, it is fast for comparing a number of values in its first argument. Testing for the first element, then the second if necessary, and so on, would tend in fact to be slower.

The extra information from the full match also allows us to test our assumption that the two sequences are synchronized if they ever have equal elements. The `randomSlippage()` function includes a `check` argument, `FALSE` by default, that optionally tests the assumption:

```
if(check && k1 <   n2
    && ( any(diff(k) != 1) || any(diff(m[k]) != 1)))
            stop("Non-synchronized .....")
```

In a sufficiently large simulation, exactly identical values could in principle occur without the generator being resynchronized.

Pseudo-random generators in C

Simulating a process that is not simply a large sample of independently generated values often leads to a one-number-at-a-time computation. The next value to be generated requires tests based on the preceding values and/or involves trying various alternatives. It's natural to look for computationally efficient software in a language such as C in these cases. Software for simulation is not trivial, however, and when written in such languages needs to be both flexible to use and trustworthy, our two guiding principles. Whether you are evaluating someone else's software or planning your own, here are some suggested guidelines.

The low-level implementation of techniques should not compromise users' flexibility, their ability to use the simulation software to explore freely (the *Mission*). That's a guideline for all low-level code, and largely means that the C code should be a small set of clear, functionally designed tools. The standard approach via the `.C()` or `.Call()` interface would be to design a set of R functions. The functions should have a clear purpose, be well-defined in terms of their arguments and together give the user a flexible coverage of the new simulation techniques.

From the viewpoint of trustworthy software (the *Prime Directive*), extra care is particularly important with simulation, because programming errors can be hard to detect. Because the computations are by definition (pseudo-) random, some aspects of the code will only be tested rarely, so bugs may only show up much later. Some special requirements come from the reproducibility aspects noted above. For trustworthiness as well as convenience, the techniques should conform to standard conventions about setting seeds and choice of basic generators, in order for results of the new functions to be reproducible and therefore testable.

C-level access to the basic R generators is supplied by a simple interface with access to the uniform, normal and exponential distributions. The official interface is described in the *Writing R Extensions* manual, and consists of the routines:

```
double unif_rand();
double norm_rand();
double exp_rand();
```

For most purposes, the uniform generator is likely to be the essential interface. It is essential for consistency with other simulation computations that the C code get the state of the generator (that is, the seed) before calling any of these routines and save the state after finishing the simulation. These two operations are carried out by calling the C routines:

```
GetRNGstate();
PutRNGstate();
```

Therefore, any C routine that does some simulation and then returns control to R should be organized somewhat like the following, imaginary example. The following snippet uses the .C() interface, to a C routine my_simulation taking arguments for a vector pars of parameters defining the simulation and a vector x in which to store and return some computed values. The lower-level routine called in the loop will do something involving unif_rand and/or the normal or exponential routines, and return one numeric value from the simulation. The simulation in the loop is bracketed by getting the state of the generator and putting it back.

```
void my_simulation(double *x, double *pars,
          double *nx_ref, double  *npars_ref) {
    long nx = *nx_ref, npars = *npars_ref, i;

    GetRNGstate(); /* initialize random seed */
    for(i = 0; i <nx; i++) {
        x[i] = do_some_simulation(pars, npars);
    }

    PutRNGstate(); /* save random seed before returning */

}
```

A more extensive computation may prefer to use C++, as is the case with several packages on CRAN. For an example of a C++ interface to the R generators, see Section 12.6, page 442.

There are many libraries of random number generators, other than those in R. However, from our guiding principles of usefulness and trustworthy software, I think the burden of proof is on having a good reason not to use the interface to the R generators. The basic generators have been carefully studied and very extensively used in practice. They include a number of currently competitive algorithms, and have facilities for introducing user-defined generators (although that's an activity probably best left to those who specialize in the field). Most importantly, they can be combined with a wide variety of other R software, both for simulation and for general support.

If you are using some simulation software in a package, I would recommend testing whether the software is properly integrated with the basic R simulation mechanism. The test is easy: set the seed to anything, do a calculation, then reset the seed to the same value and repeat the calculation. If the two values are not identical (and you really have asked for the identical computation from the package), then there is some `"slippage"` as in our example. Quite possibly the slippage is total, in that the package is using a different generator, such as that supplied with the basic C library. Unless there is a good alternative mechanism, it's a definite negative for the package.

Chapter 7

Data Visualization and Graphics

One of the main attractions of R is its software for visualizing data and presenting results through displays. R provides functions to generate plots from data, plus a flexible environment for modifying the details of the plots and for creating new software. This chapter examines programming for graphics using R, emphasizing some concepts underlying most of the R software for graphics. The first section outlines the organization of this software. Section 7.2, page 242, relates the software to the x-y plot as the most valuable model for statistical graphics with R. The next four sections provide the essential concepts for computational graphics in R (7.3, 253) and relate those to the three main packages for general-purpose graphics, base `graphics` (7.4, 263), `grid` (7.5, 271), and `lattice` (7.6, 280).

A note on terminology: The terms *graph* and *graphical* may be ambiguous. A graph can refer to a piece of graphics display or output, but it can also refer to the mathematical concept of a set of nodes connected by edges. And by extension, both uses can be applied to software related to one or the other meaning. Similarly, the adjective *graphical* can refer to aspects of either meaning or to the related software (for example, *graphical parameters* on the one hand, and *graphical models* on the other). Both topics are relevant and interesting for this book, though admittedly the mathematical one is much less central. For clarity, the terms *graphics* and *graphical* throughout the book refer to the topic of this chapter, and the term *graph* refers to the thing with nodes and edges.

7.1   Using Graphics in R

This section offers some background and suggestions mainly aimed at those who are starting to use graphics in R, or adding graphics to a project not currently using it. We begin with an outline of graphics packages in R, with some suggestions for choosing software for a particular project. We then discuss the options for output devices (page 240).

Graphics presentations are very powerful for examining some aspects of data. Their essential advantage is that the eye can absorb a great deal of information from suitable visual summaries; for example, summarizing the relationship between two variables by versions of the classic "x-y" or "scatter" plot (see Section 7.2, page 242). For exploring data, flexibility and a clear understanding of how the graphics relate to the data are particularly important. Graphics have an unequaled ability to simultaneously show patterns in the data (curves and surfaces, for example) and also to relate the data to those patterns (to show which points seem not to follow the curve). Where printed versions of models and specific summary statistics necessarily boil down the story into a few numbers or strings, graphics can leave much more of the interpretation to the viewer.

The ability in R to produce relevant graphical summaries by simple programming is one of the system's main contributions to effectively exploring data. Choosing clearly interpretable data visualization (such as the x-y plot, again) adds to the trust users can place in the data analysis. So both our fundamental principles motivate attention to graphics.

Graphics packages in R

Software in R exists to provide a wide variety of plots, describing particular classes of objects or giving visual presentations related to various statistical techniques. Many R packages provide specialized graphics. In addition, R has two general packages for basic graphics programming, representing an early and a more recent approach:

- the `graphics` package (Section 7.4), which implements the original graphics computations in the S language;

- the `grid` package (Section 7.5), which implements a newer approach to graphics computations.

For a particular project, you will usually be wise to choose one or the other of the approaches. They cover roughly the same ground, but require extra effort to use together. In addition, a third general graphics package should be mentioned:

- the `lattice` package (Section 7.6), which implements the "trellis" model of data visualization.

The `graphics` package and the `lattice` package both contain a number of high-level functions, intended to produce a complete display from one call. The `graphics` and `grid` package both contain a set of lower-level functions for constructing graphics. A number of other packages provide graphics for specialized purposes, most but not all of them based on the `graphics` package.

How to choose an approach for a specific project? The following suggestions may help:

1. Look first for an existing function that does what you want, or nearly so, and start with that. Search among the high-level functions in the `lattice` and `graphics` packages, and in other packages, for something that sounds promising.

2. Existing software can often be customized either by using optional arguments or graphical parameters, or by adding to the plot using low-level functions from the same package used by the existing function.

3. If you must do a lot of new programming or if you are concerned to end up with some high-quality new software, you should favor the `grid` package, for the flexibility outlined in section 7.5.

Basically, use existing functions if those do what you want, or can be modified through changing the arguments and/or adding some straightforward additional computations. Many R packages include specialized graphics for the objects or the analysis they support, and the majority of these are based on the `graphics` package. Both `graphics` and `grid` allow adding graphics elements to plots and both make use of graphical parameters to control drawing details.

The `graphics` and `grid` package share a common model (see section 7.3), but the `graphics` package is old in design, and somewhat fragmented and inconsistent in implementation, because it grew up during the early days of R development. The computations in `grid` use a more powerful model, often more convenient for a serious programming effort, especially if the application benefits from any of the key advantages of `grid`: manipulating graphics objects, using graphics computations recursively, and dealing precisely with the details of the graphics computation, such as the positioning and layout.

Graphics output and graphics devices

Both the traditional `graphics` package and the `grid` package eventually use low-level device software for converting the graphics to some non-R form that will then be displayed on a screen, included in a document, or otherwise made visible. If you are using R interactively, graphics will usually be shown automatically in a window, via a suitable default device for your operating system and hardware. If you need to keep copies of some of the graphics output, facilities in your R interface may provide a technique (the `"Save As"` directive in a GUI, for example); if not, applications in the operating system will usually allow you to copy the relevant portion of the screen. You will not need to select a graphics device explicitly for any of these requirements. On the other hand, you may need to be involved with devices if you want to generate a substantial amount of graphics output, if you need to create output for a specific documentation system, or if you want control over detailed appearance of the graphics output. If so, read on in this section.

Computer graphics has always had an implicit distinction between online graphics devices, to be used for interactive viewing, and offline devices for generating reports. By the mid-1960s, graphics output devices provided options for either high-quality output (via early microfilm recorders) or dynamic displays (via oscilloscopes and other "tubes"), but both were luxury hardware.

The situation has changed greatly since then. Most users of statistical computing now have monitors with both reasonable resolution and dynamic capabilities. Most users also have access to printers, usually including color, capable of quite high-quality static graphics. (Comparable capabilities would not have been available forty years ago at any price, and the closest approximations we had at Bell Labs represented a significant fraction of the research budget for computer hardware.) Graphics devices remain a relevant concept, but at a higher level. Modern devices for statistical graphics are more typically defined in terms of other software rather than hardware: the window manager for interactive displays and the formatting system for printed output.

The package `grDevices` supports a number of such devices, and is used by both basic approaches to graphics in R. See `?Devices` for a list of available devices. A suitable default device will produce plots in a window on your monitor; on Windows or Mac OS X this will be a device using the native graphics software; on Linux the X11 software is the usual default for online displays. Offline plots will be generated in one of the graphics languages or formats, typically written to a file that will then be included in a document.

The plots in this book, for example, used the `pdf()` function to create PDF files, a good choice for portable output. If you want online graphics that is platform-independent, the `x11()` device function is the best choice, but it is not required on all platforms, so you may need to arrange to install it. If you are running via a remote shell or using a network of computers, `x11()` will be the most likely choice for online display.

Most programming of R graphics is device-independent, in the sense that we describe graphics independently of the physical details of the device. Once we understand some of the options for choosing and controlling the output, such details can be ignored most of the time in our programming. Not entirely, however, and you need to watch out for hidden device dependencies in your graphics techniques (see the example on page 251). Whenever choices are made based on how the plot appears there is a danger that the choice has been influenced by the device currently in use. Color especially is highly subjective and will appear differently on different monitors, still more so between displayed and printed graphics. A technique that depends on color subtly risks a hidden dependence on the device being used when the technique was programmed (for example, the choice of partial transparency to improve scatter plots of large amounts of data depends on the display, as well as on the particular data).

The `grDevices` package also contains some other software, providing tools for controlling the rendering of graphics (color and fonts, for example). If you do need to make explicit use of ranges of color to encode information in a plot, flexible functions exist to create colors. See the documentation for `?rainbow` in the `grDevices` package, and other functions referenced there; the CRAN repository has some other packages, such as `RColorBrewer`, for specialized generation of colors. Section 7.3, page 258 presents some details and an example.

Whatever the device, R graphics follows a static, "painting", model (see Section 7.3, page 253). Graphic elements are drawn, and remain visible until painted over. Interaction can be added to allow the user to make changes, perhaps in a non-programming style using the mouse or other input techniques. But true dynamic graphics requires a different model; not least, usually a concept of graphics objects as being modified and automatically re-displayed by efficient dynamic computations. Integrating such computations with the data analysis using R is a powerful approach, but best done via an interface to software specially designed for dynamic graphics. For example, the GGobi software provides dynamic displays for high-dimensional data (more than 2 or 3 variables) and for other dynamic data visualization. Although the software is not written to use R graphics, there are interfaces between R and GGobi. See the book by Diane Cook and Deborah Swayne [10] and the Web site, ggobi.org for details on GGobi.

7.2   The x-y Plot: The Foundation of Statistical Graphics

One single idea epitomizes the value of statistical graphics, and provides a model for the computations: the x-y plot, a plot that displays pairs of data values from two quantitative variables.

First, the x-y plot brings the power and flexibility of visualization to bear on what is arguably the most fundamental goal of scientific data analysis: to understand or predict the behavior of one variable based on the observed pattern of one or more other variables. This idea recurs throughout our discussions; for example, in arguing for the fundamental nature of the data frame concept. Historically, it goes back to early scientific studies and beyond. How does the position of Mars vary with the time of observation? How does the location of sunrise vary with the days of the year? How does the time for an object to fall vary with distance? What is the relation between body and brain weight for different species? Visualizing such relations provides a richer tool for observers, more open to new insights, than a few numerical summaries.

Second, among visualization techniques, the x-y plot uses the visual encoding that we can read most informatively: position related to linear scales. Intuitively, we spend our whole lives in activities that demand locating positions from left to right and from up to down. Perception studies reinforce this intuition. We can infer quantitative information best from position; and, although we see in three dimensions, the depth perception ability is relatively weak compared to horizontal and vertical perception. Examples in this section illustrate both these points.

It's also relevant that our computer screens, and the paper pages that preceded them as graphics devices, are flat and rectangular, just waiting for an x-y plot to be drawn on them.

An x-y plot specializes to a *scatter plot* when the data values are displayed as "points" (as a symbol drawn at the locations on the plot that are linear transformations of the x and y values). In the graphics package, a scatter plot of log(brain) on the y-axis against log(body) on the x-axis is produced by the function call:

```
plot(log(body), log(brain))   ## graphics package
```

In the `lattice` package, based on `grid`, a similar plot, shown below, is produced by:

```
xyplot(log(brain) ~ log(body))   ## lattice package
```

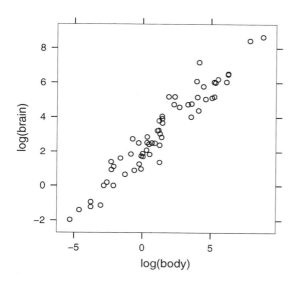

The plot in this case shows the relation between body weight and brain weight for 62 species of mammals. The dataset is included in the MASS package in R, and has been used as an example in many statistics texts; see the references in the R documentation, `?mammals`, of the dataset. That the plot uses logarithmic transformations of the variables is itself the result of the scientific analysis of this data, for which interactive use of data visualization is important.

The basic scatter plot is a powerful tool in itself, but the x-y plot can be adapted to display additional information, while retaining the power of the x-y information. Minor additions to the R functions for scatter plots can often add crucial information, through extra arguments or additional function calls. The x-y plot provides a good starting point, both visual and computational, for using graphics to explore data. The basic visual notion represents two sets of quantitative values by plotted symbols (points), using horizontal (x) and vertical (y) positions on the plot to represent numerical values. But the plot need not simply display a symbol at each of the points. Depending on the context, additional variables and/or relationships between points can be coded on the plot. Some examples are shown at the end of this section.

If the number of points is very large, a simple scatter plot may lose detail. A number of alternatives can be used to compensate: drawing the points with partial transparency; replacing individual points with symbols denoting clusters; or estimating and displaying a density function for the points. Additional information about a variable (for example, that it represents a time or a physical location) can be important in making choices about how to display the data. All the techniques still exploit the essential `x-y` graphics. All are aimed at helping us examine the relation between the variables.

The call to `xyplot()` emphasizes this aspect: the first argument to the call is an S-language formula defining the relation to be shown. You could read the formula "`log(brain) ~ log(body)`" as "`log(brain)` as related to `log(body)`". (For the general use of formulas in graphics in the context of the `lattice` package, see Section 7.6, page 280; they arise originally from software for statistical models, discussed in Section 6.9, page 218.)

Much of the presentation of scientific results takes for granted that coding numbers by position on a plot is an effective way to visualize quantitative information, probably the most effective way. Our eye and brain are used to estimating distances as we navigate through our surroundings, and gravity enforces the horizontal/vertical distinction. It's intuitively appealing that we can infer patterns from positions more naturally and in more detail than we could interpret coding via symbol size, color, or other parameters.[1] To see how widespread the use of this visualization mechanism is, look at papers in scientific journals that discuss any sort of modeling or inference from data. Even if the paper has no explicitly statistical content, chances are that plots included to support or illustrate the ideas will include those of relations visualized using `x-y` plots with curves, points or both.

Beyond the scatter plot itself, a large variety of other statistical graphics use the same idea. For example, using one coordinate for a single variable and the other for some computed variable or index gives rise to a variety of useful plots, including time-series plots, probability plots and many others. Collections of scatter plots, related to each other systematically, are essential for dealing with more than one simple `x-y` relation. Pairwise scatter plots (the "scatter plot matrix") are a step in studying datasets with more than two variables. More generally, multiple `x-y` plots can be presented together to illustrate more than one relation among variables. What is known as *trellis graphics* forms a particularly important collection of such scatter-

---

[1]See the books by W. S. Cleveland [9], [8] and references there for arguments based on perception.

plot-based methods. The `lattice` package implements the trellis graphics techniques in R. Section 7.6, page 280, discusses the `lattice` package.

The older function `plot()` plays an important role as a generic way to display objects. Its original notion, however, was again the classic scatter plot, taking two numeric vectors as `x` and `y` arguments, the first used for the horizontal coordinate and the second for the vertical coordinate of plotted symbols ("points"). The term "scatter" suggests the notion of a scatter of the points around some underlying relation between the variables. In the original S use, likewise, `plot()` took on this extended role of displaying both relations and the scatter of actual data, through optional arguments and functions for additional graphics on the plot. See Section 7.4, page 263 for the practical details of using `plot()`.

The organization of the drawing area in R graphics also reflects that of the `x-y` plot. The layout, with a central rectangular plot surrounded by margins on four sides, defines the essential structure for nearly all the high-level plots in the `graphics` package and underlies much of the trellis graphics as well.

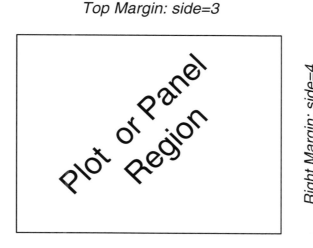

This organization follows intuitively from the `x-y` plot concept, and to a considerable extent arose originally from generalizing early x-y plot software into a general graphics capability. Once the organization is defined, however, it lends itself to a variety of other graphics that are not strictly x-y plots, from contour plots to box plots to bar charts and pie charts. The information in the plot and its relation to the data change, but the underlying organization allows us to construct and adapt these graphics in a consistent way. Later sections on the common graphics model and on the three main general packages all use this structure as a basis for understanding R graphics.

To close this section, here are two examples taking the basic x-y plot and adapting it, first to provide some extra information, and then to define a method for visualizing a class of objects. Programming details are not important here—the examples use functions from the lattice and graphics package, all discussed in the sections devoted to those packages—but the intent of the programming should be clear without worrying about details.

Example: Examining residuals

As an example of adding information to a scatter plot, let's consider examining patterns of residuals from a fitted linear model (from an artificial example). One aspect of studying residuals is to look for patterns related to the predictor variables: Are the residuals noticeably large (positive or negative) in particular regions of the distribution of the predictor variables? If so, this may suggest a better form for the model.

There are many possible techniques, including multivariate dynamic graphics using a tool such as GGobi. But a simple idea is to make x-y plots of pairs of predictor variables, but with points coded to show the size of the residuals. Areas with predominantly positive residuals and those with predominantly negative residuals are of interest.

A general visualization technique is to cut the range of a numeric variable into a factor, and then use that factor to index a suitable graphical parameter. The amount of information is reduced, but visual coding techniques such as choice of symbol or color often do not convey more than, say, 3 to 5 levels clearly. Here we will code residuals from the model by a readily visible aspect of the plotted points. There are several specific techniques; we'll examine two, the choice of plotting symbol and then, on page 258, the color of the symbol. In both cases, it's essential to use a simple coding scheme that gives comparable weight to both extremes of the extra variable. The ColorBrewer system refers to this as a *diverging scale*. The same notion applies in choosing plotting symbols. Be careful that you don't try to provide too much information and that the visual appearance does not bias the interpretation. For plotting symbols, about 3 levels is the limit; for our purposes we want to show negative, small, and positive residuals, and to give the two extremes equal visual weight. Obvious symbols such as the digits have little impact. Resist the temptation to use "+" and "-", since the second symbol is visually only half of the first. Whatever we pick, some visual experimenting will be needed. We'll use "X", "=", and "O"; the middle symbol is less strong, but we are not as interested in the middle values for this plot. For that reason, we choose to divide the scale of the residuals into 5 values, coding the middle 3 levels as "=", the negative 20% as "X" and the positive 20% as "O".

We can compute the scaled data by creating a grouping factor from the residuals. Let's assume these have been extracted into the object `resids`. To get 5 groups of equal size, we use the function `quantile()` on `resids`, with 6 equi-spaced break points on the probability scale, and adust to make the left end less than `min(resids)`.

```
qq <- quantile(resids, seq(0., 1., len=6))
qq[[1]] <- qq[[1]] - .001 # to avoid NA at the minimum residual
residGroups <- cut(resids, qq)
```

Now we can do an x-y plot, but supply extra information according to the `residGroups` factor created by `cut()`. The `xyplot()` function in the `lattice` package does this nicely using a `groups=` argument. Having told `xyplot()` how to group the displayed information, we can then specify graphical parameters to differentiate the groups: plotting character in this case, and colors on page 258.

If `x1` and `x2` are the predictor variables of interest, the plot is generated by the call:

```
xyplot(x2~ x1, cex=1.5, lwd=2, groups = residGroups,
    pch = c("X", "=", "=", "=", "O"), col="black")
```

The optional arguments to `xyplot()` include the graphical parameters `pch` and `col`, the plotting character and color parameters in the common graphics model for R (see Section 7.3, page 258). To keep color constant, we specified it as a single value, not wanting it to interfere with the effect of plotting symbol. The resulting plot is shown in Figure 7.1

There is a clearly visible pattern of increasingly negative ("X") residuals near the diagonal, and of increasingly positive ("O") residuals away from the diagonal. This pattern in the residuals suggests modifying the model to include an interaction of `x1` and `x2`.

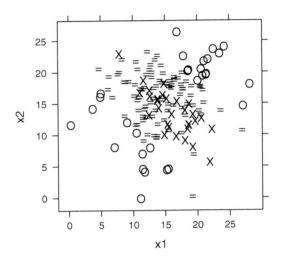

Figure 7.1: Scatter plot of residuals enhanced with plotting symbols to show large positive ("O") and negative ("X") values.

Example: Plotting method for GPS data

As another example of adapting x-y plots, let's design a function to plot tracking data from a Global Positioning System (GPS) sensor. GPS track data is a sample from a conceptually continuous path through space and time, with three spatial variables (latitude, longitude and elevation) plus date/time. In Section 9.2, page 342, we define a class, "GPSTrack", to represent GPS data; our goal in this example is a function that will provide a plot() method for objects from that class.

As in the previous example, we have more than two variables, but now the directional and time-related progress of the track is central to what the objects mean. Can we convey this information in a plot? An x-y plot is suggested by interpreting the geographic coordinates as in a map. An ordinary scatter plot of map coordinates would convey some information. Here's a start, this time using plot() from the graphics package. Here object is some object from the "GPSTrack" class. The function geoXY() transforms latitude and longitude to coordinates on the surface of the earth, measured by default from the lower left corner of the box enclosing the data. The function is part of the SoDA package, and provides a convenient alternative to choosing a particular projection. (See Section 11.2, page 419.)

Given the coordinates, we generate a scatter plot, with the *aspect ratio* set
by the parameter `asp` to make distances on the plot proportional to actual
distances.

```
> xy <- geoXY(object@latitude, object@longitude)
> x <- xy[, "X"];   y <- xy[, "Y"]
> plot(x, y, asp = 1)
```

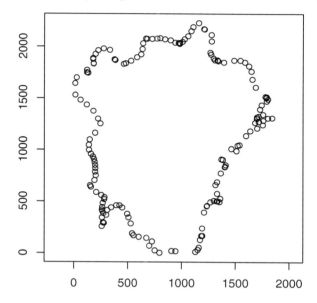

But our goal for this example was a `plot()` method that would adequately
represent objects from class `"GPSTrack"`. Several aspects of `"GPSTrack"` data
are not seen in the scatter plot, any of which might be important in some
applications. First, the object represents a *track*, that is observations taken
at successive points in time from a conceptually continuous path followed
by the GPS receiver. Directionality in space is not clear in the plot. Second,
the data includes `elevation` as a third geographic coordinate, not used here.
Third, the `time` information might be important, for example to show the
relative speed with which parts of the track were traversed. Any of these
aspects can be accommodated within the general x-y plot concept. Let's
begin by incorporating directional information from the track.

To acknowledge the continuous path, one could simply turn the plotted
points into a curve (that is, line segments between successive points) by
adding the argument `type="l"` to the call to `plot()`. However, that still does
not convey the direction of motion, and it may obscure the actual discrete
observations more than we should. An alternative is to draw arrows at each

of the points, with small but visible arrowheads indicating the direction. We'll do that, but the details are not trivial, so we've now again crossed that fundamental boundary to where we should write a function to capture our ideas.

The graphics package has a function, arrows(), to draw line segments with arrowheads on one or both ends. The nontrivial questions are how long the individual arrows should be and how large the arrowheads. The function does not do well by default on the second question. One could choose various strategies and playing around interactively is recommended. We've chosen in the example to make the arrows a fraction of the distance from the preceding point; if fraction=1 we get a continuous curve with arrowheads. Sizing the arrowheads is tricky, but we've chosen to scale them by the average length of the arrows, with an argument head that is the fraction of that distance to use. We'll define a utility function, trackArrows(), to plot the arrows, given the map coordinates and the two arguments above. Then a plotting function using the arrows could be written:

```
plotGPSArrows <- function(object,
                    fraction = .75, head = .5, ...) {
    xy <- geoXY(object@latitude, object@longitude)
    x = xy[,1]; y = xy[,2]
    plot(x, y, asp = 1, type = "n")
    trackArrows(x,  y, fraction, head, ...)
}
```

Here we use the plot() function again, but with type="n" it sets up the plot and produces the box, axes, and so forth, but does not draw the actual data, leaving the plot region blank for later use. This is often the natural way to build new x-y plots with the graphics package, as in this case, where we need only call our utility function to add the arrows.

Here is the utility function, with its own support function, arrowFrom(), to compute the starting coordinates for the arrows.

```
arrowFrom <- function(u, fraction) {
    n = length(u)
    if(n < 2)
        numeric(0)
    else
        u[-1]*(1-fraction) + u[-n]*fraction
}

trackArrows <- function(x, y,
```

```
                          fraction, head, nArrowLengths = 5, ...) {
    x0 = arrowFrom(x, fraction);   y0 = arrowFrom(y, fraction)
    x1 = x[-1];     y1 = y[-1]
    ## compute the average line length
    delta = sqrt(mean((x1-x0)^2 + (y1-y0)^2, na.rm = TRUE))
    ## and convert it to inches for arrows()
    delta = delta * (par("pin")[1]/diff(range(x, na.rm = TRUE)))
    arrows(x0, y0, x1, y1, head * delta, ...)
}
```

The computations are nontrivial mainly in that `arrows()` takes the length of
the arrowhead in inches, so our computation in terms of the x-y coordinates
needs to be scaled, using the physical size of the plot. The resulting device
dependence is inconvenient and potentially misleading; the *Prime Directive*
should cause us to worry a little, if the method were incorporated in a more
complicated graphic display. In our example:

```
> plotGPSArrows(object)
```

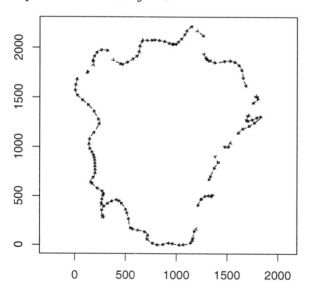

A certain amount of squinting may be needed, but the display does provide
direction information reasonably clearly.

Next, elevation information. Notice that the `plotGPSArrows()` function
includes the "..." argument and passes it down to `trackArrows()`, which
passes it to `arrows()`. This sort of flexibility is recommended when writing
new functions using the `graphics` package. The caller of your new function

can then customize the display by supplying graphical parameters. The customization allows us in this example to code elevation by the color of the arrows, another instance of cutting a variable into a factor to visualize it (page 246).

Here is another utility function, `arrowColors()`, that takes some variable (in our example, the `elevation` data), and a set of graphics colors. It computes the average value of the variable at the beginning and end of each segment, calls `cut()` to get as many levels as there are colors, and returns a vector that assigns to each arrow segment the corresponding color:

```
arrowColors<- function(v, colors) {
    n <- length(v); k <- length(colors)
    midPoints <- (v[-1] + v[-n])/2
    colors[cut(midPoints, k)]
}
```

This example has as its goal a method for the function `plot(x, y, ...)` when x is a `"GPSTrack"` object, and y is missing. Now we're at a point to write a first version of a function that could serve as the method. It must include all the arguments of `plot()`, but it's allowed to add some extra arguments that are matched from `"..."`. These will include `colors`, a vector of color parameters. Here's a function, `plotGPSTrack()`, that could be the definition of a method:

```
plotGPSTrack <- function(x, y,
                    colors = c("blue", "green", "brown"),
                    fraction = .75, head = .5, ...) {
    elevationColors <- arrowColors(x@elevation, colors)
    plotGPSArrows(x, fraction, head, col = elevationColors)
}
```

With the default value for the `colors` argument, the lowest third of the elevations will be drawn in blue, the middle in green and the highest in brown. For a discussion of choosing colors, see page 258. For an alternative way of coding elevation, via vertical segments, using the `grid` package, see page 276.

Finally, what about time, or speed? Suppose we wanted to indicate the speed with which the subject moved along the track. This is again an additional variable, but one that is intimately related to the positions. If the observations were made at roughly equal times, and we ignored changes in elevation, then the distance between successive points on the plot would be a rough indication of speed. Visually that would mean that the length of the arrow would be an approximate speedometer. If speed were the main interest, the data could be replaced by an interpolated version at equally spaced times. Without going that far, we could make the length of the arrow reflect the average speed between successive GPS observations. See function `trackSpeed()` in the SoDA package for the speed computations. A modified version of the function `plotGPSArrows()` shown on page 250, scaling the arrow lengths by speed, could have the form:

```
plotGPSArrows <- function(object,
                          fraction = 2, head = .5, ...) {
    xy <- geoXY(object@latitude, object@longitude)
    x = xy[,1]; y = xy[,2]
    plot(x, y, asp = 1, type = "n")
    speed <- trackSpeed(cbind(xy,object@elevation), object@time)
    speed <- speed * ( fraction/max(speed, na.rm=TRUE))
    trackArrows(x,  y,  speed, head, ...)
}
```

A little note on vectorizing, that is, thinking in whole object computations: Notice that the computations in `trackArrows()` do not change at all, even though the argument `fraction` is now a vector instead of a single number. All the computations involving `fraction` are whole-object, and implicitly promote single values to vectors of the required length.

7.3   The Common Graphics Model

This section presents the common elements of the model for graphics that has evolved in the S language over the years. It owes a good deal to the ideas behind the x-y plot described in the previous section, which is one reason for including that section in the chapter. This is not to say at all that the computations are limited to such plots. The model has supported a very wide range of statistical computing, implying that it is sufficiently general to handle many forms of graphics. But the x-y plot is a paradigm that may help to clarify the ideas, and it frequently provides an example in discussing the graphics model.

This is a computational model for the graphics needed in data analysis, including both data visualization and scientific graphics generally. It is not designed for engineering drawing, animation or even business graphics; although it has been used to some extent for such applications, the wealth of modern graphics software suggests using interfaces to more suitable systems. Also, the model is primarily for static graphics. Once displayed, the graphics elements remain until "painted over" by another element that intersects the same place. The static painting model is suitable if the graphics are to be used without change as both displays and documents. Dynamic and high-interaction graphics require other models for the computation.

The overall idea of graphics in R (and in the S language before that) is that of drawing on a page. The effect of evaluating a sequence of calls to graphics functions, or of drawing a graphics object with the `grid` package, is to draw various graphics elements, each on top of the previous, onto a page. When that page is finished, the software conceptually ejects it and starts on a new, clean page.

The page in turn exists on a graphics device. In the early days, devices were defined physically and the page was either literally a piece of paper in a printer or plotter, or else the surface of a display. Today neither picture is likely to be accurate. The device is generally another software system, typically a document generator or a window manager. The page in a document is defined by a document processing system (for example, the `pdf()` and `postscript()` devices produce output in the corresponding PDF or Postscript languages). Actual printing, if it takes place, is done by processing output files generated by the device function; however, the same output can be viewed interactively.

Similarly, the R software doesn't usually deal with a physical display directly; instead, a window manager is used, by default either a function using the window manager for the operating system (functions `windows()` in Windows and `quartz()` in Mac OS X), or a window manager suitable for use over a network of computers (most often `x11()`). Pages are cleared by the window manager.

The graphics model for drawing on the page can be understood in terms of three pieces:

1. the graphics *elements* that define what's actually drawn;

2. the *positioning* that determines where graphics elements will be drawn;

3. control of *drawing* to refine what the graphics elements look like.

Graphics elements

The full set of graphics elements depends on the package, but the following four are the most commonly used. They are all defined in terms of data as understood by the x-y plot; that is, in terms of pairs of x and y vectors corresponding to horizontal and vertical coordinates, mapped in some way to the current plot region.

points: A plotting symbol is added at each point defined by x-y data.

lines: A connected piecewise linear curve (i.e., connected line segments) is added, drawn through the points defined by the x-y data.

segments: A line segment is added from each point specified by a first set of x-y data to the point specified by the corresponding element of a second set of x-y data.

text: Successive text strings (the elements of a character vector, text) are added at each point defined by the x-y data.

Just what "added" means depends on the package. In the older graphics package, the graphics are drawn immediately on the current plot. In the grid package, the appropriate elements are added to a graphics object, and this object is the value of the corresponding function call. The graphics package has functions of the four names above, taking suitable x-y arguments. The grid package has functions (pointsGrob(), linesGrob(), ...) to return the corresponding graphics objects, and also convenience functions (grid.points(), grid.lines(), ...) that draw the graphics element as well as returning the object.

Positioning graphics

Positioning in the graphics model is always with respect to some rectangular region of the page, with x-y coordinates relating to the horizontal and vertical edges of the region. In the x-y plot, for example, graphical output representing the data is drawn in a rectangular region, the *plot region* in the standard graphics model. Marginal ticks, labels and titles are drawn in the rectangles above, below and to the sides.

By default, the whole page is used for the drawing, and rectangular regions subdivide that. It's also possible to specify part of the page and then to define regions inside that. In the graphics package the regions follow a fixed pattern: a figure region is defined on the page, and a plot region with margins is defined relative to the figure, as in the diagram on page 245. The grid package has much more generality, allowing regions (called *viewports*) to be rotated in the enclosing viewport and, more importantly, supporting an essentially arbitrary arrangement of nested viewports.

Within a particular region or viewport, the software has to choose actual drawing positions for the graphics elements. When using `plot()` or another high-level graphics function, we can be conveniently vague about the interpretation of `x-y` data as positions. The software can be expected to do something sensible in order to display the data provided in an informative way. In the actual graphics model, however, the correspondence between `x-y` values and plotting positions must be defined before the graphics element is drawn. In the `graphics` package the correspondence is specified as what are called "user" coordinates, the range of `x` and `y` data values to be mapped into the corners of the current plotting region. The `grid` package is again more flexible, in that a variety of different correspondences can be used simultaneously (by means of what `grid` calls different "units").

Drawing information; graphical parameters

Drawing information controls the appearance of graphics elements when they are drawn. The term *rendering* is sometimes used, but technically this implies control down to the pixel level, and it's important to keep in mind that R graphics does not generally work at that level, but rather assumes an interface to some other software to do the actual rendering. So the term "drawing" rather than "rendering" is more appropriate in our discussion.

Typical examples of drawing information include the font type and size for text and the colors used for any graphics elements. R graphics in all forms uses in effect a fixed set of named *graphical parameters*. (Fixed, that is, by the current implementation of the `graphics` or `grid` package. The set of graphical parameters has grown and to some extent changed in meaning over the years.)

A specification of drawing information in R graphics can be thought of as a named list, with the element corresponding to a particular parameter name being the value to set for that parameter. The way in which drawing information is used varies between the `graphics` and `grid` packages, but many of the parameter names and their interpretation are similar.

Individual graphical parameters often reflect the long evolution of S graphics from Fortran subroutines. The older names tend to be short, typically 3 characters. The corresponding parameter values started as either numeric values (one or a fixed small number) or else short character strings (often a single character). R has generalized some of these parameters to more natural forms, such as a string to identify a color (`col="red"`) or font (`family="serif"`). The common graphics model frequently uses numeric codes that have standardized meaning when specifying, for example, the plotting symbol (`pch`) or type of line segment (`lty`). These and similar parameters can be integer codes, with 1 typically the default choice. To complicate interpretation, many of the parameters have accreted extra conventions in the interests of flexibility. Line types include codings for customized patterns, colors accept strings encoding hexadecimal RGB specifications, and plotting characters can be a character instead of a code. For programming, we would prefer to spare our users (and ourselves) from such details. Try to give users a natural and readable way to say what they want; if the specification needs to be mapped into some arcane graphical parameters, dedicate a utility function to that purpose.

There are in fact a number of such utilities available in R. Color is probably the greatest beneficiary for graphics purposes. Several useful functions exist for generating sequences of colors that work well in many cases (for example, `grey()` for grey scales, `rainbow()` for a variety of color sequences and a number of more specialized color generating functions; see page 258).

Some other graphical parameters with numerical values are related to size and position and are more natural to interpret. Size parameters are positive numbers to be multiplied by some default. So `"cex"` determines the size of characters (symbols or text) as a multiple greater or less than 1, applied to the current default text size. A position parameter may be a number between 0 and 1, or a distance measured in specific units, such as the inter-line distance for text. For other details of graphical parameters, see the discussion in *R Graphics* (particularly the tables on pages 51 and 53 for `graphics` and page 167 for `grid`). And as always the online documentation should be the most current authority. See `?par` for the `graphics` package parameters and `?gpar` for `grid`, along with other documentation referenced by these entries.

The `grid` package has many of the same drawing parameters as the traditional `graphics` package, but avoids many other traditional graphical parameters that controlled positioning (`grid` achieves more general control via its viewport facilities and by specialized arguments for particular primitives, such as the `just=` argument instead of the `adj` parameter for positioning text.). The `lattice` package is somewhat special in that it has an extensive set of graphical parameters inherited from the trellis graphics model, partially overriding the `grid` parameters. The trellis model is discussed in Section 7.6, page 280; see also the online documentation for the `lattice` package, specifically `?trellis.par.set` and the useful graphical display of parameters from calling `show.settings()`, and for much more detail the *Lattice* book [21].

The `grid` and `graphics` packages use their graphics parameters differently. The `graphics` package keeps a graphics state associated with the device; drawing parameters are set in the device. They will be set permanently by a call to the `par()` function, or temporarily by supplying the parameters as named arguments to a function that draws graphics elements. In contrast, the `grid` package associates parameters with a viewport or a graphics object. We illustrate both styles in the examples for the individual packages. The remainder of this section discusses the use of graphical parameters to control color and font, two aspects of graphics having particularly rich possibilities.

Color parameters

Modern computer displays and printers, if they are of good quality, often do a fine job of rendering colors vividly. Color is a dramatic and memorable part of visual input, for most of us. It's natural then to look to color to convey information in statistical graphics. Through its graphics devices, R provides a general way to specify colors in graphics elements. Colors are generally provided as character strings. Common colors are given by name (`"red"`, `"blue"`, etc.; the function call `colors()` returns all the built-in names). The strings can also define colors using one of the universal color-definition schemes (such as RGB or hsv), but you should generate non-trivial color schemes via one of the tools discussed below, not directly.

There are both advantages and pitfalls to using color. Besides esthetic appeal, color has the advantage that it cuts across all graphics elements. Thus, output colored red can be linked in the mind whether it's lines, text, symbols, or filled areas that have that color. And strong color contrasts are memorable.

There is a substantial difference in the ability of different humans to perceive colors (especially for male humans), both in basic perception and in the tendency to notice and remember colors. So one needs to be careful not to code too much information into color contrasts. The caution applies particularly if we try to use color to code a continuous range or to infer quantitative information. Color shades from light to dark, or from one vivid color gradually to another, can be helpful, but don't expect them to be unambiguously interpreted in the way that position on an axis often can be.

If you need to convey information through color, do take advantage of tools for choosing the colors. The core package `grDevices` has a number of functions to create ranges of colors: for example, `rainbow()` to create a set of varied colors or `colorRampPalette()` to interpolate colors between limits. A perceptually sophisticated and trustworthy tool for certain purposes is the `RColorBrewer` package, which provides an interface to the ColorBrewer project, a systematic approach to choosing colors developed by Cynthia Brewer for filling colored regions on maps. See the Web site `colorbrewer.org` and book [3]. In ColorBrewer, three different goals are supported for color choice: contrasting but not necessarily ordered colors, called *qualitative*; a quantitative range "low to high", called *sequential*; and a two-way quantitative range "negative to positive", called *diverging*. The `colorspace` package on CRAN is more recent and general, with similar perceptual goals.

The ColorBrewer Web site allows you to see recommended color schemes of each type, for a varying number of color levels. The `RColorBrewer` package generates a character vector of R color definitions corresponding to each such scheme (the schemes are identified by a code name given on the Web page plus the number of levels). The color schemes produced are carefully chosen and valuable, but there is one important catch: They are intended for coloring in regions on maps. You need to be careful when using them for other graphics. One major distinction is that for such maps, all the relevant geographic area is colored with one of the chosen colors. But for other graphics, much of the display will remain in the background color. In particular, if you are drawing symbols, text, or lines in different colors, the background color may interfere with visibility of some of the displayed information, as the example below illustrates.

Example: Color to examine residuals from a model

The overall motto for using color remains "Keep it simple!". Color works well, but the effect should be immediate, not the result of measuring or subtle analysis. Let's revisit the plot of residuals from a model; on page 246 we used plotting characters, dividing the range of the residuals into 5 equal-sized groups. Five levels of color is about as much as one wants, so we can retain the grouping. In the ColorBrewer terminology, we want a diverging color scale, in which values at either end of the range are equally visible.

It only remains to choose an appropriate set of colors. We'll do this two ways, first from ColorBrewer and then from `colorRampPalette()`.

From the ColorBrewer Web site or from experimenting with various palettes using `display.brewer.pal()` in R, we can select a suitable scale. We need to select the desired palette by calling `brewer.pal()` with the number of levels (5) and the name of the scale. Let's use a scale going from red to green (which as a diverging scale goes through yellow, with a character-string code of `"RdYlGn"`). A scatter plot with the corresponding coding is created by indexing the colors by the groups and using this as the `col` graphical parameter:

```
resCols <- brewer.pal(5, "RdYlGn")
plot(x1, x2, col = resCols[residGroups], main = "Color Brewer")
```

This gives the upper plot in Plate 1 (following this page). The middle level, yellow on a white background, is hardly visible, as we might expect. In this application, residuals near zero were not our main concern, but generally the faint middle levels would be worrisome.

To avoid a light intermediate color, we could use `colorRampPalette()`. The `colorRampPalette()` function works indirectly, with a mechanism that may seem odd but that is in fact very much in the spirit of the S language: A call to this function returns another function. When that function is called it returns as many colors as requested interpolating the colors specified. Then these colors can be indexed by the groups as before. So the equivalent to the previous plot, using `colorRampPalette()`, would be:

```
redBlueGreen <- colorRampPalette(c("red", "blue", "green"))
resCols <- redBlueGreen(5)
plot(x1, x2, col = resCols[residGroups], main = "Color Ramp")
```

The result is the lower plot in Plate 1.

Either plot works in this example for the main purpose of showing patterns in the residual values. There is a clearly visible pattern of increasingly negative (red) residuals near the diagonal, and of increasingly positive (green) residuals away from the diagonal (visible even with plotting symbols as shown on page 248). The color ramp version is somewhat more interpretable, but still not perfect. The final green in the color ramp palette is slightly lighter and so less strong than the final green in the ColorBrewer palette. So although the second version avoided washing out points near the middle of the range, the choice of end points in ColorBrewer balances the diverging scale better. Subtleties such as this can also change depending on the display or printed medium used. Color is pleasing, but tricky.

The `lattice` functions such as `xyplot()` can use color in much the same way; `xyplot()` recognizes an extra argument, `groups=`, that does the indexing of colors and other parameters for us. The function calls then take the form:

```
xyplot(x2 ~ x1, groups = residGroups,col = resCols)
```

All these graphic coding techniques depend much more on how the coding is done than does information conveyed by the `x-y` patterns themselves. For trustworthy graphics, one should provide an explicit key to the coding. The functions `legend()` in the `graphics` package and `draw.key()` in the `lattice` package are designed to add an explanatory key to the plot itself. Calls to them can be tedious to get right, but trustworthy graphical data analysis needs the explanation.

Color Brewer

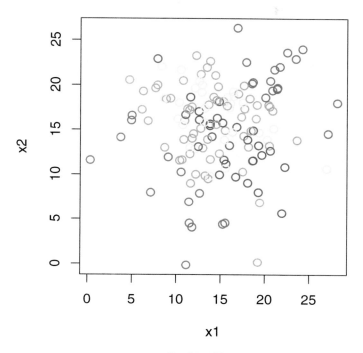

x1

Color Ramp

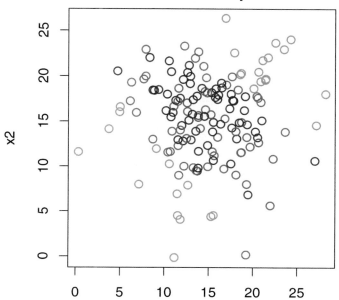

Plate 1: Coding residuals by color:
Green for large positive, red for large negative.

Font and text parameters

Early S-language graphics typically had primitive text-drawing facilities at the level of the specific device. For that matter, text handling in scientific computing generally started with an elementary model of undifferentiated characters of fixed width for printing and plotting, and with fixed-length coding internally (characters and "bytes" being essentially equivalent).

S and R have evolved since then, but computing with text has seen an equally dramatic evolution. The two main driving forces have been computer-based publication systems and the internationalization of computing. Virtually all print media (books, journals, newspapers) are generated from software systems, typically document-input software (LaTeX, Word, etc.) feeding into an output format or language (PDF, Postscript, etc.). At the same time, increasing international use of computers has prompted efforts to make computer text available in whatever human language its readers expect, in whatever alphabet is required to display the language. From an original restriction to the English-language alphabet coded in 8-bit bytes, standards have moved to coding systems sufficiently general to represent all widely used alphabets. The mapping from the human-language content to the printed or displayed graphic has two main components, the encoding scheme to interpret the stored text (based on language and locale, for example, U.S. English or a traditional version of Chinese in Taiwan), and the font that displays the text as a graphic on the screen or for printing. Fonts depend on the encoding, but usually not on details of the locale (a font suitable for U.S. English would typically work for Swiss French as well, but not for Chinese). Human languages being what they are, many exceptions and complications exist, but this general scheme applies most of the time. For a general discussion of text encoding in R, see Section 8.1, page 293.

Computing with text intersects statistical computing and programming with R in several ways, such as user input and generating text messages. For graphics, however, we can usually submerge the details under a couple of simplifications. Your graphics software usually wants to be a neutral pipeline for text, taking in single character strings or vectors of them as arguments and then displaying these as needed, typically via `text` graphics elements. The main issues for the graphics software are where to position the text and how large it should be when drawn. For this purpose, a piece of text corresponding to a character string is envisioned as occupying a rectangular region:

The quick brown fox

Looked at in detail, the rectangular region is both an approximation and somewhat arbitrary. The version shown here uses the units `"strwidth"` and `"strheight"` in the `grid` package, applied to the text plotted, in order to draw the rectangle. See Section 7.5, page 273, for a discussion of how to use units in the `grid` package. The height uses a typographical convention that measures from a "baseline" and ignores descenders such as on the `"q"` . An alternative height unit is `"lines"`, the distance between successive lines of text, which usually gives a loose rectangle, taller than the actual text.

The quick brown fox

A non-rectangular curve could wrap around the text more closely (jogging down around the "q") and other definitions of string height are possible, but the two sets of units shown are all that is easily available with current software.

The R graphics packages allow users to select fonts, a selection that will normally fall through to the graphics device software and, from there, typically to one of a few general font systems used by the device (Postscript, x11 or TrueType, for example). The device and the operating system will determine precisely which font families are available, but in any case you rarely want specific choices of font to be built into your functions or other graphics software. In the `grid` package, the parameters are `fontfamily`, which might be `"serif"` or `"sans"` or others, and `"fontface"`, which might be `"plain"`, `"bold"`, `"italic"`, or others. Setting these parameters in functions should be avoided if you want your software to be really locale-independent. (Further control of the interpretation of `fontfamily` is available for some devices; see `?X11Font` for example.) The `fontsize` parameter specifies the desired font height; this parameter is fairly innocuous in terms of locale, but the facilities in the `grid` package for using units to control position and size are a more flexible mechanism (see Section 7.5, page 273).

7.4   The graphics Package

The graphics package has widely used functions to create x-y plots, contour plots, bar charts, and other "high-level" displays. As mentioned in the introductory section, the general advice is to use the grid package for major new programming with graphics, but overriding this general advice is the good-sense principle of taking advantage of what has already been done. So, the recommended uses of graphics package software mainly involve calling existing high-level graphics functions (those that produce complete plots), possibly also controlling the appearance of such plots, augmenting them, and combining them to produce multiple plots.

If you are building a new kind of visual display from scratch, this can also be done with the graphics package software, but if detailed control over graphics is part of your design, you will usually have better results with the more modern and more object-based grid software. Using grid is recommended if you need to manipulate parts of the visual display as objects, or for some aspects of controlling the appearance of the display that are difficult to express in the graphics software (some examples are mentioned later in this section).

The graphics package contains most of the graphics workhorses for data visualization and related displays. A number of such functions are mentioned in this section but not all, and there are many additional functions and plotting methods (usually S3 methods) in other packages. Browsing online is recommended. One useful technique is to bring up the list of functions in graphics, using a browser initiated by help.start(). Then search in that page for the string "Plots"; these are most of the high-level plotting functions in the package. For more exhaustive searches, supply the same string to help.search() or to search engines such as the Web site rseek.org

The plot() function

The plot() function is probably the busiest workhorse of the basic graphics functions. If you look at the ?plot documentation in R, you will get the impression that plot(x, ...) is a function for displaying a single object. That is a very important role, but was not the original purpose of the function (and plot() was a popular tool in the earliest versions of S). Originally , plot(x, y, ...) was designed to produce the classic scatter or x-y plot of two numeric vectors discussed in Section 7.2:

```
> plot(mars$Date, mars$Declination)
```

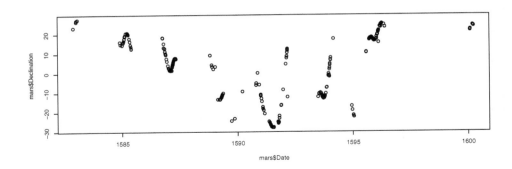

The `x-y` plot definition can be adapted via options in the call and/or the addition of lower-level graphics computations to produce a very wide variety of `x-y` plots.

Conversely, the use of `plot()` as a generic function could produce a data visualization for any class of object or indeed for any pair of classes, using S4 methods. The resulting displays need not be `x-y` plots in the graphics sense. As a result the definition of `plot()` as a function has been diluted into two quite separate ideas. The two definitions co-exist without difficulty, but keep both in mind when looking for useful graphics functions. (The evolution is an interesting example of the role of a function's purpose in developing software, as discussed in Section 3.2, page 48.)

Optional arguments in the call to `plot()` include many of the graphical parameters, such as those controlling color, character size, plotting character or symbol, and many others. The function has a few special "high-level" parameters, such as `type=` which controls how the `x-y` information is displayed. The default is to plot a character or symbol at each position, but lines and several other displays can be specified; see `?plot`. Most of the relevant low-level graphical parameters can also be supplied, optionally as vectors whose elements will be used in succession in displaying the data. Powerful variants on the plot can be designed, for example, by giving vectors parallel to the x and y data. One can display other variables in this way; either discrete levels of a factor or numeric values (depending on whether the parameter is treated as discrete or continuous). The examples in Section 7.2 starting on page 246 show additional variables coded into calls to `plot()`.

The other essential technique for adapting `plot()` to special needs is to add information to the result of the plot, using low-level graphics functions such as `lines()`, `points()`, `abline()` and others. One of the values for the `type` parameter is `"n"`, meaning not to plot the data. The call to `plot()` then

produces all the x-y display (the box, margins, axes and titles) but not the
x-y part itself. Arbitrary additional graphics can then be specified relative
to the world coordinate system and plot outline generated. The techniques
for customizing plots in this way apply to other high-level functions, at least
in part. For a general discussion see page 266.

Other high-level plots

boxplot()	bxp()	cdplot()	contours()	filled.contour()
fourfoldplot()	hist()	image()	matplot()	mosaicplot()
persp()	spineplot()	stars()	stripchart()	

Table 7.1: Some high-level functions in the graphics package

Some of the high-level plotting functions in the graphics package are
listed in Table 7.1. See the online documentation for any of these if they
sound interesting.

There are a number of functions omitted from the table for various reasons. The functions coplot() and dotchart() implement versions of two
plots from trellis graphics, and for most purposes the functions in the lattice
package are preferable (they follow the trellis model more closely and are
more flexible). Some functions, such as curve(), are essentially methods to
plot specific classes of objects, in which case defining a method is usually the
preferred approach. A few functions, such as barplot() and pie(), although
nominally high-level, are very explicit in their graphics form, and don't work
well for the kind of programming discussed in this section.

We can summarize the functions on the basis of their overall purpose.

boxplot(), bxp(), stripchart(): plot summaries of several sets of data, for
purposes of comparison of their distributions.

hist(): plots a histogram, of one set of data; see also density() in the stats
package.

contours(), filled.contour(), image(), persp(): produce various plots of
three-dimensional data, specifically based on values of a variable z
for a rectangular grid of x-y values.

cdplot(), fourfoldplot(), mosaicplot(), spineplot(): generate various plots
related to categorical data.

`matplot()`, `stars()`: produce two (very different) plots related to matrices (multivariate data).

Customizing plots from the `graphics` package

Discussions throughout this book emphasize that programming—making software do what you want—is essential for any serious study of data. Nowhere is that more true than in statistical graphics. Scarcely any data visualization can be fully successful without some adjustment, to make it communicate better or to make its appearance pleasing. We've also emphasized that programming should not be onerous, particularly at the early stages of experimenting with new ideas. The R software generally lends itself to gradual learning, from simple adjustments on towards more ambitious design. This too is reflected in graphics programming.

Initial steps in programming with the `graphics` package can be managed by modifying simple calls to the functions discussed so far. Users can customize the output of the high-level functions in four main ways:

1. by supplying optional arguments in the call that are special to the function itself;

2. by supplying other arguments corresponding to graphics *parameters* that are part of the general `graphics` software;

3. by adding output to the plot, through calls to additional `graphics` functions, either low-level functions corresponding to the graphics elements or more specialized functions;

4. by setting aspects of the graphics state globally, prior to the call, either through calls to the function `par()` or through arguments to the function that sets up the graphics device.

The techniques apply to any of the functions in Table 7.1, but most simply to the classic scatter plot based on a call to `plot()`, so we'll start with some examples of each customization mechanism, applied to the plot of Tycho Brahe's Mars data on page 263. In fact, that plot was itself programmed a little, using graphical parameters and device settings. The result of the call to `plot()` as shown on page 263, if we just type it interactively, is likely to be something like this:

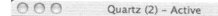

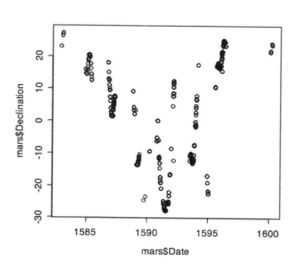

The plot is square by default, which obscures the "message" of the data, that shifting sinusoidal pattern that characterizes the planet's apparent motion. Interactively, we can stretch the width of the plot and clarify the message. Assuming we want to program the same effect, say for a `pdf` file, what do we do? The interactive feedback from resizing the `quartz()` window tells us that a width:height ratio of about 2.5 is effective. A `pdf` file is generated by calling the `pdf()` device function in R, and arguments to that function let us specify a suitable width and height:

```
pdf(file = "Examples/marsPlot.pdf", width = 7.5, height = 3)
```

It then turns out that the plotted characters are too large, smearing the shape of the curve and also lacking room to draw some of the axis labels. Character size is controlled by one of the graphical parameters, `cex=`, which multiplies the default size by a numerical ratio (a little experimentation interactively shows `0.6` of the default to be a good choice here). We choose to set the parameter permanently with a call to `par()`, and now we have the code that really produced the plot on page 263.

```
pdf(file = "Examples/marsPlot.pdf", width = 7.5, height = 3)
par(cex=.6)
plot(mars$Date, mars$Declination)
```

To illustrate the other ways of modifying graphics, let's bring in another variable in the Mars data. The actual recorded entries in Brahe's journal usually included both the date and the time of the observations, but some of them omitted the time. We might want to investigate whether those observations seem to be different. To do that, we use the text field, Time in the data frame; if its width as a string is 0 we know there is no time recorded. We'll show this on the graphics in two ways. First, we use the graphical parameter pch= for plotting symbol, this time as an argument to the plot() function. As mentioned on page 256, this parameter has a numeric form that indexes some standard plotting symbols, with the default value of 1. We'll replace this symbol with a cross (pch=3) for those observations with no time recorded. A useful technique in using graphical parameters is often to supply them as vector arguments of the same length as the number of points being plotted. In this case we can create a vector with 1 and 3 in the right place by something like:

```
noTime <- nchar(mars$Time)==0
pchTime <- ifelse(noTime, 3, 1)
```

and then giving the argument pch=pchTime to plot() puts crosses in the right place.[2] Graphical parameters can be given as arguments, such as pch=, to nearly all drawing functions in the graphics package. Some other arguments apply to so-called "high-level" functions (those that can produce a new page of graphics); for example, xlab= and ylab= specify labels for the horizontal and vertical axis labels. The automatic labels produced before are fine for the R user doing the computing, but for a plot to show others, we would prefer to set explicit labels. Specifying these gives us:

```
plot(mars$Date, mars$Declination,
     xlab = "Date of Observation",
     ylab =  "Declination of Mars",
     pch = pchTime)
```

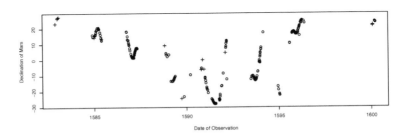

---

[2]I might as well confess that certain S-language hackers are likely to write the computation for pchTime as c(1,3)[noTime+1]. This works because logical values convert to numeric as 0 and 1, but please don't use it. The call to ifelse() is more communicative, even if it were slower, and it isn't in this case.

Next, let's consider two examples of adding graphics to a plot, first an explanatory legend on the plot telling what the two plotting symbols mean, and then a one-dimensional scatter of those observations where no time was entered (to see the distribution of those observations more clearly). The scatter might be useful either for exploring the data or for communicating what we've found to others. A legend, on the other hand, is an example of a graphics add-on that is pretty much used only for communication. As with the axis labels, the original user probably understands what the symbols mean, but another viewer will likely appreciate some explanation.

Legends are an example of an add-on graphic specifically supplied in the package, by the function `legend()` as it happens. The idea here is to add a box to the plot, containing examples of the points or lines shown, matched to some text (the `"legend"` explaining the meaning of the graphics). The call to the `legend()` function does this by supplying arguments giving the graphical parameter(s) that were used and a parallel vector of the descriptive text. There remains the question of where to put the box. It's one of those decisions that usually can't be made until you see what the plot looks like— another reason why this sort of graphics add-on usually arises only when we want to communicate the graphics to others. The R function helps with the positioning by accepting some special strings for the `x-y` position; for example, `"right"` means to put the box against the right side, centered vertically. That seems a good choice because there's some empty space there on the plot. Then the other two arguments to `legend()` are the legend itself and the corresponding parameter values, for `pch` in this case. We used standard symbol 1 where time was given, and 3 otherwise. The appropriate call to `legend()` is then:

```
legend("right", c("Time of Day Given", "No Time of Day"),
       pch=c(1,3))
```

Now for the one-dimensional scatter of the observations for which no time was entered. An attractive graphic here is to repeat these points just above the top axis, to look something like this:

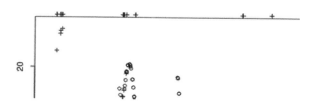

There are two fairly obvious ways to plot this scatter in the `graphics` package, neither ideal and together showing some further useful techniques in graphics programming. The most natural approach is to note that the scatter produced by `plot()` is in fact equivalent to a call to the `points()` function with the same `x-y` data. The equivalence would be obvious if `plot()` were a function written in R, but instead it's a generic and the corresponding method uses C code, presumably for efficiency. But trust me, the result is what you would get from calling `points()`, so the natural way to do the added scatter is with this function, but with the y argument chosen to specify a vertical position in the upper margin.

The catch, and a general issue to remember, is that `points()` and all standard drawing functions in the package expect to draw in the plot region, that is, inside the box. Where the `grid` package has a fairly natural way to do any drawing anywhere, the `graphics` package requires some trickery. Specifically, to draw in the upper margin, we must compute a y coordinate just above the box and we must set a graphical parameter to prevent the default "clipping" of graphics output to the plot region. The parameter is `xpd=TRUE` to "expand" drawing to the figure region. To get the needed y coordinate generally we should retrieve the graphical parameter `usr`, which is a vector of 4 numbers, the last being the maximum y coordinate. Easier but dangerous in general is just to look at the plot and pick a value, say `31` in this case, after a little experimenting. The computation to add the scatter is then:

```
points(Date[noTime], rep(31, sum(noTime)), xpd=TRUE, pch=3)
```

We have to replicate the y value the correct number of times, because plotting functions, unlike many R functions, don't recycle shorter vectors of coordinates[3] (although they do recycle graphical parameters).

The other approach to adding graphics to the margin is to find a function that already draws in the margins and adapt it to our needs. The function `mtext()` is a candidate, because it draws text in a margin, at specified coordinates. In the `graphics` package, `side=3` means the top margin, and the argument `at=` then gives the x coordinates. So we can get approximately the scatter we want with the call

```
mtext("+", side = 3,  at = Date[noTime])
```

---

[3]The alert reader may have noticed that we used a trick to replicate `31` that converted `TRUE` to 1 in calling `sum()`, just what I criticized as obscure in the previous footnote. Well, the excuse is that the alternative here is quite a long, hard-to-read expression, and it doesn't fit on one printed line.

The catch here is that word "approximately": plotting the "+" character is not quite the same as plotting symbol number 3, as you'll see if you do the above and look closely. And some symbols don't correspond to ordinary characters at all; fundamentally, we're using a version of the text() graphics element because there is no version of points() pre-defined to plot in the margins. To carry out general graphics in arbitrary regions, the grid package is more flexible. Although combining it with the graphics software is not simple, the gridBase package provides some techniques (see Appendix B to the *R Graphics* book [19]).

With the calls to points() and legend(), here's the augmented scatter plot:

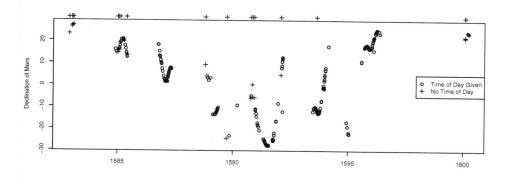

7.5 The grid Package

The grid package is a basic graphics software system, providing the essentials of the common graphics model: graphics elements to draw, a flexible system for positioning graphics via *viewports*, and a set of drawing parameters. It also supports an object-based view of graphics, by generating graphics objects, or "grob"s in grid terminology, corresponding to the graphics.

The package is suitable to be used on its own to create new data visualizations and related tools. It can also be useful to extend existing graphics, particularly those based on grid itself or on the lattice package. With somewhat more effort, it can also extend software using the graphics package.

The reference for a thorough grounding in the grid package is Paul Murrell's book *R Graphics* [19], cited hereafter simply as *R Graphics*. The present section introduces the main features, providing enough background to discuss programming with the package. It also complements *R Graphics* in relating the discussion to the themes of this chapter, especially to the common graphics model.

Graphics elements and graphics objects

Graphics elements are provided in `grid` for points, lines, segments, and text as in the common graphics model (Section 7.3, page 254). There are a few extra elements, but the main difference to keep in mind is that functions for the elements can return graphics objects as well as, or instead of, drawing the element. The package provides each element in two forms for the two purposes. So `linesGrob()` returns a `grob` representing the connected-lines graphics element, whereas `grid.lines()` also draws the lines.[4] Similarly named functions exist for other graphics elements; for example, `grid` has graphics elements to draw circles, and two corresponding functions `circlesGrob()` and `grid.circles()`.

Following the common graphics model, the arguments to the graphics elements functions in `grid` usually include `x-y` positions, provided by pairs of arguments corresponding to the horizontal and vertical positions. But `grid` provides much more flexibility than the basic `graphics` package in that the `x-y` values can correspond to a variety of units, not just to the pre-specified user coordinates for the region. This generality of positioning is in fact key to using `grid` effectively; we discuss it in detail below in the context of positioning and viewports.

In programming with the `grid` package, you can ignore graphics objects, drawing graphics directly in the older style of S-language graphics. You will still have the advantages of viewports, flexible positioning, and other techniques. However, programming in the functional and object-based style we have used in this book will often be more effective if you deal explicitly with graphics objects in non-trivial use of the `grid` software. Graphics objects are often key to reusing graphics software in a new context.

Graphics objects can be passed to functions to generate other graphics objects. Basic graphics objects are returned by the functions corresponding to the graphics elements. Graphics objects can be put together hierarchically. The general graphics object is a tree structure, a graphics tree of S3 class `"gTree"`. A graphics tree is indeed a graphics object, meaning that the facilities of `grid` can be incorporated into graphics trees; for example, they

---

[4]A note for users of S3 methods: although the `grid` package prepends `"grid."` to many function names, this has nothing to do with the S3 naming convention that would suggest methods for the `grid()` function in the `graphics` package.

can have their own parameters and viewport. Specialized graphics trees are the essential technique for creating new graphics with the `grid` package.

Positioning and viewports

All graphics in the `grid` package takes place in the context of a *current viewport*, a rectangular portion of the display window (for display devices), or of the output region on a page (for document-generating devices such as `pdf()`). The viewport concept is the key to programming with `grid`. Precise and flexible statistical graphics comes largely from manipulating viewports to match your goals and from organizing your graphics functions so they in turn can be used in other viewports in a flexible way. It will be worth going over the concept carefully. For more details, see *R Graphics*, particularly Chapter 6, and the online documentation, particularly `?viewport` and the other documentation referred to there.

A graphics device starts out with an initial viewport corresponding to the whole drawing surface. Note that `grid` has little or no concept of graphics objects that span more than one "page". Programming with graphics objects is largely restricted to defining objects within the current page. The function `grid.newpage()` will cause the window to be cleared or the output to move to a new page, if that makes sense. But within a particular graphics object, only the current page is accessible. In fact, for most purposes you will benefit from programming within an arbitrary current viewport; that is, assume your graphics functions are being called from an essentially arbitrary context. The ability to nest viewports arbitrarily in `grid` makes this approach very flexible. Your graphics function may correspond to an arbitrarily complex drawing, but that does not prevent users from then embedding that drawing in a variety of other contexts. (A graphics object to represent vertical elevation is shown on page 276.)

All positioning is defined relative to the current viewport. This includes the interpretation of `x-y` arguments for graphics elements, as well as the definition of a new viewport within the current one. If you're used to programming with the older `graphics` package, you expect positions for graphics elements to be in terms of *user coordinates*, which are called *native units* in `grid`. But native units are not the only way to give positions; be warned that they are often not even the default choice. Other units include: the parent viewport itself, as the (0, 1) interval in each direction (called `"npc"` units, standing for *normalized parent coordinates*); a variety of physical lengths, such as millimeters or inches; and size related to either strings or general graphics objects. These relative units are useful in positioning strings or graphics objects, particularly because `grid` lets you do arithmetic in mixed units. For example, you can move a distance in text-related units from a data-based position just by adding values in text units (`"char"` units in `grid`) to values in native units.

As an example, consider drawing some text in a box, as we did in Section 7.3, page 262. Two functions, `grid.text()` and `grid.rect()` will draw the text and the box, respectively. We need to tell both functions where to draw the graphics, and how large to scale them. If you look at their documentation, you will see that the functions have quite similar arguments, both taking an `x-y` position that defaults to the middle of the current viewport. If we're happy with that position, and want to plot the character string in the object, `myText`, then `grid.text(myText)` does the job. For the rectangle, the same default centering is fine, but we need to specify the width and height. Here is where thinking in terms of units is the right concept. There are a variety of shortcuts, but the general technique is to call the function `unit()`. Its first two arguments are a vector of numeric values and a string identifying which units to use in interpreting the numbers. The expression:

```
unit(x, "native")
```

says to interpret the data x in terms of the `"native"` coordinate system, which will have been set in the specification of some viewport (perhaps by a high-level plotting function). From `?unit` or the discussion in Chapter 5 of *R Graphics* you will see that units `"strwidth"` and `"strheight"`, along with the correct string, will supply scale information to any `grid` function corresponding to plotting that string. The computation to produce the first plot on page 262 is therefore just:

```
myText <- "The quick brown fox"
grid.text(myText)
grid.rect(width = unit(1, "strwidth", myText),
    height = unit(1, "strheight", myText))
```

Notice that in this example, `unit()` takes a third argument. The `"strwidth"` and `"strheight"` units have to be defined relative to a particular string, supplied as the third argument. Units are always used for either horizontal or vertical measurements in the current viewport, depending on the corresponding argument to the graphics function. In this case, the units are supplied as the `height=` argument, and will be interpreted as a vertical measurement. For native units or `"npc"` units the choice is unambiguous. But when we're using the size of a string or of a graphics object, we have to say which we mean. If a string were plotted vertically, the string width is a relevant distance for vertical units, for example. Hence there are two units for string size and two, `"grobwidth"` and `"grobheight"`, for the size of graphics objects.

As we saw on page 262, the `"strheight"` units follow a convention that ignores pieces of some characters. If the goal is to guarantee that the box includes all the plotted text, a different height is needed. For this purpose, the unit `"lines"` is more appropriate. It indicates the inter-line spacing in the current font and graphical parameters, independent of any particular text. To get the second box on page 262, just change the last line in the code above to:

```
height = unit(1, "lines"))
```

It's this flexibility of using units in general ways in general contexts that makes them a powerful tool for graphics computations.

For a slightly more challenging example, suppose we have some x-y data, through which we will draw connected lines. In addition, we have some vertical data, associated with the same n points. We'd like to draw vertical line segments to code this variable. The example arises in designing a graphics display for the `"GPSTrack"` class objects (in Section 7.2, page 252, we suggested a less informative coding via color). Here, the vertical data is the `elevation` slot. How should we scale the segments, so that information about the data in `elevation` is visible, but does not overwhelm the display of the x-y data?

The wide range of units in `grid` gives us great flexibility in specifying the desired size. As often happens with graphics computations, an appropriate strategy depends on how the resulting graphics elements are to be used. One possibility is that the curve and the segments will take up a sizable fraction of the viewing space; in other words, this is a main plot on its own. In this case we just need to choose a scale that is visually big enough to see the variation in values but not so big that it dominates the whole display. We could choose a physical size, `unit(5,"cm")` or `unit(1.5, "inches")`, say. Slightly more flexible is to use a text-related size, which might scale slightly better if, for example, we switched to an array of plots with reduced-size text. Suppose we decide to make the largest vertical values correspond to two lines of text and the smallest values to be half a line of text. First, we scale the original data, `elevation` in our example, to values on the range desired, `0.5` to `2` (note the need to ignore NAs in the data).

```
vlim <- range(elevation, na.rm=TRUE)
v <- 1.5 * (elevation - vlim[[1]])/diff(vlim) + 0.5
```

In `grid`, we scale v as units of `"lines"` (vertical spacing between lines):

```
xn <- unit(x, "native"); yn <- unit(y, "native")
segObject <- segmentsGrob(xn, yn, xn, yn + unit(v, "lines"))
```

We can now plot these segments, or use them for further computations. For the GPS data shown on page 249:

The example above illustrates arithmetic and other computations with unit objects, an important topic in `grid` graphics. To use objects of class `"unit"` generally and effectively, the key concept is that these objects allow the explicit computation of distances to be delayed until drawing time (for graphics elements) or until a viewport object is pushed. The object returned by a call to `unit()` essentially contains the arguments to the call, as an object of S3 class `"unit"`. Arithmetic on `"unit"` objects is supported by methods that similarly delay the actual computations, returning an object of class `"unit.arithmetic"`.

The mechanism used here is quite simple, but you do need to understand the concept to make use of the flexibility inherent in `grid` calculations, and to avoid surprises. An expression that combines numeric objects, graphics objects, and/or unit objects will return an object in which the numeric parts have been computed in the ordinary way, but in which the graphics objects and unit objects remain in "symbolic" form, essentially mirroring the function call that produced them. This is a simple and effective strategy because all R function calls have a consistent, list-like structure before evaluation (see Section 13.6, page 468, for a description of language objects). Methods for arithmetic involving unit objects return an object with the same structure, but with class `"unit.arith"`; by the time the method has been called, any ordinary numeric arguments will have been evaluated.

Let's look again at the computations leading to the graphics segments above. First we converted x and y, presumably numeric data, into `"native"` units. The objects xn and yn contain the numeric values from x and y, but with a special class indicating they are unit objects (and with information about what type of units).

```
> class(xn)
[1] "unit"
```

Because unit objects are not just numbers, arithmetic and other computations defined for them cannot simply carry out the computations. Instead, they essentially save the symbolic form of the computation, as an object of class "unit.arithmetic":[5]

```
> class(yn +  unit(v, "lines"))
[1] "unit.arithmetic" "unit"
```

A similar concept applies to graphics objects; again, the numeric computations needed to actually draw the lines, segments or other graphics will take place at drawing time. The graphics object retains enough information to do the computations in an object of a special class:

```
> class(segObject)
[1] "segments" "grob"     "gDesc"
```

Like unit objects, graphics objects tend to retain the structure of the call that produces them, in symbolic form. A "segments" object has components x1, y1, ..., corresponding to the arguments.

This strategy of retaining in symbolic form the computations that will eventually draw the graphics means that graphics objects and unit objects can be combined to essentially arbitrary depths: All that matters is that the symbolic, list-like structure can be scanned by the eventual drawing computations. In particular, graphics objects themselves can be used as unit objects, with the eventual width and height of the drawn object defining the unit.

For an example, let's go back to the scaling of the segments on page 276. We scaled the segments in units of text lines, which is reasonable if the combined graphics of the lines and segments occupies a large piece of the display, because then we have ensured that the segments take up a sensible amount of visual space.

A different situation arises if we want to use the combination of the lines and the vertical segments together as a "glyph" representing the three

---

[5]The classes in grid are S3 classes; hence they can have more than one string in the class. See Section 9.6, page 362, for using S3 classes with modern S4 classes.

variables. We might then plot a whole set of these glyphs to study how these variables vary with some other data, for example with two other variables that provide `x-y` positions for the glyphs. In this case the size of the segments must scale with the `x-y` data; otherwise, when the glyph becomes small only the segments will be visible. A clean way to tie the two scales together is to compute the graphics object for the lines and then relate the scale of the segments to that. The `grid` package supports such computations by having the units `"grobwidth"` and `"grobheight"`. A call to the `unit()` function with these units must supply a graphics object as a third argument. Again, the key concept is that the graphics object will be retained symbolically inside the `"unit"` object.

In the example above, suppose we decide that vertical segments should be at most around one-fifth the scale of the object representing the connected lines.

```
xn <- unit(x, "native"); yn <- unit(y, "native")
linesObject <- linesGrob(xn, yn)
segScale <- .1 * (unit(1, "grobwidth", linesObject) +
    unit(1, "grobheight", linesObject))
segObject <- segmentsGrob(xn, yn, xn, yn+v * segScale)
```

Although the scaling is for vertical segments, we used both the width and height of the graphics object in computations, effectively multiplying one-fifth of the average of width and height by the vector v, which was previously scaled to the range 0.5 to 2.0. We're trying to do something sensible if the curve drawn for the `x-y` data is very non-square. In particular, if it turns out to be long and low, we wanted the vertical segments to remain visible. But there's no claim that this solution is the best: think about alternatives and experiment with them.

In general, it should be clear now that graphics objects and unit objects can be nested to any depth, allowing for very flexible computations. The effects can sometimes be subtle. Notice above that we're ending up using the lines object three different ways, directly to draw the lines and twice indirectly in computing unit objects. There will in fact be three separate computations of the graphics object when drawing takes place. In general it's possible for such computations to produce different results, if they take place in different contexts (which is not the case here). As long as you cling to the concept that each graphics and unit object keeps a symbolic version of its computation, you should be able to understand what will eventually happen.

Graphical parameters in grid

The grid package has a set of graphical parameters, all of which control aspects of drawing; that is, of the appearance of graphics elements (lines and text). Viewports and graphics objects have a component named "gp" that contains graphical parameters specific to them. Graphical parameter objects have S3 class "gpar" and can be created by a call to a function of the same name. Arguments to the function have the names of specific graphical parameters. Graphical parameters are specified in the functions that create viewports and graphics objects.

To see the current values, use the function get.gpar(); with no arguments, it returns all the parameters as a named list:

```
> names(get.gpar())
 [1] "fill"       "col"        "lty"        "lwd"        "cex"
 [6] "fontsize"   "lineheight" "font"       "fontfamily" "alpha"
[11] "lineend"    "linejoin"   "linemitre"  "lex"
```

Most of these will be familiar from the general graphics model and from the graphics package, as discussed starting at page 256 in section 7.3. For a complete discussion, see section 5.4 of *R Graphics*, or the online documentation ?gpar.

Testing your programming using the grid package

Because the grid package is concerned with programming for graphics rather than with high-level functions for data visualization, testing out your ideas directly may seem to be less straightforward. You do need to set up suitable viewports to produce results, but just a few lines are usually sufficient. The key concept is that viewports nest; you can specify the physical size you want, then the number of lines of margin inside that, then the data coordinates, each specification will create a viewport nested inside the previous one. For our segments example on page 276, we wanted the overall graphic to be 2 by 2 inches, with 2 margin lines on each side, and using some previously computed coordinate ranges, xlim and ylim. The corresponding specification was:

```
pushViewport(viewport(width = unit(2, "inches"),
    height = unit(2, "inches")))
pushViewport(plotViewport(rep(2,4)))
pushViewport(dataViewport(xscale = xlim, yscale = ylim))
```

With the wide variety of units available, there are many variants on this; see Chapter 5 of *R Graphics*.

When the test code or example gets just a little more general, it pays to turn it into a function, just as we have seen in so many aspects of programming with R. Once again, the *Mission* applies: as we work out ideas about graphics and data visualization, let's try to make the software as helpful and reusable as we can. The concepts of viewports and units in the `grid` package help considerably.

7.6   Trellis Graphics and the `lattice` Package

Trellis graphics are techniques for statistical graphics based on the advice and ideas presented in *Visualizing Data* by W. S. Cleveland [9]. The `lattice` package by Deepayan Sarkar implements a version of trellis graphics for R, using the `grid` package for the underlying graphics computations. The functions in `lattice` represent both a data-analytic model for graphics and a computational one. They embody a very definite viewpoint on what data visualizations to produce as well as on how to produce them. The functions generally make well-considered choices of details in layout and rendering of statistical graphics, with little control required from the user. For many applications, the result will be high-quality, trustworthy graphics with minimal effort. On the other hand, trellis graphics are not ideally suited to build entirely new visualizations from scratch; for this purpose, using the `grid` package directly will typically work better.

There are many high-level graphics functions in `lattice`. For details on all of them and on the package generally, you should use the *Lattice* book by Deepayan Sarkar [21]. In this section we will discuss the overall graphics model used and some techniques for programming with the package.

The trellis graphics model can best be understood starting from the common graphics model and the x-y plot, as described in Section 7.3, page 253. Like the `graphics` package, `lattice` works with a central plot bordered optionally by axes (ticks and labels) and/or marginal text. The central graphics is often a version of the x-y plot: points, line segments or other graphics that code information in x-y coordinates. Some `lattice` functions display other graphics in the rectangular plot region (for example, 3D surfaces), but retain the same general plot/margins model.

Trellis adds to the common graphics model the use of multiple related x-y plots to make up a single visualization. Trellis calls the individual plots *panels* and lays out the panels in a rectangular array on one or more pages of output (the resemblance of the resulting rectangles to a garden trellis gave rise to the name "trellis".) Multiple panels are used for several purposes, but especially to condition the plot in each panel according to variables in addition to those used for the x-y coordinates. These variables are called the *givens* in trellis. Each panel represents some value or interval for the given variables, typically shown in the top margin, symbolically or by text. The encoding is done in a *strip* in trellis terminology, by default a shaded band on which information about the particular values of the conditioning variable may be shown. The panels in a particular display are inter-related, which allows the trellis graphics to make better use of the display space (only repeating axes when needed, for example, rather than on each panel).

So far we have considered what is displayed; let's turn now to how the computations are organized. Like grid, but unlike the graphics package, lattice produces objects representing the graphic to be displayed, rather than doing the actual drawing. The object is of class "trellis" and contains a fairly high-level description of the graphic. This is an S3 class, so don't expect to find a formal definition. In fact, it is a named list with some 40+ elements. There are around ten S3 methods in the lattice package that manipulate these objects. Most importantly, the plot is drawn by the print() method for trellis objects, either automatically if the "trellis"-class object is the result of a top-level expression, or explicitly by a call to print(). The methods are hidden inside the package's namespace. To examine the methods or debug code that uses them requires some standard trickery. First, get the namespace environment from one of the lattice functions. There is no way to unambiguously identify S3 methods, but those explicitly for class "trellis" must have names ending in ".trellis". A heuristic to find the methods is to look for the corresponding regular expression among the objects in the lattice namespace, which is the environment of an ordinary function from the package:

```
> ev <- environment(xyplot)
> ev
<environment: namespace:lattice>
> objects(ev, pattern = "[.]trellis$")
 [1] "[.trellis"             "dim.trellis"
 [3] "dimnames.trellis"      "plot.trellis"
 [5] "print.summary.trellis" "print.trellis"
 [7] "summary.trellis"       "t.trellis"
 [9] "tmd.trellis"           "update.trellis"
```

Now we can, for example, trace code in one of the methods, using the `:::` operator to access objects that are not exported.

```
> trace(lattice:::print.trellis, edit = TRUE)
```

(The printed code in this case is over 500 lines long, so we won't examine it here.)

Trellis objects are generated by calls to one of the high-level plotting functions in the lattice package; for example, xyplot(), bwplot() (a version of Tukey's box plots), wireframe() (plotting three-dimensional surfaces), splom() (scatter plots of pairs of variables), and some ten others. The visualizations involve differing numbers of variables, one, two, three, or arbitrarily many. The typical user interface for all of these, however, is made uniform via the S-language *formula* mechanism. Formulas were originally designed for use in statistical model software (introduced in the book *Statistical Models in S* [6]). Model formulas generally have the form

```
y ~ x
```

meaning that y is to be modeled by x. Trellis took over the same formula for a plot that showed the relationship of y to x, that is, an x-y plot of the variables. The conventions for S formulas included operators `+` and `*` to correspond to combinations of the groups generated in variables x and y. In trellis graphics, an additional operator was added to the formula convention: `|` meaning "given". Thus

```
y ~ x | z
```

means to show the relationship of y to x, conditional on a range of values for z.

Formulas can be extended to visualizing a single object, conditional on one or more other variables. In this case the left side variable in the formula is omitted; for example,

```
~ x | u * v
```

specifies a visualization of x, conditional on combinations of two other variables u and v. The expression in front of the `|` operator can represent a single variable or an object such as a data frame that contains multiple variables.

To see this sort of formula in use, Figure 7.2 is a box-and-whisker plot of the famous "Fisher iris data", visualizing the distribution of sepal length by a box-and-whisker summary, conditional on each combination of species and a discretized version of petal length, with three levels. First, we define u to be the 3-level version of Petal.Length, and then construct the trellis display of Sepal.length given the 3 by 3 interaction of u and Species.

```
> u <- cut(Petal.Length, breaks = 3)
> bwplot( ~ Sepal.Length | u * Species)
```

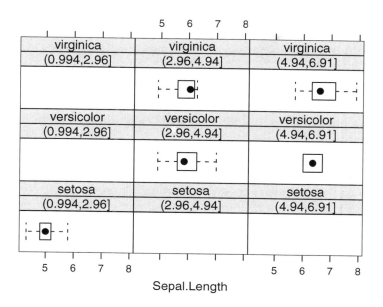

Figure 7.2: Box and whisker plot of sepal length, conditioned on petal length and species.

As an example of data visualization, this plot illustrates both the clustering of the iris data by species (all the *setosa* values and none of the other species' fall in the bottom third of the sepal length range) and the correlation between sepal and petal size (the values of sepal length shift to the right between the second and third columns of the display).

In terms of statistical computing, the example illustrates an important strength of `lattice`: producing a complex plot with a great deal of information and carefully chosen drawing details, from a simple and fairly intuitive function call.

Trellis graphics shares the common graphics model followed by most S-language graphics, including the central role for the concepts of the x-y plot. This shows up most clearly when we examine the structure of `"trellis"` objects, and also helps us understand how to control the details of trellis graphics.

Trellis objects

As noted earlier in the section, trellis graphics are organized around the notion of *panels*, each of which displays a plot, often an x-y plot. Regardless of the particular high-level trellis plot, each `"trellis"` object in effect contains a description of these panels. The components of the `"trellis"` object correspond to different aspects of the panels. Some individual components are themselves a list, whose elements are the corresponding information for each panel. In the box-and-whiskers example above, there are 9 panels, so such components would be lists of length 9. Other components contain information that applies unchanged to all panels.

The organization of the panels in trellis graphics is defined by a *panel function*. Each `"trellis"` object, g say, has a component `g$panel` identifying this function. A trellis plot is drawn by calling the panel function once for each panel: There is only one panel function in each trellis object, but the arguments with which it will be called will vary between panels. Actual drawing is done by the function `print.trellis()`, the S3 print method for `"trellis"` objects. It initiates the drawing by constructing and evaluating a suitable call to the object's panel function for each panel.

The necessary arguments for each call to the panel function are stored in the trellis object: a list of argument lists, one element for each panel, and another single argument list for the arguments whose values are common to all calls. Other components of the trellis object control a variety of graphics details, such as aspect ratio and coordinate limits.

Customizing trellis plots

The details of trellis graphics can be controlled at different levels, from straightforward optional arguments, to function calls that set parameters, to detailed modification of trellis objects or customizing the panel functions. Straightforward control is mostly done through optional arguments to the high-level `lattice` functions. These arguments are mostly described under the corresponding detailed documentation, `?xyplot`, for example. The next more detailed level of control is via the package's graphical parameters. As in the `grid` and `graphics` packages, `lattice` has some specially named parameters that can be set by users. In the case of `lattice`, graphical parameters are stored in the current trellis device, rather than in a graphics object as in `grid` or globally as in `graphics`. Trellis graphical parameters are examined or set by calling `trellis.par.get()` or `trellis.par.set()` (with named arguments for the latter).

It's probably fair to say that dealing with `lattice`'s graphical parameters requires some empirical study and some knowledge of how `lattice` uses the `grid` package. The learning step beyond using optional arguments to high-level functions is moderately steep.

The valid names for setting parameters are the names of the components returned by `trellis.par.get()`. As this book is written:

```
> names(trellis.par.get())
 [1] "grid.pars"         "fontsize"           "background"
 [4] "clip"              "add.line"           "add.text"
 [7] "plot.polygon"      "box.dot"            "box.rectangle"
[10] "box.umbrella"      "dot.line"           "dot.symbol"
[13] "plot.line"         "plot.symbol"        "reference.line"
[16] "strip.background"  "strip.shingle"      "strip.border"
[19] "superpose.line"    "superpose.symbol"   "superpose.polygon"
[22] "regions"           "shade.colors"       "axis.line"
[25] "axis.text"         "axis.components"    "layout.heights"
[28] "layout.widths"     "box.3d"             "par.xlab.text"
[31] "par.ylab.text"     "par.zlab.text"      "par.main.text"
[34] "par.sub.text"
```

Modifying the details of a particular trellis plot requires two steps. First, figure out what parameters are actually used to create the effect you want to modify. Second, within that parameter, find the underlying `grid` parameter that needs changing.

Unlike the `graphics` package, the parameters in `lattice` come at different levels and may be specific to one or a few of the high-level functions. Changing a low-level parameter will not always affect the appearance of the plot. For example, consider `"box.rectangle"`. The components of this parameter affect the box drawn in each panel of a box-and-whisker plot. You might guess the correct parameter, but the safe way to proceed is to examine the source for the appropriate panel function, `panel.bwplot` in this case. That function calls `trellis.par.get()` to get `"box.rectangle"`.

To see how to use a particular parameter, you need to examine its default contents. Many of the trellis parameters are themselves named lists of `grid` parameters; for example, in this case:

```
> br <- trellis.par.get("box.rectangle")
> br
$alpha
[1] 1

$col
[1] "#00FFFF"

$fill
[1] "transparent"
```

```
$lty
[1] 1

$lwd
[1] 1
```

These five `grid` parameters will be used in drawing the rectangle in the box symbols. You need to examine the `grid` documentation to be sure of their meaning; for example, `col` is the color for drawing the rectangle and `fill` the color for filling it in.

To modify the fill color to `"white"`, set the `fill` component and call `trellis.par.set()` before doing the plot.

```
> br$fill <- "white"
> trellis.par.set(box.rectangle = br)
> bwplot(~Sepal.Length | u * Species)
```

Remember that you need to know which parameters are really used in the particular plot. For example, setting component `col` of the `box.rectangle` parameter would change the color of the lines drawn around the box but changing the `col` component of the lower-level `plot.line` parameter would not, because the code in `panel.bwplot()` drawing the rectangle ignores that parameter.

A call to the `show.settings()` function will display the various parameter sets graphically, which should suggest what parameters are likely to be relevant. Beyond that, you may need to examine the code of the relevant function in the `lattice` package to be sure. For example, if you are doing box-and-whisker plots, you need to study the function `panel.bwplot()`, which plots such panels. In the code, you will see:

```
box.dot <- trellis.par.get("box.dot")
box.rectangle <- trellis.par.get("box.rectangle")
box.umbrella <- trellis.par.get("box.umbrella")
plot.symbol <- trellis.par.get("plot.symbol")
fontsize.points <- trellis.par.get("fontsize")$points
```

These parameters, therefore, may affect the box-and-whisker panels.

Lattice also has a set of "options", which differ from the parameters mainly in that they do not relate directly to the specifically trellis-graphics aspects of the computation. See `?lattice.options` for details.

As the example shows, controlling `lattice` output takes more work than just setting a low-level parameter in `grid` or `graphics`. The compensation is that the multi-level structure of `lattice` parameters allows more flexible control, leaving the trellis graphics unchanged except for the specific aspects modified.

For even more detailed control, one can modify the trellis object itself, either by changing specific data values or by replacing the panel function by a customized one. The panel functions are generally identified by name and found in the `lattice` package. However, you can insert a function object into the `"panel"` component. Defining your own panel function by modifying the one in the `lattice` package for this plot is a plausible strategy to modify some of the trellis graphics design. But be prepared to learn a substantial amount about `lattice` and possibly about `grid` as well.

Chapter 8

Computing with Text

Although statistical computing, following the lead of statistical theory, has tended to be defined mostly in terms of numerical data, many applications arise from information in the form of text. This chapter discusses some computational tools that have proven useful in analyzing text data. Computations in both R and a variety of other systems are useful, and can complement each other. The first section sets out some basic concepts and computations that cut across different systems. Section 8.2, page 294, gives techniques for importing text data into R. Section 8.3, page 298, discusses *regular expressions*, a key technique for dealing with text. The next two sections apply a variety of techniques in R (8.4, 304) and in Perl (8.5, 309). Finally, Section 8.6, page 318, gives some fairly extended examples of text computations.

8.1   Text Computations for Data Analysis

The computations needed most often in dealing with text data can be built up from a fairly small number of concepts and techniques. Implementations for all these techniques exist in many systems, with variations in generality and efficiency. Some of these systems are discussed in this section; later sections concentrate mainly on R itself and on Perl to illustrate working with other systems.

Text computations that aim to be used in the world at large must consider how text from human languages is represented internally in files or in systems; that is, on the *encoding* of characters. In practice, modern versions of R and other systems deal quite generally with essentially any language, at least as far as carrying out typical text computations. One does need to express the computations to take advantage of this generality. The main points are considered on page 293.

The concepts for computing with text have much in common across a number of systems, including R, Perl, Python, and UNIX-style tools. Many of the techniques in fact evolved from UNIX and were then implemented in other systems. As a result, programming with text can make use of different systems without being totally redesigned, allowing users to implement techniques in the most appropriate environment. A roughly accurate summary is that quite similar computations on text will be applied to different data structures. For example, most R functions will be designed to work on character vectors, whereas Perl computations often loop over lines of text that are read from a data stream such as a file. The programming involved may be quite similar, despite the difference in data structures, although some computations will be more natural in one form or the other. For large computations, major differences in computing time may result. We begin with an R-style exposition and examples, and then illustrate the use of one alternative, the Perl system (without prejudice to other choices; see the comments on page 291 about alternative systems).

Computational tasks

The basic computational tasks with text for data analysis divide roughly into those that match whole strings and those that search or replace substrings.

String matching is simply the computation that determines whether some candidate strings, x, are each identical to one of the strings in another object, `table`. This is exactly what the R function `match(x, table)` does, but some conceptual points need to be noted. First, there is an asymmetry in the task, compared to the equality testing operation, `` `==` ``. The `table` is thought of as containing unique strings, whereas x may be a large collection of arbitrary strings. Second, and related, the internal computations involved are not done by comparing strings pairwise. The `table` object is pre-processed, as a *hash table*, to greatly speed up the matching process. However, the `match()` function was not written to take a pre-computed hash table, and so has to prepare the table on each call. The extra computation is usually irrelevant, unless the table is very large and/or the matching must be done in many separate calls with the same table. Other techniques may be needed in these circumstances. Within R, the class of `"environment"` objects provide one mechanism. One may also choose to pass some of the matching to another system.

The computational techniques needed change when the desire is to search for substrings or patterns, that is, when multiple strings can satisfy a particular matching criterion. Word processors and editors, as well as general systems such as R and Perl, have techniques to identify substrings in text data. Typically, these come with corresponding techniques to replace the identified substrings with specified text. In word processors, the technique is often via a widget in which the user types the text for searching or replacement, but we are interested in programming, so some explicit specification is needed.

Substrings are identified in three main ways: by position (first character position and length of the substring, for example); by matching specified text; and by use of a language to match text patterns. The last is the most general, and the classic grammar to specify the pattern in UNIX-derived systems is expressed by *regular expressions*, discussed in section 8.3. All three ways of identifying substrings may be relevant. The first is the least ambiguous, and will be used as the definition of a substring in this chapter. Two helpful generalizations are to allow substrings of length zero, and to define character positions corresponding to just before and just after all the actual characters (positions 0 and `nchar(x)+1` in R terms). Matching fixed strings with a regular expression is clumsy, so the string matching software usually allows turning regular expression matching off for an argument supplying a pattern for matching. Most of the R functions for text matching have an option such as `fixed = TRUE` for this purpose.

Alternative systems for text computations

Aside from those of us doing data analysis or "quantitative" computing generally, most computer users spend most of their time dealing with text data in Web browsers, mail programs, document processing and other information/communication activities. Not surprisingly, there are many pieces of software with at least some hope of being useful tools in dealing with text in data analysis as well. In addition to text computations in data analysis software itself, there are four main classes of tools.

1. *Interactive applications:* These include editors such as emacs and simpler tools such as search-and-replace inside document systems.

2. *Shell tools:* Tools such as grep and sed function mainly as one-line commands that can be combined in a script using a command shell.

3. *Scripting languages:* These range from fairly simple and/or old (awk) to much more ambitious (Perl or Python).

4. *Low-level languages:* In practical terms, this means C and its successors, such as C++.

All of these can be useful and inter-system interfaces allow us to mix several systems. If you are particularly familiar with any of the languages, that's a strong argument in its favor. Another strong argument is the availability of software that appears to be a good fit for your particular application. For example, there are many packages in Perl and Python and some may work well as additions to statistical computing tools.

Modern scripting languages are attractive for many applications, offering a relatively simple programming interface, very much tuned for computations with text, and competitive in efficiency of computer time to programming in a low-level language, for many applications. The term *scripting language* generally means a language and system that is powerful enough for programming, but still simple enough for use in creating "shell scripts", when the programmer wants to spend a limited time in learning and writing. The same combination of power and simplicity makes such languages suitable for use with R. In contrast, low-level languages tend to involve more extended programming efforts, more learning, tougher debugging, and possibly technical problems with installation and portability.

To keep the discussion in this chapter simple and of reasonable length, examples of computing with text are essentially all in R itself or in the Perl language. This is not to assert Perl's superiority over, say, Python, but mainly reflects my own relative familiarity, along with some good practical features of the language.

Perl is an open-source system that runs readily on all the major hardware and software environments. Binary and source copies are readily available. Like R, Perl has a central Web site, `perl.org`, with pointers to downloads, packages, and other resources.

The implementation of Perl is remarkably efficient for a variety of text processing and related computations. When dealing with large quantities of text, this efficiency can be important, and it mitigates some of the advantages of code written directly in C. Indeed, most of us would be hard pressed to write C implementations of text-related tasks to compete in speed with the existing Perl code.

Perl is, however, not a perfect or "best" system for text computations. An equally good case could be made for the Python language, which covers many of the same application areas as Perl. Broadly, Python has strengths over Perl in elegance and consistency of design, as against Perl's strengths in a very large selection of available software and, perhaps, in efficiency. Perl is used in a number of the support tools for R, which may provide some additional useful software. For this reason, also, you can usually count on Perl being available on any system that can support programming with R. Finally, Perl source code can have a fairly strong resemblance to R. Admittedly, this is both good and bad, since one can trip over underlying differences. However, on balance the similarities may help in writing code that uses both systems together. Section 8.5, page 309, gives an overview of using and writing Perl software.

Encoding text data

So far, we have talked about computing with text without specifying what "text" means. R and the other systems being considered all have mechanisms for representing text, or "character data", as arguments to functions or as data in the system. In R, the fundamental object type `"character"` fills this role.

To be useful, however, these object types must correspond to the text information that users can interpret and to the data that must be processed by the systems. That data will be expressed in one or more of the human writing systems developed and used in the world. What concepts and techniques are needed to accommodate such data?

The essential concept here is usually described as *character encoding*, a mechanism for mapping the characters of a written language (as defined by some model suited to the particular language) into a set of numeric codes, and usually also into a way to write those codes to media such as files. A one-sentence historical summary gives the essential message. Character encoding was at first simple and crude, unable to handle languages in general; as computers and systems tried to accommodate arbitrary languages, there was a period of confusion and of inconsistent approaches; now, a few standards are nearly universally accepted, with the result that programmers like us will again be able to use some simple techniques, but now with an essentially universal applicability for the results.

The historic arc has been from simple to complicated and back to simple. As this book is written, we are not quite back to simplicity, but details continue to change, so the discussion here uses what will very likely be the eventual approach. If you don't care about details, the summary is that by using a locale of `"UTF-8"`, you should be able to deal with text from nearly any language and alphabet.

When the S language began, and earlier, text came in 8-bit bytes in the "ASCII" encoding (it actually used only 7 of the bits). The alphabet was upper- and lower-case Latin letters with no accents. Over the next two decades, operating systems and other software needed to incorporate other alphabets to communicate with users and to deal with text data. A variety of solutions grew up, quite a few of which are still around. The divergent approaches partly reflected concern over machine efficiency in space and time, for storing multi-byte characters and computing with them.

With cheaper storage and faster machines, and with some well-chosen techniques, one general model and one implementation of that model are now nearly a standard: Unicode and UTF-8. For most purposes, the UTF-8 encoding allows essentially any written language to be used in text data, while not greatly inflating either the space or time requirements.

The Unicode effort is quite strongly linked to the Posix standard for operating systems. So too are R itself and a number of the other systems discussed in this book. As a result, Unicode-compliant implementations of the support software for R are becoming the standard. As this is written, there are some rough edges and platform restrictions, but the eventual approach is clear. Software can deal with arbitrary alphabets by using Unicode-based techniques, and with text data encoded by the UTF-8 standard.

R has facilities to specify the encoding, through what it terms the *locale*, by calling the function `Sys.setlocale()`, as well as facilities to convert between encodings if necessary, by the function `iconv()`. The locale includes more than just the encoding; for example, it includes the (human) language expected. And indeed there are many more issues to confront than just reading text data, but for the purposes of this chapter, ensuring that the locale includes the character encoding you need will get us most of the way.

8.2 Importing Text Data

Text data nearly always starts on an external medium, either generated directly (by typing or, more frequently now, from some external device), or else exported from another software system (such as a spreadsheet or database). The data may be on files or Web pages, or it may be generated dynamically as *data streams*, sequences of characters being read from some active source. To deal with the data, the first step must be to bring it into whatever language we plan to use.

The term "importing" describes this in general. Non-programming systems, such as word processors or spreadsheets, typically have an **open** or import menu in their user interface, offering a choice of formats recognized by the application. A format in the list will correspond to a known file format used by that application (or one of its competitors) for exporting or saving data to a file. The import works in a single step, giving the user a complete document now in the application's internal form. The user's responsibility only extends to selecting the format, and that is typically suggested by the file suffix (for example, ".xls" is the usual suffix for files used to save Excel spreadsheets).

Programming languages, including R, offer the user a much wider range of choices, indeed in some sense an unlimited range. The user must decide where the text should come from, by specifying the input file or other source; what the imported data should be, in terms of an object or structure in the language; and what format information the software should use in processing the input to define the data. Most users would prefer to avoid making these choices. Fortunately, a number of software tools in R, and in other systems, do in fact allow us to get most of the way back to the simplicity of non-programming applications, provided we do know that the imported data has some appropriate structure.

A prime example is importing spreadsheet data into R. We do have a suitable class of object for much spreadsheet data, namely the "data.frame". Not everything in a spreadsheet maps naturally into a data frame, but the sort of data most amenable to data analysis often does. A simple two-step computation is possible for importing such data from many systems. First, the data is *exported* from the spreadsheet program or similar application, choosing an appropriate export format. Then, an R function also matched to that format reads the data in a single call.

Spreadsheet programs and many other software systems can export tables in some standard formats, such as the "comma-separated-values" or ".csv" format. The R function read.csv() reads such data and returns a data frame. For an example and details, see Section 6.5, page 173.

Importing spreadsheet data is the most common such whole-object import example, but not the only one. If you have other external text data that should map naturally into an R object, look for a direct import function in the usual sources, such as the Web-based search lists. The *R Data Import/Export* manual on the R Web site covers a number of formats, not all for text data.

The ".csv" files are a special case of files that correspond to data frames in the general sense, that is to repeated records of the same set of variables. Likewise, the read.csv() function is a specialization of the function read.table(). The more general version allows for different conventions about the delimiters between fields, the presence or not of a header line, and other variants. The ".csv" files used for exporting and importing data have adopted some conventions, such as for escaping quote characters in strings, that are different from the traditional S-language and UNIX-based conventions. The R functions to read files generally recognize the ".csv" conventions, but you would be wise to check specifically in the relevant detailed documentation.

If a data frame or similar table is not the right concept for the data you need to import, you may need to work at a somewhat lower level. The two workhorse R functions for input are scan(), which reads fields of specified types, and readLines(), which simply reads lines of text as character strings. The scan() function is the original basic input function in the language. If the data being imported has little structure, then scan() is both fast and flexible. To read numeric data, in fields separated by blanks, newlines, or other white-space characters, for example, from a file "numData.txt", is simply:

```
scan("numData.txt", numeric())
```

The second argument to scan() is an object that is taken to be the template for the type of data. It's either from one of the atomic basic object types, "numeric" and "character" being the most likely, or else it's a list. In the former case, nothing matters about the object except its type, which tells scan() to interpret each field as an elementary value of that type. The use of a list as the second argument provided an early version of the table-style later handled by read.table(). The elements of the list give the object types for successive fields on each line, and scan() then returns a list with corresponding elements for each field. Usually, read.csv() or read.table() will be simpler to use, but scan() does have considerable flexibility, through a large number of optional arguments.

Example: Importing data with variable line formats

A fairly common pattern for data is to have individual lines whose structure varies, so that the data as a whole does not correspond to a simple table. Suppose each observation includes a variable number of replicated values for some variable. Then if the data is on a file with one line per observation, the lines will have a variable number of fields.

Different approaches to such data may be preferred depending on how complicated the structure is, on how much control you can exert over the format of the external text file, and on how large the input data will likely be. Solutions within R can be programmed flexibly for moderate complexity and moderate size by reading individual lines and then breaking them up by per-line calculations. The function readLines() does the first of these tasks efficiently. A variety of tools may then help with the second task; that is, breaking up character strings into fields. The function strsplit() specializes in splitting strings, usually according to a regular expression (see Section 8.3, page 298).

The programming details will depend heavily on the details of the text format. If you can exert some influence, your job will be easier. For example, suppose for the moment that the data consists of a number of ordinary, single-valued variables plus one variable with repeated observations. If the file can be organized to have the repeated observations on a separate line, following each line of the regular variables for the same observation, one can use readLines(), and then process the regular and the repeated values separately. That reduces the latter problem to reading repeated values *only*, and that in turn is done by a simple use of strsplit(). We begin then with a function splitRepeated(), for the second step, given the lines of repeated values:

```
splitRepeated <- function(lines,
          separator = "[[:space:]]+",
          numeric = NA) {
    value <- strsplit(lines, separator)
    if(!identical(numeric, FALSE)) {
       warned <- FALSE
       opt <- options(warn = -1); on.exit(options(opt))
       nValue <-  withCallingHandlers(lapply(value, as.numeric),
               warning = function(cond) warned <<- TRUE)
       if(!warned || identical(numeric, TRUE))
           value <- nValue
       options(opt)
       if(warned && identical(numeric, TRUE))
         warning("NAs introduced in coercing to numeric")
    }
    value
}
```

The function takes a regular expression to pass on to strsplit() as a separator. The default expression is interpreted as one or more white space characters, and is an example of the use of character classes in regular expressions (see page 301). It's the explicit equivalent of the default separator for function scan().

Because repeated observations are often of numeric data, the function attempts to interpret the imported data as numeric, unless told explicitly not to by the argument `numeric = FALSE`. The function `as.numeric()` will try to convert character string data to numeric and will produce `NA` and a warning message if one of the fields can't be interpreted as a number. By default, `splitRepeated()` treats the data as numeric if all the fields can be interpreted as such; that is, if there was no warning from `as.numeric()`. The technique for detecting the warning is a call handler. See Section 3.7, page 75, for this part of the example. The user can force numeric fields by supplying `numeric = TRUE`.

Given both ordinary variables (one value per observation) *and* some repeated observations, the next simplest pattern is to have one line of ordinary variables, followed by one line of repeated values. That can be reduced to the previous situation by reading in all lines and giving the even-numbered lines to `splitRepeated()`:

```
allLines <- readlines(con)
allLines <- matrix(allLines, nrow = 2)
repeatedObs <- splitRepeated(allLines[2,], ...)
regularVariables <- textConnection(allLines[1,])
```

Two techniques are used here. The first uses the fact that matrices in R are stored by column, meaning that a 2-row matrix has every odd element in the first row and every even element in the second row, and therefore giving a simple way to split the data. See page 326 for more on this technique. The second technique turns the odd-numbered lines into a text connection that allows us to apply any other input function to these lines (`read.table()` or `scan()`, for example). For text connections as objects, see Section 5.5.

For another approach to mixtures of repeated and non-repeated values, see Section 8.6, page 318. Arranging to put the repeated values on separate lines may involve some non-R techniques if the data does not start out in this form.

8.3 Regular Expressions

Regular expressions are a mechanism for encoding pattern-matching instructions into a character string, using certain printing characters not as literals but to define matching rules. The use of regular expressions is extremely widespread, particularly in any software influenced by the UNIX software tradition. It's likely that most readers of this book already have some acquaintance with them. The description in this section should be adequate for many programming tasks, but more detail is available from many sources, including the `?regex` documentation in R. Because Perl relies heavily on regular expressions, books and online documentation related to Perl are other good information sources.

Regular expressions essentially form a programming language for software that matches patterns in text data. Like expressions in R, regular expressions have a set of rules that allows them to be parsed and interpreted. The following description of regular expressions is intended to help you to build up an expression to correspond to a pattern that you understand informally. The description is not a formal or even semi-formal definition of a regular expression, but in my experience it covers much of what is needed in practice. Different languages may extend the definitions in incompatible ways, but most modern treatments of regular expressions will include at least what is shown here.

R doesn't use a special class for regular expression objects, so they are normally passed around as character strings, usually only a single string. In other languages, Perl for example, regular expressions may be integrated with the grammar of the language, not necessarily as an object. This section takes an R-like view in which `pattern` is a string to be interpreted as a regular expression.

In R, regular expressions will be applied by functions to text data, which will be an object of type `"character"`, x, or will be coerced to such an object. Each element of x is then a character string, to which the regular expression will be applied for either *matching* or *substitution*. In either case, applying the pattern to each string in x identifies a substring that is the match of `pattern` to the text, if the match was successful. Substitution operations take in addition a second text data argument, `replacement`, and return the result of substituting `replacement` for the matched substring, if any.

The Perl use of regular expressions is similar, in that operators take regular expressions and (single) strings as arguments for matching or substitution. The similarity may be disguised because Perl allows the matching and substitution to be written in a non-functional way, making the expression look like a command in one of the UNIX editors. The arguments in Perl are not necessarily objects, and substitution usually takes place in the string, rather than by returning a function value. But the major difference is in the rest of the programming context, where Perl and other scripting languages use less of a "whole object" view, so that operations with regular expressions are often applied to lines read from a data stream.

Regular expressions are requests to the function or operator to find a matching substring in a text string. The pattern is read from left to right, and each piece of the pattern (each *subexpression* of the expression) will be matched to the text.

Subexpressions include the following atomic patterns.

- Single characters that match themselves. If the character is one of the special characters (see below), it must be preceded by a backslash to become non-special.

- Bracket expressions, enclosed in square brackets. They match any of the characters defined by what's between the brackets. The character "^" as the first character is special; if it is present, the bracket expression matches any character *except* those defined by the rest of the bracket expression.

  Otherwise, each element is a single character, a character class (see page 301), or a range. Ranges are defined by two characters separated by a hyphen, but because they depend on how text is encoded, avoid them. You can nearly always use character classes instead.

- The character "." matches any character.

- Anchors. There are two, "^", again, but this time outside a bracket expression it matches the start of the string; and "$", which matches the end of the string.

Subexpressions can be *quantified* by following the subexpression with a quantifier. This says how many repeats of the subexpression will be matched. Three single characters are quantifiers: "*", matching zero or more repeats; "+", matching one or more repeats; and "?", matching zero or one repeats. Quantifiers can also be braced expressions giving either the number of repeats or a range, such as {4} to match exactly four occurrences of the preceding subexpression or {1,4} to match from one to four occurrences.

Because many of the special characters in regular expressions are also part of the S language grammar, it's important to *escape* the character if you need it to be interpreted literally. Special characters include:

    { } [ ] ( ) * + - | ? \ .

If any of these occurs literally as part of a pattern, you must precede it with a backslash to make it non-special. One further character, "&", is a special character in the `replacement` string and must be escaped to appear literally there.

This is far from the full grammar of regular expressions, but in my experience it is enough for most matching requirements, so let's stop here and go on to substitutions. For substitution only, one further special form is important, using parentheses to label subexpressions in the pattern. Thus "(*subexpression*)" matches the same text as "*subexpression*" but labels it. The labels are successive integers, matching the first parenthesized subexpression, the second, and so on, working from left to right in the matched substring.

The result of matching a pattern to a string is a substring, that is, a position i and a length n in the string. When we defined substrings on page 291, we allowed zero-length substrings, including the position at the beginning and end of the string, which can be matched using anchors. In substitution, the matched substring is removed and the `replacement` string provided is inserted in its place. But first, the replacement string is processed, using two special patterns in the replacement text. The single character "&" will be replaced by the substring that matched `pattern`. Escaped digits, that is the substrings "\1", "\2", ..., will be replaced by the first labeled substring, the second labeled substring, ...

Character classes

A character class in a regular expression is denoted by one of a number of reserved names, enclosed between "[:" and ":]". A character class is equivalent to writing out the corresponding sequence of characters. For example, "[:blank:]" is defined to be the character class containing the space and tab characters. In a bracket expression, it's equivalent to typing those two characters. Note that a character class is not itself a bracket expression: A bracket expression to match space or tab would be "[[:blank:]]". Character classes are important for making your regular expressions independent of locale, and should be used instead of ranges in bracket expressions whenever possible.

A number of computations in R depend on identifying alphabetic or alphanumeric characters (for example, the syntactic definition of a name in the language). It's important for good programming with R to remember that the answer is not universal; instead, it depends on the *locale*. The current locale defines names to include whatever characters are naturally alphanumeric in the language and script being used. In particular, letters need not be restricted to the usual 52 characters in the R objects `letters` and `LETTERS`, or the equivalent character range in a regular expression, "[a-zA-Z]". To make sure your programming will adapt to the locale, always use predefined character classes "[:alpha:]" and "[:alnum:]" for alphabetic and alphanumeric regular expressions. The definition of a letter depends on the text encoding of the locale, with the intention of allowing things that look like names, in the intuitive sense, to act as names where possible. Thus, for example, in a locale recognizing accented letters (such as UTF-8), tête is a valid name:

```
> tête <- head # a French version of the function
> tête(letters)
[1] "a" "b" "c" "d" "e" "f"
```

The definition of a name in the R version of the S language is any string consisting of letters, numbers, and the two characters "." and "_", with the first character being a letter or ".". As a regular expression this is:

```
nameRegexp <- "^[.[:alpha:]][._[:alnum:]]*$"
```

Another character class needed for regular expressions in R is "[:space:]", which stands for all the characters that can be interpreted as "white space", such as a blank, a tab or a newline. See ?regex for the standard character classes and Section 8.1, page 293, for locales and encoding.

Character classes are important for good programming with regular expressions, but unfortunately they make regular expressions even less readable, because of the double use of square brackets. For example, the regular expression matching one or more consecutive white space characters is

```
"[[:space:]]+"
```

The dual role of square brackets allows bracket expressions to contain any combination of character classes and individual characters, but the double-square-bracket form is the most common. Perl uses a different notation for character classes, preceding single letters by a back-slash; for example, \s is a character class equivalent to [:space:]. And Perl documentation actually uses the term "character class" for what is called a "range" above.

Example: Regular expressions to match object names

Suppose we want to find all the binary or unary operators available in R, in the base package. The task is not trivial, and there are several approaches. The rigorous approach is to study the formal grammar for the language, which will list the specifically recognized operator forms, but a grammar in the yacc form is not easy reading; understanding exactly what is included will be a challenge. We could, of course, examine the documentation, but that leads to several trails and we can't be sure we have followed them all.

A third, heuristic approach starts with the names of all the objects in the base package and peels away names used for other purposes. Operators have either special names, such as "+", or follow the convention of a name that starts and ends with the character "%". None of these corresponds to names that are syntactically legal for several other purposes, such as the following.

1. Regular syntactic names, as defined in `nameRegexp` above.

2. Replacement operators, such as "dim<-", which have names consisting of a syntactic name followed by "<-"

3. S3 methods, which end in a dot followed by the name of an S3 class.

We will construct regular expressions for each of these three cases, and eliminate the corresponding object names. We could do all this in a single regular expression but the result would be less readable and more prone to error. The general pattern illustrated by this example is to combine regular expressions with other features in the language, whether in R, Perl, or elsewhere, to obtain as simple and trustworthy a computation as possible. In this case we construct the regular expressions and apply them, using `grep()`, to eliminate the different possibilities.

```
> maybeOps <- objects("package:base", all.names=TRUE)
> nameRegexp <- "^[.[:alpha:]][._[:alnum:]]*$"
> maybeOps <- maybeOps[-grep(nameRegexp, maybeOps)]
> nameGetsRegexp <-  "^[.[:alpha:]][._[:alnum:]]*<-$"
> maybeOps <- maybeOps[-grep(nameGetsRegexp, maybeOps)]
> S3MethodRegexp <- "[.][[:alpha:]][._[:alnum:]]*$"
> maybeOps <- maybeOps[-grep(S3MethodRegexp, maybeOps)]
> maybeOps
 [1] "!"      "!="     "$"      "$<-"    "%%"     "%*%"    "%/%"    "%in%"
 [9] "%o%"    "%x%"    "&"      "&&"     "("      "*"      "+"      "-"
[17] "/"      ":"      "::"     ":::"    "<"      "<-"     "<<-"    "<="
[25] "="      "=="     ">"      ">="     "@"      "["      "[<-"    "[["
[33] "[[<-"   "^"      "{"      "|"      "||"     "~"
```

We ended up with a few extra names, but the output is now small enough to sort through visually. In addition to the desired operators, we have various functions related to `` `[` `` and `` `[[` ``, which are operators but not binary or unary; and also some functions that implement parts of the language, `` `{` `` and `` `(` ``.

Some of the individual regular expressions, such as S3MethodRegexp for S3 methods, may be useful in other contexts as well. Name matching for S3 methods matches any string that ends in a "." followed by a name. S3 methods have this form but so could an ordinary function. For example, plot.Date() is a method for plot() but plot.xy() is not, and plot.function() could be but in fact is used specially by the plot() function. There is, in fact, no sure way to identify a function as an S3 method (one of the reasons not to program with them, if you can avoid it, when trustworthy software is important).

8.4   Text Computations in R

R has functions for the basic text computations outlined on page 289:

```
match(x, table) # matching strings
grep(pattern, x)
sub(pattern, replacement, x)
```

These respectively match character data x to the values in table, search for regular expression pattern in x, and replace the substrings matching pattern with replacement. The grep() and sub() functions will treat pattern as a literal string if given the optional argument fixed = TRUE. There are many other text-related functions in the various R packages. See ?strsplit and ?substr, for example. A good place to look for others is the search engine at the R site: search.r-project.org or the more general search at rseek.org.

Using the functions above allows text computations in R similar to those in other systems; Section 8.6 has some examples. The remainder of the current section consists of two examples of text computations in a more specifically R style. Most of the details needed relate to R programming, rather than to elaborate text manipulation.

Example: Removing terms from a model formula

The first example arises when one wants to update a statistical model; in particular, the task at hand is to remove from the current model all the terms that involve a particular variable. We will then fit a new model and compare the two to understand the role of the deleted variable. In our very first programming example, Section 3.1, page 39, we worked on this problem and ended with a nice little function, dropModel(), on page 42. We left undefined a function it calls, dropFormula(), which works out a formula for dropping all the terms involving the variable. Now we'll fill in that gap.

When individual variables are factors, their interactions with other variables may be included in the model as well. The formula language for R has compact ways to express such interactions. For example, if the formula was y ~ x0 * (x1 + x2), then there are in fact two terms involving x1; namely, x1 itself and its interaction with x0, a term that is labeled "x0:x1" in output from the models software (in an analysis of variance table, for example).

To remove a variable, we must remove all the terms that include that variable. The task is to find all the term labels that involve the variable, and to construct a formula where each of these terms is preceded by a minus sign. In this example we want the formula ~ . -x1 - x0:x1.

To get at the term labels, we can use the `terms()` function. It returns an object that describes all the terms implied by a formula. This object is used by the statistical models software to set up numerical fitting, but as often happens the object-based approach to programming pays off in different uses of the object. Here's the term object for the formula above.

```
> terms(~ x0 * (x1 + x2))
~x0 * (x1 + x2)
attr(,"variables")
list(x0, x1, x2)
attr(,"factors")
   x0 x1 x2 x0:x1 x0:x2
x0  1  0  0     1     1
x1  0  1  0     1     0
x2  0  0  1     0     1
attr(,"term.labels")
[1] "x0"    "x1"    "x2"    "x0:x1" "x0:x2"
   etc.
```

Now we can see the two terms involving x1, giving us a way to construct the drop formula.

In fact, two attributes of the terms object have the information we need: "terms.label", containing string labels for each term; and "factors", a matrix with rows and row labels corresponding to variables, and columns and column labels corresponding to terms. The elements in the matrix are 1 if and only if the variable for that row is found in the term for that column. We can see those two attributes in the printout above. Check the documentation ?terms (which points you to ?terms.object) to see the details.

These two attributes give rise to two alternative computations of about the same complexity. One is to construct a regular expression that matches those labels in which the relevant variable occurs. The other, which we will use, does a more R-style computation, using the "factors" matrix, which actually has the desired information explicitly.

Each row of "factors" identifies the terms containing the corresponding variable. So if we pick off the column labels corresponding to a 1 in the row for the variable we want to drop, that's the correct set of term labels:

```
> formula <- y ~ x0 * (x1 + x2)
> fMatrix <- attr(terms(formula), "factors")
> whichTerms <- fMatrix["x1",] == 1
> colnames(fMatrix)[whichTerms]
[1] "x1"      "x0:x1"
```

These are the terms we need to drop from the model in order to remove the variable x1. The corresponding formula for update() is ~ . - x1 - x0:x1.

The function paste() can generate this expression as a character string given those labels. Evaluating that string as if it was typed to R then gives us the formula we want. This is done in two steps, first calling parse() with argument text=, and then eval to evaluate the parsed expression. If the text could have been more than one expression or the evaluation could have depended on the context, you have to be more careful. See the function evalText() in the SoDA package.

We are now in a position to write the function dropFormula() taking a formula (or a fitted model) and returning a formula suitable for a call to update():

```
dropFormula <- function(original, drop) {
    factors <- attr(terms(as.formula(original)),
                    "factors")
    row <-  match(drop, rownames(factors))
    whichTerms <- factors[row,] == 1
    labels <- colnames(factors)[whichTerms]
    text <- paste("~ . ",
                  paste("-", labels, collapse = " "))
    eval(parse(text = text))
}
```

Notice the nested calls to paste(): The inner call pastes "-" in front of each term label and then collapses the character vector (of length 2 in the example) into a single string, so that we get only one "~" pasted in front in the outer call. This sort of manipulation is common when dealing with text in R. If it gets too complicated, interpret that as a suggestion that some other text-manipulation tools might be more convenient.

Example: Merging documentation sections

Our second example illustrates text computations that fit well with R: the data is naturally organized as R character vectors (lists of them in this case), and the operations work with these objects relatively directly, rather than iteratively modifying the text inside the strings.

The objective is to generate automatic documentation outlines for several related functions. It's often useful to document closely related functions together. Users can be led to choose the function for their needs, and shared information such as common arguments can be documented in one place. For example, the functions `get()`, `exists()`, and `assign()` perform closely related tasks and have many common arguments, but also some inconsistencies that often confuse users. They are not documented together but doing so would probably help users to avoid some common errors.

To get started with such documentation, we would like a function that produces a documentation outline in one file for several function objects. The existing function `prompt()` generates documentation outlines, but only for a single function. The function `promptAll()` in the SoDA package associated with this book provides the same facility for several functions.

This example looks at a portion of the design for `promptAll()`, based on merging the output of `prompt()` for each of the functions. Starting with a function object, `prompt()` infers the formal arguments, and uses these to create sections referred to as `usage` (the calling sequence) and `arguments` (a list of items for each argument), along with other documentation sections. These are normally written as a file in the R documentation markup language, which is roughly a dialect of LaTeX. However, a useful option to `prompt()` is `filename = NA`, which causes the documentation to be returned as a named list instead of being printed. The `"arguments"` component of the list is the arguments section of the documentation, as a character vector, one element per line of the documentation.

The trick for `promptAll()` is to merge the lists from the individual calls to `prompt()`, to create one documentation object with the same format. We want to keep all the relevant information but not to repeat duplicated lines. In particular, the `arguments` section should merge the unique information, but only have repeated argument names appear once.

The example deals with the subproblem of merging corresponding sections for several functions, to be done by a function `mergeSections()`. Its first argument, `input`, is a list, each element of the list being the same section for a different function. To see how the computations might work, let's look at one section for one function, the `arguments` section of the `prompt()`

output for get():

```
> prompt(get, filename = NA)$arguments
[1] "\\arguments{"
[2] "  \\item{x}{ ~~Describe \\code{x} here~~ }"
[3] "  \\item{pos}{ ~~Describe \\code{pos} here~~ }"
[4] "  \\item{envir}{ ~~Describe \\code{envir} here~~ }"
[5] "  \\item{mode}{ ~~Describe \\code{mode} here~~ }"
[6] "  \\item{inherits}{ ~~Describe \\code{inherits} here~~ }"
[7] "}"
```

You might do the same computation for exists() and assign(), and compare the results. There are two important points. First, the beginning and end of the text is always the same; in fact it's the required invocation of the \arguments{ } command in the documentation markup language. Second, each of the other lines differs only by the name of the argument. This gives us a test for repeated argument names: If the same argument name appears in two functions, the exact same string will be generated, meaning that identical character strings will appear in the prompt() lists for the two functions.

Our goal is to list all the arguments from all the functions, with no duplicates, inside one invocation of \arguments. Here's the specific idea: split the section for the first function into the fixed start and end plus the variable middle part, then for each later function insert the new argument names at the end of the middle section.

How to do this in R? It's pretty easy. The input is a list with one element for the section in each function, the elements being character vectors having one string per line, as usual. We'll use the function match() to find any new arguments not in previous elements, and we will concatenate these with the middle part that has been built up so far.

One more point in making a useful function. Examining the documentation outline shows that the same pattern applies to other sections, for example usage. What differs is how many lines of fixed text at the beginning and at the end need to be kept to wrap around the lines generated for these functions (one at the beginning and one at the end for the arguments section). By making these arguments to mergeSections(), we get a function that can be called by promptAll() for several sections. Finally, an argument sep says what if anything should be inserted between the output for successive functions; by default, it's an empty line.

Here's a version of the function.

```
mergeSections <- function(input,
    keepFirst = 1, keepLast = 1, sep = "") {
  item <- input[[1]]
  start <- item[seq(length=keepFirst)]
  end <- item[seq(length=keepLast, to=length(item))]
  middle <- character(); all <- c(start, end)
  for(i in seq(along=input)) {
    item <- input[[i]]
    item <- item[is.na(match(item, all))]
    middle <- c(middle, sep, item)
    all <- c(all, item)
  }
  c(start, middle, end)
}
```

A few points of detail need mentioning. The `match()` function returns `NA` for a non-match, so indexing with `is.na(match(...))` gets unique lines. We update an object, `all`, with all the unique lines so we don't need to strip off the first and last lines from each section; they just fall out with the test for unique lines. And we iterated over all the sections after extracting the start and end pieces, rather than doing some clumsy work outside the loop just to save one step in the iteration.

We can reflect again on the aspects that make this example comfortable for programming in R. The iteration involved is over objects, while the computations for each object are expressed directly. The computation in this sense would be called naturally *vectorized* (discussed in general in Section 6.4, page 158). In particular, we never need to iterate over lines of text. It's key that `input` is conveniently set up as a list of the relevant vectors. That computation is done in the calling function, `promptAll()`, taking advantage of the optional `filename = NA` for `prompt()`.

Notice that nobody is writing files here: When possible, text computations in R should work from text objects and return text objects as their results. It's easy to convert these to files, but less easy at times to convert the files back to usable objects.

8.5   Using and Writing Perl

This section covers briefly some of the main points in using existing Perl software and in building on it. We begin with basic techniques, sufficient for some simple and typical uses of Perl in computing with data. After this is a short discussion of two convenient ways to interact with Perl in order to develop your own software: either through Perl's own debugger or through an inter-system interface from R . Next, we give some more extended examples to demonstrate both techniques in Perl and a few more points about organizing computations. If you're new to Perl, you should be able to imitate the examples, but do go to a good tutorial or manual to get a more extended exposition. And if you're not new to Perl, please scan this section anyway; the brief explanations shouldn't hold you up very long, and we do pick and choose Perl computations that work well with the programming style in the rest of the book.

After the examples, we will look at Perl slightly more formally, but still quite selectively, emphasizing some aspects that differ from the style and programming model of R, and that may therefore trap the exploring R programmer.

The basics: Reading, writing, and functions

Although Perl can be used in many ways, it began as an extension of other tools that processed text files. The style of these tools was to read information a line at a time from the input, process the line, and then write the processed line to the output. Such basic UNIX tools as sed and awk work this way. It remains a good model for using Perl as well, although that model can be extended greatly, particularly by using Perl functions. Processing text in this form is one of Perl's strengths, and something it does more naturally than R.

Perl has a syntax similar to that of R and other C-style languages. To give the flavor of typical useful Perl computations, the next part of the section presents a simple example, first as a stand-alone program, then in a functional form.

Here is a Perl program that reads lines of input, removes simple HTML commands (`"tags"`), and writes the modified lines to the output. The substitution is done by matching a regular expression to the form of an HTML tag, that is, text enclosed in angle brackets.

```
while($line = <STDIN>) {
    $line =~ s/<[^>]*>//g;
    print $line;
}
```

If the program were stored in the file `"htmlOut.prl"`, it could be run by the shell command:

```
$ perl htmlOut.prl < dataWithHTML.txt > dataCleaned.txt
```

The input data on file `"dataWithHTML.txt"` will be processed by the Perl script and the output written to file `"dataCleaned.txt"`.

Let's examine how this little program works. If you are unfamiliar with Perl, the details may be helpful. For more details, there is also a wealth of Perl documentation available, including extensive online man pages.

Perl reads and writes by using *filehandles*, very special Perl types that are analogous to connections in R. Like connections, filehandles are created by opening a file, creating a pipe, or connecting to a socket or similar object. Like connections, filehandles can be opened in different modes depending on the sort of input and/or output desired. Some filehandles are predefined, including STDIN, the standard input in the usual sense of UNIX or C. It's no coincidence that both connections and filehandles build on the behavior of input/output in C. R and Perl are both providing some basic C-style facilities, in a higher-level form.

Reading a line from a filehandle is a special operator, denoted by angle brackets, as in <STDIN>. Each call to this operator reads the next line from the filehandle and returns the line as a string. In our example, the line of text is assigned to a Perl variable, $line. Ordinary Perl variable names always appear with the preceding $, partly to distinguish them from function names.

The style of assigning inside the condition of a loop is typical in Perl; when the program reaches the end of the file, the read operation returns a null, treated as FALSE. (Perl treats many things as FALSE, including empty strings, the number zero, and null elements. Beware: nasty programming bugs can result if you think only a boolean FALSE will cause a condition to fail.)

The first line inside the loop modifies the string by using a special assignment operator, "=~". The right side of the call to the operator is a substitute expression, similar to those used in UNIX-style editors (vi, sed, and others). It substitutes an empty string for all instances of the regular expression consisting of a left angle-bracket followed by anything up to and including the first right angle-bracket. The effect is to remove any HTML commands completely contained in the line of text. The program then prints the modified line of text, to standard output by default. The text already includes a newline character (just which character depends on your operating system and possibly your locale), so no explicit newline is added.

So here we have a very simple but complete Perl program to remove most HTML commands from files. It's not a seriously useful program; for one thing, it does no checking for the proper structure of an HTML file, but it does illustrate the fundamental Perl style. As soon as we want something more ambitious or want to reuse the computations in other applications, it's wise to structure the Perl code in terms of functions, just as in R. Which raises the question: How alike or different are R and Perl in terms of functions? After all, the little example above doesn't seem all that functional when examined in detail. We called s a function (and it is a Perl function) to perform a substitution in a string, but it looks more like the corresponding command in a text editor. And the call to print had a space, not a parenthesis, before the argument. How deep are these differences, and how important in practice? The answer, roughly, is that there are some important differences in the computational model for the two languages, but fortunately you can avoid worrying much about the differences if you keep things simple and follow examples of working Perl code as much as possible.

Meanwhile, on to writing functions. Perl functions are not created as ordinary objects, but instead by the special sub expression. The syntax of this expression is simply the sub keyword follolwed by the name of the new function followed by the body of the function as a braced set of subexpressions. The previous computations could be organized as a function, htmlOut say, with the main program now a loop that modified each line of input via a call to the htmlOut function.

```
sub htmlOut {
    my($text) = @_;
    $text =~ s/<[^>]*>//g;
    $text;
}

while($line = <STDIN>) {
    $line = htmlOut($line);
    print $line;
}
```

The expression my(...) creates local variables; the expression @_ refers to the arguments in the call to our function; see page 315 for more detail on these mechanisms.

Testing and debugging Perl code

As noted in Chapter 1, R's standard model for computation is interactive exploration, a session with R in which the user supplies expressions, R evaluates them and displays the results. Batch scripts—fixed programs to do the same or very similar complete computations repeatedly—are special constructions, and relatively rare. Perl has the opposite situation. Standard

computation is a Perl *program*, a file of source that Perl runs, typically when
invoked as a shell-level command:

```
$ perl htmlOut.prl
```

as we did in the example above.

How then, can one conveniently develop, test and debug new software
in Perl? Two convenient ways are to use Perl's own debugger or to do most
of your computing in R, passing test data to Perl via some inter-system
interface. Which is more convenient depends on the application and on
your own tastes. If you're primarily working in R and inserting a few, fairly
self-contained Perl computations, the interface will be straightforward. If
you need to work out a more extended set of Perl techniques, and these can
be tested pretty much on their own, the Perl debugger may allow quicker
changes in the Perl content.

Let's begin with the Perl debugger, or more correctly with Perl used in
debug mode, initiated by invoking the `perl` command with the -d option.
The debugger is designed to debug a Perl program, and you have to give it
one to get into the interaction. To run the program `htmlOut.prl` above, but
in debug mode,

```
$ perl -d htmlOut.prl
```

However, if you have only a partial set of functions, or would like to start the
debugger from scratch, you can give a dummy program, as an expression on
the command line. The following, giving it the expression 1 as a complete
program, is about the minimal typing:

```
$ perl -de 1

Loading DB routines from perl5db.pl version 1.22
Editor support available.

Enter h or 'h h' for help, or 'man perldebug' for more help.

main::(-e:1):   1
  DB<1>
```

At this point, you can type complete Perl expressions, which will be evaluated when you enter a newline. It's roughly like interacting with R, although
in some ways not as convenient. For example, expressions cannot be continued over multiple lines and there is no automatic printing. On the other
hand, you are in a debugger, whose commands provide you with many compensating conveniences. To print an expression, make it the argument to
the debugger command p:

```
    DB<2> p 1..5
    12345
```

The Perl debugger has many of the usual commands for a C-style debugger, such as b to put a break point at the call to a function, and s to step a line at a time through the code in the function.

Intersystem interfaces to Perl

So much for using Perl directly. What about using Perl from R? There are several possibilities.

Given a stand-alone, executable file of Perl source code similar to our "htmlOut.prl" example, the simplest interface uses the system() function to run Perl on the relevant data. Given some text in the R character vector htmlIn, the computation could be:

```
    > noTags <- system("perl htmlOut.perl", intern = TRUE,
    +      input = htmlIn)
```

The intern = TRUE option causes the output to be returned as a character vector, one element per line.

Running a Perl program on each R function call will be unsatisfactory if we need to test a variety of Perl functions or to keep data in Perlbetween calls from R. The Perl program can have command-line arguments to get some flexibility, but anything nontrivial will quickly become tedious to implement and change. In addition, the per-call computational overhead of running the Perl program may become significant if the computation being done is fairly small, and has to be done repeatedly.

An alternative approach is to use the general inter-system interface, RSPerl, available from the omegahat repository, at the Web site omegahat.org/RSPerl. The simplest way to think of this interface is that it makes essentially any Perl function available to be called from R. Typically, the interface will be used by writing a corresponding R function that manages the arguments and invokes the Perl function. There are a number of advantages to this approach, which is discussed in general in Chapter 12. It submerges most of the details of the inter-system interface, leaving us with functions that behave essentially like any R functions. It also provides a level of generality in what we can do in Perl that is difficult to attain with any more specialized interface.

The price of using the RSPerl interface is essentially that we now have three pieces of software involved, not two. The interface needs to be installed in the environment where you (or those using your software) are working.

This is essentially a one-time overhead, but it has to be done for each computing environment, and can involve problems at a lower level (for example, C libraries) than simply running Perl itself.

Functions, variables, and data in Perl.

Perl has an essentially fixed set of "things" to which a named variable can correspond. The important ones are: scalars (which include strings), arrays, hash tables, and functions. Any variable can be used in any way at any time (using a non-function as a function generates an error; most other invalid uses produce undef). For each of the four types, preceding the variable name with a corresponding special character tells the Perl evaluator how to use the variable: "$" for scalar use, "@" for array, "%" for hash, and "&" for function. It's important to understand what "use" means here: it is the computation in the expression—what Perl calls the *context*—that counts, not the implicit "type" of the data currently contained by the variable. For example, to create an array with a particular variable name is to use the name in an *array context*, implying the "@" form:

```
@dmy = (7, 3, 4);
```

On the other hand, to extract a (scalar) element from the same variable is a scalar use, implying the "$" prefix:

```
$dmy[0];
```

The most important array is @_, containing the flattened concatenation of all the arguments to the current function call.

As in R, much of the programming in Perl consists of calls to functions. The mechanism used determines much of the style of programming required in the language, and also relates directly to how data is organized. Perl has no formal arguments for functions. Instead, all the actual arguments are concatenated into a flat list of scalars, assigned as the local Perl variable named "_".

Perl has a general, low-level mechanism to create *references*. An expression consisting of a backslash preceding any form of a variable name creates a scalar reference to that data. So, for example, \@dmy creates a scalar quantity that contains a reference to the array dmy. By dereferencing the scalar, one gets back to the array.

There are several ways to dereference in Perl. One general way is fairly easy to remember: Following any of the four special characters by an expression in braces says to evaluate the braced expression and use the value as a

reference to the type of data implied by the special character. For example,
consider the expression:

```
my(@fields) = @{$_[0]};
```

This expression says to assign as an array the quantity referenced by the
first element of the array named "_". Remember that this array contains all
the arguments in a function call.

Therefore, if function `f` had the above line in its code, and it was called
in the form:

```
f(\@dmy);
```

the array `@fields` would be assigned the array data computed by dereferencing the first argument. This creates a copy of the original array, so that
computations in the function can alter an array or hash without having side
effects outside the function itself.

Passing and using arguments with this semantic style maintains essentially the "functional model", in that changes made to the array in the
function are local. This is only one way to handle arguments. Other applications may *not* want to copy a hash or array, in which case the references
will be passed directly. If the object wisto be used as a proxy in R for an
object in Perl that needs to be maintained and updated, it's the reference
itself that is needed. Let's look at an example.

Example: Perl functions for counting chunks of text

As a small but typical example, let's look at a technique for counting patterns in text. This might be part of a toolkit for analyzing text data, using
Perl. The concept is that prior to calling the function we're about to write,
the analysis has found a stream of instances of certain text patterns. The
patterns may be fixed strings or they may be regular expression patterns; either way, by this point we just have a vector of character data, each element
of which represents one occurrence of the corresponding pattern. What we
want now is to update the *distribution* of the patterns, which we'll represent
as a table of counts. The new data may be in the process of being added to
the current distribution, but if we're keeping a running window of current
data, it might also be dropped. We'll write functions for both.

Section 12.4, page 436, develops an interface function to use these techniques from R.

A Perl `hash` is an object in which scalar values are assigned and extracted
corresponding to string-valued keys. A `hash` works well to represent a distribution if we arrange that the value corresponding to a pattern (that is,

to the string representing the pattern) is the count of how many times the pattern has occurred. Because we want to update the distribution, it makes sense to keep the hash in Perl from one call to the next; therefore, we pass in a reference, and return that reference as the value of the call.

The other argument is an array of the new data, chunks. We could pass that in as a reference and dereference it, but it happens to be the last argument, and a typical Perl trick is just to append the entire corresponding object to the argument list. The last argument doesn't need to be a reference; the array elements will be flattened out in the call and then re-assembled into an array. Here's a version of the code:

```perl
sub chunks_add {
    my($tref, @chunks) = @_;
    my($chunk);

    foreach $chunk (@chunks) {
      $$tref{$chunk} = $$tref{$chunk} + 1;
    }
    return $tref;
}

sub chunks_drop {
    my($tref, @chunks) = @_;
    my( $chunk, $count);

    foreach $chunk (@chunks) {
      $count = $$tref{$chunk} - 1;

      if($count > 0) { $$tref{$chunk} = $count;}
      elsif ($count == 0)  {delete $$tref{$chunk}; }
      else {die
    "Decrementing a chunk (\"$chunk\") not in the table";}
    }
    return $tref;
}
```

We would be justified in working fairly hard to make this computation efficient; fortunately, Perl has done a very good job of implementing hash tables, so the basic lookup implied by {$chunk} will do fine for most conceivable applications.

Notice that there are no explicit hash objects in the two routines (hash object names would start with "%"). That's a bit startling and not ideal for reading the code, but natural to the use of references in Perl. Whenever we

access or set an element of the hash table, we refer to the scalar element
(a leading `"$"`) of the reference to the table, which is itself a scalar, `$tref`;
hence, the prevalent idiom of `$$tref{$chunk}`.

These routines do some error checking, and use the standard Perl `die`
statement. If that sounds a bit drastic in code intended to be used from
R, not to worry. The `RSPerl` interface does a nice job of wrapping the
resulting error message and exiting the calling R expression cleanly, with no
permanent damage.

8.6   Examples of Text Computations

In this section we examine or re-examine some examples, looking both at
R and Perl. Choosing and designing computations for text data involves
many tradeoffs. Nearly any example can be treated in multiple ways, more
than one of which might be suitable depending on the experience of the
programmer and/or the size or detailed characteristics of the application.

The examples illustrate some of the choices and the tradeoffs they involve.

Data with repeated values

A common departure from strictly "rectangular" or data-frame-like structure comes when some variables are observed repeatedly, so that the observation is not a single number or quantity, but several repetitions of the
same quantity. If the number of repetitions varies from one observation to
the next, the data has a list-like structure: in R terminology, each observation is an element in the list consisting of a vector of the values recorded for
that observation. Either R or Perl can deal with such data in a simple way.
The differences are useful to consider.

To import such data, there must be a way to distinguish the repeated
values from other variables. The simplest case diverts the repeated values to
a separate file, written one line per set of repeated observations. In Section
8.2, page 296, we showed a computation for this case, based on reading the
lines of repeated values as separate strings and then splitting them by calling
`strplit()`. Here's an alternative, allowing a more flexible form of data. In
this version, successive lines may have different formats, provided each of
the lines is interpretable by the `scan()` function. The lines might come in
pairs, with the first line of each pair having non-repeated variables and the
second the repeated values.

For example, the first line might be data for a state in the United States, with the abbreviation, population, area, and center (as in the `state` data of the R `datasets` package). The following line might list data for the largest cities in the state, say the name, population, and area for a variable number of cities. The first ten lines of such a file, using commas as separators, looks something like this:

```
AL,4447100,50708,32.5901,-86.7509
Birmingham,242820,149.9,Montgomery,201568,155.4,Mobile,etc.
AK,626932,566432,49.25,-127.25
Anchorage,260283,1697.3
AZ,5130632,113417,34.2192,-111.625
Phoenix,1321045,474.9,Tucson,486699,194.7,Mesa,396375,etc.
AR,2673400,51945,34.7336,-92.2992
Little Rock,183133,116.2,Fort Smith,80268,50.4,North Little etc.
CA,33871648,156361,36.5341,-119.773
Los Angeles,3694820,469.1,San Diego,1223400,324.4,San Jose,etc.
```

How would we read in such data? The state data and the city data, separately, could each be read by a call to `scan()`. That function takes an argument, `what`, which is a template for the fields (see Section 8.2, page 296). For the state data:

```
what = list(abb = "", population = 1, area = 1,
            latitude = 1, longitude = 1)
```

and for the city data:

```
what = list(name = "", population = 1, area = 1)
```

Let's assume some pre-processing has been done if necessary, so that the city data for each state is on a single line. The technique for reading repeated values in this approach is to apply `scan()` repeatedly, with a separate `what` argument each time. Let's show the function, `scanRepeated()`, and then analyze how it works:

```
scanRepeated <- function (file, what, ...) {
    lines <- readLines(file)
    scanText <- function(text, what, quiet = TRUE, ...) {
        con <- textConnection(text, "r")
        value <- scan(con, what, quiet = quiet, ...)
        close(con)
        value
    }
```

```
        mapply(scanText, lines, what, MoreArgs = list(...),
               SIMPLIFY = FALSE)
}
```

The `what` argument in this case is a list whose *elements* are the individual `what` arguments to `scan()`; in the state and city data:

```
what = list(
    list(abb = "", population = 1, area = 1,
         latitude = 1, longitude = 1),
    list(name = "", population = 1, area = 1)
)
```

The workhorse is the function `mapply()` from the R base package. This repeatedly calls the function supplied as its first argument, `scanText()` in this case, with the first element of `lines` and the first element of `what`, then with the second element of each, and so on. Arguments to `mapply()` will be recycled, so that all the odd-numbered lines of the file will be scanned with the first element of `what` and all the even-numbered lines with the second element. Arguments supplied as `MoreArgs=`, however, are passed down directly. The use of `MoreArgs` in `scanRepeated()` allows the call to pass arbitrary arguments down to `scan()`.

The rest of the `scanRepeated()` function sets up the data for `mapply()` in two simple steps. First, all the lines of the file are read in. Second, a local function `scanText()` is defined to treat each resulting character string as a `"connection"` object in a call to `scan()`, which returns the vector of data values in that line. Each call to `scanText()` from `mapply()` will open a line of text as a separate connection. To be neat, we explicitly open and close the text connection; this is not strictly required, but is a good practice. To be very conscientious, we would have used `on.exit()` to close the connection in case of an error.

It's interesting to compare this computation with the approach in Section 8.2, page 297, where we turned the vector corresponding to `lines` into a matrix and then used a single text connection and a single call to `scan()` to read in all the odd-numbered lines. That computation ought to be more efficient for large files, because `scanRepeated()` will require more calls to `scan()`, 49 more in the state-data example. On the other hand, `scanRepeated()` is more general, in that it can handle many different patterns of repeated and non-repeated fields via different `what` arguments. As an exercise, consider writing a fancier version of `scanRepeated()` that takes an argument to specify that certain elements of `what()` have no repeated fields. This version could combine the best of both examples, but you may need to think carefully about the best organization for the value returned.

A similar Perl computation can be written for either version of the example. In fact, a computation analogous to `splitRepeated()` on page 297 often serves to illustrate the Perl notion of an "array of arrays", somewhat analogous to a list in R.

```
sub split_repeated {
  my($input, $output, $sep) = @_;
  my($line, @value, @fields);
  while($line = <$input>) {
    @fields = split($sep, $line);
    push @value, [ @fields ];
  }
  return @value;
}
```

The concept is similar to the R implementation: take each line and pass it to a function that splits the fields. Make the vector (array in Perl) the corresponding element of the result. As usual, the Perl computation is iterative, a line at a time. There are some touchy details for those not familiar with Perl, such as putting square brackets around the `@fields` expression when pushing it as the new last element of the `@value` array. A similar function could be written analogous to `scanRepeated()`. Iteration being encouraged in Perl, there is no need to involve an explicit apply-style function as we did in R.

For large applications, the Perl computations will be more efficient. Both R and Perl apply a function to each line of text, but such iteration has less overhead in Perl, particularly for built-in functions. The catch with the Perl version, for R users, is what to do with the generated data. For some applications, a suitable technique uses the RSPerl interface to maintain the object in Perl, with further computations applied as appropriate. (The example in Section 12.4, page 436, uses a similar strategy.)

Parsing strings as dates

To illustrate both computations in Perl and their use in data analysis, let's consider interpreting some strings as calendar dates, when we do not know in advance the style in which the dates are being written. The task may seem trivial, but only if you have never needed to deal with such data in any extensive application. Several features make the example interesting.

There are many variants in formatting dates, both between and within different geographic regions. The sixth day of the month of May in the year 1976 might be written in at least the following ways.

```
5/6/76
6/5/76
May 6, 1976
May 6, 76
6.v.1976
1976 May 6
1976-05-06
```

The second string, a valid British form for May 6, is also a valid form for June 5, 1976, in the United States. And May is an easy month because nobody abbreviates the name. If the date had been in September, the month could be written in full, or as "Sep", or as "Sept", with or without trailing ".". To keep the example simple, we are also ignoring the time portion of a typical date-time string.

Both R and Perl have software for handling dates. In particular, Perl has a variety of modules on its CPAN archive, including `Date::Manip`, an extensive collection of functions for transforming and manipulating strings representing dates.

Most of this software, however, makes some assumptions about the date format, or expects the user to specify either the format or enough information to disambiguate the format. Also, the Perl packages tend to work with a single date at a time, whereas most computations in data analysis will encounter a vector of date strings (which is relevant in that the interpretation of a single string in the form "5/2/76" is ambiguous, but a subsequent string of the form "5/22/76" resolves the format to be the American version).

The SoDA package has a small collection of Perl software to, first, figure out the format of an array of date strings, and then to convert them to numeric dates. Let's examine some of the basic computations used in that software, illustrating some useful features of Perl in the process.

Here are a number of simple Perl functions and objects to recognize the individual fields holding day, month, or year.

```
%roman = (
        i => 1, ii=>2, iii=>3, iv=>4, v=>5,
        vi=>6, vii=>7, viii=>8, ix=>9, x=>10,
        xi=>11, xii=>12);

sub monthRoman {
    $roman{$_[0]};
```

```
}

sub monthText {
    $Months{$_[0]};
}

sub monthNumber {
    my $string = $_[0];
    $string =~ /^([1-9]|1[12]|0[1-9])$/ ?
    $string+0 : undef;
}

sub dayNumber {
    my $string = $_[0];
    $string =~ /^(0{0,1}[1-9]|[12]\d|3[01])$/ ?
    $string+0 : undef;
}

sub year4Digit {
    my $string = $_[0];
    $string =~ /^\d{4}$/ ?
    $string+0 : undef;
}

## will choose 20th or 21st century, whichever
## is nearer:  this year + 50 is the boundary
$bdyYear = ((localtime)[5]) % 100 + 49;

sub year2Digit {
    my $string = $_[0];
    if($string !~ /^\d{2}$/) {
    return ;
    }
    my $year = $string + 0;
    ($year < $bdyYear) ? 2000 + $year : 1900 + $year;
}

@dayFuns = (\&dayNumber);
@monthFuns = (\&monthText, \&monthNumber, \&monthRoman);
@yearFuns = (\&year4Digit, \&year2Digit);
```

The first definition, %roman, is a hash table (*hash* in Perl). It maps each of the Roman numerals up to 12 into the corresponding number. The following definition of function monthRoman takes its first argument and tries to select the corresponding month number from the hash table. Any argument that is not one of the Roman numerals will fail to match in the hash. As often in Perl, the result is a special value, undef. All the functions above follow a common and useful Perl convention of returning undef to indicate failure.

To review some basics: Perl functions don't have a formal argument list. Instead, there is a special Perl array with the name "_" that contains the actual arguments. The expression $_[0] extracts the first element of this array. As with R, functions in Perl return the last expression evaluated, with the option of using an explicit return expression instead. For more basics, see any good introduction to Perl. Here are some of the main points in the computations for this example.

The function monthText looks up the month as a number, from a hash table (not shown) containing both month names and their accepted abbreviations. This is the key data structure in our approach that would allow dealing with non-English text. One could augment the hash table with as many languages (or *locales*) as convenient, without changing the logic.[1] Alternatively, appropriate tables could be loaded on demand for the current locale. Perl, like R, has facilities for dealing with general alphabets that allow substantial international flexibility.

The remaining functions all recognize valid numeric codes for month, day, and year. They return the corresponding numerical value, or undef if the match fails. All of them use variations on regular expressions, including extensions, such as the {4} modifier, in function year4Digit, that says to match exactly 4 occurrences of the preceding pattern. The preceding \d is Perl's notation for the character class written as [:digit:] in other languages (see page 301).

Notice that we used Perl for a variety of computations with text, in addition to its well-known facility with regular expressions. The two hash-table functions are both more flexible and simpler than any equivalent regular expression. Think of a natural way to express your computation and then see if Perl has an analogous mechanism: Perl's famous motto is *TMTOWTDI*, *T*here's *M*ore *T*han *O*ne *W*ay *T*o *D*o *I*t.

Below all the function definitions on page 323 are three lines creating three Perl arrays. Each array holds *references* to some of the functions. The character "&" before each name identifies it as a function, and the character "\" before that creates a reference to the function. The top level of the Perl code for recognizing dates (not shown here) takes triples of fields and determines whether each field could be any of a day, a month, or a year. It

---

[1]Well, assuming that no two languages used the same text for a *different* month.

does this by calling each of the functions in the array; if any of them returns anything other than undef, the field is still in the running. For testing day format, there is only one function; for a month there are three, allowing numbers, names, or Roman numerals; for a year, either two or four digits.

As the code proceeds through lines of date input, some possibilities will fail. Eventually, we expect that just one of the patterns such as (day, month, year) or (month, day, year) will remain valid. At that point testing is over and the code can translate the dates in the desired standard form. See the file "perl/dateForm.perl", in the installed SoDA package for the details.

As in this example, Perl is often adept at implementing relatively fuzzy computations, although sometimes with code that the *Prime Directive* would find dangerous; here too, our example illustrates the point. Arrays of references that are asserted to point to compatible functions that return consistent types of values are not a formally defined class. Perl does in fact support a version of OOP that can be useful when more structured and verifiable programming is needed. Other scripting languages, such as Python, might be more appropriate in such applications, however.

Example: Converting fields to lines

Let's consider the task of converting fields of text input in free format into text with a fixed number of fields per line. The conversion is required to import data via utilities that enforce a line-oriented view, such as the read.table() function in R or the data import mechanism in Excel (see the discussion in Section 6.5 starting on page 166). The line-oriented view helps to prevent user errors and is also easier to program for the import software. However, it's natural to generate the data in a free-format mode; for example, if one wants to include fields of narrative text, multi-line fields are likely. So our goal is some software to convert from free-form to line-oriented text, preferably software that can be adapted easily to explore various forms of input data (the *Mission*). First, a simple formulation in R, then a version in Perl that may be more suited to large-scale applications.

For either version, we have to formulate the task more precisely. This is actually a nontrivial step, because different formulations suit one or the other system better. If the goal really is to provide input for an import procedure, the natural formulation is to copy from one connection (R) or filehandle (Perl) to another. We also have to decide the form of the solution, for example, perhaps a function taking the input connection and other information as arguments. A function is the natural form for R, because functions are the basic unit of programming. Perl also deals well with functions, but we might prefer a solution as a free-standing Perl program. We'll allow the details to vary between the two systems, because that will turn out to be helpful.

The R function has four main arguments:

```
fieldsToLines(input, nfield, sep, outputSep)
```

where `input` is a connection for the free format input, `nfield` is the desired number of fields per line, `sep` is the input separator character, and `outputSep` is the field separator for the output. We will define the function to return the desired output connection as the value of the call; a somewhat unusual approach for most languages but natural for a functional language such as R.

R can implement this function with a simple and elegant computation. If we browse among R input functions, we quickly see that `scan()` can read free-format input if we specify the field-separator character. There are a few limitations to `scan()`, to be noted, but basically we can read in all the fields as a character vector by:

```
text <- scan(input, what = "", sep = sep)
```

Now we want to group the elements of `text`, `nfield` items at a time, making each group into a line. Here we need to think in "whole object" terms. We would like to deal with the data in an object where we can talk about groups of `nfield` items easily. A natural choice is a matrix where either rows or columns correspond to the groups. Either would work, but we can use the knowledge that R stores matrices by columns to make the actual computation trivial:

```
text <- matrix(text, nrow = nfield)
```

The lines of text we want correspond to the columns of the matrix: The first `nfield` fields are the first column, and so on. For the output connection, each line is formed by pasting together the items in the column, separated by the `outputSep` character. The R function `paste()` will do this, with argument `collapse=outputSep`. We have to call `paste()` separately for each column, which could be done in a loop but is just what function `apply()` is designed for:

```
output <- apply(text, 2, paste, collapse = outputSep)
```

The call to `apply()` calls the function `paste()` for each column of `text`, and passes along the extra argument `collapse` as well; see `?apply` for details.

We defined the goal as creating a new connection from which other software can read the data a line at a time. R can do this in one trivial way, because the single call `textConnection(output)` turns the character vector into a text connection, from which other R computations can read just as they would from a file. Now we can put the computations together into a function definition.

```
fieldsToLines <- function(input, nfield, sep = "",
                          outputSep = if(nchar(sep)) sep else " ",
                          addQuotes = FALSE, ...)
{
    text <- scan(input, what = "", sep = sep, ...)
    if(addQuotes)
      text <- shQuote(text)
    text <- matrix(text, nrow = nfield)
    output <- apply(text, 2, paste, collapse = outputSep)
    textConnection(output)
}
```

The R solution is neat and uses the features of R in a natural way. But it has two intrinsic weaknesses: The computations may be somewhat inefficient for high-volume processing, and the flexibility is limited by the use of `scan()`. With respect to the latter, one problem is that newlines can only be included in fields by following the particular quoting rules of `scan()` and generally white space in fields will be trouble if the default output separator is used. The optional argument `addQuotes = TRUE` will cause all the fields to be surrounded by quotation characters on output, using the function `shQuote()`. Quotes are needed if you want to have white space inside fields and the output separator is the default `""` (which would treat any white space as a separator). Quotes are also needed for any separator if any input fields have embedded quote characters (single or double quotes) or newlines.

Notice the addition of a `"..."` argument, passed on to `scan()`, which allows users the full flexibility of `scan()`. Even so, the option of treating newlines as intrinsically not significant is not available.

With respect to efficiency, we can analyze the computations with respect to *vectorizing*, the heuristic goal in R of expressing computations in whole-object terms using efficient functions. The implementation is not bad, with no explicit loops and, except for the `apply()` call, only functions that deal with whole objects at the C level (`scan()`, `shQuote()`, `matrix()`, and `textConnection()`). The use of `apply()` does cause a separate R call for every record of the output connection; although `paste()` too is a C-based function, there will be some moderate overhead. More fundamentally, returning the value as a text connection limits the computations intrinsically to what can be held in memory. A larger-scale version could be written in R, by reading a limited amount of input at a time and writing the transformed data to a file instead of a text connection. But at this stage an implementation in Perl may be more natural and may scale better to really large volumes of data.

So saying, let's formulate the task for Perl. Where in R the natural formulation is in whole-object terms, Perl has advantages for a line-by-line treatment. We'll formulate the problem in terms of writing to an output filehandle one or more lines, formatted with `nfield` fields per line. Whereas in R it was natural to read in all the data and restructure it as an object, in Perl we would rather identify a smaller unit of computation that can be used iteratively to do the whole job. A natural unit of input in this problem is just enough to create at least one line of output. We don't know how many lines of input will be needed, and once we have enough, we may need to generate more than one line of output. Furthermore, we have to expect that some fields may be left over for the next unit of input. For all these reasons, we need some place to keep data temporarily; in other words, a buffer. A Perl array is a natural structure for a buffer. As we split input into fields, we can store these in an array and output elements from the array when there are enough.

One more detail: Text may be left over from the end of the last input line after we do the output. This text is a part of the next field, and needs to be pasted together with the first field on the next unit of input.

As with all the Perl examples in this section, the programming style leans towards a functional form. All Perl calls will be written in functional form, and we will define the solution as a function, `&fields_to_lines`, that processes a unit of input. The arguments to the function are the input and output filehandles, the number of fields per line, and the strings to use as input separator, output separator, and in place of newlines.

Here's an implementation. The basic idea is to build up an array of fields by reading lines of input, using the usual Perl syntax of enclosing the filehandle in angle brackets, namely, `<$input>` to read from a filehandle passed in as an argument and kept in the local variable `$input`. Once enough fields have been read, one or more lines of output can be written. In order for our function to be used to copy a whole file, we need to detect the end of an input file. The function is called for its side effect of writing onto the output, so we can use a return value of 0 to indicate end-of-file and of 1 otherwise, making a call to the function natural in a `while()` loop.

The rest of the implementation is largely a matter of getting the details right: allowing for an arbitrary number of input fields, and remembering to join the end of one line to the beginning of the next. The buffer is an array, separate from the function. We give it a long name, `@fields_to_lines_buf` to avoid conflicting with other variables in the Perl module containing the code. Including an argument `$lineSepAs` for translating the line ensures we get the last partial field on each line. It's not expected to be obvious, but you can cause newlines to be interpreted as end-of-field by making this argument the same as the field separator, `$sep`. And to retain newline characters in the fields use the newline expression, `"\n"` for `$lineSepAs`. Here's a complete listing:

```perl
sub fields_to_lines {
  my($input, $output, $nfield,
     $sep, $outSep, $lineSepAs) = @_;
  my($line, @fields, $fieldNo, $lineNo);
  ## read input until there's enough for a line of output
  while (@fields_to_lines_buf  < $nfield) {
    if(!($line = <$input>)) {
       return(0); # end of input
    }
    chomp($line);
     @fields = split($sep, "$line$lineSepAs");
    if ($sep != $lineSepAs) {
      ## append first field of this line to last field in buffer
      my($last) = pop(@fields_to_lines_buf).shift(@fields);
      push(@fields_to_lines_buf, $last);
    }
    @fields_to_lines_buf = (@fields_to_lines_buf, @fields);
  }
  ## now write out as many lines as there are
   while (@fields_to_lines_buf  >= $nfield) {
     for ($fieldNo = 1; $fieldNo < $nfield; $fieldNo++) {
     print $output shift(@fields_to_lines_buf),$outSep;
    }
    print $output shift(@fields_to_lines_buf),"\n";
  }
  return(1); # not the end of the input
}

@fields_to_lines_buf = ();
```

Two points of typical Perl style are worth noticing.

- Perl switches easily between strings and arrays, as we do here. The function `split` takes a separator and a string (the line of input here) and creates an array of the fields defined from the string.

- Arrays in Perl are typically manipulated by iteratively removing elements from either the front or back of the array (functions `shift` and `pop` respectively). To build up arrays, one can do the reverse by adding elements to front or back (`unshift` or `push`), or concatenate arrays by writing them as a list in parentheses separated by commas.

Chapter 9

New Classes

This chapter presents techniques for defining new classes of R objects. It and the closely related Chapter 10 on methods represent a more serious level of programming than most of the earlier discussion. Together, the techniques in the two chapters cope with more complex applications while retaining the functional, object-based concepts of programming with R.

Section 9.1 presents motivation and an example. Section 9.2 introduces the essential techniques: creating the class (page 334), slots (336), inheritance (336), class unions (338), new objects (339), documentation (341), and an example (342). The material in this section should be sufficient to start programming with classes.

Later sections review inheritance (9.3, 344) and virtual classes (9.4, 351). Section 9.5, page 359, discusses methods for initializing and validating objects. Section 9.6, page 362, provides techniques for programming with S3 classes. Two additional examples complete the chapter (Section 9.7, page 369; 9.8, 375).

9.1 Introduction: Why Classes?

Defining formal classes and methods is an extra burden, compared to just plunging in to analyze the data, or even compared to programming by writing functions to encapsulate the analysis. Why bother? Indeed, I've encouraged you to get started in a simple, convenient interaction with R functions and with other software. As you become more involved with software for data analysis, however, creating related classes and methods responds to both of our guiding principles: making the analysis more natural and convenient (the *Mission*) and making the results more trustworthy (the *Prime Directive*).

The key challenge is dealing with complexity and growth: how to expand the computing capabilities in a way that is easy to use and leads to trustworthy software.

Example: Global positioning system (GPS) data

As a motivating example, let's consider a source of data that is widely used, simple, but still challenging; in other words, typical of data that is interesting but that might not at first appear to need formal treatment. The data comes from tracking output produced by devices using the Global Positioning System (GPS). GPS receivers are devices that provide locational and navigational information either used by the receiver itself (for example, for navigation) or as input to computers or other devices. Applications range from the very practical to the scientific to the recreational:

- GPS data on position and motion assist navigation for planes, boats, and motor vehicles, or for hikers on foot.

- GPS data provides tracking information recording the movements of the receiver, for example to study the behavior of birds or animals.

The navigational applications undoubtedly sell the most GPS hardware, but because we're concerned with exploring data, we will emphasize the tracking applications. These have already produced some important scientific advances, in several cases expanding our concept of the mobility of species in the wild. While navigational applications usually hide the actual track data under a user-friendly combination of maps and/or computer voices, tracking applications do generally need to worry about the data, particularly when tracking is being done under difficult circumstances.

Conceptually, GPS technology computes the co-ordinates of a device, the GPS receiver, in space and time. The receiver uses radio signals to estimate distance to orbiting satellites, along with accurate time information. The data involved in this computation is itself fascinating, but not what the user normally sees nor what we will consider here. We are concerned with the output from the GPS receiver. The receiver is programmed to record its position at a sequence of times, as that position is computed based on the available satellite connections.

Position in GPS data is defined with respect to the surface of the earth, usually computed and returned as *latitude*, *longitude*, and *elevation*. Notice that these are, geometrically, a system of spherical co-ordinates in space. A standard convention is that the first two variables are in degrees, with negatively signed values for south of the equator and west of the meridian through Greenwich. Elevation is the distance above or below the surface of the earth.

A reasonable starting point is with track files exported from a GPS receiver. There are many formats, both public and proprietary. Here's a fragment from a tracking file:

```
T   05/27/2005 10:42:00 40.76637 -74.54335 185.7
T   05/27/2005 10:42:18 40.76658 -74.54337 191.4
T   05/27/2005 10:42:41 40.76685 -74.54344 197.7
T   05/27/2005 10:43:02 40.76710 -74.54358 198.6
T   05/27/2005 10:43:20 40.76730 -74.54370 199.6
T   05/27/2005 10:43:46 40.76752 -74.54388 204.4
T   05/27/2005 10:44:01 40.76776 -74.54385 207.3
T   05/27/2005 10:44:26 40.76805 -74.54384 208.7
T   05/27/2005 10:44:54 40.76836 -74.54382 213.1
T   05/27/2005 10:45:25 40.76866 -74.54365 216.0
```

In the example we'll deal with, the output for location and time from a GPS track appear as five columns, separated by white space, for the date, time, latitude, longitude and elevation. The leading "T" field just identifies the line as track data. We can infer, if we haven't been told, that the date is in the "mm/dd/yyyy" form. A little more investigation is required to know that elevation in this case is in feet, not meters. There are a few extra issues not shown here: blank lines indicate loss of signal, which may be important; a few lines of header information and other lines (not starting with "T") are also in the file.

Allowing for such details, we can imagine computations in R to read in such data. The function scan() could create a list with components for each field; function read.table() and its variants could create a data frame; in Section 6.5, page 182, we read some similar data. With a little work we can end up, say, with a data frame object gps1, having variables date, time, latitude, longitude, and elevation.

So, is there any need to invent a new class for this application? Yes, because the existing classes fail to capture some essential properties of the data, making computations less convenient and potentially error prone. Consider the first summaries we're likely to need: printed and plotted displays of the data. GPS data is nearly always plotted on a map. Plenty of software in R and in other systems generates maps, but using that software requires some programming, when all we really want is to say `plot(gps1)`. The temptation is just to use the position information as `x-y` information:

```
with(gps1, plot(longitude, latitude))
```

That may produce a reasonable plot, but it treats the two variables as a scatter of rectangular coordinates, which they are not, ignoring their physical relation and the sequential nature of the tracking. (A good, sensible and fully general plotting method is not trivial. Section 7.2, page 248, explored some possibilities.) A class and a corresponding method for `plot()` are the best way to package the details of the data and of the computations, leaving the user needing only to say `plot(gps1)`.

Similarly, when we come to trustworthy analysis, a simple data frame is not adequate. Data frames support many very general modifications of the data. You can extract arbitrary subsets of both rows and columns. Numeric variables can be transformed or combined in arbitrary ways. But does that make sense for our `gps1` object, if the result is still to be considered a valid record of GPS track data? Definitely not. The three geographic coordinates have physical reality; a cautious interpretation would prohibit any transformation of the individual coordinates. Rearranging the rows is less obviously pernicious, but also distorts the notion of the data as tracking information. Date and time values are not arbitrary; they represent the concept of a continuous track for the physical receiver, of which our data show a constructed sample. A `"GPSTrack"` class can prevent destructive or misleading modifications of the GPS data, either because the modifications can't be done or because they produce an object that no longer claims to represent tracking data.

We'll pursue the GPS example later in the chapter, starting on page 342, to illustrate some techniques for dealing with new classes.

9.2 Programming with New Classes

A new class is created, and saved, by a call to the function `setClass()`, in its simple form:

```
setClass(Class, representation)
```

where `Class` is the character string name of the class to be created, and `representation` defines the information to be provided in objects from the class.

First, a brief aside about what `setClass()` actually does. Unlike most computations in R, this function is called for its side effect: it assigns an object containing the definition of the new class. The class-definition objects, like objects containing method definitions and some other constructions, are referred to as *metadata*. Metadata objects are ordinary objects, in that you can manipulate them with expressions in R. But the implementation hides metadata definitions, partly so that a class and a function can have the same name, as has traditionally been done. For example, `"matrix"` is both the name of an important class of objects and of a function that generates objects from that class.

So you should be aware that `setClass()` is misbehaving by the standards we've set for functional programming, by doing an assignment behind your back. It's not a major issue for what actually happens; one could define all the same techniques and ask the programmer to carry out the assignment, by making explicit the way metadata is hidden. The result would be philosophically cleaner, but quite a bit more trouble for the user.

Because the assignment is the essential step, it matters where the call to `setClass()` takes place. The usual and preferred situation is to call `setClass()` from the top level; typically from a source file that is part of a package's R code or evaluated by a call to `source()`. In this case, the assignment takes place in the global environment, usually what you want. If you need to call `setClass()` from inside another function, you should provide a `where=` argument; see the documentation for `?setClass`. But the essential recommendation is to keep it simple; define classes at the top level, usually in the source code for a package.

There is another message here as well. Defining a new class is in many ways a more serious piece of programming than much of what we have discussed in previous chapters. While the number of lines of code needed are often not large, it all tends to count. The design of the new class will affect the ease with which it can be used. You will benefit from more advance contemplation than we have suggested, for example, when writing a new function. You may want to try several different versions before committing to one; different ways to define essentially the same structure will arise often in this chapter.

The amount of programming involved in using a new class may be much more than that involved in defining the class. You owe it to the users of your new classes to make that programming as effective as possible (even if you expect to be your own main user). So the fact that the programming style in this chapter and in Chapter 10 is somewhat different is not a coincidence. We're doing some more serious programming here.

Class representation

With these asides out of the way, let's examine the basic things you will be doing in the call to `setClass()`. The call specifies what information can be found in an object from the new class. This information is organized into *slots*. The call to `setClass()` determines the names of the slots in the new class, and requires each slot to itself correspond to a specified class. As a result, software working with a valid object from the class can extract or replace a named slot, confident that the object will have the named slot and that each slot when extracted, will be an object that contains all the information implied by the slot's class.

We will see that the slots in a new class can be defined both directly, by naming them, and through inheritance, by asserting that the new class contains all the slots in an existing class.

We call the information about names and classes for the slots the *representation* information for the new class. The first two arguments to `setClass()` are the name of the new class and the representation information.

For a very simple example, let's create a new class named `"track"` that has two slots named `"x"` and `"y"`, both of the slots being numeric vectors (class `"numeric"`).

```
setClass("track",
    representation(x = "numeric", y = "numeric")
)
```

With this definition, new objects can be created from the class. If `tr`, say, is any such object, then it's guaranteed to have a slot `tr@x` and a slot `tr@y`, and both are guaranteed to be numeric. Suppose the idea is that x and y represent coordinates for some observed track being followed, perhaps by an animal wearing a recording device. The class is too trivial to be useful on its own, but just for that reason it helps illustrate some basic points in the discussions of this chapter. A less trivial extension of the example is the GPS data (which we will take up again on page 342).

Class inheritance

As a simple class is used and found useful, variations on it nearly always suggest creating a class that *extends* the first class, that is, a new class that contains all the information from an existing class. This is done just by specifying one or more existing classes in the `contains=` argument to `setClass()`. So, to define a new class that has the information in our previous "track" class, but in addition has a third numeric slot, z, for tracking with three coordinates:

```
> setClass("track3",
+   representation(z = "numeric"),
+    contains = "track")
[1] "track3"
> getClass("track3")

Slots:

Name:       z       x       y
Class: numeric numeric numeric
```

The new class has all the slots from the classes it contains, plus those specified directly. Most importantly, methods defined for the contained class can be used for the new class as well.

An object, say tr3, from class "track3" will have three slots, the two inherited and one specified directly. We can say of any such object that it "is" also an object from class "track", by which we mean that tr3 can be supplied to any method where an object of class "track" was expected. It's this assertion that makes inheritance such a powerful tool in extending existing software.

The classes specified for slots in the representation argument can be any class that has been defined. In contrast, there are some inherent restrictions on classes in the contains= argument. Classes supplied here must be either:

1. Other S4 classes, defined and imported into the environment where the new class is being created; or,

2. One of the basic R object types, but not those types that are references or nonstandard; for example, not "environment" or "symbol" (the object type for class "name"). Also, the new class can contain at most one such basic object type, whether directly or indirectly.

The restrictions in the second item are required because the type of objects from the new class is that of the basic data class. For example, if a new class contains class "numeric", the type of objects from the class will be "numeric", and the various built-in computations for that object type will generally be inherited by the new class. Therefore, containing more than one such class would make the object type undefined. Objects from a class that does not contain any of the basic data classes have object type "S4".

The `contains=` argument should not include an S3 class; these are fine for slots, so long as they have been defined by `setOldClass()`, as discussed in Section 9.6, page 366. However, they do not make sense as inherited classes, for two reasons. First, there is no information available to specify what contents objects from the class have, in terms of guaranteed slots. In fact, a number of S3 classes either have inconsistent slots from object to object, or use nonstandard mechanisms for defining the properties of the objects. Second, S3 method selection will not be aware of the inheritance of an S4 object, so all S3 methods will fail to be inherited.

It's common to call the inherited class a "superclass" of the new class and conversely to call the new class a "subclass" of the inherited class. We'll use that terminology because it is convenient and common.

The uses (and occasionally the dangers) of inheritance are an important topic. Section 9.3 discusses the concepts and techniques in detail, and goes on to some other techniques for relating class definitions.

With representation and inheritance we have the essential ingredients for creating new classes. The rest of this section introduces some additional techniques and variations.

Virtual classes and class unions

Not all useful classes correspond to actual objects. A *virtual* class often represents some structure or concept about objects, without fully specifying how those objects are represented. Methods can be written for virtual classes and then shared by all the actual classes that contain the virtual class. Virtual classes can also be slots in other class definitions, allowing the slot to contain an object from any subclass of the virtual class.

A common special case of a virtual class is one that exists only to represent a conceptual property shared by other classes. This virtual class has no slots defined and therefore makes no restrictions on which classes extend it. In R, these are referred to as *class unions*, the term borrowed from a similar construction in C. Class unions are created directly by the function `setClassUnion()`:

```
setClassUnion("OptionalFunction", c("function", "NULL"))
```

This creates a class called `"OptionalFunction"` and says that both classes in the second argument implicitly extend the new class. The union can now be used, either as a slot in further class definitions or in the signature of a method definition. Objects from any of the classes in the union can be supplied as slots or actual arguments for the method.

In the "OptionalFunction" example, we might want to write some software that optionally transforms x by a user-supplied function, say as an argument named `transform` to our function. If the user doesn't want to supply a transform, how do we indicate this? We could have a second argument, set to TRUE if the transform was to be done, but this is an extra burden on the user. We could do the transform anyway and have a "do nothing" function, but this is slightly inefficient and ugly. If the argument corresponds to "OptionalFunction" in a method signature, however, then we can use a computation of the form:

```
if(!is.null(transform))
  x <- transform(x)
```

A similar motivation applies to slots in a new class. Suppose we want the optional function to be a slot in a descriptive object, for example, a model definition. Just as with the argument, we would like a way to indicate in the object itself whether the transformation should happen. Defining the corresponding slot to be a class union allows the user to easily supply either no transformation or a function when creating the model definition.

Class unions are virtual classes that only relate to behavior, with no implications about the information in objects, in the sense of slots. However, virtual classes can include a partial specification of the slots. Actual classes extending such virtual classes will have these slots and, usually, additional information as well.

Virtual classes with slots are often valuable in thinking about new directions for computing with data. Rather than prematurely deciding everything that needs to be implemented for a new idea, we can begin with the most important concepts, incorporating those into a virtual class. Experiments with actual classes that contain the virtual class can then allow alternatives to be explored, without confusing the original ideas. If some alternatives are abandoned, the rewriting will be less difficult and (particularly important) less error-prone if the original key concepts remain.

Any class can be declared to be virtual, either by having a completely empty representation, or by explicitly including "VIRTUAL" in the `contains=` argument to `setClass()`.

For details on virtual classes and class unions, see Section 9.4, page 351.

Generating objects from classes

Once a non-virtual class has been created, objects from that class can be generated by a call to the function `new()`, with the name of the class as the first argument. If that is the only argument, `new()` returns the proto-type object from the class. If other arguments are supplied, `new()` passes the prototype object and those arguments on to the function `initialize()`. Methods for `initialize()` are an important tool in designing classes, but the default method is itself quite flexible. It can be given arguments that are either;

1. named with one of the slot names, in which case this argument is assigned as the corresponding slot; or,

2. unnamed arguments from one of the superclasses of this class.

In the second case, all the slots inherited are assigned from the corresponding slot in the argument. (In fact, the initializing computations used by `new()` try to interpret some other cases as well, but for most purposes you should stick to either slots or objects from inherited classes.)

Slots not explicitly specified in either of these ways will have the values in the default or *prototype* object from the class definition. The prototype object can itself be specified by using the `prototype=` argument to `setClass()`. The notion of a prototype is usually that it specifies objects corresponding to some of the slots that are different from the defaults for the slots' own classes. Once again, the implementation tries to interpret a number of different objects as prototypes, but the safe approach is to use the corresponding function `prototype()`.

When you define a new class, you may also want to define a correspond-ing method for `initialize()`. You can choose arguments for that method to suit the way you want people to think about objects from your class. The arguments need not be the same as the slot names. Using this flexibility is a good idea, for example, if you have a number of classes that imple-ment alternative versions of some basic ideas. Users should be thinking in terms of the concepts, while the software underneath is responsible for the alternative implementations of the concepts. There are a few points of style in writing `initialize()` methods; in particular, you should remember that `initialize()` may be called for a subclass of your class, having additional slots you can't anticipate. You should allow the flexibility for additional slots to be specified. For the technique and examples, see the discussion of methods for `initialize()` in Section 9.5, page 359.

Slots and slot classes

Formal classes provide guarantees about the contents of objects through the class specification for slots in the class definition. A slot can be assigned either in the initial creation of an object, via the implied call to `initialize()`, or later on by replacing the slot explicitly. Slots are accessed or replaced by the "@" operator; for example, `tr1@x` returns the slot "x" from object `tr1` and

```
tr1@x <- xx
```

replaces it with the object `xx`.

Specifying the class of the slot in the definition guarantees that the assignment will only succeed if the replacement value *is* an object of the specified class, whether the assignment takes place in `initialize()` or later on. The meaning of the requirement is literally as stated; in the example, the assignment will succeed only if

```
is(xx, "numeric")
```

would evaluate to TRUE. Notice that so long as the condition is satisfied, the object is assigned to the slot. In particular, the object can come from a class that extends the specified class. It will generally be unchanged, still an object from the subclass. If `xx` came from an S4 class that contained `"numeric"`, but that had other slots as well, the new slot in `tr1` will be that object, with its class and its other slots unchanged. See Section 9.3, page 348 for the underlying concepts related to coercing an object to a class.

Documentation for classes

To see documentation for a class, as for most documentation, a Web browser interface usually works best, either an actual browser or the similar interface provided by a GUI. Starting from the documentation for the package containing the class definition, look for the name of the class in the alphabetic index. Class documentation is listed under the name of the class, followed by `"-class"`, for example:

```
track-class
```

Click on this to see documentation for class `"track"`.

To request documentation for a class in an R expression, precede a call to the operator `` `?` `` with the documentation type, `"class"`:

```
class ? track
```

requests documentation for class `"track"`. Browser interfaces to documentation and the `help()` function have not yet learned about documentation types. To use those, supply the class-type documentation topic shown above; that is, `"topic-class"`, and in this case:

```
help("track-class")
```

See Section 10.4, page 389, for similar documentation for methods.

This chapter is about defining new classes, and at this point, about documenting them. To start the process, the function `promptClass()` will create a documentation skeleton from the metadata defining the class, similarly to the use of `prompt()` for functions. The call to `promptClass()` specifies the name of the class; optionally, you can also supply a file or other connection to which the skeleton documentation should be written. However, the function knows the convention for naming class documentation files, so my suggestion is to let `promptClass()` name the file, and then move that file to the `"man"` directory under your source package directory.

For example, to put a skeleton of documentation for our `"track"` class into the source package `"SoDA"` (and following our pattern of putting packages into the `"RPackages"` subdirectory of the user's login), we can call `promptClass()` and then use the `system()` command interface to move the file to its correct destination:

```
> promptClass("track")
A shell of class documentation has been written
    to the file "track-class.Rd".

> system("mv track-class.Rd ~/RPackages/SoDA/man/")
```

The documentation shell contains entries for slots and superclasses, plus other general information. As usually with documentation shells from the `prompt` family of functions, you need to replace the stubs in the documentation with actual information.

Example: GPS data (continued)

Here is an example of defining a class for the GPS tracking data introduced on page 332. In the treatment without a specific class, such data is read as a `"data.frame"` object. But general data frame operations are not meaningful if the object is to continue to be a valid example of tracking data. Arbitrary extraction of rows or variables contradicts the concept of the track as a sample of continuous motion. The numeric variables representing position should not be subject to arbitrary numerical transformations, as permitted when treating a data frame as a two-way table. Defining a special class lets us be more restrictive about the computations defined for such objects.

A natural way to think of this data as an R class is to take the three position variables to be numeric. Time, in the sense of date-and-time as it occurs in GPS applications, is not a built-in R object type, and there are some choices. We will use a class "DateTime", defined as a union that includes the standard S3 classes for time (see ?DateTimeClasses).

At this point we can define a GPS class in a straightforward way:

```
setClass("GPSTrack",
    representation(latitude = "numeric", longtitude = "numeric",
                   elevation = "numeric", time = "DateTime")
)
```

The class has four slots with the obvious names, containing numeric data for the three position slots and with the standard time class for time data.

Time is always known accurately as part of the GPS technology. Some GPS receivers infer continuous motion information, usually defined in terms of direction (on the earth's surface) and speed, and include such motion information in their track output. We have not included it here, and for many scientific tracking purposes it would not be meaningful. But an extension to the "GPSTrack" class having slots for motion data would be useful for some applications.

Example: Binary representation of numeric data

In Section 6.4, page 161, some R functions are defined to produce the binary representation of numeric data, as an exercise in *vectorizing* computations. The computational exercise was to infer the pieces of an internal representation for numeric (floating-point) data. Each number is modeled as having an integer exponent, a sign (± 1), and a binary fraction, considered as a field of bits. A class definition with corresponding slots might have the form:

```
setClass("binaryRep",
    representation( original = "numeric",
        sign = "integer",
        exponent = "integer",
        bits = "raw"))
```

This class is designed to record the results of computing the representation, and to carry along the original numeric data as well. Although the computations generating the representation naturally generated considerable intermediate swell (because bits had to be computed as numeric values), the end result uses the "raw" built-in object type for the bits, getting some efficiency of storage and protecting the bits from being treated numerically by storing them as "raw" values, that is, bytes. The R classes for "sign" and `"bits"` slots are more general than the valid values they can contain; for these purposes, a validity method is useful. Section 9.5, page 361, discusses such methods, including an example for this class.

Because the main goal of the class is to examine numerical data, a method to show the results is key, printing the representation in a fairly compact but complete form:

```
setMethod("show", "binaryRep",
        function(object){
            cat("Object of class \"", class(object), "\"\n")
            sign <- ifelse(object@sign < 0, "-", " ")
            pasteBits <- function(bits)
              paste(ifelse(bits>0, "1","0"),collapse="")
            bits <- matrix(object@bits, nrow = length(sign))
            bits <- apply(bits, 1, pasteBits)
            lines <- paste(format(1:length(sign)),": ",sign,".",
                           bits, " * 2^", object@exponent,
                           " (", object@original, ")", sep="")
            cat(lines, sep="\n")
        })
```

Converting the bits to a printed form is made simpler by the common trick of turning the vector into a matrix, with columns representing the bits for successive numbers.

9.3   Inheritance and Inter-class Relations

New class definitions in a call to `setClass()` can specify that the new class will contain all the information of an existing class, so that objects from the new class will have each of the slots in the existing class, with the same slot names and slot classes. Some simple examples were introduced starting in Section 9.2, page 336. The concept of inheritance extends well beyond such examples. It is arguably the single most important mechanism in programming with classes and methods in R. It's also perhaps the concept that generates the most confusion when programmers start to exploit it.

In this section we look in more detail at inheritance and similar mechanisms for converting between classes, beginning with an attempt to nail down the concept as clearly as possible and deal with the variety of terminology used to talk about inheritance.

The concept of inheritance

In the S language and in other languages and systems, a number of terms are used to convey the concept of inheritance. In this book, we use several, emphasizing different aspects of the one underlying mechanism. Let's consider the simple example, using the `contains=` argument to `setClass()`, shown on page 336:

```
setClass("track3",
    representation(z = "numeric"),
    contains = "track")
```

The term *inheritance* itself is particularly concerned with behavior, that is with methods. The `"track3"` class inherits all the methods for the `"track"` class; that is, any method can (we assert) be applied to an object from the new class, by using the object as if it were from the earlier class. Inheritance in this sense is an automatic result of the rules for method selection in R: If there is no method directly defined for the new class, an inherited method will be used. The designer of the new class will need to decide which methods should not be inherited, and define methods explicitly to prevent inheriting the existing methods.

The term *contains* relates to the content of the objects. The slots in the earlier class definition appear automatically in the new class. In the sense of the term in mathematics, the set of slots in the new class contains the set of slots in the previous class. When other techniques are used to specify class inheritance, as discussed on page 347, the sense of contains may be less literal, but it remains part of the concept that all the information implied by the previous class can be retrieved from an object having the new class.

It's useful to borrow some other terms in discussing inheritance. Terminology dating back to the Smalltalk system states that, when a class, $\mathcal{B}$, extends an existing class, $\mathcal{A}$, then an object from class $\mathcal{B}$ *is* an object of class $\mathcal{A}$ (abbreviated to "is an $\mathcal{A}$" in most discussions). In contrast, if one of the slots in the definition of $\mathcal{B}$ is of class $\mathcal{B}_1$, say, then the Smalltalk term is that an object from class $\mathcal{B}$ *has* an object of class $\mathcal{B}_1$.

The Smalltalk terminology remains helpful and useful even today, in emphasizing the conceptual differences. Notice how much more is implied by the "is a" relationship than by the "has a" relationship. Bringing the discussion back to R, we're saying that any computation defined for an object of class $\mathcal{A}$ can be applied to an object of class $\mathcal{B}$. Not just applied to, but with the value of the computation being valid. As some examples will illustrate shortly, this assertion provides a very powerful tool, but also carries some risks. (If the computation can be applied, but the result is not valid, we've violated the Prime Directive.)

Yet another common terminology calls the new class, $\mathcal{B}$, a *subclass* of class $\mathcal{A}$, and $\mathcal{A}$ a *superclass* of $\mathcal{B}$. This terminology is also useful as well as unavoidable in many discussions of inheritance. For example, it's convenient to refer to "all the known classes that extend class $\mathcal{A}$" as "the known subclasses of class $\mathcal{A}$". But the idea behind the subclass/superclass terminology is somewhat the opposite of our discussion so far. The idea can be related to the concept of subsets and supersets in mathematics.

One can think of a class $\mathcal{A}$ in terms of all the objects x that exist such that is(x, $\mathcal{A}$) is true. Whenever $\mathcal{B}$ extends $\mathcal{A}$, then the set of objects corresponding to $\mathcal{B}$ will in fact be a subset of the objects corresponding to $\mathcal{A}$. All the $\mathcal{B}$ objects are also in the set of $\mathcal{A}$ objects, but not the other way around. In this sense it's natural to refer to $\mathcal{B}$ as a subclass of $\mathcal{A}$. Similarly for the term superclass: the set of objects belonging to or inheriting from class $\mathcal{A}$ is a superset of the objects corresponding to $\mathcal{B}$.

Perhaps a more intuitive way to remember subclass and superclass, however, is to think of drawing a picture of class inheritance on a page, starting at the top. The picture starts with the simplest classes in the relationships, since only these can be defined from scratch. Now, below these, we draw the classes that contain these classes, with lines connecting each class to its superclasses. Then, next down the page the classes that depend on the classes so far. The vertical position of a class directly reflects its inheritance relations: Those classes above a class and connected to it are its superclasses; those classes below a class and connected to it are its subclasses.

However you manage to sort out the terms, do try to get comfortable with the concepts. The networks of super- and subclasses provide essential concepts for understanding how the objects in a project are modeled and managed. Let's state the general concepts one more time, from one more, slightly different perspective. An object from a particular class should have all the behavior implied for each of the superclasses of that class. Conversely, a class shares all its behavior with its subclasses, but each of these will typically have some additional behavior as well.

Simple inheritance

"Simple" inheritance, by naming inherited classes in the `contains=` argument when defining a new class, is the preferred mechanism for specifying inheritance, and works for most applications.[1] Simple contained superclasses are the easiest to understand, so this should be the first concept to try out.

An advantage of simple inheritance arises in computations that select a method for a function or assign a slot in an object, when the class specified for the method or slot is a superclass of the actual object's class. The actual object must be interpreted as if it came from the superclass. When the inheritance is simple, the actual object is used *without change*, making for a more efficient computation but more importantly allowing objects from the actual subclass to be returned from a method or extracted from a slot.

In the example on page 345, class "track" was made a superclass of a new class, "track3". Whenever an object, x say, is generated from "track3", one can use x as an object from class "track". All the slots of class "track" are present with the same definition. When a method is called that expects an actual argument from class "track", an object from class "track3" can be supplied instead, without any change . A similar interpretation is placed on an object inserted into a slot. The class definition specifies a class for the slot. Only objects from that class or from a subclass are valid, but objects from a class that contains the required class are inserted without change into the slot.

An alternative mechanism for simple inheritance was shown on page 338: a call to `setClassUnion()`. This creates a class that only exists as the union of other classes. The class union is a superclass of all the members: The assertion is that objects from any of the member classes behave correctly for methods defined for the union. Calls to `setIs()` can add classes to the union. Class unions are special in that they add a superclass to the definition of existing classes, even potentially to basic object types and other classes whose definition is "sealed". It's a subtle mechanism, but often useful.

As with the use of the `contains=` relationship, a class union defines a simple inheritance: Members of the union are simple subclasses of the union. If a method is defined for the class union or if a slot is specified to be of the class union, an object from any of the member classes of the union can be used, without change. The slot application is, in fact, one of the valuable uses of class unions: to allow more than one kind of object in a slot, without abandoning control altogether.

---

[1]Superclasses can also be specified in the call to `setClass()` as unnamed arguments to `representation()`. There is no difference in the result. The use of `contains=` makes the inheritance clearer when reading the code and is the preferred mechanism. The alternative is allowed by the S language, and may be needed to define the representation object on its own, outside the call to `setClass()`.

Coercing one class to another

A relationship can exist between two classes when both are actual, non-virtual classes but with different representations. Neither class contains the other, but the classes can be related in terms of all or part of what they mean, in which case it might be useful to *coerce* an object from one class to the other.

Coercion has two forms, direct and replacement:

```
as(x, "track")
as(x, "track") <- value
```

The first expression returns an object from class `"track"`, The second replaces the part of x corresponding to class `"track"`. When x comes from a class that contains `"track"`, the method for both computations comes from the class definitions: selecting the correct slots from x for direct coercion and replacing the correct slots from `value` (implicitly, from `as(value, "track")`). Notice that coercion really does change the object from the subclass, whereas method selection and use in a slot left it unchanged. The latter behavior can be obtained explicitly by using the `strict = FALSE` option to `as()`.

If x does not come from a subclass, there will not be an automatically defined method for either form of coercion, but a mechanism exists to specify the methods, by calling

```
setAs(from, to, def, replace )
```

with `from` and `to` the names of the classes, and `def` and `replace` being the methods for direct coercion and replacement. The first method has one argument, being the object to be converted; the second is a replacement method with arguments `from` and `value`. Supplying a replacement method is optional.

Defining coerce methods for two classes by calling `setAs()` does not imply that the first class is a subclass of the second, but R does allow that extra assertion by a closely related mechanism, the `setIs()` function. This takes optionally methods `coerce` and `replace` interpreted as direct coercion and replacement. But it has the added effect of adding class `to` to the superclasses of class `from`. Objects from the `from` class will now inherit behavior automatically, for method selection and slot assignment for example. However, this is not *simple* inheritance in the sense discussed above. When an object is selected for a method or used in a slot, it must be explicitly converted to the `to` class, losing some of the advantages of simple inheritance. For this and other reasons, the automatic conversion of a class to another by explicit coercion has proven to be less appropriate in most applications than defining a common superclass for the two classes. An example will illustrate.

A recurring theme in this book is the *data frame* concept, originally implemented in the S language by the S3 "data.frame" class, but which arises in many contexts with different implementations. In Section 9.8, page 376, an S4 class "dataFrame1" is defined with the same information content as was prescribed for the "data.frame" class in the book *Statistical Models in S* [6]. Having a formal definition of the same concept allows the use of more modern tools with data frame data, but how should the old and the new classes be related? A simple approach would be to define a conversion method from old to new (and perhaps from new to old). The method(s) could be made available for use by the as() functions, by supplying them in calls to setAs(). One could also define a method to initialize the "dataFrame1" class from a "data.frame" object.

One could go further and assert that "data.frame" is a subclass of the new class, by setIs("data.frame", "data.frame1", ...). The assertion makes some sense, in that the informal S3 class can have other, unspecified attributes (and sometimes does), so that it is in that sense more general than the formally defined class. Remember that inheritance the other way doesn't work: an S4 class can not effectively contain an S3 class because, among other problems, S3 methods will not recognize the inheritance.

Because the S3 class has no formal description, the inheritance must be explicit, with a method for coercion and replacement. The same would be true if both classes were formally defined, but used a different representation for the information. Whenever explicit conversion is required, experience suggests you should consider instead defining another class that is independent of either explicit representation, and make that class a superclass of both current classes. Methods can then be defined for the new superclass that rely only on shared behavior. These methods will work for either of the subclasses, and retain the advantages of simple inheritance. Defining a common superclass makes particular sense for this example. As emphasized throughout the book, data frames are a very general concept in software for data analysis, from classic "data.frame" objects to spreadsheet and database applications.

A more extensible approach is then to define a virtual class, probably a class union, that has no assumed representation but is expected to have methods based on general data-frame properties. We'll pick up this discussion and consider such a class in the example of Section 9.8, page 375.

Multiple inheritance

Saying that the new class can extend more than one existing class is allowing *multiple inheritance*. Not all class systems do allow multiple inheritance, but for a functional language, I believe that the flexibility provided makes the mechanism essential.

Objects in R exist to be used in functions. When the behavior of functions is meaningfully related to the class, corresponding methods express some aspect of the class, such as its numerical behavior, how subsets of data are specified, and so on. *Multiple* inheritance says that objects naturally inherit different aspects of their behavior from different, essentially unrelated sources. In a functional language, these aspects of behavior are expressed as functions, such as arithmetic operators, subset operators and many others. In a class system for such a language, methods for these functions need to be shared by all classes that share the same behavior. And that sharing is made possible when the methods are defined for a common superclass. Different aspects of behavior may require different superclasses, and so multiple inheritance.

However, multiple inheritance does introduce potential ambiguities, if the aspects inherited are not clearly distinguished. Specifically, the new class may inherit more than one possible method for the same function call. R has a rule for choosing one of the methods (see Section 10.6, page 405), but it's more important to avoid class definitions where such ambiguities are a serious problem. Well-designed classes choose superclasses that contribute distinct aspects of the new class' behavior. It's less likely that both superclasses will make sense in the same method context. If they do, the preferred meaning for the new class should be clear, or else the two inherited aspects are not themselves clear. It's a good practice if such ambiguities arise to specify the behavior for the new class directly, via its own method for this function.

Contained classes must have been defined when `setClass()` is called. Some languages allow recursive class definitions; that is, a class can inherit from itself, directly or indirectly, which the R restriction prevents. Direct recursive use usually doesn't make sense in R for ordinary classes; among other problems, it prevents an automatic definition of the prototype object for the new class. Even undefined classes for slots provoke a warning, since again it's not possible to define a valid prototype object if a slot specifies an undefined class. See Section 9.7, page 369, however, for an approach to recursive class definitions.

9.4 Virtual Classes

In R, a virtual class is simply one for which you can't use the function `new()` to generate objects. The metadata for the class definition has an explicit slot to indicate whether the class is virtual. There are three main kinds of virtual classes and three corresponding ways to create them.

1. Class *unions*, created by `setClassUnion()` have no slots, but exist so that other classes can be declared as members of the union, and so share its methods.

2. Old-style, "S3", classes have no formal definition, but are specified in a call to `setOldClass()`;

3. Arbitrary class definitions may contain the special class `"VIRTUAL"` ; the term *mix-in* is often used to describe classes of this form.

Virtual classes may appear in method signatures, or as slots or superclasses of a new class (but see page 363 for the fine print on S3 classes).

Class unions

Class unions were introduced in Section 9.2, page 338, with the example:

```
setClassUnion("OptionalFunction", c("function", "NULL"))
```

Specifying `"OptionalFunction"` for a slot in a class definition allows the slot to define some computation, but also to indicate unambiguously that no computation should be done. The "optional thing" motivation for a class union is especially simple, but a similar idea works for a number of other techniques as well. If a slot could either be a pre-computed numerical summary or a function to compute that summary, a class union of `"numeric"` and `"function"` would work similarly:

```
setClassUnion("parameterSpecification",
  c("numeric", "function"))
```

The idea this time is that a parameter can be specified either as fixed numerical values or as a function that creates these values from the current object's contents. If a slot in another class is specified as having class `"parameterSpecification"` then the actual slot contents will be either numeric or function. To benefit from such flexibility without introducing many tests of the actual object's class, define a related generic function, say `updateParameter()`, which has methods for each of the member classes of the union. Then calling `updateParameter()` will recompute the desired parameter if it was specified as a function and simply return the value if it was specified as a constant.

Class unions can also link classes that are related by the ability to do certain calculations, but are not assumed to have any common slots. Our continuing example of data frame objects illustrates the value, and also the challenges, of this approach. A `"dataFrame"` class union would represent classes that implement the essential two-way layout of variables by observations. Some further discussion is in the example in Section 9.8, page 375.

A class union is a special type of class definition, with a special privilege: A class union can be defined as a superclass of another class, even if the definition of the other class is sealed. Sealed classes cannot be changed; for example, `"data.frame"` is such a class:

```
> isSealedClass("data.frame")
[1] TRUE
```

But the call to `setClassUnion()` is allowed an exception. If a class union is created containing `"data.frame"`, as in Section 9.8, page 375, `"data.frame"` has a new superclass:

```
> extends("data.frame", "dataFrame")
[1] TRUE
```

This exception is essential to using class unions (if we couldn't include basic classes as members, unions would be largely useless). Also, because class unions have no slots, the union cannot conflict with the representation of any of its member classes.

A class union can itself be sealed, by calling `sealClass()`. If it is not sealed, additional members can be included later on, by calling `setIs()`:

```
> setIs("dataFrame2", "dataFrame")
> getClass("dataFrame")
Extended class definition ( ?ClassUnionRepresentation? )
Virtual Class

No Slots, prototype of class "NULL"

Known Subclasses:
Class "data.frame", directly
Class "dataFrame1", directly
Class "dataFrame2", directly
Class "anova", by class "data.frame", distance 2
```

As the output of the example illustrates, class unions will also implicitly include those classes that contain or otherwise extend the directly specified members of the union.

S3 classes

The first, informal version of classes for the S language was introduced in the book *Statistical Models in S* [6]. Objects were assigned a class attribute consisting of one or more character strings; a method dispatch mechanism looked for method names matching one of the strings. Although there are a number of disadvantages to S3 classes (above all the absence of any definition of a valid object), they are widely used and unlikely to disappear soon.

To make use of S3 classes with the techniques of this chapter, it is necessary to construct corresponding S4 classes. These have the same name as the S3 class and are always virtual classes. Because there is no definition of the class, `new()` can't generate a corresponding object. The virtual class is created by a call to `setOldClass(Classes)`, where `Classes` is the value that the class attribute would have; for example,

```
setOldClass("data.frame")
```

to declare the S3 `"data.frame"` class. All classes declared in this way inherit from class `"oldClass"`, identifying them as S3 classes. Such classes can be used for slots in the definition of formal classes and can appear in method signatures. In recent versions of R they can also be used in the `contains=` specification of superclasses. For more details, see Section 9.6, page 362.

Mix-ins

Any ordinary class definition can create a virtual class, by including the special class `"VIRTUAL"` in the `contains=` argument to `setClass()`. Such virtual classes are useful in describing computational structure that is not complete in itself, but must have additional class information "mixed in" in order to fully define a class.

A class definition that is completely empty (no slots and no contained classes) is also made virtual, but note that any class that contains a virtual class is not made virtual automatically. You must explicitly include `"VIRTUAL"` in the superclasses.

Example: Traceable objects

As a fairly serious example of the use of virtual classes and inheritance, including multiple inheritance, let's consider the mechanism for tracing evaluation in R, which centers on the mix-in class `"traceable"`, a virtual class with a single slot:

```
setClass("traceable", representation(original = "function"),
         contains = "VIRTUAL")
```

In any interactive environment for programming, one may want to inspect a computation as it occurs. Debugging systems and debugging modes for programming languages have long provided mechanisms, usually involving "breaking" execution at certain points, such as specified lines in the source code. A functional system provides an opportunity for building such facilities directly in the language itself. R uses the `trace()` function to create versions of functions or methods that include interactive browsing or inspection, or for that matter any computation desired. The traced versions are specified from the command line of the session and then untraced when no longer needed. The result is a flexible and open-ended debugging mechanism. The use of `trace()` is discussed in Section 3.6, page 67. Here we're concerned with the mechanism, which illustrates the power of inheritance.

Suppose we want to trace the evaluation of a function, say `f()`. There are many things we might want to do, such as to use an interactive browser at some stage during the call to `f()`, whether on entry, before returning, or at some intermediate point. In a programming language like C, you would need to run your computations through a debug application and insert break points in the appropriate places. In R, you continue to evaluate expressions in the same way as always. Interactive debugging is enabled by creating a new version of `f()`, a step that is done by a call to the `trace()` function. For example,

```
trace(f, exit = quote(browser()))
```

says to redefine `f()` to evaluate the expression `browser()` just before exiting. The `trace()` function in fact allows this expression to be abbreviated to just `exit = browser`, but this is just a short form for the general idea of specifying an unevaluated expression to be inserted. We might want to print some information in addition to or instead of interacting:

```
trace(f, quote(cat("f:",narg(), "arguments")),
      exit = quote(browser()))
```

And we might want the action to be conditional on some test. Instead of building up various special techniques for breaks and debugging, R uses the one mechanism of redefining the function to be studied.

Because the function is an object, `trace()` operates by constructing a new version of the object that is temporarily assigned in place of the original. In essence the new version can be any modification of the function's body (you aren't allowed to change the arguments). R constructs the new version either automatically or in response to some editing by the user (if the call to `trace()` included the option `edit = TRUE`).

To make the mechanism work, it must be possible to undo the tracing, or to replace it with a different form of tracing. And the mechanism should allow us to trace methods as well, because these are essentially function definitions. Inheritance, and in particular multiple inheritance, provides a clean solution.

The call to `trace()` replaces the function by a new object, from class `"functionWithTrace"`. This class extends class `"function"`; in particular, its data part is the modified function definition. The evaluator treats it as a function, so all calls to `f()` still work, but call the modified version. In addition the new object has a slot that saves the original definition, allowing a call to `untrace()` to undo the tracing.

So far, it sounds as if class `"functionWithTrace"` can just be defined by adding a slot to the basic class `"function"`. Virtual classes and mix-ins enter the picture because ordinary functions are not the only objects that need to be traced. To debug a method, for example, the tracing code must be inserted in the method definition. The mechanism is the same: The function `trace()` finds the method that would be selected, constructs a modified method that includes the tracing behavior and re-assigns it, effectively by calling `setMethod()`. Once again a slot `original` in the traced object contains the original version.

But method definitions are not just functions. They too come from a class that extends `"function"`, in their case by having information about the *signature*, the classes for which the method was defined and also the classes for which the method is being used. (If you want details see Section 10.6, page 405.) Specifically, the untraced method has class `"MethodDefinition"`. To retain all the method-related capabilities, the traced object must extend class `"MethodDefinition"`, requiring another class for method definitions with trace, say `"MethodDefinitionWithTrace"`. Now virtual classes and mix-ins become relevant. Rather than just define the trace mechanism separately for functions and methods (and there are still more classes of extended functions to be handled), the cleaner solution is to encapsulate the use of an

"`original`" slot in a virtual class, "`traceable`" and have all the new objects
come from classes that contain class "`traceable`".

The definition of "`traceable`" is extremely simple:

```
setClass("traceable", representation(original = "function"),
          contains = "VIRTUAL")
```

Class "`functionWithTrace`" contains both classes "`function`" and "`traceable`";
class "`MethodDefinitionWithTrace`" contains both "`MethodDefinition`" and
"`traceable`":

```
setClass("functionWithTrace", contains= c("function", "traceable"))
setClass("MethodDefinitionWithTrace",
        contains= c("MethodDefinition", "traceable"))
```

Given an object to be traced, function `trace()` can construct a new object
from the corresponding original object and save the original for untracing:

```
objectT <- new(traceClass, object)
objectT @ original <- object
```

Here `traceClass` has been set to the suitable class, "`functionWithTrace`",
"`MethodDefinitionWithTrace`", or others. The discussion of `new()` on page
339 mentioned that an object from a superclass could be an argument, with
the result that all of the information from that object would be copied into
the new object. Because `object` comes from a superclass of `traceClass`, the
function or method definition information will automatically be copied into
`objectT`. Here the behavior of mix-ins becomes essential; otherwise `trace()`
would need to know all about all the possible object classes.

A few details: The actual code for `trace()` uses an initialization method
for "`traceable`" to insert the tracing computations, using the techniques
discussed in Section 9.5, page 359. And for compatibility with older R code,
the computations are not in `trace()` itself but in a function it calls. If you
want to see the real thing, look at `methods:::.TraceWithMethods`.

Example: Creating classes dynamically

The preceding example has yet another interesting point to raise. You may
have remarked that each new class extending "`function`" will have to have
a corresponding "`...WithTrace`" class defined in order for `trace()` to work
correctly with objects from the new class. This seems a nuisance, and requires more knowledge of the inner workings than one would like to impose
on a programmer who just wants a slightly different class of function-like

objects. Is it possible to automate the construction of classes? And if so, is it a good idea?

The answer to the first question is: Yes, it's quite feasible to automate such manufacture of classes. Because classes are created by a call to a function, a programmer is perfectly at liberty to generate classes during a session. We need to know what the new class definition should be and where to save the definition.

Is it a good idea? Generally, no. For most purposes, stick to the standard approach: Define classes explicitly by calls to `setClass()` done at the top level of the code for your application or package. The class definition will be permanently and unambiguously part of your software; for trustworthy use of classes in R, this is as it should be.

Having said that, class definition is done by R functions, and therefore can be used in many contexts. Some applications, such as this one, do invite us to stray from standard practice. Trace computations are already using some special trickery, all in the aid of flexible debugging and experimenting as part of programming with R. Bending the principle here is in a good cause, that of making other software more trustworthy.

As an example, dynamically creating classes for tracing is interesting in that it points up some of the questions to ask, which reinforce the general message to stick to the standard approach when possible. One question is whether the mix-in class can really be defined solely from the components of the mix, another is whether the process of creating the class in question is a reasonable overhead. The question of where to save the class metadata also needs to be considered. Let's develop dynamic class software for the tracing mechanism to illustrate the technique and the requirements.

Given a class that extends `"function"`, we have a standard form for the corresponding traceable class, simply a mix-in of this class and class `"traceable"`. This suggests a very simple computation to create a traceable class, given an object that we want to trace: paste `"WithTrace"` on to the name of the object's class to get the name of the traceable class, and call `setClass()` to create this class with two superclasses, the object's class and class `"traceable"`, just as the examples above do for `"function"` and `"MethodDefinition"` objects.

You should always ask when creating classes automatically whether you know enough from just the pieces to feel safe using the new class. In this example, is there enough information just from the definition of the two superclasses to be sure the constructed traceable class behaves correctly? Probably yes, but a slight change in the context would pose a problem worth considering. What happens when we `untrace()` the new object? The implementation for `untrace()` assumes it gets the same information used by `trace()`, including the name of the function and in the case of a method definition the signature. It does not use the class of the traced object to determine how to do the untrace computation. Other extended versions of functions may require some additional computation when tracing is done or undone. If neither of the actions of `untrace()` for ordinary functions or for methods suited some future extension of functions, then a different version of `untrace()` might be needed.

When defining classes dynamically, another question is where to store the definition. When a call to `setClass()` appears in the source for a package, the class definition becomes one of the objects provided with that package. Whenever the package is loaded or attached, the class definition is there. But now the new class is created during a session. What environment should it be stored in? There are several choices, none of them entirely satisfactory. It might be stored in the same environment as the object's class; often, the environment of some package that defines the object's class. There are two problems. First, this environment lasts only through the current session, so the same class will have to be defined for each session in which it is needed. Second, packages with a namespace normally *lock* their environment, so that assignments there are prohibited.

It's always possible to assign the definition into the global environment of the session. This can potentially be saved between sessions and it's not sealed, because top-level assignments would then be impossible! A disadvantage is that the association with the object's class is now broken, so that saving and running a new session can result in a class in the global environment that inherits from a class in a package not currently loaded. Also, the saved session normally only applies when R is run from the same directory. Copies of the traceable class are likely to be needed in many places. For various reasons similar to this problem, it's a general design recommendation that packages should not store package-specific objects in the global environment.

The code for generating trace classes dynamically currently stores the new class, for the session only, back where the original class was defined or, if this environment is locked, in the base package environment, `baseenv()`, which is not locked because it contains some objects that may be modified in the session.

9.5   Creating and Validating Objects

Once a class has been defined by a call to `setClass()`, objects can be created from the class by calling the function `new()` unless the class is a virtual class. For our first simple example,

```
setClass("track", representation(x="numeric", y="numeric"))
```

calls to `new()` could include:

```
new("track")
new("track", x=dd$days, y=dd$decl)
new("track", y = rnorm(1000))
```

Arguments named `x` and `y` are expected to be legal objects to use in the slots of the same name. If any slots are unspecified, they remain as defined in the class prototype, here the default objects of class `"numeric"`, numeric vectors of length zero.

It's often the case that we would prefer to customize the user interface for generating objects from a class, to make the arguments more natural for users. Also, there may well be conditions for an object from the class being valid, beyond those implied just by the call to `setClass()`. In our simple `"track"` class, for example, it may likely be a requirement that the two slots have the same length. Both object creation and validation can be customized for new classes. It's useful to discuss the topics together, because they raise similar points for consideration, particularly about inheritance.

Customizing new object creation

A number of mechanisms exist for customizing objects created from a class.

- As noted in Section 9.2, page 339, the prototype object can be specified by the corresponding argument to `setClass()`.

- Methods can be written for the function `initialize()`, which customize the call to `new()` itself.

- A class can also have a companion generating function, typically with the same name as the class, although this is just for user convenience, not a requirement.

The function `new()` creates an object from a class definition. The implementation of `new()` begins by constructing an object, `value`, which is a copy of the prototype in the class definition. Then, it initializes the contents of this object according to the remaining arguments to `new()` by evaluating the expression:

```
initialize(value, ...)
```

Notice that `value` is already an object from the class. Therefore, the computations in `initialize()` can be customized by specifying methods for the first argument corresponding to our defined class.

The default method for initialize allows either arguments with the same names as the slots in the class, or unnamed arguments from one of the superclasses of this class. In the latter case, all the inherited slots for that class will be set. After any unnamed arguments are handled, explicitly named slots will be set, meaning that explicit information always overrides inherited information. See the detailed documentation, `?new`.

You can generate a skeleton for an initialization method by:

```
> method.skeleton("initialize", "track")
Skeleton of method written to initialize_track.R
```

The formal arguments are `.Object` and `"..."`. Method definitions can have named arguments in addition to `"..."`. For our `"track"` class, we might choose to make x and y explicit arguments. That would allow default values to be inferred if only one set of data was supplied, for example, by setting y to this data, and x to the standard sequence 1, 2, ..., `length(y)`. (The logic here is similar to that in the function `plot()`.) Here is an implementation of that method:

```
setMethod("initialize", "track",
    function(.Object, x, y, ...) {
        if(missing(y)) {
            y <- x; x <- seq(along=y)
        }
        callNextMethod(.Object, x = x, y = y, ...)
    })
```

Note that `"..."` is retained as an argument, and that the computed x and y slots, along with any other arguments, are passed down to the next method for `initialize()`.

The style of the example provides two benefits that apply in most methods for `initialize()`. First, the use of `callNextMethod()` ensures that any special initialization for superclasses of this class are not lost. (See Section 10.4, page 391, for `callNextMethod()`.) Second, including the `"..."` argument provides for the opposite consideration. The class you are defining may at some point itself be contained by one or more subclasses, which you or your users define. If the subclass does not itself have an `initialize()` method defined, users may supply named slots from the subclass definition and these arguments will be passed on to your method. You need to pass them along in turn, so that some method (probably the default) will eventually deal with them.

Testing for Valid Objects

Class definitions have implications for the contents of objects generated from the class. Some of these can be inferred from the `setClass()` definition itself; others are implicit constraints reflecting the meaning of the class to its users. In the first category are the asserted classes for the object's slots; in the second the expectation that the slots are related in some way, as in requiring x and y to have the same length, in our example. The default method for `initialize()` and the replacement function for slots both check slot classes against the class definition, but additional requirements have to be programmed, as a validity method for the class. The existence of programmed validity methods also raises the question: When should an object be tested for validity? Testing too often can create substantial overhead, particularly in a system such as R which does nearly everything through a single mechanism, the function call. In addition, intermediate computations such as replacing a slot may have to create a temporarily invalid object, pending further changes.

The approach taken in R is to have a function, `validObject()`, that performs a general validity check. This function is only called automatically in a few contexts, primarily when an object is generated from the class by a nontrivial computation (specifically, when some optional arguments are included in the call to `new()`). Otherwise, it's left to users or to application functions to call `validObject()` when an object's validity might be in question.

A validity method is a function supplied either as the `validity=` argument to `setClass()` or via a separate call to `setValidity()`. The two mechanisms have the same effect, the difference being simply a question of convenience in programming. The validity method gets as its single argument an object nominally from the asserted class.

It should return `TRUE` if the object satisfies the requirements and a character vector describing the nature of the failure(s) otherwise. In writing validity methods, you only need to check constraints specific to this particular class. By the time your method is called, you can assume that all checking for both the validity of the object's slots and for any constraints imposed by superclass definitions has been carried out without finding problems.

The simple `"track"` class (Section 9.2, page 336) had two numeric slots representing the two variables being observed. It's at least plausible to require the same number of values in both slots, in which case a corresponding validity method could have been included in the class definition:

```
validTrackObject <- function(object) {
  x <- object@x;  y <- object@y
  if(length(x) == length(y)) TRUE
  else
    paste("Lengths of x (", length(x),
          ") and y (", length(y),
          ") should have been equal", sep="")
}

setClass("track", representation(x="numeric", y="numeric"),
    validity = validTrackObject)
```

Note that validity methods should not themselves generate errors or warnings. Their purpose is to provide as much and as specific information as possible about what seems to be wrong. They should continue, where possible, even after finding one problem. If there are multiple failures, the first detected may be a consequence of the real flaw, and not give the most useful feedback to the user.

9.6   Programming with S3 Classes

The version of S that was developed around 1990 introduced a simple class/method mechanism into the software for the first time. The mechanism has come to be known as "S3" classes and methods. This section discusses using S3 classes in combination with formal methods and classes.

The class/method mechanism described elsewhere in this book, which has grown up since about 1998, is recommended rather than the informal S3 mechanism for any new computing. The S3 mechanism was simple to implement and was added to the version of S at the time with relatively little change to other code. It does not allow many of the techniques we need to produce clear and reliable software. Most particularly, there is no information about what structure can be expected in objects of a given class. An S3 class is defined by the presence of the class name in the corresponding `class` attribute of some objects. More than one string may be included in the attribute, in which case the object "has" the class of the first string and inherits from the classes named by the remaining strings, in the order they appear.

The S3 class/method mechanism was the basis for a large amount of software, either implemented in R as that system developed or explicitly programmed for R since then. The defects of the system would have to be much greater than they are before a mass conversion of this large body of software would be likely. (I would encourage those planning on a major overhaul of S3-style software to consider re-design in terms of the current mechanism. Future reliability and ease of maintenance can repay the conversion costs.)

The older approach to classes had no `setClass()` and no constraint on inheritance. Instead, each object could have a class attribute, a character vector with one or more string elements. The object inherited from all these classes, with the first string being thought of as "the" class of the object.

In order to make use of S3 classes in S4 computations, the first and most essential step is to declare the S3 class structure explicitly, using the function `setOldClass()`. Commonly used S3 classes in package `stats` and in the `base` package should have been pre-declared.

The statistical models software in the `stats` package is a major source of S3 classes. For example, linear regression models will have class `"lm"` if there is one variable being fit, but will need special methods for some computations if multiple variables are fit. To handle multivariate regression, the object representing the fit has a class with two strings, `c("mlm", "lm")`. The idea is that if a method for class `"mlm"` exists, this is chosen in preference to one for class `"lm"`, but otherwise the `"lm"` method applies.

To make use of these classes would require calling `setOldClass()`:

```
setOldClass(c("mlm", "lm"))
```

(In fact this declaration is provided in the `methods` package.) Class `"mlm"` maps into an S4 class that contains `"lm"`, also mapped into an S4 class.

```
> extends("mlm")
[1] "mlm"        "lm"         "oldClass"
```

This unambiguously defines class `"mlm"`, if every object x with `"mlm"` as the first element in `class(x)` has `"lm"` as the second element, and nothing else, and if all objects with `"lm"` as the first element of `class(x)` have only that string in `class(x)`. There is no mechanism to enforce these sanity requirements. They usually hold, but exceptions exist, as noted on page 367.

The virtual S4 classes created in this way are usually safe as:

1. classes in signatures for methods;

2. a slot in new class definitions.

3. a superclass of an S4 class (supported in version 2.8.0 of R or later).

Further details need to be considered in some cases. First, you may want to combine S3 and S4 classes and methods for a function; sometimes this requires turning S3 methods into S4 methods, or at least considering which methods will be chosen. You may want to turn an S3 class into an S4 class, either for better programming or because you need assurances not provided by the approach above (for example, to create a new class with guaranteed structure); see page 366. And occasionally, S3 inheritance is inconsistent, requiring more extended modifications for any use at all (page 367). This happens when the first string in the S3 class is followed in different objects by different strings; in other words, the S3 class seems to have a variable inheritance from one object to another. It really does happen.

Turning S3 methods into S4 methods

Defining "true", S4 methods for a function that has S3 methods as well usually works fine. To understand what's happening, you should realize that the S3 generic function containing the call to `UseMethod()` is just an ordinary function object in S4, not a generic function object. When S4 methods are first defined for the same function, a new generic function object is created and the previous function becomes the default method, just as it would for any ordinary function.

Suppose the function, `f()` say, is now called with an argument that would match an S3 method. First, the list of S4 methods is examined to find a match. Normally, none of the S4 methods will match (unless you intended to override the S3 method), and the default S4 method will be dispatched. Because the default method is the old version of the function, evaluating that method will now call `UseMethod()`, and dispatch the appropriate S3 method. A small amount of extra computation is needed to do two method dispatch computations, but otherwise all should be as expected. (It's unlikely that you will detect the time for the extra dispatch if the method itself is doing any serious amount of computation.)

To determine the available S3 methods look for function objects whose names are the function's name followed by "." followed by the class name. For example, a method for `plot()` for class `"lm"` would have the name `plot.lm`. However, nothing prevents the same name pattern from being used for other purposes (neither `plot.new()` nor `plot.curve()` are in fact S3 methods, for example). So be careful.

When you can, it's generally best to leave the S3 methods alone; once the S4 default (that is, the S3 generic function) is called, methods should be selected using the standard S3 rules. One possible problem is that an S4 method might be chosen rather than the default, for an object destined for an S3 method.

This is fairly unlikely, but can happen, usually because an S4 method is defined for a superclass of the S3 method's class. For example, suppose x has S3 class `"mlm"` and you have an S3 method for function `f()`, namely `f.mlm()`.

The S3 `"mlm"` class inherits from class `"lm"` and the S3 inheritance has been declared via `setOldClass()`. But if you define an S4 method for `"lm"` for `f()`, that method will be selected over the default for an object of class `"mlm"`. Maybe in fact you wanted this to happen, but it's at least as likely that you meant to leave the direct, S3 method for class `"mlm"` in place. If so, you need to convert the method to an S4 method.

If you want to convert an S3 method to an S4 method and get the same result as before, there are a few details to consider. The temptation is to simply use the existing function:

```
setMethod("f", "mlm", f.mlm)  # Not recommended
```

However the preferred alternative is to *call* the S3 method:

```
setMethod("f", "mlm",
  function(x, y, ...) f.mlm(x, ...))
```

(assuming that `f()` has arguments `x, y, ...`).

There are a few subtle reasons to prefer the second form, and just occasionally you must use it. You must call the method if the arguments to `f.mlm()` are not legal as an S4 method for `f()`. Such a situation is more likely than you might expect. Because S3 methods can only dispatch on the first argument to the function, there is a temptation to define S3 generics with only one named argument and `"..."`:

```
f <- function(x, ...) UseMethod("f")
```

But S4 methods can and do depend on more than one argument, and methods can be defined for `"..."` in version 2.8.0 of R or later. So converting `f()` to an S4 generic function might well suggest adding or dropping named arguments to get the full benefit of methods:

```
f <- function(x, y, ...) standardGeneric("f")
```

In fact, exactly this happened, replacing `"f"` with `"plot"`.

Turning **S3** classes into **S4** classes

Declaring an S3 class with a call to `setOldClass()` creates a virtual S4 class
corresponding to the S3 class. An alternative is to design an explicit S4 class
to contain formally the same information as one finds informally in the S3
class. If the class in question is important enough that you want to write
some S4 methods for it, defining an analogous S4 class has the advantage,
compared to just using `setOldClass()`, of providing an explicit guarantee of
the objects' contents, rather than the vague hopes that are the best you can
do with S3 classes. The price is that something explicit now needs to be
done for S3 methods to apply to the new class.

The S3 class `"data.frame"` relates to the fundamental data frame concept
considered throughout this book, of repeated observations on a defined set
of variables. Section 9.8, page 375, defines a class `"dataFrame1"` that is one
approach to bringing data frames into S4 classes. The `"dataFrame1"` class
has an explicit definition that replicates what is found in a `"data.frame"`
object:

```
setClass("dataFrame1",
    contains = "list",
    representation(row.names = "character", names = "character"))
```

Data frames represent a widely applicable concept and a thorough treatment
would need to deal with different requirements, most likely via a class union,
of which `"dataFrame1"` would only be one member. Nevertheless, we can use
it as an example.

Having created an S4 class related to the S3 class, and presumably defined some methods involving it, how should you manage the relation between the two classes? Should there be inheritance, that is automatic conversion between the two classes? In recent versions of R (2.8.0 and later),
one can register the S3 class with its slots, *if* we are guaranteed that all
objects have the asserted slots (see `?setOldClass`, including a version of
`"data.frame"`). But in general, with no formal definition from which to infer
slots, we have no guarantee that the S3 class has well-defined analogies to
slots. If not, the S3 class can not be reliably treated as an S4 class.

It's possible to define explicit inheritance the other way, which allows
objects from the S3 class to use methods for the S4 class. A more cautious
approach is to define explicit coercion via `setAs()`, and then to provide S4
methods that use the coercion, suitable in examples where there are no
guarantees as to what the S3 class object contains nor what it is expected
to contain (remember the *Prime Directive*, trustworthy software). For example, the model-fitting software in R constructs `"data.frame"` objects with

extra attributes to represent a model, but leaves the class of these objects as `"data.frame"`. Given such uncertainties, the audit trail of the computation will be clearer if we can see the conversions. A new S4 class would be required in this case (see the discussion starting on page 378 below).

Where possible, the `setAs()` definitions should make use of known methods for the S3 object, rather than making assumptions about the contents. For example, to coerce a `"data.frame"` object to class `"dataFrame1"`:

```
setAs("data.frame", "dataFrame1",
     function(from)
       new("dataFrame1",
            as.list(from),
            row.names = rownames(from),
            names = colnames(from))
     )
```

Because the coercion uses `new()` to create the `"dataFrame1"` object, we know that the result is valid; we know this literally, in that `new()` with arguments specifying the contents of the object ends up by calling `validObject()`. The rest of the information in the new object should come from computations with known results for the S3 class. There's no universal rule to apply, given that S3 classes and methods have no meta data and no general validity mechanism. Here we rely on the very basic use of a list for the data and on the requirement, explicitly stated in *Statistical Models in S*, that every data frame has row names and column names.

Inconsistent S3 inheritance

When a class is formally defined, the classes from which the new class inherits are unambiguously specified. The `contains=` argument to `setClass()` specifies the classes from which this class inherits directly; if those classes were in turn defined to contain other classes, more classes will be added to the inheritance indirectly. Every object created from the new class will have this same "tree" of superclasses.

A call to `setOldClass()` creates a similar superclass relationship for the multiple strings that might appear in an S3 class attribute, such as `c("mlm",  "lm")`. So long as the inheritance implied by the multiple strings is consistent over all objects using these S3 class names, no problem arises. Class `"mlm"` maps into an S4 class that contains `"lm"`, also mapped into an S4 class. But the class strings are attributes on individual objects, not constrained by a single class definition. Nothing enforces consistency, and inevitably inconsistency does happen occasionally.

A particularly striking example comes from the S3 classes used to represent date/time information. These have names starting with "POSIX"; not exactly intuitive but referring to the standard, [16], defined in 1991 as an extension to the POSIX definitions for an operating system interface. The standard leads to representations for a particular time, either in seconds from the beginning of 1970, or in text format with fields for year, month, and day (for a particular time zone). There are two such classes, "POSIXct" and "POSIX1t" corresponding to the two representations. These objects are useful in many applications and vital for some, when precise and unambiguous computations on actual times are required.

The function Sys.time() returns the current time in the "POSIXct" representation. Other functions convert and operate on the two representations; see ?POSIXt for details. Because the standard is widely used, interfaces to other systems can also expect to produce times in formats compatible with these classes.

So far, so good. But if you create one of these objects and examine its class, a strange beast emerges, a two-tailed monster in fact.

```
> z <- Sys.time()
> class(z)
[1] "POSIXt"   "POSIXct"
> class(as.POSIX1t(z))
[1] "POSIXt"   "POSIX1t"
```

While documentation refers to objects of class "POSIXct" and "POSIX1t", what is actually produced in the standard interpretation of classes are objects that all have class "POSIXt", except that in one case this class extends "POSIXct" and in the other "POSIX1t".

The intent presumably was to define methods for "POSIXt" that applied to either class. Unfortunately, any such method eliminates the chance to refine that method for either of the more specialized classes. Without disparaging useful software for such anomalies, they can not be incorporated into the S4 class-and-method system; in particular, setOldClass() will be stymied. What should one do, if the existing software is too entrenched to change (quite likely the case with "POSIXt", part of the R base package)? The best compromise may be to introduce additional classes matching the anomalous classes but with correct hierarchical behavior. Valid objects in the S4 sense must come from the new classes But the computations in the S3 methods may still be inherited from any of the existing classes, provided an S3 object is generated from one of the newly defined classes.

Consider `"POSIXt"` as an example. In this case, we need two new classes. To emphasize that they are meant to take over from the existing classes shadowed by `"POSIXt"`, let's call them `"POSIXCt"` and `"POSIXLt"`, just capitalizing one more letter in each case. (Ordinarily, ambiguity of this sort would be discouraged, but here it emphasizes that this is emergency repairs on a weird situation.) To make minimal changes, the new classes could be left as S3 classes, with `setOldClass()` now able to express the definitions:

```
setOldClass(c("POSIXCt", "POSIXt", "POSIXct"))
setOldClass(c("POSIXLt", "POSIXt", "POSIXlt"))
```

Objects created with the first of these three-string S3 class attributes will inherit all the methods that applied to the previous objects of "class" `"POSIXct"`, but now legitimate hierarchy applies, so that `"POSIXt"` methods can be replaced by specialized methods for class `"POSIXCt"`.

9.7 Example: Binary Trees: Recursive or Not?

A number of R packages deal with various forms of *graph structures*, objects defined in terms of nodes and edges. The packages take many different approaches, from interfaces to implementations in other languages such as C++ to a variety of strategies in R itself. Examples include packages `graph` in BioConductor and `igraph` in CRAN. This section looks at a simple special case, the binary tree, to compare two approaches, a recursive view and a "flattened" view more usual in S language structures.

If you have dealt with tree-like objects in some other languages, you may be used to definitions that are essentially recursive. For example, a binary tree can be defined recursively to consist of two subtrees, each of which can be either a leaf (that is, some sort of atomic non-tree data) or another binary tree. Usually, a single leaf is also valid, as a special case.

You can express the same notion in R as well, and a class union is an elegant way to do it. Whether this sort of construction is a good idea takes a bit more thinking. Tradition among users of the S language says that recursion of this form is computationally slow. Let's examine how it's done first, and then ask when you might want to use or to avoid the mechanism. The question can be studied by comparing a recursive implementation with a non-recursive one, as we will do on page 370.

We will make the main class a virtual class, specifically a class union, which may be surprising. There are several reasons, but the essential one is to create a recursive definition without violating the rule that a class must be defined before being used.

For the moment, suppose we're dealing with binary trees built on text data, and only want to allow character vectors as leaf nodes. The main class will be called `"textTree"`. Here's the definition. We begin by defining the leaf class explicitly. It too will be a class union, initialized to allow ordinary character vectors. Later applications can add other classes of leaf node.

```
setClassUnion("textLeaf"  "character")
```

Now we proceed to define the `"textTree"` class and also a strict version:

```
setClassUnion("textTree", "textLeaf")

setClass("strictTextTree",
    representation(left = "textTree", right = "textTree"))

setIs("strictTextTree", "textTree")
```

We proceed in three steps because R will not let us insert an undefined class as one of the members of a class union, and will also warn if we define a slot of a new class to be an undefined class. So we set up the class union, with only the leaf class included, then use the union to define the strict non-leaf version of the tree with a left and right subtree. Finally, the strict tree class is added to the class union to complete the recursive definition.

Before we worry about efficiency, there is one feature of such definitions that should be noted. The class that will be used most often in programming with this set of classes is the virtual class, the class union `"textTree"`. The non-virtual class is a helper class, although an important one.

Method specifications can use the distinction between the general, virtual class and specific subclasses. We can define a particular computation for text trees by defining alternative methods for all or some of `"textTree"`, `"strictTextTree"`, and `"textLeaf"`. Methods would have `"textTree"` in the signature if we wanted to allow an arbitrary tree, but `"strictTextTree"` if we wanted only to deal with non-trivial trees.

Recursive versus non-recursive class definitions

Recursive-style class definitions such as the binary tree class above naturally organize information in an implicit way. The very notion of the recursive class is that the immediately visible slots are partly or entirely a few objects of a similar class. Computing with such objects tends to be a process of navigation, doing something on the current object, then perhaps doing the same thing or a related computation on one or more of the "children" objects. Languages such as Lisp make extensive use of such computations, often without explicitly defining classes for the purpose.

A more traditional approach to such information in the S language is to lay out all the relationships explicitly; instead of slots that contain children of similar classes, the slots will define all the structure explicitly. Typically, the recursive-style computation is then replaced by an iterative computation over the data defining the structure.

To see this comparison, let's define a binary tree class with no recursion. Once again, we think of the tree as a collection of nodes. Each node can be a leaf, or it can have two other nodes as its children. In the non-recursive definition, the nodes are an index and the slots correspond to different kinds of information for the nodes. We define one slot to contain all the leaf information: the slot "leaves" is a vector with all the leaf data as elements. The only other information we need is the tree structure itself. One of many ways to define that is by a two-column matrix, nodes, whose rows correspond to the non-leaf nodes in the tree. Each row has two numbers that identify the two children of this node. Our example uses a traditional technique in the S language to code this information. For example, the R function hclust(), which performs hierarchical clustering on a set of observations, returns an object using this form to encode the tree representing the clustering.

An element in the matrix nodes is negative if the child is a leaf node and positive otherwise. A positive entry is another row in the matrix nodes. A negative entry is the negative of the index in leaves. A corresponding class definition might be:

```
setClass("treeB",
    representation(leaves = "list", nodes = "matrix")
)
```

Many other choices are possible: it would be a little clearer to have two numeric vector slots, say left and right for the sub-nodes, but a single matrix is often convenient for computation. In fact, the specific choice above happens to be a traditional one in the function hclust(), which returns an object of S3 class "hclust". The merge component of the object corresponds to what we are calling the nodes slot in our class definition. See ?hclust. The object also has component label that corresponds to slot leaves.

If you run example(hclust), it will leave behind a cluster tree, assigned as hc. Each node of hc corresponds to a cluster containing some subset of the states of the United States. You can look at the nodes information as hc$merge. Because the tree is created by successively merging clusters, the first few nodes have only leaves as subtrees (in this case the leaves are states of the United States):

```
> hc$merge
         [,1]  [,2]
  [1,]   -15   -29
  [2,]   -17   -26
  [3,]   -14   -16
  [4,]   -13   -32
  [5,]   -35   -44
  etc.
```

Node 5 contains leaves 35 and 44. Farther down,

```
  [13,]   -37    11
  [14,]   -27     2
```

Node 14 merges leaf 27 with node 2, which was defined above.

The recursive and non-recursive classes essentially hold the same information. The non-recursive definition is simpler to state, but that is partly deceptive. The recursive form is largely self-describing and it's hard to construct an object from the class that is structurally invalid, in the sense that there is no binary tree of this form. With the non-recursive definition, the explicit use of node and leaf indices is both a strength and a weakness: a strength, in that a number of computations can be done fairly directly from the object, without recursion; and a weakness, in that the validity of the object is not at all obvious and not in fact trivial to check. Nothing in the structure prevents a later row in the nodes for hc from containing, say:

```
  [16,]     2    14
```

But subtree 2 was already a child of subtree 14; as a result, there are two paths from node 16 to node 2, meaning that the object no longer represents a tree, but a general network.

An essential tradeoff between the two definitions is therefore that the recursive form gives a direct, logically straightforward, and trustworthy way to navigate the tree structure, at the cost of having to do separate function calls for each step of the navigation. That cost can be quite high if the number of nodes is large. Each node corresponds to a separate R object (all contained in the top-level tree object, but still each having the overhead in space and computation of a separate object). In the non-recursive form, each node just adds an element to a vector and a row to a matrix. The complexity of the structure is independent of the size of the tree.

The non-recursive form often does not require navigation as such, particularly for summaries or visualization that take the structure as given. On the other hand, computations are likely to be less clear when we do need to navigate the tree, and the danger of erroneous computations producing an invalid object is likely to be higher. When the computations involve extracting or replacing a subtree, the recursive form shines. Such operations are typically a single step, once one has navigated to the desired node.

To see the non-recursive form at its best, let's consider computing some additive summary for all nodes of a binary tree. An additive summary is any measure such that the value for a particular node in the tree is the sum of the values for all the leaf nodes under that node. (The logic we will derive applies to any summary of a binary tree, additive or not, if the value for a node can be computed from information about the two subnodes merged to form that node. But the additive case is easier to describe.)

Let's return to tree `hc`. Suppose we wanted some additive statistic for each cluster, say the total population or area of the states in the cluster.

We'll define a function that produces such a summary, starting from the corresponding data for the leaves (the states in this case) and from the information about the tree given by the `nodes` matrix.

The key to programming such functions is to iterate, starting with the simplest set of nodes and at each iteration adding up the information for nodes whose children were done at earlier iterations. Nodes made from merging two leaves can be done on the first iteration, because we start with the leaf data. Then all the nodes made from merging leaves or first-round nodes can be done on the second iteration, and so on. The number of iterations is what's called the *depth* of the tree, the maximum number of steps from the root node to a leaf. This number is usually much smaller than the total number of nodes; in "balanced" trees, it's of the order of the logarithm of the number of nodes.

The mechanics of the computation turn out to be startlingly simple when computing a vector of `counts` for some additive summary. Remember that we chose to represent leaf nodes by their negative index, and non-leaf subnodes by the corresponding (positive) row in the `nodes` matrix. Suppose there are n_L leaves and n_N non-leaf nodes. For the summary computation, we want a vector of $n_L + n_N$ counts for both leaves and nodes. So we change the coding, now using $i, i = 1, \ldots, n_L$ for the leaves and $n_l + i, i = 1, \ldots, n_N$ for the nodes. It's easy to convert, just change the sign for the leaf nodes and add n_L for the others.

To start with, we know the first n_L counts for the leaves, and we set the remaining values to `NA`. Then all we need to do on each iteration is to add the counts for left and right children of each node, whether those children are leaves or other nodes of the tree. On the first iteration, only the leaf nodes

will have a count that is not NA. But the addition will give us the correct
value for any node made by merging two leaves. On the next iteration, those
nodes will have non-NA counts, letting us compute the values for the next
set of nodes. Here is the corresponding function:

```
binaryCount <- function(nodes, leafValues) {
    nL <- length(leafValues)
    nN <- nrow(nodes)
    left <- nodes[,1]; right <- nodes[, 2]

    left <- ifelse(left<0, -left, left + nL)
    right <- ifelse(right<0, -right , right + nL)

    count <- c(leafValues, rep(NA, nN))

    while(any(is.na(count)))
        count <- c(leafValues, count[left] + count[right])

    count[-seq(length=nL)]
}
```

It may seem magic that we just do the same computation each time in the
loop. The computation works simply because adding two values produces
NA if either of the individual values is NA, so all the counts that are not yet
known just stay NA. To see the mechanism in action, we use the trace()
mechanism to print the value of sum(is.na(count)) (which is the number of
remaining NA values) on each iteration.

```
> nodeArea <- binaryCount(usTree@nodes, Area)
1: 49
2: 32
3: 21
4: 15
5: 11
6: 7
7: 4
8: 2
9: 1
```

See Section 3.6, page 70 for the tracing technique.

The same mechanism works for any element-by-element computation
which treats NA values that way. For more general summaries, we'd need to
replace only the values for which both subnodes were currently non-NA, but
otherwise the same logic applies.

One further detail of the example may seem wasteful. In each iteration, we recomputed the sum of all the counts, even those that had been successfully computed earlier, and were therefore no longer NA. The apparently more economical computation would be to replace the while() loop with:

```
while(any(is.na(count))) {
    remaining <- is.na(count)
    count[remaining] <- count[left[remaining]] +
                  count[right[remaining]]
}
```

In fact, it is not obvious which of the two versions takes more processing time. The second version trades off two extra subset operations and a replacement against a call to c() and a simple assignment in the first version, in addition to calling `+` with a smaller vector. A general point in thinking about efficiency in R is that primitive functions such as arithmetic are very fast. In this case, all the computations involved are either primitives or built in to the evaluator. It's not at all clear which version will be faster. What is more important, here and in many examples, is that you should not worry about such efficiency questions prematurely. If you start to apply much more complicated summary calculations than the simple additions here, then perhaps you should take care to compute only the values needed. However, the original version was simpler, giving it an edge in being trustworthy and error-free.

9.8 Example: Data Frames

The data frame concept permeates statistics, and science generally. Section 6.5, page 166, describes the concept and relates it to both statistical and other software. The general idea is that of meaningful *variables* on each of which corresponding *observations* are made, resulting in a conceptual two-way layout of data values, by convention with variables as columns and observations as rows. Software as diverse as spreadsheets and relational database systems share versions of this concept.

This section explores some class definitions related to the concept, including two approaches starting directly from the S3 class "data.frame", used in software for statistical models and for trellis graphics. Many other applications of the concept to programming with R arise, notably in the interfaces to other systems with similar concepts, such as spreadsheets and database systems (Section 6.5, page 173).

Given its wide reach, the data frame concept fits naturally with an abstract umbrella under which any specific implementation might fit. In R, the natural umbrella is a class union, with the S3 class as a member:

```
setClassUnion("dataFrame", "data.frame")
```

S4 classes can then be designed and added to the class union. Methods for the class union itself could use an agreed-upon set of functions (such as the `[` operator with two indices, and its replacement version). Functions `dim()` and `dimnames()` would require methods as well. Member classes of the union would be required to have a consistent method for each function. On the other hand, the goal is to avoid assumptions about how the actual representation of variables and observations is carried out. For example, computations for the class union would not rely on treating the object as a list of variables; these work for `"data.frame"` objects, but converting an arbitrary representation to such a list might be unwise or even impossible.

Once the class union has set out its requirements, then methods can be written for the union making use of the corresponding functions. These methods both extend the software for the member classes and also provide validation tests for those member classes. For example, a validity method for `"dataFrame"` could be written, and would apply to any member class that did not override it. See the `validDataFrame()` function in the `Examples/dataFrame.R` file of package SoDA, which is one possible such validity method.

Let's look next at two approaches to specific S4 classes derived from the `"data.frame"` class. The S3 `"data.frame"` class used a list to represent the data itself; each element of the list corresponded to a variable. The variables were implicitly required to represent the same set of observations. Both the columns (variables) and the rows (observations) were required to have character-string names, either specified or created by default. R now allows row names optionally to be integer, largely to speed up some operations. Our version could incorporate this by using a class union for row names, but for simplicity we'll omit that option.

As a first formal definition corresponding to `"data.frame"`, here is an implementation that follows the S3 class explicitly, with slots corresponding to the attributes of a `"data.frame"` object:

```
setClass("dataFrame1",
    representation(row.names = "character", names = "character"),
    contains = "list")
```

The content of a `"dataFrame1"` object, in fact, appears to be exactly the same as you would expect for the corresponding `"data.frame"` object, except of course for `class(x)` itself. Specifying the `"names"` slot explicitly is needed because S4 classes that extend `"list"` interpret lists as simple vectors, without a names attribute. It's incorrect to interpret names as intrinsic to list vectors, although understandable given the long use of named lists in the S language and especially in the `"pairlist"` object type in early versions of R.

Because class `"dataFrame1"`, like the S3 class, does extend class `"list"`, it inherits some computations that can be used in defining methods for the matrix-like behavior expected from data frames. The method for `dimnames()`, for example, could be essentially

```
list(x@row.names, names(x))
```

which relies on inheriting the `"list"` method for `names(x)`. Similarly, the method for `dim()` is

```
c(length(x@row.names), length(x))
```

These definitions provide much of the data frame behavior required of the class. A method for operator `` `[` `` and its replacement version would also be required; in fact, the S3 methods `` `[.data.frame` `` and `` `[<-.data.frame` `` do essentially the right computation.

Extending the basic `"list"` class simplified some of the programming when the `"data.frame"` class was introduced. The penalty for that was that some low-level software might be inherited that produced incorrect or at least questionable results. For example, consider the operator `` `$` `` to extract or replace a named element of an object. The default method (a primitive function in the `base` package) will apply automatically because the class definition extends `"list"`. But the code for replacing a named element is inherited also—the default method for the replacement function `` `$<-` ``—anything at all can be inserted as a variable, potentially destroying the validity of the object.

Inheritance means that the new class inherits every method for its superclass, except for explicitly defined new methods. If some inherited methods do not behave correctly, we are in grave danger of producing untrustworthy software. In the case of the S3 `"data.frame"` class, safety has required defining many methods for the class, including all the obvious ways to insert variables (at last count, the `base` package alone had 38 methods for `"data.frame"`!). Among these is a method for `` `$<-` `` that ensures the replacement value has the correct number of observations.

An alternative class definition would avoid inheritance, requiring more work to implement the basic computations but avoiding dangerous inherited methods: a tradeoff between ease of programming (the *Mission*) and

trustworthy software (the *Prime Directive*). A non-inheriting definition of
a class to represent data frames might look like:

```
setClass("dataFrame2",
    representation(variables = "list",
      colNames = "character", rowNames = "character"))
```

With this definition, none of the replacement operators for vectors or arrays
will be automatically available. Those that treat the object as conceptually
a two-way table will be needed, as in fact they were with the previous version
of the class. But the `$` operator is not naturally relevant, it just happened
to be inherited in the previous version. For the second version, we might
well omit any methods for `$`.

With the non-inheriting definition but with the internal structure essentially the same, the methods we do write may not look very different. With
class "dataFrame2", most extraction and replacement operations, for example, will begin by extracting the "variables" slot and then operate on that as
a list. The same computation for class "dataFrame1" could be implemented
in several ways. A clear version would start by turning the data into the list
of variables, with other information removed, so the reader could be assured
that the following computations used only the computations for basic lists.
In this case the inheriting and non-inheriting implementations only differ in
how they get to the underlying basic list:

```
variables <- x@variables
```

for class "dataFrame2" versus

```
variables <- as(x, "list")
```

for class "dataFrame1". For either class, the computation is likely to end by
constructing a new object from the recomputed variables. Aside from the
different slots in the two classes, the computation is essentially specifying
the same information.

Extensions to data frames

Extensions to the original data frame in S3 came from two directions: from
its role in the software for models; and from the use of the class more generally to represent statistical data. In model fitting, the "data.frame" class
was used in more than one version, sometimes with extra "slots" (attributes)
added but with the same class. This would be illegal with an S4 class, and
in fact caused some clumsiness in the original software.

One example was the `model.frame()` function and objects. The software in S for fitting models combined a data frame and a `"formula"` object in a call to one of several model-fitting functions to produce an object describing the fitted model. The different types of model generally shared a "model frame" intermediate object combining the data and formula, the latter based on a `"formula"` object usually supplied by the user. In Section 3.1, page 38, a linear model was constructed from a formula and the `clouds` data frame. The call to `lm()` used would have constructed a model frame as an intermediate step:

```
[1] "clouds"
> mf <- model.frame(formula, clouds)
> class(mf)
[1] "data.frame"
> names(attributes(mf))
[1] "names"     "terms"     "row.names" "class"
```

The model frame object still has class `"data.frame"`, but a new attribute has been added, an object of class `"terms"` (an S3 class that extends `"formula"`). This sort of ambiguity about object contents is one reason to prefer programming with S4 classes when possible. The ambiguity contributes to some of the clumsier details of the model software; for example, the `model.matrix()` function expects a model frame, but also requires a formula as an argument.

In a rewriting of the model-fitting software to use formal classes, it would be natural to provide model frames as a formal class that extends the data frame class.

```
setClass("modelFrame",
    representation(terms = "terms", contains = "dataFrame"))
```

One implementation question in such examples is whether to create another class union for the extension . The choice above says that we will always implement the model-frame aspect by a specific `"terms"` slot, regardless of how the underlying data frame was represented. For model frames, that choice seems appropriate, because the model frame is largely an internal class of objects used in standard computations. In other applications one might want to preserve the option to implement the added information in different ways, which would argue for the analog to `"modelFrame"` to be a virtual class.

Data frames outside models

The S3 `"data.frame"` class has been used heavily and successfully since its introduction, and not only for fitting models. Many of the datasets made available with R are provided as `"data.frame"` objects: the majority of those supplied with the "recommended packages" from CRAN, for example. Section 6.5, page 168, gives some practical discussion of the use of `"data.frame"` objects in R.

Other changes in the treatment of `"data.frame"` objects were motivated by using the class to represent data following the general concept (variables and observations) but arising in a wide variety of circumstances. Because the concept is shared, roughly, by both spreadsheet software and relational database systems, the `"data.frame"` class was a natural choice for importing data from these systems. The original model-fitting applications restricted variables to be numeric or factor, but more general use of data frames required lifting that restriction. The main technique for doing so was to add options to the R function `read.table()` and its specializations, `read.csv()` and `read.delim()`. The logical flag `as.is` would switch off the interpretation of text as factors, and the more general `colClasses` argument specifies the desired class for variables (see the examples in Section 6.5, page 168). The implementation of the general options allows essentially any class for a variable, with the software implicitly requiring that the class have a method for coercing from character vector.

For a formal treatment, a more general solution would be to provide a formal mechanism for ensuring that the variable could be treated correctly. A class, say `"DataFrameVariable"`, would encapsulate requirements on classes to be used for variables in a data frame. Methods would be required for coercing from `"character"` and for selecting a subset of observations (just the ` [ ` operator for vectors, but other definitions could be used to allow, for example, matrix variables). The `"DataFrameVariable"` class would be another class union, defined to include constraints on valid member classes.

Chapter 10

Methods and Generic Functions

This chapter describes the design and implementation of generic functions and methods in R, including basic techniques for creating methods, the definition of generic functions, and a discussion of method dispatch, the mechanism by which a method is chosen to evaluate a call to a generic function. Section 10.2, page 384, describes the fundamental mechanism for creating new methods. Section 10.3, page 387, discusses important functions that are frequently made generic; Section 10.5, page 396, provides more detail on the generic functions themselves; Section 10.6, page 405, discusses method selection—the matching of arguments in a call to the method signatures.

The chapter is closely related to Chapter 9, and cross-references between the two will be important.

10.1 Introduction: Why Methods?

A fundamental goal in programming is to increase the capabilities of the software without increasing the complexity for the user. With a functional system like R, the danger is that just writing more and larger functions harms both ease of exploration and trust in the software. Searching among many similar functions leaves the user baffled to find and choose an appropriate one. Multi-page R functions challenge even expert readers to understand the computations. One technique to manage complexity is to emphasize the generic behavior of a function: What is its purpose and what information does it use? The purpose can often be extended to new applications by defining *methods* that implement the generic behavior for different inputs; specifically, for different classes of objects appearing among the arguments to the function.

The functional approach to object-oriented programming centers on two basic concepts: the *class* of objects and the *generic function*—a function along with a collection of methods. The methods specify what calculations the function should do, when it is called with arguments from specified classes.

New generic functions can be defined explicitly and older functions can be turned into generics. In the latter case, the earlier function typically becomes the default method, producing compatible results for objects not covered by the new methods. As applications stimulate new classes to represent novel kinds of data, methods will often be created for the new classes. These methods frequently define how to print, plot, or summarize the new data. Where the classes are naturally interpreted as behaving like vectors, matrices, or structures, methods can be created for extracting and replacing subsets. Objects representing numeric information may have methods for arithmetic and numerical computations.

The process can start from the function side too. Statistics research or novel applications may suggest a fundamental computation for which a new function is needed. This function may achieve some general goal, but the details of how (the method) will often depend on the kind of data to which it is applied.

Example: Methods for statistical models

The classic, original example of defining methods comes from the work on statistical models in S, which inspired the first approach to classes and methods in the S language. The challenge of creating software to formulate, fit and assess statistical models led naturally to both new classes of data and new functions.

The S language approach to statistical models imagines a model as composed of three pieces:

1. the data to be used, organized as a `"data.frame"` object;

2. the structural `formula` that expresses a relation among variables in the data;

3. the statistical form of the model (e.g., linear model, additive model) along with other specifications for fitting.

The statistical model software in S and later in R organized the computations around some choices for the third item. For each major form of model handled, a corresponding function would generate a fitted model given a formula to express the structure and a specification of the data. The function lm() returned a fitted linear model in the form of an object of class "lm"; function gam() generated an additive model of class "gam"; and so on.

Given the fitted models,there are some key actions that naturally suggest corresponding functions: printing and plotting; predictions for new data; and updating the model for changes. For example, the stats package has a function update() to modify an existing fitted model for changes in the formula or the data. Its arguments are the current fit plus one or more of changes to the formula, new data, or other modifications. Such a function is naturally generic—its purpose and the arguments that it requires are generally meaningful, but the methods to implement the function will vary according to the class of the fitted model, and potentially according to other arguments as well.

To implement update() without using methods would be more difficult and less trustworthy. Either users would have to choose separate functions for each class of models or the single function would incorporate all the computations for all models. In the second case, as research or novel applications introduced new kinds of models, these would not be easily added. Both conceptual simplicity for the user and the discipline of a consistent interface for the implementations would suffer. In terms of our two principles, both the expressive power for data analysis (the *Mission*) and the trustworthiness of the implementation (the *Prime Directive*) benefit from the organization into generic functions and methods.

The stats package used S3 methods, whose signatures are only the first argument of the function, but a modern implementation could usefully make the methods for predict() depend on other arguments as well, such as the newdata supplied.

To summarize, method definitions contribute in two ways to software for data analysis:

1. To class definitions, by defining their behavior with relevant functions, either existing or new;

2. To the definition of generic functions, by defining their behavior for either new or existing classes.

10.2   Method Definitions

A method is specified by a call to `setMethod()`, typically in the form:

```
setMethod(f, signature, definition)
```

The call includes three pieces of information:

- the generic function `f` for which this is a method;

- the method `signature`, that is the classes that arguments should match;

- the method `definition`, a suitable function to be called when the signature matches the classes of the actual arguments in a call.

You can use the utility function, `method.skeleton()`, to write a file with an appropriate call to `setMethod()`, to create a new method. The utility will create a skeleton definition with the correct arguments. Its use is recommended, particularly when you're just starting to program with methods.

Let's look at an example: `Arith()` is a group generic function used to define methods for arithmetic operators (Section 10.5, page 403 discusses these). Suppose we want to write a method to evaluate calls when both arguments to the arithmetic operator come from a new class, `"trackNumeric"`. To generate a skeleton of the appropriate definition:

```
> method.skeleton("Arith", c("trackNumeric", "trackNumeric"))
Skeleton of method written to Arith_trackNumeric_trackNumeric.R
```

The utility constructed a name for the file (we could have supplied one). The file contains:

```
setMethod("Arith",
    signature(e1 = "trackNumeric", e2 = "trackNumeric"),
    function (e1, e2)
    {
        stop("Need a definition for the method here")
    }
)
```

The file generated has filled in the signature by matching to the eligible formal arguments, and created a dummy method definition. Now we can fill in the body of the definition, replacing the call to `stop()` with the computations we want.

Next, let's consider each of the three main arguments to `setMethod()` to get an overall understanding of how methods work.

Generic function

All methods are associated with a particular generic function, sometimes located in this environment or package and sometimes located in another package. The generic function may have been defined originally as such, or it may have been originally an ordinary function that was then set to be a generic function to augment its behavior. In either case, the `setMethod()` call in effect registers the new method as part of the generic function's definition. There's plenty of detail to understand here, but for the moment the key concept is that including `setMethod()` calls in your package means that the corresponding methods will be part of that function when your package is used. During any R computation, the generic function will have a collection of methods, one of which will be selected to evaluate each call to the function.

The argument `f` to `setMethod()` must identify which generic function in which package is meant. Nearly always, it's enough to give the name of the function, meaning that a search from the environment where `setMethod()` is called will find the correct function. But in principle more than one generic function (in different packages) can have the same name. Because R packages are not all required to use one global set of function names, duplicate names are inevitable. Each of the corresponding functions has its own set of methods. When you define a new method, it's likely that your package has arranged to use one particular generic function for each name. Ensuring such consistency is one of the main advantages of using the `NAMESPACE` mechanism, which allows your package to be explicit about where a particular function definition comes from.

Method signature

The signature says when to use the method, by supplying instructions for matching the class of arguments in a call to target classes for this method. The method signature associates each of a subset of the function's formal arguments with a particular class. The intuitive meaning is that this method can be selected if the corresponding actual arguments match those classes. Section 10.6 discusses just what "match" means, but the idea is that the class of the actual argument should be the same or the actual argument should come from a subclass of that specified in the signature.

The subset of formal arguments eligible to appear in method signatures is usually all the formal arguments, in order, except "..." (which, if used, matches all the arguments corresponding to "..." to the class in the signature; only in R 2.8.0 and later, see `?dotsMethods`). A generic function can have an explicit definition of the arguments allowed in method signatures; see Section 10.5, page 399. Some arguments cannot be used in method signatures because the function uses them symbolically, so that the argument cannot be evaluated in the ordinary way to find its class.

For convenience, the classes in the signature can be supplied with or without argument names in the call to `method.skeleton()` (or in fact, in the call to `setMethod()` itself). The rule for associating elements of the signature with formal arguments is the same as for a call to the function: Arguments can be named or unnamed, with unnamed arguments matched by position. If you are in any doubt about the arguments, it's wise to base the source code on the output from `method.skeleton()`.

As with the name of the generic function, so with the names of the classes: the same name could be used for different classes, in different packages. R will look for an appropriate class definition in the context of the `setMethod()` call.

Method definition

The method definition is a function that will be used instead of the generic function when the method signature is the best match to the objects in the call. The method function is not "called" from the generic in the usual sense. The arguments in the call start off already matched and evaluated, as they were in the call to the generic when the method was dispatched. To be precise, the actual arguments in the signature of the generic function are all evaluated when the method is selected (see Section 10.6, page 405 for details). Missing arguments are not touched, just noted. In particular, default expressions play no role in method selection, and are not evaluated then. Formal arguments that are not eligible to appear in method signatures are not evaluated at this point either.

The method definition must have all the formal arguments of the generic function, in the same order. The call to `setMethod()` will verify that the arguments are correct. Two techniques are available that appear to be exceptions to this rule, one to omit irrelevant arguments and the other to add arguments in addition to or instead of `"..."`. In fact, both techniques work by modifying the supplied definition to one with the correct set of formal arguments, but with the definition of the method and the signature modified to produce the desired result. See page 393.

10.3   New Methods for Old Functions

When defining a new class of objects, you are likely to apply existing functions to these objects. The new class may be an extension of a class of objects provided by an existing R package. For example, you might be extending existing software that deals with sparse matrices (package `Matrix`) or some classes dealing with microarray data (many of the BioConductor packages). Or the new class may be developed independently as part of your own software work. As noted in Chapter 9, any new class will need some methods to print or plot objects. In addition, classes that extend those in existing packages will need some methods for functions from those packages, to express how the new class differs. For matrix-based classes, for example, methods to insert or extract data and for at least some of the numerical matrix computations are likely. Your software will be calling `setMethod()` to create new methods for functions that exist in other packages, both packages included with R and packages from other sources.

The concept is that your method will become part of the function's collection of methods, just for the session usually. I think of this as a request from your software that the generic function accept this new method. Being a generic function implies a willingness to accept such requests, provided the method is valid for this function. (In practice, software in the R evaluator inserts the method in a table associated with the generic function, either when `setMethod()` is called or, more often, when a package containing the method is loaded.) The `Matrix` package has a generic function `Cholesky()`, for example, that is intended to compute objects representing the matrix decomposition of the same name. If you had a new class to represent special matrices then you might want to add a new `Cholesky()` method for that class:

```
setMethod(Cholesky, "myMatrix",  etc.)
```

If the function is not currently generic, you may still legitimately want to create a method for your new class. In nearly all situations you can and should create such methods, but the process requires additional action from the methods software.

Conceptually, adding a method to an "ordinary" function is a request that the function use this method when the actual arguments match the method's signature, while behaving as before for all arguments that do not match. The simple mechanism that approximately answers this request has two steps: to create a generic function with the same arguments as the original; and to make the original function the default method for the new generic. Then `setMethod()` can be used in the usual way to define one or more methods. Most functions that are not already generic have a corresponding *implicit generic function* either inferred automatically or specified explicitly (see Section 10.5, page 401). Just calling `setMethod()` activates the implicit generic. Alternatively, you can create a generic function with an intentionally augmented argument list, but this is a different function and must live in a different environment.

The function `chol()` and the `Matrix` package give an example. This is another version of the Cholesky decomposition, differing from `Cholesky()` in the way it represents the result. Function `chol()` is an older version, with S3 methods, found in the `base` package. The `Matrix` package defines a number of methods for this function, after creating a generic version of it. The generic function is actually somewhat more general in that it adds an argument `pivot`, and explicitly calls the function from the `base` package in the default method. As a result a new `chol()` function is created in the `Matrix` package. Adding an argument is necessary if you want to define methods using it; in this case, the original `chol()` had only x and "..." as arguments. However, having two versions of the function is potentially confusing. Other things being equal, try for a solution that retains the implicit generic version of the function.

The creation of a generic function works fine in nearly all cases, but there are some subtle differences in behavior from the earlier non-generic situation. The evaluator must examine the actual arguments, as noted on page 386, in order to select a method. The mechanism of "lazy evaluation" for arguments—that arguments are evaluated when needed—no longer applies as it would have for most non-generic functions. The arguments are needed right away. See Section 13.3, page 462 for lazy evaluation, and Section 10.5, page 396 to adjust the generic function for special cases.

Often the non-generic function will actually be an S3 generic function; for example, the functions in the `stats` package for examining and updating statistical models are nearly all S3 generics. The S3 generic becomes the default method in S4 terms, just as it would for any non-generic function. Therefore, an S3 method will be used only if no explicitly specified S4 method matches the actual call; in most practical cases, that is the natural behavior. Notice that you should not define S3 methods for S4 classes: The danger of doing so is that S3 generic functions have no way to detect inheritance in S4 classes.

You can promote the S3 method to an S4 method if you want, provided that the S3 class, and any other S3 classes that inherit from it, have been declared by calls to `setOldClass()`. See Section 9.6, page 362.

Methods for basic operators and primitive functions

Special considerations apply when defining methods for operators and other *primitive functions*. These do not exist as ordinary function objects; in particular, they have no formal argument list, `formalArgs()` returns `NULL` for them. That does not prevent writing methods for most of them, however. Starting with `method.skeleton()` is still recommended.

```
> method.skeleton("[[", "dataFrame1", "elementDataFrame.R")
Skeleton of method written to elementDataFrame.R
```

(We supplied the file name in the call, because dealing with files that have special characters in the name may be inconvenient on some systems.) A few primitive functions do not permit methods (`missing()`, for example). Also, for operators and numeric transformations, writing methods for the group of functions may often be a good idea (Section 10.5, page 404).

Primitive functions are special also in the way that methods are dispatched, both modern methods and S3 methods. For the sake of machine efficiency in using these functions, particularly with basic data types such as vectors, the primitive implementation in C is always called, regardless of whether methods have been defined. Code built in at the C level examines the actual arguments to detect possible methods; if there is a matching method, a call to the appropriate method will be constructed and evaluated. Otherwise, the evaluation drops through to the C implementation of the primitive, that is, of the default method.

10.4 Programming Techniques for Methods

This section collects a variety of topics that arise in writing methods, particularly as you progress towards software that others may use or that integrates multiple methods.

Documentation for methods

To find documentation for existing methods, a Web browser usually provides the best interface, either an actual browser or the similar interface provided by a GUI. Special documentation topics are constructed for methods, as they are for classes (see Section 9.2, page 341). Method documentation is listed under the name of the generic function, followed by a comma-separated list consisting of the class names in the signature and ending with `"-method"`. So if the generic function is `plot()` and the signature is `c("track", "missing")`, then the documentation for the method would be listed under

```
plot,track,missing-method
```

The same documentation topic (quoted) can be passed to the `` `?` `` operator or the `help()` function.

Documentation for the method in question does have to be written in order for users to look at it, unfortunately. As with functions and classes, a utility function, in this case `promptMethods()`, will initialize a file of such documentation for the programmer to fill in. For example, suppose we have written some methods in our package for function `plot()`. To generate a documentation file for these, we build and install the package, and then attach it (in position 2 on the search list as will happen by default). Then:

```
> promptMethods("plot")
A shell of methods documentation has been written
to the file 'plot-methods.Rd'.
```

By default, `promptMethods()` picks up the methods from the first package on the search list that has some. If our package was SoDA, for example and had methods for x being either `"track"` or `"track3"`, and y being `"missing"`, the file would contain these lines (among others):

```
\alias{plot-methods}
\alias{plot,track,missing-method}
\alias{plot,track3,missing-method}
\title{ ~~ Methods for Function plot in Package `SoDA' ~~}

\section{Methods}{
\describe{
\item{x = "track", y = "missing"}{ ~~describe this method here }
\item{x = "track3", y = "missing"}{ ~~describe this method here }
}}
```

You could fill in the file as is, or move the relevant lines to another documentation file first.

Methods and default values

Arguments in generic function definitions can have default expressions, which are passed down to the selected method. The following example illustrates several points about such defaults.

```
> setGeneric("xplot", function(x, xlim= xlimit(x))
+     standardGeneric("xplot"))
> setMethod("xplot", "numeric",
+     function(x, xlim = range(x,na.rm = TRUE))
+         plot(x, xlim=xlim))
```

Let's imagine that `xplot()` is a generic function we want for a variant of regular plotting, and `xlimit()` is some parallel function for computing limits on the plot.

First point: the default expression has no effect on method selection. In a call of the form `xplot(x)`, method selection uses the special class `"missing"` as the actual class for argument `xlim`. The class resulting from evaluating the default expression, `xlimit(x)`, is irrelevant.

Second, a method definition can include a default that overrides the default in the generic function, as we see in the method defined for signature `"numeric"`. The default expression in the generic function will not be evaluated in this case. Unfortunately, the R mechanism for handling defaults currently prevents a method from introducing a default expression unless the argument in question already had a default expression in the generic function. In the example, the method could not introduce a default for argument `x`. (Future improvements to R may eliminate this defect—check the online documentation `?Methods`.)

Third, the default expression is evaluated according to the standard lazy evaluation rules. Default expressions differ from actual arguments in this respect; actual arguments have to be evaluated to select a method, but missing arguments always match class `"missing"`. Otherwise, both logical consistency and efficiency would suffer. Given the definitions for `xplot()` above, a call with a numeric `x` object and `xlimit` missing would result in a call to `range()`, but not until needed, down in the call to `plot()`.

Calling methods from methods

The functions `callGeneric()` and `callNextMethod()` will result in a call to another method for the current generic function. In the first case, one simply calls the function, with different objects as the arguments, resulting in a selection of a method, usually not the same as the current method. In the second case, the generic function is called, often with the same arguments, but with the currently defined method excluded. Both `callGeneric()` and `callNextMethod()` can be called with any set of arguments, and both interpret a call with no arguments by passing down the same arguments as in the current method.

The two mechanisms are similar in form, but they shine in different circumstances: `callGeneric()` is essential in many methods for group generic functions (Section 10.5, page 404); `callNextMethod()` works well when we want to build up the current method by changes to a method for one of the superclasses.

Let's look again at the `initialize()` method in Section 9.5, page 360:

```
setMethod("initialize", "track",
    function(.Object, x, y, ...) {
        if(missing(y)) {
            y <- x; x <- seq(along=y)
        }
        callNextMethod(.Object, x = x, y = y, ...)
    })
```

The method definition uses the technique discussed on page 394 to add two formal arguments, x and y, that are not in the generic function `initialize()`. The motivation is to allow users to supply these arguments without names, and also to allow default values to be computed if only one of the two is supplied. The method adjusts for missing y with the same idea used by `plot()`, making a sequence of the same length as x and treating x as y. It then passes explicit x and y slots to the next method.

The next method happens to be the default method in this case, but using `callNextMethod()` is simpler to program than explicitly extracting the default method. It's also more reliable, in that it remains valid even if the class should later acquire a superclass with an `initialize()` method. Both the *Mission* and the *Prime Directive* benefit.

When the functions `callGeneric()` and `callNextMethod()` are called with no arguments, the current arguments are passed on in a constructed call to the generic function or selected method. Specifically, the formal arguments included in the current call will appear in the constructed call, and only these. If the generic function `f()` had formal arguments x, y, z, ... and the current call supplied just x and y, then the constructed call would have the form:

```
f(x = x, y = y)
```

Argument-less calls to `callGeneric()` and `callNextMethod()` are convenient when the current method does some adjustments and then proceeds to use some other methods. Two warnings need to be kept in mind, though. First, calls without arguments are ambiguous if the method in fact has different arguments from the generic (as was the case in our example above). Because the local formal arguments are different, there may be no unambiguous way to pass on the "..." arguments. Best to give explicit arguments, as we did in the example. Second, you need to be careful with `callGeneric()`, to be sure that suitable changes have been made to some of the original arguments; otherwise, an infinite loop will result.

The common use of `callGeneric()` is with group methods, where the actual generic function recalled will depend on which member of the group was called originally. See Section 10.5, page 404 for group methods.

To conclude this section, we discuss two techniques that appear to be exceptions to the key rule that the formal arguments of a method must agree exactly with those of the generic function. The first allows irrelevant arguments to be omitted from the method definition, forcing the corresponding arguments to be missing in the call in order for the method to be selected. The other modifies the `"..."` argument in the generic: adding arguments, replacing `"..."`, or omitting it.

These techniques can be helpful in making your method definitions clearer and in allowing users flexibility in calling them. However, they only appear to violate the rule; in fact, the method definition supplied is modified by utilities called from `setMethod()` to behave as usual, while conforming to the intent of the definition supplied. Both techniques are in a sense only cosmetic, because the same computation produced by the modification could be programmed directly. If you find the techniques convenient, use them. But if you find the modified code confusing (for example, hard to debug), it's better to go back to the strictly standard method definition.

Omitting irrelevant arguments

Some of the arguments to the generic function may make no sense in a particular method. For trustworthy programming, the method should force those arguments to be missing in the actual call. Just omitting the argument from the signature of the method does not accomplish this: The interpretation is that the argument corresponds to class `"ANY"`, so that the user can supply any argument at all, but the argument will be ignored! Instead, supply the special class `"missing"` in the signature for the method. A call that has an actual argument corresponding to this formal argument will never be selected in this case.

Such arguments may be omitted from the definition of the method. The omission is interpreted to imply class `"missing"` for the argument in the signature. A classic case for irrelevant arguments is the operator `` `[` ``: in addition to argument x for the object, it has two explicit index arguments, i and j, includes `"..."` for additional index arguments, and then has an argument `drop=` at the end of the argument list. Generally, none of the index arguments except x and i are relevant for most methods other than those for matrix- or array-like classes. It's cluttered and confusing to include all these arguments in methods for which they are irrelevant. They can, in fact, be omitted. For example, here is a method for this operator for the"trackNumeric" class:

```
setMethod("[",
      signature(x = "trackNumeric", i = "ANY", j = "missing"),
      function(x, i) {
            x@.Data[i]
      })
```

The code is certainly much simpler and easier to read. It's optional to omit the "missing" elements from the signature in the second line as well, but argument j has been included here to emphasize the meaning of the method.

Keep in mind, however, that it's all essentially cosmetic. The actual method definition stored has the full argument list, and the signature will be modified if necessary to force the omitted arguments to be missing. In fact, both the techniques mentioned above are being used here. Arguments j and drop are in the signature for the generic function, and will be added to the method signature with class "missing". But argument "..." is never in the signature; it will be forced to be omitted by the technique for modifying argument lists.

Modifying argument lists in methods

When a method has been selected for use in a call to a generic function, the body of the method is evaluated without re-matching the arguments in the call. Therefore, the formal arguments of the method must be identical to the formal arguments of the generic function.

On the other hand, details of a particular method may suggest some extra arguments that would not be meaningful for the function generally; for example, parameters related to a particular numerical method or options that only make sense for certain classes of objects. One might want to match these arguments in the usual way, named or unnamed, as if they had been formal arguments. You can, simply by calling a helper function written with the special arguments included, and passing "..." to that function. However, sometimes it is clearer to write the method itself with the modified arguments.

Method definitions accommodate these modified arguments by a technique that does not really change method dispatch itself, but allows programmers to add extra arguments and/or to drop the "..." argument. The mechanism simply turns the programmer's method into a local function and constructs the actual method definition to call this function. Extra arguments are matched from the "..." argument to the generic function, using standard R argument matching. For this mechanism to work requires several conditions.

1. The generic function must have "..." as a formal argument.

2. The formal arguments of the method definition must include all the formal arguments of the generic function, in the same order, with the possible exception of "..." itself.

3. Any extra arguments to the method definition must appear just before, just after or instead of the "..." argument.

These requirements just state conditions needed for the argument matching in the call to the local function to work correctly.

For a simple example, consider the `initialize()` method for class `"track"`, previously used to illustrate `callNextMethod()`:

```
setMethod("initialize", "track",
    function(.Object, x, y, ...) {
        if(missing(y)) {
            y <- x; x <- seq(along=y)
        }
        callNextMethod(.Object, x = x, y = y, ...)
    })
```

The formal arguments to `initialize()` are `".Object"` and `"..."`. The default method requires all the `"..."` arguments to be named with the names of slots in the class definition. For class `"track"`, the slots are `"x"` and `"y"`, interpreted as the coordinates.

The `"track"` method for `initialize()` allows one or two sets of coordinates to be given in the usual positional form, and treats one set of coordinates as a curve at equally spaced points (the same logic as used by function `plot()`). The method definition will be treated as if it had been written:

```
function (.Object, ...)
{
    .local <- function (.Object, x, y, ...)
    {
        if (missing(y)) {
            y <- x
            x <- seq(along = y)
```

```
            }
            callNextMethod(.Object, x = x, y = y, ...)
        }
        .local(.Object, ...)
    }
```

The call to the next method (which will be the default method, because class "track" contains no superclasses) always names the coordinates. See page 392 for the callNextMethod() aspect of the example.

The "..." argument is retained, allowing additional arguments, even though none would be legal for class "track" itself. This is a good idea for all initialize() methods, because it allows the method to be used with a subclass of "track". For example, a call to new() for class "track3" (page 336), which contains "track", could continue to use the initialize() method for "track", but only if other slots could be specified and passed down to the default method. Remember that nearly any method you write could be inherited, with objects coming from a subclass of the class you specified. Various tactics allow for this possibility; for example, you should generally use the object's actual class in computations, not the class you specified to setMethod().

In the example for operator `[` shown previously, the "..." argument was deliberately omitted, in contrast to the initialize() example. With the operator, additional arguments would not be passed down to another method, so omitting "..." lets R catch invalid argument names, which would otherwise be silently eaten up by "...".

All these details are just part of the continuing, essential process of thinking about your software and how it might be used.

10.5   Generic Functions

A generic function inherits the behavior of an ordinary R function, particularly from the user's view. When the function is called, actual arguments are matched to the formal arguments, and the function returns a result or does some other computation for the user. If the function is well designed, it has a clear functionality in terms of the arguments and the results.

Generic functions differ in that the computations include dispatching a method according to the classes of the actual arguments. The complete generic function, then, consists of the function itself plus the collection of methods for that function currently defined and active. The generic function nearly always comes from a particular R package, but the methods for that function may be distributed over several packages, and the active methods may depend on what packages are being used in the current session.

This section presents techniques for detailed control over generic functions. The function is created either directly or by conversion of a non-generic function. Options in direct creation include doing additional computation before or after dispatching a method (page 399) and controlling which arguments may appear in method signatures (page 399). This control can also be specified implicitly, for a function that is not (yet) generic, to ensure that all methods defined for this function will be consistent or to restrict the arguments that may be used (page 401). Generic functions can be organized as groups, with the option of defining methods for the group generic that then apply to all functions in the group (page 403).

Creating a generic function

At this point, we need to clarify the distinction between a generic function as an object, versus the key action that it takes, namely to dispatch a method corresponding to a call to the function. When we are using methods or even writing them, this distinction is usually unimportant, because the computations we are responsible for begin when the method is evaluated. In defining a generic function, we may need to be more precise.

Method dispatch—selecting a method and evaluating its body in the current context—is done in R by a call to `standardGeneric()`, with an argument that essentially always must be the name of the function. Also, you cannot just insert a call to `standardGeneric()` in an arbitrary piece of R code. The call must come from a generic function object. During an R session, this object will contain the currently active methods for the corresponding function in a suitable form for method dispatch (specifically, in a table that includes both direct and inherited methods for various classes of arguments). The generic function is created as a side effect of the call to `setGeneric()`.

Generic functions are defined in two common ways, either by converting an existing non-generic function or by defining a new function in terms of its arguments and perhaps its default method. The first case is simpler, frequently not requiring any information other than the name of the function.

In either case, the generic function is defined by three choices:

1. the formal arguments;

2. the *signature*, that is, the subset of the arguments that can be used in defining methods; and,

3. for nonstandard generic functions, the body of the function. A standard generic function does no computation other than dispatching a method, but R generic functions can do other computations as well before and/or after method dispatch.

In addition, the call to `setGeneric()` can provide the default method for the function; that is, the method corresponding to class `"ANY"` for all arguments.

With an existing function, default choices are often used for all the above. For example, the function `plot()` can be turned into a generic by:

```
setGeneric("plot")
```

The implicit generic will be used; in this case, the signature will have arguments x and y and a standard generic will be created. The previous non-generic version of the function becomes the default method. Calling `setMethod()` for a function that is not currently generic, without explicitly calling `setGeneric()`, has the same effect.

A signature can be specified in the call to `setGeneric()` as an ordered subset of the eligible formal arguments. See page 399. Otherwise, the signature consists of all the formal arguments except `"..."`, in the order they appear in the function definition. Methods cannot be defined for `"..."`, which is substituted into a call rather than matching a single object.

The argument `useAsDefault` specifies a default method:

```
setGeneric("plot",
    useAsDefault = function(x, y, ...)graphics::plot(x, y, ...))
```

In practice, `useAsDefault` is useful mainly when no non-generic version of the function exists. In that case, the arguments for the default method also define those for the generic function and, normally, the generic signature as well.

There is a subtle difference between the default method above and the previous version, where the existing function on package graphics was copied over as the default method. The explicit version uses operator `` `::` `` to call the current function named `"plot"` on package `graphics`, even if that has changed since the generic function was created. It's unlikely to make a difference in this case, but one choice or the other might suit the overall design with functions that are more likely to change than `plot()`.

An explicit generic function form can be supplied, as the argument `def` to `setGeneric()`. The body of the function definition supplied as this argument will contain only a call to `standardGeneric()` when a standard generic function is desired. The generic function `Schur()` is defined in the `Matrix` package:

```
setGeneric("Schur",
    def = function(x, vectors, ...) standardGeneric("Schur"))
```

Supplying `def` is often used to prevent a default method from being defined. In this case, function `Schur()` returns a particular form of matrix decomposition, and so is meaningful only when `x` is some form of matrix object or something that can be similarly interpreted. Arbitrary objects should produce an error, as they will in the absence of a default method:

```
> Schur("hello, world")
Error in function (classes, fdef, mtable)   :
    unable to find an inherited method for function "Schur",
    for signature "character", "missing"
```

Users might benefit from a default method that stopped with a more specific error message, but an error is the key requirement.

Nonstandard generic functions

By definition, a standard generic function consists only of the dispatching call to `standardGeneric()`. For conceptual simplicity and to some extent for efficiency, most generic functions should be standard generics. However, other computations can be included, so long as a (successful) call eventually calls `standardGeneric()`. To create a nonstandard generic function, supply the definition as the argument `def=` in a call to `setGeneric()`.

One reason for having a nonstandard generic is to apply some checks to the value of the call to the method. In this case, `standardGeneric()` will be called first, and its value then used in later computations. The function `initialize()` is an example; it does some checking that the generated object is valid.

The simplest such case, to require the value of the function to have a particular class, can be handled automatically by including the argument `valueClass` in the call to `setGeneric()`.

Generic signature

The signature of the generic is the ordered set of formal arguments for which methods can be specified, usually all the formal arguments in order, except for `"..."` (see `?dotsMethods` to use `"..."`). Suppose the generic function has formal arguments:

```
> args(f)
function (x, y, z, ...)
NULL
```

Then the default signature would be equivalent to `expression(x, y, z)`. The `setGeneric()` call can include a `signature` argument to override the default.

The main reason to do so is to remove from the signature any argument for which lazy evaluation is required. If an argument appears in a method signature, the argument must be evaluated immediately in order to select a method. For consistent behavior regardless of what methods have been defined, all the arguments in the signature of the generic function are evaluated when a method is selected.

When creating a generic function from an existing function, therefore, one needs to identify arguments requiring lazy evaluation. These are frequently treated specially depending on the unevaluated form of the argument, such as treating unevaluated names as strings. A good clue is a call to `substitute()` involving the argument. The functions `library()` and `require()`, for example, use the argument `"package"` literally, by examining `substitute(package)`. A generic version of these functions could not include `package` in the signature without breaking current use. Similarly for the function `help()`, a call such as

```
help(Startup)
```

shouldn't normally work, because there is usually no object named `Startup` and if there was, the call has nothing to do with it. The function uses lazy evaluation to examine the first argument as an unevaluated expression. In retrospect, these functions might have been better without the special features, to behave more consistently with standard R evaluation, but they are unlikely to change. Methods cannot be written for such functions without ensuring that the corresponding arguments are excluded, because all arguments in the generic function's signature must be evaluated in order to select a method.

Some uses of lazy evaluation are simply to test explicitly for missing arguments rather than supplying a default expression. Since missing arguments are not touched in method selection, the same code could still be used in a method where this argument defaulted to class `"ANY"`. Alternatively, you could have methods for class `"missing"` corresponding to this argument and implementing the same action, perhaps more clearly.

Technically, it's possible to retain lazy evaluation for any argument, by introducing code into the generic function to deal with the argument before a method is selected. If one wanted to examine the argument by calling `substitute()` for example, that examination needs to be done before calling `standardGeneric()`. I would not recommend this approach unless you are really sure it makes sense. The combination of sometimes using an argument unevaluated and sometimes dispatching a method on the same argument has a strong potential for confusion and untrustworthy computations.

Note that the order of names in the generic signature is significant. The signature of methods must correspond to that order; that is, if a method signature is supplied as one or more unnamed strings (the usual case), the classes match the names in the generic signature. For this reason, it's probably not a good idea to reorder the arguments in the signature, even if a later argument is more likely to appear in a method signature. The chance of confusing your users about what method they are actually creating is high. It's usually better to leave the generic signature in the same order as the formal arguments.

Implicit generic functions

It's important that all methods defined for a particular function from a particular package deal with the same generic function. If you in your package define some methods for `plot()` from the `graphics` package, and I do so also in my package, our intention is usually that those methods apply to the same generic `plot()` function. If so, they had better agree on its properties, such as the generic signature and whether this is a standard generic function.

For this reason, all functions are considered to correspond to an *implicit generic function*. The simple conversion of, say, the function `with()` on the `base` package to be a generic function corresponds to:

```
setGeneric("with")
```

By definition, the result corresponds to the implicit generic version of `with()`.

If nothing else is done, the implicit generic follows all the default rules outlined in this section: a standard generic, whose signature is all the formal arguments except `"..."`. That's nearly always fine, but for just the reasons outlined in the section so far, there may be functions for which something else is needed. R provides the implicit generic function mechanism for these cases.

The function `with()` is a case in point. Its second argument is an expression that is used literally, and so must not be in the generic signature. On the other hand, `with()` is not a generic function, so the signature must be specified implicitly. If `with()` was in our personal package, we would define what the generic version should be. This information is stored in an internal table; when `setGeneric("with")` is evaluated, the desired generic is retrieved and used. Notice that the table is conceptually associated with the package owning the original function. No matter what other package defines methods for the function, it's this version that is used.

If a call to `setGeneric()` defines a version of the generic that is not identical to the implicit generic, the new generic function will not reside in the original package; instead, a new function will be created in the package that had the `setGeneric()` call. Having a separate version is potentially confusing, but sometimes necessary if the new package requires method selection on an argument not in the original function (as in the `chol()` example on page 388). Note that the new generic is created whether the implicit generic has been specified directly or has been left as the default. Consistency is the essential requirement.

Implicit generic functions are encountered most frequently for functions in the core R packages (`base`, `graphics`, etc.), for traditional functions in the S language. Call `implicitGeneric()` to see a particular implicit generic function:

```
> implicitGeneric("with")
standardGeneric for "with" defined from package "base"

function (data, expr, ...)
standardGeneric("with")
<environment: 0x29ad924>
Methods may be defined for arguments: data
```

Creating a new non-default implicit generic function corresponding to a function in your own package can be done most easily by creating a generic version of the function, in the source for the package, just as you would normally, by calling `setGeneric()`. You can even define some methods for the function, so that when additional methods are defined these are also available. Once you have defined the generic version, a call to `setGenericImplicit()` will restore the non-generic version of the function and also save the generic version to be used whenever another package or a user's source code defines a method for this function.

As an illustration, here is a function that constructs a formula to drop terms from a model (for a related example, see Section 3.1, page 39):

```
> updFormula <- function(model, var) {
+         var <- as.character(substitute(var))
+         tnames <- colnames(attr(terms(model), "factors"))
+         hasVar <- grep(paste(":",var,":", sep = ""),
+                 paste(":", tnames, ":", sep=""), fixed = TRUE)
```

```
+          fText <- paste("~ .", paste("-", tnames[hasVar], collapse = " "))
+          eval(parse(text = fText)[[1]])
+      }
>
> setGeneric("updFormula", signature = "model")
>
> setMethod(updFormula, "formula", function(model, var) {
+          eval(parse(text = paste("~ . -", as.character(var))))
+      })
>
> setGenericImplicit("updFormula")
```

We chose to treat `var` in the argument list as a literal; not necessarily a good idea, but common in R functions to save users from typing quotation marks. As a result, we had to ensure that `var` was not in the signature for the generic function. We added a method to this generic version, to treat the case that `model` was a formula object. Finally, a call to `setGenericImplicit()` reverts `updFormula()` to the non-generic version. The generic, including the defined method, is saved as the implicit generic, to be restored when a call to `setGeneric()` or `setMethod()` occurs.

Groups of generic functions

Generic functions can belong to a group, specified by the `group=` argument in the call to `setGeneric()`. If specified, this identifies a group generic function; the function created in the call is a *member* of that group. Methods defined for the group generic are used for a call to the member function, if that function has no directly specified method for that method signature.

A number of group generic functions are defined in the `methods` package itself. For example, `Arith()` is a group generic function for all the arithmetic operators (`` `+` ``, etc.), and `Compare()` is a group generic function for the comparison operators (`` `==` ``, `` `>` ``, etc.). Group generic functions nest, so that the function `Ops()` is a group generic that includes `Arith()` and `Compare()` among its members. To see the known members, use the function `getGroupMembers()`:

```
> getGroupMembers(Compare)
[1] "==" ">"  "<"  "!=" "<=" ">="
```

New group generic functions can be created by calling `setGroupGeneric()`. The functions created are never called directly, and their body is just a call to `stop()`.

Group generic functions in effect create an inheritance structure for functions, for the purpose of method selection. The essential rule is that a group generic method matches a specific signature less well than a method for the member of the group with the same signature, but better than a method inherited from superclasses. And, naturally, the direct group generic matches better than the group that the direct group belongs to. In a call to `>`, for example, a method for `Compare()` would match before one for `Ops()`, for a specific signature.

Methods for group generic functions

Methods written for group generic functions usually require recalling the underlying generic function with some modified arguments. Group generic methods are useful when we observe a computational pattern that applies to all or many member functions, after substitution of the specific function into the general pattern. In this respect, the methods are analogous to the *templates* found in various programming languages.

The chief mechanism for inserting the individual generic into the general pattern is `callGeneric()`. As an example, consider our simple `"track"` class (Section 9.2, page 336). Suppose we decide to implement comparison operations for these objects, comparing the two slots, x and y. There are six functions in the `Compare()` group: equals, not equals, and four comparison operators. Equality requires corresponding elements of both slots to be equal, and similarly the value of `!=` is `TRUE` where either element is unequal. For the other comparisons, we want a value of `TRUE` if `TRUE` for both the x and y elements, `FALSE` if `FALSE` for both, and `NA` otherwise.

The first two methods can be defined as:

```
setMethod("==", c("track", "track"),
          function(e1, e2) {
              e1@x == e2@x &
                e1@y == e2@y
          })

setMethod("!=", c("track", "track"),
          function(e1, e2) {
              e1@x != e2@x |
                e1@y != e2@y
          })
```

We could go on to define the four remaining methods individually, but in fact they have the same pattern. That pattern can be expressed as a method for the Compare() group generic:

```
setMethod("Compare", c("track", "track"),
        function(e1, e2) {
            cmpx <- callGeneric(e1@x, e2@x)
            cmpy <- callGeneric(e1@y, e2@y)
            ifelse(cmpx & cmpy, TRUE,
                    ifelse(cmpx | cmpy, NA, FALSE))
        })
```

(Working out how these methods implement the verbal description is a good exercise in understanding comparisons and logical operators in R. Try them out on the data examples in the SoDA package.)

The group generic methods would apply to `==` and `!=` as well, but the existence of explicit methods for these operators, for the same signature, guarantees that the group methods will not be called.

10.6 How Method Selection Works

This section describes method selection in somewhat more detail than the examples earlier in the chapter. The details may help to explain why certain methods are selected, and also why at times warnings appear about ambiguous choices of methods. The important conclusion, however, is that from our principles of effective and trustworthy software, it's usually a mistake to depend on the details of method selection. Better in most cases to define a few more methods to resolve any ambiguous situations.

The method selection mechanism maintains a table (an R environment) in which the available methods for a particular generic function are stored, indexed by strings formed by concatenating identifiers for classes. In fact, there are two tables, one containing all the methods that can be called, and another containing the methods explicitly defined. The latter all come from a setMethod() call in some package, for this function or for a group generic function that includes this function as a group member. The table of callable methods contains all these, plus methods selected so far by inheritance, when no explicitly defined method existed. Both tables are stored in the generic function object during the R session. Methods are added to the table of defined methods when packages that contain methods for this function are loaded or attached, or when a setMethod() call occurs for this function.

Methods are indexed by the signature defined by the call to setMethod(); that is, by a class associated with each of the formal arguments in the signature of the generic function. For example, the function `plot()` has an implicit signature of the formal arguments other than `"..."`; that is, `c("x", "y")`. The classes are represented by character strings, usually just the string name of the class, but possibly including the package name if the same class name is defined in more than one package. (The further possibility of having two packages of the same name is not handled, either here or in other situations.) For the examples in this chapter, we make things simpler by assuming that a particular class name only arises from one package.

When a request to select a method for this function occurs, the *target signature* corresponding to the actual arguments is computed, and matched against the table of callable methods for the function. Notice that only the actual arguments are used. If an argument is present, it is evaluated and the class of the result goes into the target signature. If the argument is missing, class `"missing"` goes into the target signature, not the class that an evaluated default expression might have. The evaluation of actual arguments normally takes place when `standardGeneric()` is called.

It's an important consequence that lazy evaluation is not available for arguments that are in the signature of the generic function. Arguments that require lazy evaluation should be omitted from the generic signature (the best solution) or examined before method selection (Section 10.5, page 399).

In the internal implementation of `standardGeneric()`, if the target signature is found in the table of callable methods for this generic, that method is selected and used to evaluate the call to the generic. If the target signature is not found, the computations proceed to look for an inherited method. If one is selected, that method is then copied into the table of callable methods and indexed by the target signature, where it will be found directly on the next call with the same target signature.

Inherited methods

When no exact match of the target signature is found, all qualifying inherited methods are assembled and compared to find those that have the least "distance" from the target signature. A candidate method qualifies for inheritance if, for each argument in the signature, the class in the candidate is equal to or a superclass of the class in the target. In addition to candidates directly defined for the generic function itself, candidates will be added from the group generic functions for this function, taken in order if there are several generations of group generic. The default method, if there is one, always qualifies, but if there are any other qualifying candidates, the default method is not considered further.

The distance between a candidate signature and the target is computed currently as the sum of the distances for each class inheritance. Class inheritance distance is essentially the number of generations of inheritance. Classes contained directly in the target class have distance 1, those contained in the directly inherited classes have distance 2, and so on. Class "ANY" is considered to have a distance larger than any of the actual inherited distances.

There can be more than one qualifying candidate with the same distance. If some, but not all, of these are from group generic functions, those from group generics are now discarded. If more than one candidate remains, the selection is considered ambiguous. The current implementation issues a warning, but picks one method arbitrarily (currently it's just the first on the list, which is in effect the result of lexically ordering the superclasses of the target classes).

Once an inherited method is selected, it is saved in the table of all callable methods—not in the table of explicitly defined methods, which is used for inheritance computations. It would be an error to use inherited methods to compute further inheritance, because the distances would not correspond to those in the original table. But saving the selection means that future selection for the same function and target signature will find the selected method immediately.

Let's look at an example. Suppose we have a class "trackNumeric" that represents some numeric variable recorded at points on a track, with the track represented by the simple class introduced in Section 9.2, page 336. The "trackNumeric" class has a very simple definition, it just contains class "numeric" (for its data) and class "track":

```
setClass("trackNumeric",
        contains = c("numeric", "track"))
```

Now let's write some methods for the arithmetic operators involving this class. The group generic function Arith() has arguments e1 and e2. A simple method where e1 was of class "trackNumeric" and e2 of class "numeric" might just replace the data part with the result of calling the generic function on that part and on e2. Let's not worry yet about details, but just assume there is some method for signature:

```
c("trackNumeric", "numeric")
```

A similar method would apply when e2 was "trackNumeric" and e1 was "numeric", defining a method for signature:

```
c("numeric", "trackNumeric")
```

Let's assume these are only the two methods defined. Suppose now that `z` is an object from class `"trackNumeric"`, and consider the evaluation of two expressions involving `z`:

```
zz <- z -mean(z); (1:length(z)) * z
```

The methods for the group generic will be used for both `` `-` `` and `` `*` `` because there are no methods specifically for those operators, other than the default method. Because `mean(z)` is of class `"numeric"`, no inheritance is required to select the `c("trackNumeric", "numeric")` method.

The class of `1:length(z)` is `"integer"`, so no method is defined. Two methods could be inherited, `c("numeric", "trackNumeric")` and the default method, corresponding to `c("ANY", "ANY")`, but as always the default is discarded when there are other candidates. So selection is immediate.

On the other hand, let's consider a computation where both arguments are from `"trackNumeric"`, such as:

```
zz / z
```

Because `"trackNumeric"` extends `"numeric"` at distance 1, both our defined methods have distance 1 from the target signature. The choice is ambiguous, a warning will be issued to that effect and the first of the two methods used.

In this specific computation, either method returns the same result. However, the warning is justified if we look more closely. What should happen when the two objects are from the class, but do not have identical `x` and `y` slots? It's hard to argue generally that one should throw away the structure of the second argument, or that `zz + z` and `z + zz` should be different. The important message is that we really should have worked a little harder and produced a third method, for signature:

```
c("trackNumeric", "trackNumeric")
```

Just what that method should do takes some thinking; one plausible strategy would be to only allow the case that both `x` and `y` match between the two arguments. More realistically, `"trackNumeric"` provides a handy example to study method selection, but a better practical approach to data collected over a track would likely be a vector structure class (Section 6.3, page 154).

Attaching packages

Each generic function contains a table of its methods. Usually, the generic function is associated with a package. Methods may be defined for the generic, however, in other packages or by non-package calls (from the global environment). The underlying concept is that the generic function accepts and stores the method definition, in what is essentially a response to a request implied by the `setMethod()` call. For example, class definitions will often include methods for function `show()` to handle automatic printing of objects. This generic function belongs to the `methods` package. The table of methods for `show()` is maintained in the generic, in its package of origin, regardless of where the `setMethod()` call originated.

When packages are attached the methods in that package are integrated into the appropriate generic function. Similarly, for packages with a namespace, loading the namespace causes methods in the namespace to be installed in generic functions. Therefore, the methods associated with a generic are not fixed, but may change during the session as packages are loaded or unloaded.

Methods for primitive functions

Primitive functions in the `base` package provide method dispatch by a similar mechanism to regular functions, but directly from the C code in the R application. Aside from a few primitives that do not support methods, such as the function `missing()`, implicit generic function definitions exist corresponding to primitive functions.

```
> getGeneric("[")
standardGeneric for "[" defined from package "base"

function (x, i, j, ..., drop = TRUE)
standardGeneric("[", .Primitive("["))
<environment: 0xf355a94>
Methods may be defined for arguments: x, i, j, drop

> get("[")
.Primitive("[")
```

Notice that, although the generic functions are available, they are not inserted into the base package's namespace. Users' calls still access the non-generic primitive; from the underlying C implementation of the primitive, code may be called to test for method dispatch.

The C code initiating method dispatch for primitives introduces some restrictions on the signatures for valid methods. The object corresponding to at least one of the arguments in the function's signature must be an S4 object before the method dispatch code will search for an applicable method. The effect is to prohibit S4 methods for primitive functions unless the signature contains an S4 class (and not just an S3 class registered by setOldClass()). The motivation was probably machine efficiency, but an argument can be made from the *Prime Directive* as well. Certainly for basic R object types, the behavior of primitive functions can reasonably be taken as part of the system definition. Prohibiting changes to that behavior is a reasonable precaution. The prohibition for S3 classes is perhaps more debatable.

Most methods utilities recognize a primitive function object as a reference to the corresponding generic function. Functions such as showMethods() and selectMethod() should work as usual. The design goal is that methods for primitive functions can be used essentially as for normal functions, aside from the restrictions noted above.

Chapter 11

Interfaces I: Using **C** and **Fortran**

This chapter and the following one discuss techniques for making use of software written in other languages and systems. This chapter covers calling software in C, Fortran, and to some extent C++. Given that R's implementation is based on a program written in C, it's natural that techniques are available for incorporating additional C software not available for general interfaces. This chapter describes several. The simplest interfaces are to routines in C or Fortran that do not include R-dependent features (Section 11.2, page 415). For greater control, at the cost of more programming effort, C routines may manipulate R objects directly (Section 11.3, page 420). Functional interfaces to C++ are discussed in Section 11.4, page 425, although the difference in programming model in this case is discussed in Section 12.6, page 440. For trustworthy software, the interfaces to C and Fortran should be registered as part of initializing a package (Section 11.5, page 426).

11.1   Interfaces to **C** and **Fortran**

Since the core of R is in fact a program written in the C language, it's not surprising that the most direct interface to non-R software is for code written in C, or directly callable from C. All the same, including additional C code is a serious step, with some added dangers and often a substantial amount of programming and debugging required. You should have a good reason.

The two reasons usually cited for going to C are greater computational efficiency and the need for computations that are unavailable in R, but available in C, C++, or Fortran. The second reason is more compelling, but the efficiency advantages may be compelling as well.

Before getting started, it's worth reviewing the pros and cons of importing such code.

Against:

- *It's more work.* Software using the C interface should be developed as part of an R package, so that the package development tools in R can take over some of the details in compiling and linking. Even then there will be more work involved in making changes. And debugging will require more effort as well.

- *Bugs will bite.* These are ancient and relatively low-level languages. Programming problems are more likely. And, the consequences can be much worse than bugs in R: It's quite easy to kill the R session with a memory fault, for example.

- *Potential platform dependency.* Writing software that works on the various platforms that support R may be more difficult for arbitrary C computations, particularly when input/output or interactions with the operating system are involved.

- *Less readable software.* A subtler point, but in a sense the most insidious: Most sizable code in C and related languages is largely unreadable, at least to the ordinary user of R. Does it work as advertised, or are we introducing less trustworthy software, to the detriment of the *Prime Directive*? This is an issue even with the base code supplied with R, but in that case much effort has gone into finding reliable algorithms and the scrutiny of hundreds or thousands of users may give us some added security.

In Favor:

- *New and trusted computations.* There is a great deal of software written in these languages. We can add some important computations, provided the software can interface effectively to R. Interfacing to well-chosen computations can help us explore, as is our *Mission*.

And, countering the second item in the previous list, introducing a well-tested algorithm, particularly in place of a less-validated computation, can make software more trustworthy, enlisting the *Prime Directive* in favor of the new code.

- *Speed.* The overhead of a call to an R function is many times that of a call to a C function, so that if the computation done each time is roughly similar, the C or Fortran implementation may be much faster. Identifying "hot spots" where it's actually worth the effort to replace the R computation is a challenge, but the reward can sometimes be large, making a computation feasible on realistic problems.

- *Object references.* Another efficiency issue, but mainly concerned with memory. C and the other languages generally pass references to objects; if the computations iteratively modify those objects, the equivalent R implementation will often make more copies of the objects, potentially slowing or even preventing the computation for large applications.

Weigh the relevance of the pros and cons in any specific situation, naturally including your own degree of familiarity with the languages involved in general and with the actual software in particular.

As noted, incorporating an existing, trusted or well-tested set of code, particularly if it has a straightforward set of arguments, may be a winning strategy. I would be more hesitant about implementing from scratch a C version of a computation on a general feeling that it should be a lot faster.

The different interfaces

In fact, there are four different types of C software to consider, and in addition two other languages that get special attention, Fortran and C++, giving us six topics to consider:

1. the .C() interface for C routines independent of R object structure;

2. the .Call() interface, an S-language interface for programming in C;

3. the .External() interface, a version of the internal R function call mechanism;

4. special C-language code for registering routines to be called from R.

5. the .Fortran() interface for calling Fortran subroutines;

6. a mechanism for using the C interface with C++ code.

The general interfaces in this are .Call(), .External(), .C(), and .Fortran().

The key question for programming is: How to communicate the needed data between R and the compiled routines. All four of the general interface functions have the same form of arguments.

```
.C(name, ...)
.Fortran(name, ...)
.Call(name, ...)
.External(name, ...)
```

Aside from some special control arguments discussed below, the call supplies the character-string name of the routine to be called, followed by arguments that correspond to the arguments of the routine. All the interface routines also take an optional PACKAGE= argument that is not passed on to the routine but that specifies the name of the package in which the routine was compiled. Only the dynamically loaded code for that package will be searched. For example:

```
.Call("det_ge_real", x, logarithm, PACKAGE = "base")
```

The .Call() interface will find the C routine "det_ge_real" by looking in the package "base", and will generate a call to that routine with the two arguments provided. The package base in this case stands for all the compiled code included with the core R application itself.

Other than the special control arguments, the names of the arguments are not used in preparing the call to the C or Fortran routine, and in particular are unrelated to the argument names of the routine itself. The number of non-control arguments must equal the number of arguments in the subroutine definition (special programming techniques in C do deal with variable argument lists). The number of arguments, and in some cases the types, will be checked before the call, if the routine has been registered, as discussed in Section 11.5, page 426.

The essential distinction among the C interface functions is whether the C code is written to manipulate R objects or in an R-independent form. Both options have a long history in the S language, and both are available.

The R-independent approach restricts the classes of objects in R and the corresponding argument types in C or Fortran, but otherwise the routine called has no need to deal with the structure of R objects. The .C() and .Fortran() interfaces use this approach. In the other approach, the .Call() and .External() interfaces both expect the C routine to use R-dependent code. The programmer then needs to manipulate the references to R objects, using utilities provided as part of the R environment.

11.2 Calling **R-Independent** Subroutines

The implementation of the .C() and .Fortran() interfaces passes each of the arguments to the called routine as a simple array (Fortran) or pointer (C) to data of a type that corresponds to one of the basic types in R. Table

R Object Type	C Type	Fortran Type
logical	int *	INTEGER
integer	int *	INTEGER
double	double *	DOUBLE PRECISION
complex	Rcomplex *	DOUBLE COMPLEX
character	char **	CHARACTER*255
raw	char *	none

Table 11.1: Corresponding types for arguments to .C() and .Fortran().

11.1 (adapted from the *Writing R Extensions* manual) shows the correspondences. Object type relates to how the basic vector is actually stored; for example, data that is considered "numeric" is usually stored as "double" but can also be forced to be "integer". It rarely makes a difference in R and in any case one should usually let the software decide. However, it makes a definite difference to C or Fortran. The actual argument to .C() or .Fortran() must correspond to the declaration of the routine, or the computed results will be nonsense.

At the time of writing, the programmer is responsible for matching types. In principle, much of this could be automated using parsing tools, so we can hope for extended tools in the future. Meanwhile, you usually need only apply the corresponding as.*Type*() function.

Here is a .Fortran() example. The Fortran routine GEODISTV takes 4 arrays of type DOUBLE PRECISION representing two sets of latitude and longitude coordinates and returns the corresponding geodetic distances in array DIST. It also takes an INTEGER argument N for the lengths of the arrays:

```
SUBROUTINE GEODISTV(LAT1,LON1,LAT2,LON2,DIST, N)
DOUBLE PRECISION LAT1(1), LON1(1), LAT2(1), LON2(1), DIST(1)
INTEGER N
```

etc.

This is a small subroutine in the SoDA package that in turn calls a subroutine taken from Dan Kelley's oce package.[1] That subroutine goes back through

---

[1]myweb.dal.ca/kelley/pub/sof/oce/index.php

several previous versions to a technique published in 1975 (see the comments in the source code: Fortran algorithms often have a long history). The computation produces the geodetic distance between points on the earth's surface. We use it in our computations for "GPSTrack" data.

The justification for including this code is convincing: The computations are nontrivial (accurate modeling of the earth's surface) and the Fortran code has a long history of use and testing in the geographical sciences. The GEODISTV routine simplifies the calling sequence (omitting 4 arguments) and vectorizes the computations by computing distances for the whole array in one call from R. It's typical that some extra Fortran code is added to make the interface more effective. Although the code is R-independent in terms of the structure of R objects, only rarely in Fortran and virtually never in C are the original routines set up conveniently for a call from R.

The routines must have arguments that are all pointers (C) or arrays (Fortran) of one of the types in the table. This is usually more natural for Fortran subroutines, which typically do deal with simple vectors, and where single values are passed by the same mechanism, than for C. Existing C code is likely to come in another form, and to need a wrapper routine before being usable.

The interface to GEODISTV adds a computing capability to R that would be difficult to implement directly and less trustworthy once implemented. And it leads to a cute little function that plots data using geodetic coordinates; see page 419.

Function geoDist() in the SoDA package calls the interface to GEODISTV:

```
res <- .Fortran("GEODISTV",
     as.double(lat1), as.double(lon1),
     as.double(lat2), as.double(lon2),
     dist = double(n), as.integer(n),
     PACKAGE = "SoDA")$dist
```

The value of the .Fortran() call is a list of all the arguments with values as they were on exit from the routine. If arguments are named, those names will be passed on to the list. So in the above example, $dist would extract the output values of the corresponding argument.

Here's a C example, adapted from the digest package on CRAN written by Dirk Eddelbuettel. The actual interface in that package uses .Call(), and we will look at an interface of that form below. In fact, the underlying computations are somewhat better suited to .C(), which makes the comparison interesting. Here's the underlying code and the .C() interface; after introducing the alternative on page 422, we'll compare them.

The underlying C computation here takes an R object and produces a "hash" string based on the contents of the object. The `digest` package does this by first serializing the object into a string (potentially a very long one). Then one of several hashing algorithms is used to produce a fixed-length string. The technique could be useful for an application that wanted to compare a number of objects by their *content*, as opposed to R environments, which hash the *name* for the object. Any application that wants to keep track of unique objects could build on this tool to create a table indexed by object content. The fixed-length strings are hash codes, and the application will need to convert these into a complete mechanism by dealing with non-identical objects that hash to the same value (a very common programming exercise). The hashing algorithms are individually available as C routines. It's a neat technique, because the `digest` computations get complete generality for free. The built-in serialization code deals with any R object, and converts it into a character string. By using the serialization step in R as a preliminary, the `digest` computations also work for any object.

To build up a C interface from R, we start with a C definition of the overall task,[2] parameterized naturally for C:

```
static char * digest_string(
        char *txt,
        int algo,
        int  length) {
        . . . . . . .
}
```

The routine `digest_string` takes a character string `txt`, an integer code for the algorithm to use, and an optional length for the string. It returns a (fixed-length) output hash string.

This is a natural way to code the computation, but not what `.C()` can handle directly. A wrapper routine in C is needed, in this case say `R_digest_C`:

```
void R_digest_C(
        char ** Txt,
        int * Algo,
        int * Length,
        char ** Output) {
    static char *output;
```

---

[2]The formulation in this chapter extracts essentially all the underlying computation into an R-independent routine, to illustrate the alternatives, whereas the original `digest` package uses more extensive R-dependent C code.

```
    output = digest_string(*Txt, *Algo, *Length, output);
    *Output = output;
}
```

The R code that invokes this routine takes responsibility for ensuring that each of the arguments matches the assumed type, as in Table 11.1. Here is the relevant part of the function:

```
val <- .C("R_digest_C",
            as.character(object),
            as.integer(algoint),
            as.integer(length),
            output = character(1),
            PACKAGE="digest")
    return(val$output)
```

As in the preceding .Fortran() example, this uses a match between the R object type in the table and either the corresponding as.*Type*() function or the generating function for this type.

The pattern shown in these two examples is recommended for most uses of these interfaces.

1. Find or write a routine that does the computation (digest_string in the example).

2. Write a routine (R_digest_C in the example), callable through .C() or .Fortran(), that translates the input arguments for the first routine and, if necessary, arranges for output arguments to receive the value of the underlying routine. Each of the arguments to the interfacing routine must have one of the declarations in the appropriate column of Table 11.1.

3. Write an R function that calls the second routine. Each of the arguments in the call must be guaranteed to have the correct object type, either by coercing or generating an object. The same function will then extract the output to return as a value, from the list of arguments (possibly modified) returned by .C() or .Fortran().

For this pattern to work requires that the value make sense as one or more basic vectors. C code that returns a more complex C structure as its value may require some R-dependent code to transfer the information to an R object. Alternatively, consider leaving the object in C, returning a proxy object to R, and providing R-callable tools in C to deal with the proxy (see Section 12.4, page 435 for the general idea).

There are two special named arguments to .C() and .Fortran(), both logical flags. Passing NAOK=TRUE allows missing values to be passed on to the routine. By default, any missing values will generate an error. In Fortran numeric data, NA satisfies the test for "not-a-number", ISNAN() (Section 6.7, page 191). Otherwise, C and Fortran do not themselves understand R's NA, so some special code must be applied to deal with them.

The other flag controls duplication of the arguments by the interface. By default, copies of the data are made and passed down to the routines, to protect the validity of any R objects. If you are certain—really certain— that no computation will change any of these values, you can save some memory by supplying DUP=FALSE. However, it's generally a bad idea. The *Prime Directive* says that trustworthy software is essential; saving memory allocation is secondary, and often not that significant in typical situations.

Even with the .C() interface, there is one topic that probably should be done in an R-dependent way: error handling. The simplest approach is to use the R support routine error. See page 423 for an example. Note that to use this routine, you should #include the file "R.h".

Addendum: The geoXY() function

Here is a little function included in the book mainly because I think it's cute, but also because we use it in several examples involving *G*lobal *P*ositioning *S*ystem (GPS) data. In turn, this function uses the geoDist() function's interface to Fortran, and illustrates the value of access to a somewhat ancient computational algorithm. The function takes latitude and longitude coordinates for n points and returns a matrix whose rows are x and y *geodetic coordinates*. The computational issue is how to work with data in the form of latitude, longitude and elevation—the standard form for GPS data. Such data are quite well-defined but cannot be used directly for most computations; for one reason, the variables are not in commensurate units, the first two being in degrees and the third in, say, meters. You can't just plot latitude and longitude, though people do. Particularly in polar regions, the meridians of longitude are not parallel. The usual approach is to transform the data by one of many classic projections (see the package mapproj on the CRAN archive, for example). But this means choosing a projection, and the appropriate choice depends on where the data are on the globe.

Instead, we use a system of coordinates on the surface of the earth, relative to a chosen, but arbitrary, origin (by default we will use the lower-left (southwest) corner of the latitude-longitude box enclosing the data). This is not a flat projection, but a well-defined transformation, independent of the actual data. If the data points themselves only span a small fraction of the globe, then the error of plotting the x, y values as if they were flat will be small, regardless of where the data points are located. This is the reason we use `geoXY()` in the plotting methods for class `"GPSTrack"` (see Section 7.2, page 248, for example).

The definition of the computation for a given latitude and longitude is as follows. The x coordinate is the distance from the origin to a point with the latitude of the origin and the longitude of the data. The y coordinate, similarly, is the distance from the origin to a point with the longitude of the origin and the latitude of the data. In both cases, "distance" means the geodetic distance (the distance along the surface of the earth), just what `geoDist()` (on page 416) computes; in addition, the distance will get the same sign as the difference of the latitude and longitude values and will be scaled to whatever units are desired, meters by default. All this is directly analogous to the pencil-and-ruler way of finding ordinary coordinates from a flat map, but done on the surface of the earth (well, to be precise, on the geographer's abstract version of that surface). Here is the code.

```
"geoXY" <-
function(latitude, longitude,
         lat0 = min(latitude, na.rm=TRUE),
         lon0 = min(longitude, na.rm=TRUE),
         unit = 1.) {
    lat0 <- rep(lat0, length(latitude))
    lon0 <- rep(lon0, length(longitude))
    yDist <- geoDist(lat0, lon0, latitude, lon0)
    xDist <- geoDist(lat0, lon0, lat0, longitude)
    cbind(X= xDist * sign(longitude - lon0)/unit,
          Y = yDist * sign(latitude - lat0)/unit)
}
```

The function is included in the SoDA package, with more details in the online documentation `?geoXY`.

11.3   Calling R-Dependent Subroutines

In the R-independent interfaces, the routine being called defines the types for the arguments by declarations in C or Fortran, the usual approach in these languages. The routine does no checking dynamically; all such coordination falls to the R code and the implementation of the interface.

In contrast, the `.Call()` and `.External()` interfaces expect all arguments to have just one type in C; namely, a reference (pointer) to a general R object. In the C code pointers to all R objects are declared `SEXP`; all the arguments to the interface are of this type and the routine must return a valid pointer of the same type, which the routine will usually have constructed. Checks on the actual objects during execution will be done by the called routine.

The advantage of these interfaces is generality: Essentially any computation can be carried out with any objects as arguments. A disadvantage is the added complexity of the C code, which now takes on argument processing, structure manipulation, and various tasks usually left to R code or done automatically. Such computations present even more opportunities for errors than general computations in C. They do, however, allow you to manipulate R objects and to deal with variable-length argument lists, so if you are keen to use these techniques at the C level, one of these interfaces will be required.

Next, the choice between the two interfaces. The main difference is in the mechanism for passing the arguments from R to the C routine. In the `.Call()` interface, all the `"..."` arguments are passed to the routine, as with `.C()`. The `.External()` interface passes a single pointer to the list of arguments to the routine. It is the responsibility of the called routine to work through the argument list to get at individual arguments. There are some C macros for the purpose, basically plucking off the first element of the list and the list minus the first element. If you have programmed in Lisp, the style will be familiar, even the names of the macros are taken from Lisp.

The `.External()` form is more work, so it is unlikely to be preferred, except for one important advantage: its list-style treatment of arguments can handle a variable number of arguments. The `.External()` interface is suited to computations that naturally treat their arguments iteratively, for the same reason. We will use `.Call()` in the examples here; for instructions on using `.External()` see the *Writing R Extensions* manual or the code that implements **base** package functions with variable argument lists (such as the routine do_bind).

Finally, any application of these interfaces will need some special C code, which in practice means some macros that mimic R expressions to manipulate objects, and that provide a few additional operations. Here also there is a choice. The `.Call()` interface and C macros for managing objects were originally described for the S language in Appendix A of *Programming with Data* [5], in the form now used in S-Plus. The C programming support available with R includes an extended version of the same macros. To use them you must `#include` the file `"Rdefines.h"` in your C source files in directory "src" of a source package.

A different set of macros and routines grew up in the implementation of R itself. They are described in the *Writing R Extensions* manual, with examples scattered through the core code for R. The file "Rinternals.h" has these definitions, and must be included to use any R-structure computations (but "Rdefines.h" includes it automatically). The two sets of macros are likely to be used with the corresponding interface functions, although they can be combined.

The macros replicate some basic computations in R: allocating objects of the basic object types, coercing to those types, or testing inheritance. For example, for "numeric" vectors there are macros:

```
NEW_NUMERIC(n)
AS_NUMERIC(x)
IS_NUMERIC(x)
```

Macros also give a pointer to the data values in the object, following the correspondence in the second column of Table 11.1. For example:

```
NUMERIC_POINTER(x)
```

returns a "double *" pointer to the data in the vector x. Single data values can also be accessed, as NUMERIC_VALUE(x), for example. Analogous macros exist for the other types, substituting LOGICAL, INTEGER, CHARACTER, COMPLEX, LIST, or RAW for NUMERIC. Individual elements of the various types can be obtained by indexing the various pointers. However, to set an element of a vector safely, use the macro SET_ELEMENT(x, i, value), as in the example code below.

Most importantly, however, note that these interfaces do not duplicate arguments, unlike the .C() interface. Using any of the SET macros can do very bad damage if you do not either duplicate the object x or ensure carefully that modifying it is allowed.

In writing such C code one point is most important in avoiding errors, and is not found in the S reference since it applies to R only. Whenever any computation could possibly allocate R storage dynamically and the result is not assigned at the R level, the use of the corresponding C reference must be protected by the PROTECT and UNPROTECT macros. The reason is that the storage would otherwise be released if R happened to do a garbage collection of dynamic storage during the computation. The error is particularly nasty because it will occur unpredictably, not every time. The use of the macros is best illustrated by an example.

We return to the example on page 416, this time using the .Call() interface to call a C routine digest:

```
SEXP digest(SEXP Txt, SEXP Algo, SEXP Length) {
  FILE *fp=0;
  char *txt = CHARACTER_VALUE(Txt);
  int algo = INTEGER_VALUE(Algo);
  int  length = INTEGER_VALUE(Length);
  SEXP result = NULL;
  char output[41];

  digest_string(txt, algo, length, output);
  PROTECT(result=NEW_CHARACTER(1));
  SET_ELEMENT(result, 0, mkChar(output));
  UNPROTECT(1);

  return result;
}
```

Let's deal with PROTECT first, then some other points brought out by the example. The call to NEW_CHARACTER(1) allocates an R object. A pointer is assigned in the C code, but nothing has told the R evaluator that this object must be protected; if the system happened to do a "garbage collection" to compact storage, it would throw the object away, leaving us with an invalid pointer and disaster looming.

The rule is that any such value must be passed to the PROTECT macro before doing any other computation that might involve R storage allocation. Once the object has been assigned in R or returned to the evaluator, protection is not needed. The programmer must UNPROTECT the number of objects currently protected before returning from this routine.

One further point is worth noting. This particular operation is made slightly more complicated because the object is a character vector. R does not in fact store character strings as character buffers, as Table 11.1 would suggest, but as a special structure. To turn character data into an element of an R vector, you must call mkChar().

Having now implemented the example with .C() (on page 416) and .Call(), let's compare the two. Although .Call() was the interface in the digest package, once the underlying C algorithm has been isolated as the routine digest_string, there is almost no remaining need for R-dependent interface code. Using .C(), the arguments are coerced in R, any efficiency loss being minor. Allocation is also done in R, without the complexity and potential errors of protection in C. Even the special requirements of character data are handled automatically.

An important programming step that does need some R-dependent code hasn't been shown yet: error handling. The routine digest_string detects some invalid input situations, such as an invalid integer code for the algorithm to use. General C and Fortran code don't manage error handling suitably for R (never use the Fortran STOP statement, for example). Once could develop some special procedures for communicating errors, but the simplest approach is to call the C-level error handler for R, as `digest_string` does:

```
error("Unsupported algorithm code");
```

Where error handling is desirable with the .C() interface, I would suggest using this routine, even in code that is otherwise R-independent. You should avoid in any case a C computation that would terminate the process, such as a call to the routine `exit`. To use `error`, you should `#include` the file `"R.h"`. The routine takes a string as its first argument, which can contain C format items and corresponding additional (scalar) arguments to match, in the style of utilities such as `sprintf`. For other versions and Fortran use, see the *Writing R Extensions* manual.

Object structures in C

In addition to the macros dealing with basic vectors, `Rdefines.h` has macros to GET and SET various properties, such as:

	Get	**Set**
Slot	GET_SLOT(x, what)	SET_SLOT(x, what, value)
Attribute	GET_ATTR(x, what)	SET_ATTR(x, what, value)
Length	GET_LENGTH(x)	SET_LENGTH(x, value)
Names	GET_NAMES(x)	SET_NAMES(x, value)

There are similar macros for specialized classes of objects (matrices, time-series and factors): GET_DIM(x), etc., substituting DIM, DIMNAMES, TSP, or LEVELS.

Each of the arguments must be type SEXP, including what for names (which can be either a character vector of length 1 or a name, called a "symbol" in C code for R). To be safe, always coerce the object to which the argument refers to the correct type or class in advance.

Calling R from C

Computations in C may receive or construct an R expression that needs to be evaluated. Optimization and related model-fitting techniques are natural examples. The mechanism for such an evaluation is, basically, the evaluator used in ordinary R computations, namely the `eval` utility, which is a C routine taking an expression and an evaluation context as arguments. If the expression has to be modified or constructed in C, note that the C form for the expression uses the original R version of a list structure, directly inspired by Lisp. In order to construct the expression, or even to insert a reference to an object into an existing expression, you need to know about the Lisp-style convention for navigating such objects. The basic notion is that one navigates a list one element at a time, accessing the first element (the head of the list) by macro CAR and the rest of the list (the tail) by macro CDR. For details, look in the "Calling R from C" section of the the *Writing R Extensions* manual manual, and study some of the examples in the main source code for R itself (such as do_slot and its neighbors in file attrib.c). Clearly, this is an advanced topic.

To actually carry out the evaluation, consider the C routine R_tryEval. Like the try() function in R, this will trap any errors in the evaluation, and signal the calling C code, without actually interrupting your C computation. The extra protection may be important if you need to do some cleanup before exiting.

11.4 Computations in C++

Formally, an interface to computations in C++ is a minor extension of the interfaces to C. However, C++ has a very different programming model, so that more ambitious interfaces may need to use an object-based approach, as discussed in Section 12.6, page 440.

Suppose we start with some code written in C++. To create an interface to this code via either .C() or .Call(), we write the C interface routine as usual, but compile it in a C++ source file (usually stored with suffix ".cpp"), enclosing the C code in the **extern "C"** declaration, which tells the C++ compiler to treat subroutine names as C names (among other things). The C++ files go into the src directory of the source package, as would ordinary C or Fortran.

For example, suppose we have some C++ model-fitting software and want to run it from R, through:

```
.Call("my_fit", formula, data, start)
```

The corresponding code in the C++ file would be of the form:

```
extern "C" {

#include <R.h>
```

```
#include <Rinternals.h>

SEXP my_fit(
    SEXP formula,
    SEXP data,
    SEXP start) {

    ......

    return result;
}

} // end extern "C"
```

Aside from using the C++ compiler, the procedure is essentially identical to that for ordinary C interfaces.

More interesting questions arise when we consider what the interface computation does. Since C++ was used to implement the code, it's likely that the programming model of that language was considered appropriate for the computation. For example, in the context of model fitting, C++ would be particularly suited to an iterative process of refining a model. One would create an object from the appropriate C++ class, and then invoke a variety of methods to advance the model estimate, as well as other methods that might plot, summarize, or produce other derived results from the model object. In the terminology of Chapter 12, these are *object-based* computations and assume a *reference* to the object.

As we will discuss in Chapter 12, interfacing to such software presents a choice between a functional interface, as we have discussed so far, and an interface that treats the foreign object directly, usually via a proxy in R for the C++ object (in this case). Both approaches have advantages, but as the computations become larger and more seriously iterative the object view becomes more appealing.

For a detailed example of interfacing to C++, see Section 12.6, page 440, using Greg Ridgeway's gbm package for generalized boosting models.

11.5   Loading and Registering Compiled Routines

When compiled code in C or the other related languages is to be used in a package, it must be dynamically loaded into the R program at the time the package is loaded or attached. In the case of a package with a NAMESPACE (the recommended choice), the directive to dynamically load one or more shared libraries is added to the NAMESPACE file. For package SoDA:

```
useDynLib(SoDA)
```

This loads the file, for example "Soda.so", compiled from the package's own "src" directory. You can also load other library files by supplying the name of the file as the argument to other "useDynLib" directives. If the package has no NAMESPACE, shared libraries are loaded by calling the function library.dynam(); in this example,

```
library.dynam("SoDA")
```

Either way the library file's suffix (".so") is left off, for portability.

The package mechanism also allows and encourages packages to *register* entry points in C and Fortran that will be called from R. Registration, which is in addition to loading the shared library that contains the compiled routines, stores information about entry points to be called via the various interfaces. There are several reasons why you should do so, including somewhat increased efficiency, but the most compelling is to get at least some protection against errors in the call from R. It's an advantage to have an interface to compiled code but there is no doubt that the interface is error prone. Worse yet, errors in passing arguments to C can easily cause addressing errors in the R evaluator that will terminate your session, losing all previously computed results.

The registration mechanism can catch some of these errors; for example, you can register the number of arguments to the subroutine, allowing the evaluator to catch calls with the wrong number of arguments. For the .C() interface, you can supply the intended types of the arguments, as is done in the example below for the routine R_digest_C.

Registration of routines currently itself requires writing some raw C code. For current details see the *Writing R Extensions* manual under "Registering native routines" in the concept index. The requirements are quite picky and known to give serious problems if not strictly followed. However, once it works, you have substantially increased the trustworthy nature of your interface to C and Fortran.

The following code implements the initialization file for package SoDA, including registration for the three example routines discussed in this chapter:

```
#include <R.h>
#include <Rinternals.h>
#include <R_ext/Rdynload.h>
```

```
void F77_SUB(geodistv)();
void R_digest_C(char **, int *, int *, char **);
SEXP R_digest(SEXP, SEXP, SEXP);
void R_power(double *val);

static R_FortranMethodDef FortEntries[] = {
    {"geodistv", (DL_FUNC) &F77_SUB(geodistv), 6},
    {NULL, NULL, 0}
};

static R_NativePrimitiveArgType digest_type[4]={STRSXP,INTSXP,INTSXP
static R_NativePrimitiveArgType power_type[1] = {REALSXP};
static R_CMethodDef cEntries[] = {
        {"R_digest_C", (DL_FUNC) &R_digest_C, 4, digest_type},
        {"R_power", (DL_FUNC) &R_power, 1, power_type},
        {NULL, NULL, 0, NULL}
        };

static R_CallMethodDef callEntries[]  = {
        {"R_digest", (DL_FUNC) &R_digest, 3},
        {NULL, NULL, 0}
        };

void
R_init_SoDA(DllInfo *info)
{
  /* Register routines, allocate resources. */
  R_registerRoutines(info, cEntries /* Centries*/, callEntries /*CallEnt
             FortEntries, NULL /*ExternEntries*/);
}

void
R_unload_SoDA(DllInfo *info)
{
  /* Release resources. */
}
```

Chapter 12

Interfaces II: Between R and Other Systems

This chapter discusses general inter-system interfaces between computations in R and those done in other languages and systems. "Other" generally has two senses here: The implementation usually involves communicating with another application; and more fundamentally, the computational model for the other system may be different from that in R.

The chapter discusses several approaches, the best choice depending on the other system and on the nature of the particular task: file or text-based (Section 12.2, page 432), functional (12.3, 433), or object-based (12.4, 435). Moving down the list generally provides greater flexibility and efficiency, paid for by more effort in installing the interface and programming the application. The programming model of some systems needs to be considered explicitly, as with OOP systems (Section 12.5, page 437), and C++ in particular (12.6, 440), and with database or spreadsheet systems (12.7, 446).

With our emphasis on programming with R, most of the examples invoke computations in another system *from* R, but a number of the packages implementing the interface support communication *to* R as well. In addition, some applications benefit from interfaces that avoid R altogether (Section 12.8, page 450).

12.1   Choosing an Interface

Chapter 11 discussed computations in R that called routines written in C or related languages. These routines could be called directly in the R session, so long as the routine was loaded with a package or from a library, thanks to the fact that R itself is implemented in C.

Once we think of software in other languages and systems, the picture changes. Now we are communicating in a more equal sense: The other system will typically have its own ideas of how programming is expressed (its "programming model") and quite likely its own ideas of objects and data. We have a number of choices to make in communicating between the systems.

Many such systems are of potential value for data analysis. Interfaces to some important systems are summarized in Table 12.1. Unless noted, the

System	Applications	Package	Source
Perl	Text, WWW, coding, interfaces, . . .	`RSPerl`	omegahat
Python	(similar to Perl)	`RSPython` `rpy` (to R)	omegahat Sourceforge
Java	User interfaces, events, graphics, . . .	`rJava` (from R) `JRI` (to R) `RSJava`	CRAN RForge omegahat
C++	Algorithms, processes	`.C()`, `.Call()`	(built in)
Oracle, MySQL, . . .	Relational databases	`ROracle` `RmySQL`	CRAN CRAN
Tcl/Tk	User interface	`tcltk`	(built in)

Table 12.1: Some inter-system interfaces. (Web pages for the sources: `cran.r-project.org`, `omegahat.org`, `sourceforge.net`, `rforge.net`)

interfaces provide for communication both from R and to R. Communication from R generally means that the user calls an R function that then invokes the other system as an application, communicates with a running evaluator for that system, or invokes some built-in or compiled code. Communication in the other direction usually involves embedding or dynamically linking R to a process or application running the other system. Installing an interface in this form does require some extra steps beyond a minimal installation of R, so that the embedding or linking of the R software is possible. Interfaces that are built-in run as code in the R process itself; for these interfaces, communication to R is usually through the mechanisms for evaluating function calls in R from C.

This chapter concentrates on obtaining computations in R from other systems, given our focus on building software for data analysis, and on programming with R.

Forms of interface

There are many variations in how the computations are done and communicated. We can usefully group these into three types.

1. *Text based*: In this form, text is communicated including a command that the other system executes. Text output from the command is communicated back. In effect, this is the model provided by the function `system()` in R, also sometimes referred to as the "Unix pipe" model for computation.

2. *Function based*: One or more functions in R communicate requests to the other system and return a resulting value. Usually, the arguments to the R functions identify a function or something similar in the other system and then provide arguments to that function. The interface functions to C, such as `.C()`, are the paradigm for this approach.

3. *Object based*: At least some of the computations may create and refer to objects in the other system. In particular, there may be what we call *proxy* objects in R that stand for objects in the other system.

The three models for communication are listed in order of increasing generality, in terms of what can be done, and also of an increasing level of organization required. Setup requirements also tend to increase as we go down the list, although these also depend on which system is involved.

Text- or file-based interfaces can often avoid installing an explicit interface package, in two ways. If it's sufficient to occasionally export data from one system and import it into the other, one can use the techniques of Section 8.2, page 294, on importing text or those of Section 6.5, page 173, on exporting and importing in spreadsheets and database systems. If the other system can be invoked as a "shell" command, one can use the `system()` function as described in section 12.2. Otherwise, and generally for both function-based and object-based interfaces, there must be an intersystem interface package, such as those in Table 12.1. The interface package needs to be installed on your computer, if it isn't already. Installation may

not be quite as simple as with other packages, since both R and the other
system must be available in a compatible form. If you encounter problems,
check the hints and instructions on the package's Web site and also search
for relevant discussions on the R mailing lists. Unfortunately, there are no
definitive techniques for all situations.

The distinctions among the levels are not rigid; each level is capable of
implementing the next level down, at least partially. We could also have
added a fourth level, *Component based.* In this model, the interfaces are
made up of components that advertise services or methods. Interfaces of
this form have much promise for future work, but at the time of writing the
activity is either restricted to the Windows operating system (DCOM) or to
specialized communication systems that are not much used with statistical
computing.

12.2   Text- and File-Based Interfaces

Interfaces can be established from R to any system that can be invoked
as a shell-style command. The function `system()` is the general tool to
invoke a command. How well an interface of this form works in practice,
however, depends on the other system and somewhat on the platform. Shell
commands are at the heart of the UNIX operating system's programming
model, and are fully compatible with Linux or Mac OS X; on Windows some
extra software may need to intervene to provide UNIX-style commands, but
the `system()` function itself has been designed to be platform-independent.
The function provides for specifying standard input as a character vector in
R, or any class of objects that can be interpreted as a character vector. The
catch, particularly on Windows, is that the commands invoked via `system()`
must be available. If you plan to do any significant programming with
non-R software on Windows, see the Appendix on the Windows toolset in the
Installing and Administering R manual at the R Web site.

Interfaces to scripting languages such as Perl or Python often fit easily into
a command-style interface. In Section 8.5, page 310, a simple Perl program
was shown that removed HTML tags. In the form shown, the program used
the UNIX style of reading data from its input and writing to its output,
which fits naturally with the `system()` function, using its `input=` argument
to specify the standard input.

A command-style interface for Perl and similar languages must start the
interpreter for the language each time and open files or other connections for
input and output. If the application involves many evaluations of small text

processing jobs, a more efficient mechanism is to start the interpreter and give it successive tasks directly—the approach of the functional interface. A functional interface may be more natural as well, if there are several related tasks to be requested, since those may naturally map into corresponding functions or methods in the other system.

The balance shifts in favor of text-based interfaces when the text comes from an external source and is either extensive or structured in a non-trivial way by another language. Both conditions often apply. If the text arises as a document or data stream in some markup or display language (XML or HTML, for example), extracting the relevant text for R may need some flexible programming in Perl.

12.3 Functional Interfaces

Functional interfaces, such as `.Perl()` in the `RSPerl` package, allow the R programmer to execute a function or similar programming construction in another system, and retrieve the result in R. At a basic level, the arguments and result may be treated as R objects, provided there are unambiguous analogs in the two systems. This level is functional, in the sense we use the term frequently in the book: the effect of the computation can be entirely described functionally, in terms of the arguments and value with no discussion of side effects.

In a simple functional interface, all arguments will be converted to the foreign system and all results converted back. This is the model for the `.C()` interface to C. If we examine the way that interface works a little more closely, it will illustrate the essential points to understand in other interfaces with a similar model.

Each of the arguments to be passed through `.C()` is required to be an array of one of the basic vector datatypes (those listed in Table 11.1 on page 415). Furthermore, all results are returned by the C routine by modifying the contents of these arrays. So only a very special set of routines will qualify. The strategy may not be perfect, but it is one approach to managing the different programming models of C and R.

Interfaces to other systems will also impose some restrictions in order to make a simple functional interface possible. For a particular interface, see what the documentation says about converting arguments and results. Some experimentation may be needed, and perhaps some extra techniques to convert objects you need to work with. For example, tables of objects indexed by strings are important in many systems (*hashes* in Perl and *dic-*

tionaries in Python, for example). If you are supplying such data as an argument or getting it back as the value of a call, you need to know whether there is an automatic conversion and, if so, what the corresponding object in R will be. If there are no practical conversions for objects appearing as arguments or as the value returned, then you may need to use the notion of proxy objects in the other system as discussed in the next section. Even if a conversion is possible, there may be computational advantages to the object-based approach.

For a specific example of a functional interface, consider `.Perl()`. This function in package `RSPerl` constructs and evaluates a call to a Perl function. For a simple functional interface to work in this case, it's important to understand how arguments are passed to a function in Perl. Basically, the argument list is a single array of scalars, either basic types such as numbers or strings, or else references to other Perl objects. The `.Perl()` interface applies some heuristics to interpret arbitrary R objects, but these inevitably are imperfect; for trustworthy software, don't rely on them. Supply the argument as a list, each element of which is a single basic value or a reference to a proxy object, and ensure that each value has been coerced in R to a type that corresponds to what the Perl function expects as that element of the argument array.

Consider the Perl function `&quotewords` in the `Text::ParseWords` module. Given an array of strings representing lines of text, it returns the separate words in all the text, based on specified delimiters and taking account of quotes to group words together. This function appears to take three arguments, with Perl types as follows:

```
&quotewords($delim, $keep, @lines);
```

where `$delim` is a string with the delimiter as a regular expression, `$keep` is a flag saying whether to keep quotes, and `@lines` is an array of the text to process. Watch out, however: The third argument is an array, and not a reference to an array, and Perl flattens all the arrays in argument lists. So if the third argument is a vector of n strings, Perl in effect expects $n + 2$ scalar values as arguments. Don't give `.Perl()` three arguments, the third being a character vector of arbitrary length; that might generate an array reference. Instead, we need to pass a list with $n + 2$ "scalar" elements, as is done by the simple interface function in R:

```
quotewords <- function(x, delim = "\\s+")  {
    .PerlPackage("Text::ParseWords")
    .Perl("quotewords", .args = c(list(delim, 1), x))
}
```

The .`args` argument to .`Perl()` is interpreted as a list, each element of which will be one element in the argument to the Perl function. The call to `c()` concatenates a list of 2 elements with the character vector, which has the desired effect of converting the latter to a list of length-1 vectors.

12.4 Object-Based Interfaces

Objects are certainly involved in the functional interface described above, but there is no need for the user to consider objects in the other system that are not convertible to local classes of data. In the interface defined for C by .`C()`, there is no attempt to consider C types that have no analog as R objects. The interface to Perl provided by .`Perl()` is more general, in that objects can be returned that do not correspond to R objects and Perl functions can expect such objects or references to them as arguments.

The ability to refer in R to an object in another system, even when it does not correspond exactly to any R object, opens up many valuable techniques; after all, it's often precisely the ability to do computations outside the current system's tools that makes an inter-system interface valuable. We call the R reference a *proxy* object, standing in for an object reference in the other system. And the proxy object is indeed a reference; that is, it refers to some object in the other system that can be modified, in most cases, and such that the reference will then be to the modified object. In contrast, the functional model applying to most R computations deals with objects, not references, so that modifications are local to the function involved.

The form of the proxy object reference—how its contents are extracted or modified—depends on the other system. Section 12.6, page 440, discusses proxy objects for "object-oriented" systems and Section 12.7, page 446, for relational database management systems, two important special cases. In the rest of this section, we will look at object references for Perl, which is a simpler case in some respects and so can usefully introduce general points that will apply to the other systems as well.

The most basic issue with proxy objects is to arrange for them to be created and to persist for as long as they are needed. (And then, in some cases, to arrange that they will not persist after they are needed.) When you are computing in R, such questions don't usually require your attention in any detail. If you need some object, you assign it a name in the current context, inside a function that you are writing or interactively at the top level. Assignments inside a function persist until the call to that function returns, then R will clean up at some point without your intervention.

Proxy object references, in contrast, are generated first in the interface. An object will be created in the other system and a reference to that object will be passed back as the proxy in R. Something will likely have happened in the other system so that the reference persists there, otherwise your proxy object would not be of much use. Then what? On the R side, you would assign the proxy like any object. However, can you count on the foreign object it refers to persisting and disappearing along with the proxy? In computing terminology, what is the *scope* of the object referred to? Many of the inter-system interface packages will maintain a table of such references (RSPerl and rJava, for example). In addition, packages may to varying degrees arrange to delete the referenced object and/or to modify the proxy when the reference is no longer valid. The RSPerl package arranges to zero-out a reference when the proxy object is saved, so that using the reference in a new session will just warn you about a zero reference, rather than giving an addressing error because the pointer referred to the old process.

In general, you should read the documentation for the particular interface package carefully and/or do some experiments to see when objects in the foreign system are saved and whether the user is expected to explicitly delete them. Fortunately, the really serious danger is that the object will be prematurely deleted, and this is less likely. Most interfaces use a mechanism such as a hash table or global environment to assign the object when passing back a reference. The reference should then persist through the life of the current session. Users of the interface may need to arrange for explicitly deleting objects no longer needed. The issue here is one of wasting memory, potentially serious for efficiency but at least not likely to destroy valuable information.

As an example, let's write an interface to some Perl routines for text data.

Example: Perl functions for counting chunks of text

In Section 8.5, page 316, we showed two Perl functions that took a reference to a Perl hash object and an array of strings. The hash contains counts of strings. The functions either added or subtracted to the appropriate count for each of the new strings. The intent is to maintain counts of patterns in text.

R functions chunksAdd() and chunksDrop() in package SoDA are interfaces to the Perl functions. A slightly simplified version of chunksAdd() is:

```
chunksAdd <- function(
    table = .PerlExpr("\\%{0};", .convert = FALSE),
    data = character(),
    convert = length(data) == 0) {
  if(!is(table, "PerlHashReference"))
    stop(
      "Argument table must be reference to a Perl hash object;",
      " got an object of class ", class(table))
    args <- c(list(table), as.list(as.character(data)))
  .Perl("chunks_add",  .args = args, convert = convert)
}
```

The function takes three arguments: `table` is the proxy for the hash; `data` is the new data; `convert` is a flag saying whether to return the reference or convert the hash (which RSPerl does by making a named vector of, in this case, the numeric counts). If `table` is omitted the function initializes it to an empty hash. Omitting the `data` argument, on the other hand, is the easy way to get the converted counts back, without modifying the hash—that's why the default for `convert` is TRUE when no data is being added.

The function assembles the proxy reference and the new data as a list, which when transmitted to Perl will give the suitable argument array for routine `chunks_add`. Initialization (of the table) and most error checking are done in R. That reflects our general preference for programming with R, including its facilities for interactive debugging. The Perl code can do error checking as well, and does, validating the individual data items. But as a general rule, giving the other system as clean and well-checked a set of arguments as possible is likely to save you time learning about debugging other systems.

See the code in package SoDA for more details.

12.5 Interfaces to OOP Languages

Throughout this book, the term "object-oriented programming" and its acronym OOP are reserved for the languages or systems with a programming model having the following features.

1. Objects are generated from class definitions. The data content of the objects is usually defined in terms of named slots which have a specified class or type. The terms *property* or *attribute* may be used instead of *slot* depending on the system.

2. Programming with these objects is exclusively, or at least largely, done by invoking methods on the objects.

3. The definitions of the methods come from the definition of the object's class, directly or through inheritance.

4. Although it's not a requirement, nearly all OOP objects are passed by reference, so that methods can alter the object.

The OOP programming model differs from the S language in all but the first point, even though S and some other functional languages support classes and methods. Method definitions in an OOP system are local to the class; there is no requirement that the same name for a method means the same thing for an unrelated class. In contrast, method definitions in R do not reside in a class definition; conceptually, they are associated with the generic function. Class definitions enter in determining method selection, directly or through inheritance. Programmers used to the OOP model are sometimes frustrated or confused that their programming does not transfer to R directly, but it cannot. The functional use of methods is more complicated but also more attuned to having meaningful functions, and can't be reduced to the OOP version.

Languages such as Java use the OOP model as essentially their only programming style. Other languages such as Perl, Python and C++ have added OOP programming to a functional or procedural language. Interfaces from R to these languages open up many new computations.

Method invocation usually has a different appearance from a function call, emphasizing that the method definition comes from the class definition. Usually, the expression for the object comes first, then some operator symbol, then the name of the method followed by a parenthesized list of additional arguments. The dot, ".", is a common choice for the operator symbol, used by Java and Python, among others. In these languages, a method named `print` defined for an object x might be called in the form:

```
x.print()
```

C++ and Perl (version 5) use the operator "->" instead of "." (but the proposed Perl6 uses ".").

Invoking methods in the OOP system

Interfaces from R to systems that support the OOP programming model must provide a mechanism to invoke methods. The requirements vary from one system to another but are basically that one starts with a proxy reference in R to an object in the other system, along with the name of the method, and any additional arguments the method requires. For systems supporting both functions and OOP methods, some indication may be needed as to which is wanted. It is quite feasible to mimic the syntax of method invocation in R, but as this book is written most interfaces don't do so, but instead use their functional interface.

For example, in the rJava interface package, the function .jcall() invokes Java methods. The equivalent to the example above would be:

```
.jcall(x, method = "print")
```

Similarly, in the RSPerl package, the function .Perl() handles methods if given a proxy object via the ref= argument:

```
.Perl("print", ref = x)
```

In either case, the interface code will arrange to dispatch the appropriate method in the OOP system applied to the OOP object for which x is the proxy.

Finding the "appropriate" method is the job of the foreign system. In some systems (Java, for example) there will be metadata which determines the method corresponding to the method name and the class of the object. In other systems (current Perl, for example) an interpreter for the language will evaluate the equivalent method invocation. In any case, the R software does not select the method, as it would for an R generic function.

Constructors and class methods

The notation for invoking a method in an OOP language suggests that the method belongs to the object. In fact, nearly all OOP systems associate the methods with the *class* of the object, not with the instance (the individual object itself). Method dispatch uses the known class of x to select a method with a given name; the selection will be identical for all objects with the same class. The object for which the method is invoked plays two roles: it defines the method, but only through its class; and it is passed as an argument to that method. (For example, the discussion of "method invocation" in the *Programming Perl* book [25] describes the mechanism.)

If programming is only by invoking methods on objects, how are new objects from a class generated in the first place? Methods whose purpose is to generate new objects are usually called *constructors* in OOP languages. Some languages have a separate syntax for constructors (Java, for example),

but a more revealing version has constructors invoked as a method, but on
the class itself, with no instance involved. Such methods are called *class
methods* to emphasize that they are invoked by providing the name of the
class in place of an object. So if Chunks is a class in Perl and new() is a class
method that generates a new object from the class, that method is invoked
on the class name, whereas an ordinary method, say add() is invoked on an
object from the class (to be precise, in Perl, a reference to such an object).
The following piece of Perl code creates an object and invokes one of its
methods.

```
my $counter = Chunks->new();
$counter->add(data);
```

The class method is invoked on the literal "Chunks" whereas the instance
method is invoked on the variable "$counter". Class methods in Java are
distinguished in a similar way, but by the use of declarations rather than
through syntax. Constructors are the obvious example of a class method,
and no ordinary class can get along without them. Other class methods can
exist in most systems as well, and would be invoked in a similar way.

Functional interfaces from R, such as .jcall() or .Perl(), will expect
a class method if the argument referring to an object is a character string
(the name of a class), rather than a proxy object. Constructors are often
supplied as a special case, with their own interface function (.jnew() and
.PerlNew(), for example).

12.6   Interfaces to C++

The C++ language started as a preprocessor to C, and is still compiled into
object code compatible with C. The close relation between the languages
and the fact that R is itself based on an implementation in C simplify some
aspects of interfacing to C++. Instead of calling a general interpreter for
the other system or communicating with another process, the computations
will use one of the C interface functions, .C() or .Call(). The interface
code in C++ can be included in the standard src directory where C code
would be kept, but in a file with a suffix such as "cpp" that identifies it
as C++. We began the discussion of interfacing to C++, therefore, in the
previous chapter, in Section 11.4, page 425. We continue it here because the
computational model for C++ is similar to other OOP languages and because
some extra steps are needed to write the interfacing C code.

As shown in section 11.4, the usual approach is to write some special code
in your package that contains one C-callable routine for each computation

needed from C++. The mechanism is simple: Write the new C code in a C++ source file and enclose the definitions of the C routines in a declaration that says the external names should be interpreted as C, not C++:

```
extern "C" {

}
```

While using this mechanism, there is a range of possible strategies as to how much of the C++ structure to make available to the R user, from "None" to a mirror image of the C++ methods, and corresponding questions about the R objects that should be returned to the user.

As an example, and to make the general approach clearer, let's look at the CRAN package gbm written by Greg Ridgeway. This package provides an interface to some C++ code, included with the package, for "gradient boosting", a technique for fitting statistical models. For the statistical techniques, see Chapter 10 of *Elements of Statistical Learning* [15] and the overview documentation for the gbm package. All we need to keep in mind is that the techniques iteratively refine a statistical model using the general structure we've discussed in Section 6.9, page 218, including a formula and optionally an associated data frame. The user can fit a model with an expression of the form

```
gbm1 <- gbm(formula, data, ...)
```

The formula and data arguments are similar to linear regression models and the like; in addition, there are a number of arguments special to the boosting techniques. After fitting, the user has access to plotting and other general summaries, as well as specialized performance analysis for boosting. The function gbm.more() continues the iterative fitting of an existing model. The gbm package is valuable as a bridge between the specialized computations of the C++ software and the familiar ideas provided in R for dealing with statistical models.

Functions gbm() and gbm.more() both call a C routine that creates and manipulates a CGBM object from a C++ class, CGBM, representing the models. C++ methods exist to construct and initialize the objects, to iterate fitting and to provide utilities such as prediction. The interface to the C++ computations in the R function gbm.fit() uses the .Call() interface to call the C subroutine gbm:

```
gbm.obj <- .Call("gbm",
        Y = as.double(y),
        # ... and many more arguments ...
        PACKAGE = "gbm")
```

Here is a sketch of some important steps in the C routine gbm. Arguments, allocation of R objects and error checking have all been omitted, but what's left gives an idea of the essential steps, and helps illustrate alternative strategies.

```
extern "C" {

SEXP gbm (
    // The corresponding arguments
    ) {
    CGBM *pGBM,

    // initialize R's random number generator
    GetRNGstate();

    // initialize some things
    gbm_setup( .... );

    pGBM = new CGBM();
    pGBM->Initialize( .... );
    pGBM->iterate( .... );
    gbm_transfer_to_R( .... );

    // dump random number generator seed
    PutRNGstate();

    delete pGBM;
    return rAns;
}

} // end extern "C"
```

The call to GetRNGState is a core R routine that initializes the random number generator in C to its current state (see Section 6.10, page 234); the gbm_setup call does other initialization. As with any estimation procedure using simulated random values, some extra steps would be needed to make the results reproducible; see Section 6.10, page 229.

The next lines of C++ code create and work with the object representing the model: the new expression creates the object, and the methods Initialize() and Iterate() do what their names imply. As usual in OOP computations, the object referred to by pGBM is modified to reflect the iterative fitting that has been applied. The routine gbm_transfer_to_R copies information from that C++ object into various components of the R version of the model. The C++ directive `delete` removes the object now that information has been copied.

One point to note is that the single C routine `gbm` takes the key C++ object, `pGBM`, through its entire lifetime: initializing, iterating, extracting information to return to R, and finally deleting it. The R object representing the model does not contain any proxy to a C++ object.

Hiding the C++ structure from the user has the effect, in this package, of emphasizing the similarity to other software for models in R. Users new to the package will find much of the functionality familiar, with no need to adjust to a different programming model. Their ability to explore data with these techniques will be enhanced, and that is indeed the *Mission*.

For applications in which the user needs to control computations at the level of individual C++ methods, a different organization is needed.

C++ objects in R

Once we decide not to insulate R users from the C++ objects and methods, we need a way to represent such objects. The C++ object is handled by a pointer (a reference, to sound more elegant), which will not be manipulated at all in R. In the example sketched above, `pGBM` was a pointer to an object of C++ class `CGBM`. To handle such objects in R, data of the `"externalptr"` type is the natural choice. Objects of this basic type have a single pointer as their value, only set and used in C. A value is inserted in such an object by C code and left untouched in R functions. To create explicit access to the objects and methods requires only two basic programming techniques.

- An initializing routine returns the pointer to the object, in the value field of an `"externalptr"` object;

- To each C++ method to be called from R there corresponds a C-callable routine of a known name, designed to be invoked via a `.Call()` interface and taking as its arguments the `"externalptr"` object plus whatever other arguments the method requires.

There are other ways to do it, but these choices are simple and natural.

The R package will usually have one function for each of the routines implied by these steps, each function using the `.Call()` interface to call the corresponding routine. A minimal rearrangement of the `gbm` example above to expose the C++ structure in R would have four new routines, each wrapping a corresponding C++ method:

1. gbm_new, a constructor to create and initialize an object of the C++ "CGBM" class;

2. gbm_iterate, a routine to invoke the Iterate method on the object;

3. gbm_results, a routine to return in R form the information in the current object;

4. gbm_delete, a destructor to delete the object.

The invocation of methods in the gbm routine is now broken up into separate user-callable pieces. Each of the four routines has its value and all arguments declared as pointers to R objects, conforming to the requirements for any C software to be called from the .Call() interface (see Section 11.3, page 422, for an example).

```
extern "C" {

SEXP gbm_new ( SEXP ext, ....
    ) {
    GetRNGstate();

    // initialize some things
    gbm_setup( .... );

    CGBM *pGBM = new CGBM();
    pGBM->Initialize(  .... );

    R_SetExternalPtrAddr(ext, (void *)pGBM);
    return ext;

}

SEXP gbm_iterate ( SEXP ext)
{
    CGBM *pGBM = (CGBM *) R_ExternalPtrAddr(ext);
    pGBM->iterate( .... );
    return ext;
}

SEXP gbm_results(SEXP ext)
{
    CGBM *pGBM = (CGBM *) R_ExternalPtrAddr(ext);
    gbm_transfer_to_R( .... );
    // construct list as in routine gbm
```

```
        return(rAns);
    }

    SEXP gbm_delete(SEXP ext)
    {
        CGBM *pGBM = (CGBM *) R_ExternalPtrAddr(ext);
        delete pGBM;
        return ext;

    }

} // end extern "C"
```

Each of the four C routines takes as an argument a pointer to an R object of class "externalptr" and returns the same object. The constructor, gbm_new fills in the pointer value with the newly allocated and initialized object; all the other routines extract the corresponding pointer and operate on the C++ object. (The two routines R_ExternalPtrAddr and R_SetExternalPtrAddr are R utilities that extract and set the pointer contained in an "externalptr" object.) Everything else in the example, including the code we haven't shown in this sketch, essentially rearranges the same computations done before, but now the programming model is that computations in R will control the sequence of creating, iterating, extracting and deleting.

The R software to complete the interface can be as simple as one function for each C routine, doing little more than using .Call() for the corresponding routine. If there are additional arguments to the C++ method, however, these need to be coerced to the correct datatype, either in the R function (usually the best place) or in the C routine. The construction and initialization of the CGBM object, for example, takes a number of inputs that would be arguments to gbm_new and to the corresponding R function. Here's a sketch of a fairly minimal version.

```
    gbmNew <- function( x, y,
        .... (Many more arguments)) {
        .Call("gbm_new",
            new("externalptr"),
            as.double(x), as.double(y),
            .... )
    }
```

The arguments all need to be carefully coerced to a specific basic datatype since the C routine gbm_new just passes the arguments on without checking them. The first argument is the "externalptr" object into which the C++

pointer will be inserted, and the object then returned, to be supplied in future calls to the other routines in the interface to the C++ class.

We now have a working interface to the C++ software, but usually one more layer is desirable: an R class for the objects. C++ proxy objects don't go through a single interface function, in contrast to the case for Java or other external systems; because the interface can use the standard C interface functions, no metadata is provided automatically to identify the C++ class corresponding to the object. The responsibility falls to the programmer, and for many reasons the extra effort is worth taking. In this example, a class corresponding to the C++ class would have a slot for the `"externalptr"` proxy, plus whatever additional slots are needed to complete the definition of the model (including states for the random number generator, in order to make the computations reproducible, as discussed in Section 6.10, page 229). Note that `"externalptr"` objects do not follow the standard R model to be duplicated when needed, so that the new class can not extend `"externalptr"`.

For extensive C++ software it would be better to create the mappings to C and to R automatically. Why take a chance on human error in reading the C++ definitions? As this book is written, we aren't quite able to hand over the job, but some promising work has been done, based on data available from the gcc compiler; see, for example, the `RGCCTranslationUnit` package by Duncan Temple Lang at the omegahat Web site. Check out the current status if such automation would be helpful in your application.

12.7   Interfaces to Relational Database Systems and to Spreadsheets

Database and spreadsheet programs share typical roles and data models in their relation to data analysis, even though they differ from each other in form. The typical role is as a data repository: These are the systems where the data often resides, where the underlying process keeps information. We need to interface to these repositories to have direct access to the data.

The data model suitable for both kinds of programs is the general *data frame* model discussed many times in the book; that is, the notion of some defined observable variables, for each of which values will be recorded for a range of observations. Spreadsheets and relational databases essentially visualize data frames as tables, with columns for variables and rows for observations (not that either the creators or the users of these systems would necessarily think of their data in terms of variables and observations). It's natural then that interfaces to these systems should relate tables to data frames, both in the general sense of this book and in the narrower sense of the "data.frame" class of objects.

The simplest interface from database and spreadsheet programs to R is to create files from the other system that can be read as data frames in R, in other words a text-based interface. There are a number of possible file formats, but the most widely available and convenient to use are the *comma-separated-values files* and the *tab-delimited files*. These are both standard file formats, which can be read into and exported from nearly any spreadsheet program and many database systems. Section 6.5, page 169, showed how to read such files into R, how to import and export the files in spreadsheet programs (page 173), and how to create tables from database systems (page 178).

For spreadsheet programs, this form of interface is the way to start, so long as a text-based interface is suitable for your application (mainly, that you can live with getting a copy of the non-R data and that rapid, dynamic change in the data is unlikely). Follow the discussion in Chapter 6. For database programs, such files may still be a reasonable option. Importing data from a ".csv" file is usually straightforward, but exporting a table to one may not be as simple, depending on the particular program. If your database setup does support easy export, you can follow the same route. (For example, MySQL supports ".csv" files as one of its engines; if that option is suitable to your application, it could provide an excellent interface.)

For spreadsheet programs, and in particular for Excel, some more specialized options may be available. On the Windows platform, the R-DCOM interface provides a very flexible and potentially very sophisticated communication mechanism based on the notion of components and services. On a non-Windows platform, the practical interface is to use the data export/import features in Excel.

Interfaces to database systems

For most database systems, interface packages allow flexible access with less human intervention than required to export tables explicitly. These interfaces support a functional or object-based view. Whole tables can be accessed straightforwardly. Portions of tables can be accessed using the standard query language, SQL, as supported by all major database systems. SQL was introduced briefly in Section 6.5, page 178. If you are willing to program in SQL, a functional interface is available for very general queries. Access can be functional (returning the result as a data frame) or object-based, using proxy objects as the basis for further queries or incremental

access. An additional advantage is that the related R packages provide a
uniform programming interface from R to the major database systems.

The packages use a standardization provided by the DBI package of David
James. This package defines a uniform interface for the R programmer, via
generic functions and virtual classes. Functions in the DBI package define
access to databases, tables, SQL queries, and other computations, expressed
in an essentially identical form regardless of the actual database system.
The specific database interface package implements methods and defines
subclasses to realize the programming interface for a particular database
system. If the specific interface is "DBI-compliant", software can be written
once and used on any of the database systems. Compliant interfaces exist
for Oracle (ROracle), MySQL (RMySQL), and SQLite (RSQLite).

The key concept is the mapping between a *table* in the database system
and a data frame in R. Related tables are organized into a *database*, as files
are organized in directories (in some database systems this is actually the
implementation). The DBI package reflects this organization, top-down from
choosing a database system, to specifying a database, to techniques that
manipulate individual tables.

The database system corresponds to a *driver*, created and kept through
a session. If we're using the SQLite system:

```
drv <- dbDriver("SQLite")
```

The driver is now used to open a *connection* to a particular database in
this system. Depending on the system, you may need to supply user and
password information, as well as the name of the database. SQLite just needs
the name of the database:

```
conn <- dbConnect(drv, "myDatabase")
```

It's relevant that we call these database connections; they do act much like
the R connections in Section 5.5, page 131. The difference is that data
transfer uses the facilities of the database system here rather than low-level
input and output. The units of data are tables. So, if "MarsData" has
been established as a table in "myDatabase" to hold our example of the Mars
declination data, then reading the whole table is just a call to dbReadTable():

```
> mars <- dbReadTable(conn, "MarsData")
> dim(mars)
[1] 923  21
```

Similarly, functions dbWriteTable(), dbExistsTable(), and dbRemoveTable()
perform the operations their names suggest. The concepts here are again

closely tied to the ideas of the S language, and in particular to the basic computations on environments as databases in Section 5.3, page 124.

Database tables may be very large, so that suitable access must be to a selected portion of the table. Also, a database may contain related tables and a selection may combine information from more than one of them. This is the stuff of classical relational database computation and the SQL language. Queries more complex than transferring whole tables will need to be expressed in SQL, but can be transmitted via the dbSendQuery() function. This takes as arguments a connection and a string containing the SQL query. If myQuery is an object containing such a query, the result of the query is obtained as:

```
res <- dbSendQuery(conn, myQuery)
```

We introduced SQL in Section 6.5, page 178, but for learning how to write queries, I'm afraid you will have to look up some books or other references on SQL itself. Whatever the actual query, the result is conceptually another table-like data object made up from information in one or more tables in the database. Query results are not data frames, however. In the terminology of this chapter they are proxy objects, standing in for an object in the database.

The only thing you can do in general with the result is to call function fetch() to fetch a specified number of "records" from the result. A record is a row of the implied table and the result of the call is a data frame with that many rows and with whatever columns were defined by the query.

The fetched results can be processed anyway you like. The paradigm is to check for the end of data by calling dbHasCompleted(), and then to fetch as much data as you want to handle at one time. If you wanted to just create the entire data frame:

```
> out <- NULL
> while(!dbHasCompleted(res))
+    out <- rbind(out, fetch(res, n))
```

However, if you really wanted to do this, just call dbGetQuery() instead of dbSendQuery(). The direct use of fetch() is usually to do some computations that don't require the entire data frame.

The concepts and terminology derive from the old days when records really were records, perhaps on a magnetic tape. As a consequence, bare SQL in this form does not support general manipulations of results, although database systems often do support various extensions. The simple version is adequate for many applications, and does scale well to very large datasets.

Once you have mastered enough SQL for your applications, the DBI-based interface should be straightforward to use.

As with regular connections, but sometimes even more, it may be essential to close down your connection to the database when computation is finished:

```
> dbClearResult(res)
> dbDisconnect(conn)
> dbUnloadDriver(drv)
```

12.8   Interfaces without R

Other users, not just those of us doing data analysis, can benefit from intersystem interfaces; as a result, many systems offer convenient access to other software. Keep these in mind for applications where there is no need to bring data into R from another system just to pass it on to a third. Using an interface between the other two systems can simplify programming and save computing time.

For example, many systems will have interfaces to both spreadsheet software and relational databases, for the same reasons such interfaces are useful in R: that's often where data resides. This gives us some more choices whenever data in a database or spreadsheet is to be used eventually in some other non-R computations: Either access the data indirectly through R or write some code in Perl to access the data directly, in addition to the text manipulation software.

As an example consider applying some text manipulation in Perl to data residing in a relational database. What are some tradeoffs to guide the choices?

- If the original data from the database is not needed in R for other purposes, there will be some computational efficiency to direct access, particularly if the programming style of access is made more natural for the other system (see the example below). My usual caution about "efficiency" applies: Does it matter in this case?

- The additional programming effort required for direct access will vary. If R creates a data frame from the database and then presents part of it in a different form, such as a single variable, the existing Perl code will not likely be directly usable given Perl's approach to a database interface.

The best solution in different applications can vary from ignoring R for database access (when only the results of the Perl-processed data are needed) to using only R for database access (when the data needed for Perl is more naturally supplied as columns of the data frame formed in R).

To see the different styles of database access, we can compare typical use of the DBI package in R and the DBI module in Perl. The two share a name and a basic design: to act as an interface to relational database software, including the SQL query language, with programming that is independent of the specific database system. They also take a similar approach to the initial programming required. The user establishes a connection to a particular database. In the OOP form of Perl, one invokes the connect() method of the module:

```
my $dbcon = DBI->connect('DBI:MySQL:myData');
```

As with the function dbConnect() in the DBI package, this returns a connection that can then be used for all queries on this database in this session.

The next step in both systems is to obtain a result set, the database's version of the result of executing a query. Using the DBI package in R, we call dbSendQuery(). The actual SQL is essentially the same for access from Perl, but the standard approach includes an intermediate step to *prepare* the query. The prepared but unexecuted query is returned as an object.

```
my $query = $dbcon->prepare($someQueryString);
```

Preparing is essentially compiling the SQL query; one can leave parameters (typically to be filled in by names) unspecified. The execute() method of the query then creates the result set; if there are parameters in the prepared query, these are supplied as arguments to execute(), as in:

```
$query->execute($thisName);
```

We are now at the same state that the interface from R would be after evaluating a call to dbSendQuery(), with two minor differences. The standard DBI interface in R does not include preparing queries, although specific database interface packages may do so; also, the Perl execution of the query does not return a result set as an object, but instead modifies the $query object to be ready for fetching data.

In both interfaces, the actual data transfer takes place by fetching rows from the result set. As usual, the Perl method is oriented to iteration: The method fetchrow_array() always fetches a single row, which is returned as a Perl array. The elements of the array are the (scalar) values for each variable in the result set, for the next available row. The R function `fetch()` fetches an arbitrary number of rows, as a data frame.

It's the one-row-at-a-time nature of the Perl fetch that suggests organizing the Perl computation differently when accessing data from a database rather than from R. In the first case, typical Perl style would do all the immediately relevant computations on all the variables, incrementally one row at a time, rather than collecting one or more variables as separate arrays. The second approach is feasible, but then it may be simpler just to collect the data in R.

Chapter 13

How **R** Works

This chapter takes a modest look under the hood at the R engine, that is, the program that runs R. As with an automobile, you can use R without worrying very much about how it works. But computing with data is more complicated than driving a car (fortunately for highway safety), and at some point you may need to make some basic choices between different approaches to your computation. Understanding something about what actually happens will often show that some approaches suit the system better than others.

The essential part of the R program is the evaluator (Section 13.2, page 454). As throughout the book, two interacting concepts are key, functions and objects: on the one hand, the function calls that provide the actions, distinguished between functions written in R (Section 13.3, page 460) and primitive functions (13.4, 463); and on the other hand, the objects, referenced through assignment, that are the arguments and results of the actions (Section 13.5, page 465).

Beyond the evaluator, two additional concepts are important: the language (Section 13.6, page 468); and the management of memory for objects (Section 13.7, page 471).

13.1 The **R** Program

To use R, you will start up a corresponding "program". In the early days, and still often in UNIX/Linux operating systems, this meant invoking an R program from an interactive shell. The user then typed R expressions or "commands" to that program. More typically now, you will start up R in a window, by clicking on the corresponding program or its icon in a tool bar. The resulting graphical user interface (GUI) may provide a variety of features including documentation windows or perhaps menu-driven computations. But the heart of the GUI will still likely be a window in which you can compose expressions for R to evaluate. The process of evaluating expressions is in turn the heart of how R works, and we will spend most of the chapter exploring aspects of that process.

When the program is reading user-typed expressions, its outer layer is responsible for somewhat more than just evaluating the expressions. The traditional computing description is a "read-parse-evaluate" loop. That just means that the program *reads* user input, tries to *parse* the corresponding text as an expression, and then tries to *evaluate* that expression. This three-step operation continues, until the R session ends, when the user decides to quit or (rarely, one hopes) because the program is terminated.

The reading and parsing are important, but for understanding how R works, they are only an outer layer around the object-based computations at the heart of the system. Part of the R software consists of code to interpret text in terms of R's version of the S language and to generate corresponding expressions (see Section 13.6, page 468).

The key concept is that expressions for evaluation are themselves objects; in the traditional motto of the S language, *everything is an object*. Evaluation consists of taking the object representing an expression and returning the object that is the value of that expression. Once you have that concept in mind, many useful and elegant computations become easier to imagine. For example, computations in R can generate or modify expressions and then ask for the evaluation of the expression objects.

As another example, a variety of tools to help study and debug programs in R are themselves R functions that use the objects representing functions and expressions to give users interactive views of what's being computed—all done within the language itself and as a result, available for further specialization and enhancement.

13.2   The R Evaluator

The evaluation part of the R program consists of passing the object resulting from parsing the current expression to the R evaluator. The evaluator is part of the internal program, but it also exists as the `eval()` function. In either case the evaluator takes an object, usually from one of the classes that represent expressions in the language, and returns the result of evaluating that object. This section outlines the properties and behavior of such objects, in terms of the evaluator. For the story on objects in general, start with Chapter 5.

If how R works comes down to evaluating objects, then evaluating objects largely comes down to evaluating function calls. The reason is that nearly all expressions look like function call objects when they come to be evaluated. Before moving on to function calls, we need to discuss the main exceptions: constants, names, and promises.

Constants

These are the expressions that evaluate into themselves. For the most part, their behavior is obvious, but R has a few peculiarities that need to be noted. Numerical and string constants occur most frequently. Neither of them is anything special as an object, they are simply vectors that happen to have length 1. The distinction is in the range of expressions that parse directly into these objects.

Numerical constants are written in decimal fraction or scientific notation, but not with a leading sign. Thus, `3.14` is a constant, but the expressions `-3.14` and `+3.14` are calls to the functions `` `-` `` and `` `+` ``. Complex numbers are also understood by the language, in the form $x \pm yi$, where x and y are numerical constants. Technically, these are not constants, but once again calls to the `` `+` `` or `` `-` ``; the only complex constants that can be written in the language are of the form yi.

You rarely need to know if an expression is a constant, except when writing your own tools to deal with language objects. To test a particular expression, use `class(quote(...))`.

```
> class(quote(3.14))
[1] "numeric"
> class(quote(-3.14))
[1] "call"
```

String constants as objects are just character vectors of length 1. The expressions recognized by the parser as strings are quoted text, enclosed by one of the quotation characters, """ and "'" The characters between the enclosing quotes are interpreted according to the locale, that is, the text encoding set for your local installation of R (see Section 8.1, page 293). In addition, strings can contain escaped characters, using the UNIX-style backslash escape sequences. For the grubby details, see `?Quotes`.

R has also added to the S language a third kind of quote, "`", called the "backtick" in R documentation. The parsed expression enclosed in backticks is not a string but an object of class `"name"`, and obeys the evaluation rules for names.

```
> class(quote(`[`))
[1] "name"
```

Backticks are useful when supplying names as arguments, avoiding problems if the object names are not syntactically legal names, as defined below.

The evaluator can encounter all sorts of other constants; by definition, anything guaranteed to be equal to itself after evaluation is a constant. The evaluator has an explicit list of the internal object types known to be constants; when it encounters such an object it does nothing with the contents but marks the object to prevent it being overwritten by a replacement computation. (See the discussion of replacement functions on page 465.) In typical computations, the evaluator knows what has been evaluated and tends not to re-evaluate objects. However, any special mechanisms, such as calling `eval()` directly, can indeed result in re-evaluation. For this reason, you need to be careful if a function returns a name, function call or other language object that you do not want evaluated. The safe approach hides such objects in a component, slot, or element of another object.

Names

These are expressions that identify objects. They can appear literally in input to the parser either as a syntactic name or as any string enclosed in backticks. A syntactic name in R may contain letters, digits and the two characters `"."` and `"_"`, but must start with a letter or `"."`. For fans of regular expressions, this can be translated as:

```
"^[.[:alpha:]][._[:alnum:]]*$"
```

The character classes `"[:alpha:]"` and `"[:alnum:]"` stand for alphabetic and alphanumeric characters, and should be used when dealing with letters in regular expressions. See Section 8.3, page 301. The backtick quote mechanism allows arbitrary non-empty character strings to act as names in the language, a useful extension since special operators (e.g., `` `+` `` or `` `%%` ``) and replacement functions (e.g., `` `diag<-` ``) are assigned as function objects even though the corresponding strings are not syntactically names.

Names are evaluated by looking for an object assigned with the corresponding string value. The precise definition of "looking for" is a key aspect of how R works, and a full understanding will involve several aspects; however, the essential concept is that the evaluator looks in the environment of the current evaluation (sometimes called either a *frame* or a *context*), first for the objects contained in that environment itself, and then step by step back through the enclosing environments. Inside a call to an R function the local environment contains the arguments and any local assignments. The enclosing environment is the environment of the function, typically the namespace (if any) of the package containing the function or the global environment otherwise. For more details on environments, see Section 5.3, page 119.

Some names are associated with the special object "...": The "..." name itself is only legal in another function call, in which case it is expanded to the list of corresponding arguments. In addition, there is a special notation allowed to refer to the first argument that matched "...", to the second, and so on: The name ..1 refers to the first matching argument, ..2 to the second, etc. You should probably avoid this obscure convention, which can usually be done by writing a function with some ordinary argument names, and calling it with "..." .

Also special are a variety of constants, which appear to be names but which are parsed directly into the actual objects:

```
TRUE FALSE NA # logical constants
Inf NaN       # numeric constants
NULL          # NULL constant
```

Notice that NA is a logical constant, but NaN is a numeric constant. The former is used to indicate missing elements in vectors of several object types, and its "logical" type avoids accidentally promoting a vector to a numeric type. The constant NaN is an R version of the standard representation for an undefined numerical result (see Section 6.6, page 188).

Promises

You should never literally see these objects in R, but they play an important role in evaluation. The semantics of the S language says that the arguments in a function call are not evaluated until they are needed, a mechanism known as *lazy evaluation.* The two main instances of "needed" are the evaluation of arguments in a call to a primitive function and the selection of a method in a call to a generic function. When arguments are evaluated, they should then not be re-evaluated.

R implements the semantic requirements by assigning each formal argument name a special object of type "promise". The object includes the expression whose value will be computed and the value itself, once it has been computed. The essential property is to delay computation until a request for the value is received, and then to do the computation, but only once. The ability to work with promises directly is deliberately limited (otherwise very bizarre behavior in the evaluator could result). For how promises affect the evaluation of function calls see Section 13.3, page 462.

The mechanism of promise objects was created to implement the lazy evaluation model of the S language, but it has been used for other purposes as well. The `"LazyLoad"` directive in the `"DESCRIPTION"` file causes a database of the R objects in a package to be created at `INSTALL` time. The actual objects loaded when the package is attached during a session are promises that, when evaluated, access the object from the database. The mechanism has the combined advantages of computing the objects during installation, not during attach, while initially loading only the small promise objects into the session, reducing the memory requirements of large packages. The `"LazyData"` directive works similarly for objects installed from the `"data"` directory in the source package. Promises are loaded for the data objects when the package is attached, again minimizing initial memory requirements while relieving users of the need to call the `data()` function to get the object.

Programmers can use the promise mechanism by calling `delayedAssign()`. When the motivation is saving memory or computing time, the technique is something to consider, if only rather late in the development process. For explicitly delaying evaluation, a clearer and more trustworthy approach is to store unevaluated expressions explicitly and then to call `eval()` or a similar function for the evaluation.

Everything else

Everything else looks like a function call to the evaluator, providing a nice uniformity for computations. The uniformity probably reflects a historical connection of early work on R with Lisp, where syntax as well as semantics makes expressions look uniformly like function calls. The S language uses the more common C-style notation, but this is merely syntactic convention. Thus assignments are calls to the corresponding function, such as `` `<-` ``:

```
> `<-`(xx, 1.5)
> xx
[1] 1.5
> `=`(y, 1+1)
> y
[1] 2
```

Similarly, control structures such as `if(....)...else....` and `for(....)....` are equivalent to function calls with the relevant subexpressions as the arguments:

```
> `if`(xx < 1, "Small", "Big")
[1] "Big"
```

The key concept is that, although the function-call expressions above go through a different parsing route than would the more normal way of writing the same computation, the evaluation stage of the read-parse-evaluate cycle is identical.

You can use the function-call organization for tools that construct R language objects in R itself. The objects have a class corresponding to the specific purpose (`"if"`, etc.), but their internal type is always `"language"`. For manipulation purposes you can create the object by giving `quote()` a corresponding expression or by calling `new()` with the class string (the latter is more convenient if you need to create objects of various language classes).

```
> ff <- new("if")
> class(ff)
[1] "if"
> typeof(ff)
[1] "language"
```

The function-call objects can be indexed like vectors, even though technically `"language"` is not a vector type. The first element of the object is the function, which can either be a function object or, much more often, a name. A name here means the class, not the syntactic name. The parser converts any style of quoted name for the function being called into a name object.

The evaluation of the function call begins by looking for a function corresponding to the name. The rules for "looking for" are the same as the general rules for evaluating names mentioned above, except that the evaluator silently ignores any object found that is not a function, allowing local non-function objects with the same name as non-local functions, a concession motivated by people's tendency to assign objects names such as `"c"`.

Now the evaluation depends on what sort of function object was found. The fundamental distinction is between functions defined in R itself versus certain types of primitive functions. If you work with language objects in any detail, whether in debugging or in developing new tools, you will usually need to deal separately with the two cases, so in the next two sections we branch the discussion accordingly.

13.3   Calls to **R** Functions

As noted in the previous section, the evaluation of every function call in
R and of most other nontrivial expressions generates a function call object,
passing along zero or more arguments as expressions. The evaluation of calls
to ordinary functions, including all those that R programmers will write,
follows the same essential mechanism, described in this section. There are
also special *primitive* functions built into the core of R itself that behave
differently; Section 13.4 describes how these work, but such functions exist
only in the core, and cannot be created in users' packages.

The term *closure* is used in R to describe both the object type of the
function object and also a programming technique using those objects in a
special way. The class of an R function object is `"function"`, but the internal
type of a non-primitive function, as returned by `typeof()`, is `"closure"`. To
avoid confusion, this book usually reserves the term closure for the programming technique, which is described in Section 5.4, page 125. When we talk
about function objects, we mean a function defined in R; to talk about the
primitives we specifically refer to *primitive* functions. These, by the way,
also have class `"function"`, but different internal types, as discussed on page
464. They are objects, also, but with much less structure.

A call to an R function is evaluated in three steps. Understand these,
and you understand the most important aspect of how R works.

1. The argument expressions in the call (the *actual arguments*) are matched
   to the formal arguments in the function definition.

2. A new environment is created and an assignment is made there for
   each of the formal arguments, containing the actual argument if any,
   and also any default expression if the argument was missing and there
   was a default. The enclosing environment of the new environment is
   the environment of the function object (a crucial point that we will
   discuss below).

3. The body of the function is evaluated in the new environment, and
   the result is returned as the value of the function call.

As a historical note (and to help understand compatibility between R and
S-Plus), note that the steps correspond to a model for evaluation of function
calls in the S language, presented in the form of some pseudo-S computations,
in the book *The New S Language* [1, Section 11.2]. Leaving out a few details,
the essentials were:

```
New.frame(amatch(definition, expr), expr)
value <- Eval(body)
Pop.frame()
value
```

Here `expr` is the actual call, `definition` is the function object, and `body` is the function body of that object. The first line of the example corresponds to steps 1 and 2 above, with `amatch()` carrying out the argument matching in step 1. In the S model, the evaluator has a list of the ongoing evaluations (the list returned by `sys.frames()`); `New.frame()` puts the matched arguments into a new frame, and makes that the current frame, in which `Eval()` will evaluate the body of the function, after which `Pop.frame()` gets rid of the frame.

R adopts this model, but with the crucial addition of the function environment in step 2, which affects the way names are looked up. The function's environment is the environment in which it's created, for regular functions. Generic functions each get their own environment (for method selection purposes) but the parent of that environment is the function environment, just as with non-generic functions. It's this *function environment* that is crucial for evaluation in R.

In the S model, names are searched for first in the current frame (as in R), but then essentially in the global "environment" of the current session. R searches in the function environment instead. For functions that are sourced into the R session the function environment is the global environment, and so name lookup basically follows the S model. The same is true for functions from packages, unless the package has a `NAMESPACE`.

However, R uses function environments in two important techniques that differ from the S approach. If a package uses the `NAMESPACE` mechanism, functions have an environment specific to the package, and unconnected to the dynamic global environment of a session. Namespaces are valuable in clarifying the meaning of functions in a package. The namespace only includes explicitly imported objects and the `base` package. Therefore, the result of a call will not be altered accidentally by conflicting functions attached during the session. Section 4.6, page 103, discusses how to use the namespace mechanism in a package. You can test whether a package has a namespace by trying to get it:

```
> getNamespace("methods")
<environment: namespace:methods>
> getNamespace("gam")
Error: package 'gam' does not have a name space
```

The other common use of enclosing environments is what is called the *closure* programming technique. In the usual version, an object is set up that contains some functions as components. These functions were created during a function call, not at the top level of the session, so the function environment is that of the call, now preserved in the object. This gives a mechanism for sharing and modifying objects in that environment. Section 5.4, page 125, discusses how it can be used.

Step 3, the evaluation of the function body, proceeds as a standard evaluation. It is specialized to the current function call via the objects assigned with the names of the formal arguments. These are the "promise" objects mentioned on page 457. They implement the *lazy evaluation* concept that the expression for the actual argument or default is not evaluated until needed, and then not re-evaluated.

A promise object has: an expression; an environment in which the expression will be evaluated; a value (initially an internal reference interpreted as "undefined"); and a "seen" flag (initially off). In processing a request to evaluate a promise, the evaluator simply returns the value, if it is not undefined. On the first encounter (the first time the argument is needed in evaluating the body of the function), the evaluator proceeds to evaluate the object's expression in its environment. For arguments supplied in the call these are the actual argument and the caller's environment. For missing arguments the environment is that of the call itself and the expression is the default if there is one; otherwise an error results. Before starting the evaluation of the expression, the "seen" flag is turned on. This flag is checked if another request for the value is encountered while the value is still undefined; if it is on, an error for "recursive default argument reference" results.

When is a promise evaluated? There are two main cases.

1. A primitive function call, including parsed versions of special language expressions, evaluates an argument that includes the name, directly or indirectly;

2. In method selection, an actual argument in the signature of the generic is evaluated that includes the name. Default expressions for missing arguments are not evaluated at this time; method selection uses class "missing" for these.

Note that in both cases, it's the occurrence of the name assigned to the promise that triggers the request to evaluate it. For the first case, the argument may have been given to a primitive function directly or included in a call to another function resulting in that argument eventually needing evaluation. Therefore, to be cautious, you should assume that an argument may be evaluated as soon as it's included in any function call, unless you explicitly know otherwise. On the question of which arguments to primitives are evaluated, see the comments on primitives of type "special", on page 464. To resolve the second case just print the generic function. Its show() method says which arguments can be included in methods.

Whether an argument is considered missing is normally determined from the promise object associated with that argument. If the argument name does not correspond to a promise, it is usually not considered missing. Thus, if you assign explicitly to the formal argument x, then missing(x) will be FALSE from then on, regardless of what the function call said. Consider:

```
f <- function(x = 1) {
  missing(x)
}

g <- function(x) {
  if(missing(x))
    x <- 2
  missing(x)
}
```

The call f() returns TRUE, the call g() returns FALSE.

13.4 Calls to Primitive Functions

R contains a fixed set of objects that can be called as functions but that do not correspond to an object with formal arguments and a body. These are referred to as the "primitive" functions; if you print one, it looks like a call to the function .Primitive(). Some tools in R, such as automatic printing, tend to hide the special nature of primitive functions, making them appear like ordinary functions. The test function is.primitive() will identify them. To find out what the primitive objects are, let's apply is.primitive() to each of the objects in the base package.

```
> allObjects <- objects("package:base", all=TRUE)
> primitives <- sapply(allObjects,
+     function(x)is.primitive(get(x)))
> primFuns  <- allObjects[primitives]; primFuns
  [1] "!"           "!="          "$"
  [4] "$<-"         "%%"          "%*%"
```

```
 [7]  "%/%"              "&"               "&&"
[10]  "("               "*"               "+"
[13]  "-"               ".C"              ".Call"
 etc. ...
```

The primitives include a variety of operators, mathematical functions and other, well, primitive computations. These include some language constructions that are treated as function calls (the uniformity helps provide consistent behavior in the evaluator). Examples include `if()` and `` `{` ``.

Evaluation of a call to one of these functions starts off in the usual way, but when the evaluator discovers that the function object is a primitive rather than a function defined in R, it branches to an entirely different computation. The object only appears to be a function object with formal arguments and a call to the function `.Primitive()` with a string argument. In reality, it essentially contains only an index into a table that is part of the C code implementing the core of R. The entry of the table identifies a C routine in the core that is responsible for evaluating calls to this specific primitive. The evaluator will transfer control to that routine, and expects the routine to return a C-language pointer to the R object representing the value of the call. Exactly how this works depends on the internal type of the primitive. There are two: `"builtin"` and `"special"`. To find them, we can split the primitive functions in the `base` package using the function `typeof()`:

```
> functionTypes <- split(primFuns,
+                sapply(primFuns, function(x)typeof(get(x))))
> names(functionTypes)
[1] "builtin" "special"
> sapply(functionTypes, length)
builtin special
    149      39
> functionTypes$special
 [1] "$"          "$<-"          "&&"       ".Internal"
 [5] "<-"         "<<-"          "="        "@"
 [9] "UseMethod"  "["            "[<-"      "[["
[13] "[[<-"       "break"        "browser"  "c"
[17] "call"       "expression"   "for"      "function"
[21] "if"         "interactive"  "log"      "missing"
[25] "nargs"      "next"         "on.exit"  "quote"
[29] "rep"        "repeat"       "return"   "round"
[33] "seq.int"    "signif"       "substitute" "while"
[37] "{"          "||"           "~"
```

The difference between the evaluation of "builtin" and "special" primitives is that the arguments to a primitive of type "builtin" are evaluated and passed to the routine as a list of objects, whereas the arguments to a primitive of type "special" are passed directly from the call as a list of unevaluated expressions. The primitive object for `+` is a "builtin" and that for `if` is a "special", as you might expect since only one of the branches of an if expression will be evaluated. A special primitive can choose to evaluate its arguments if and when it chooses. A general rule is impossible, but most cases are intuitively reasonable, like `if`. Less obvious is that all assignments are evaluated by a "special" primitive that evaluates the right-hand side immediately, including the case that the assignment is being handled by a replacement function written in R. See Section 13.5.

And, if you then would like to know just what one of the functions does, that can also be answered, by looking in the source for R itself.

Admittedly, the computations are written in a form of C that is not exactly for the faint of heart. The implementations use the internal structure of R objects and also tend to be very detailed, as we would hope for functions near the center of the system. All the same, I would encourage the exploration for anyone with a general understanding of programming in C or similar languages, and with an interest in how computations are done in R. Start with a source copy of R, stored in directory $RHOME, say. In a text editor, look in the file "names.c" in directory $RHOME/src/main. This contains the table mentioned before. There will be a C structure element shown for each primitive function. The first member of the structure is the quoted name of the primitive; the second is the C entry point to evaluate the call. The entries for the `+` and `if` primitives, for example, are:

```
{"+", do_arith, PLUSOP, 1, 2, {PP_BINARY, PREC_SUM, 0}},
{"if", do_if, 0, 0, -1, {PP_IF, PREC_FN, 1}},
```

The remaining elements in the structure are perhaps somewhat too far down in the internals, even for this chapter. But if, for example, you want to understand some really detailed issue about how R deals with arithmetic operations, look for the routine do_arith in the source files.

13.5 Assignments and Replacements

Assignment expressions are calls to the assignment operators: `<-`, `=`, and `<<-`. The first two are synonyms, just there to make those familiar with one or the other symbol feel more comfortable. (The parser accepts mirror-image versions, `` `->` `` and `` `->>` ``, but just translates them to point left. These are historic leftovers from the days before inline editing.)

The operator `` `<<-` `` is a *non-local assignment* operator. It behaves differently from regular assignment and breaks the functional style, in that you cannot figure out what is happening to the object on the left of the assignment by looking only at the function in which the assignment takes place. Therefore, non-local assignments are frowned on from the functional programming perspective, and can be considered dangerous to the *Prime Directive*. However, they are used in programming techniques such as *closures* (Section 5.4), so one should at least be aware of how they work.

All these assignments translate into calls to the function of the same name as the operator, and of type `"special"`, with the left- and right-side operand expressions being the first and second argument. So any assignment using `` `<-` `` calls the function `` `<-`() ``, and always with two arguments. The effect of the evaluating the call may be an *assignment* that associates a value with a name, or a *replacement* that takes the current object assigned the same name and returns a new object to replace that one. In the assignment case, the first argument is a name; all three operators assign the value of the second argument to that name, the only difference being where the assignment is done.

Replacement expressions

If the first argument (i.e., the left side of the assignment) is a call, evaluation results in a call to the corresponding replacement function. However, the right side of the assignment (the value to be assigned) is always evaluated first, before examining the left side. (The reason is the rule in the language's grammar that nested assignments associate to the right. The right side is evaluated first, in case it is also an assignment.) The practical relevance is that lazy evaluation never applies to the final argument, `value`, in replacement functions.

The replacement function mechanism means that any assignment of the form $f(\ldots)$ `<-` *rhs* is translated into an ordinary assignment: specifically,

```
tmp   <- `f<-`(tmp , ..., value=rhs)
```

So an arbitrary replacement can be defined by simply creating a function with the special name and suitable argument list, as described in Section 5.2, page 117. If the first argument to *f*, in turn, is a name, then *tmp* is effectively just that name. However, replacement expressions can nest function calls on the left side, for example,

```
diag(z$a) <- NA
```

In this case, the evaluator arranges to extract the object z$a, pass it to the replacement function `diag<-`(), and then replace the value returned by that call, using the replacement function `$<-`().

Any function can appear in this nested form of replacement operation, but only if it exists both as a regular function and the corresponding replacement version. If we wanted to evaluate

```
diag(foo(z)) <- NA
```

we need both foo() and `foo<-`().

Non-local assignments

A local assignment always takes place in the environment where the call is evaluated. Non-local assignment takes place in the *enclosing* environment of the call if there is currently an object of the same name in that environment. If not, the enclosing environment of that environment is examined, and so on until an environment is found that has an assignment for this name, which is then the environment used for the new assignment as well. If there is no current assignment, the assignment takes place in the global environment. The logic here guarantees that a non-local replacement will occur in the environment containing the object, but the effect is rather odd when a simple assignment is intended. If you know where you want the new object, a clearer style uses the assign() function directly. Even better, avoid non-local assignments without a good motivation.

The point of the R behavior becomes clearer from looking at an example. A function definition may create some new functions locally, during the call. If so, these functions have as their environment the environment of the call to the parent function. The children functions can then communicate with the parent and with each other by doing non-local assignments to variables with known names, provided those variables have already been created. Here's a very simple example: The splitRepeated() function (shown on page 297) wants to know whether any warnings took place in multiple calls to as.numeric(). By using calling handlers (see Section 3.7, page 75) it arranges for a function to be called when a warning takes place. The function is created in the call to splitRepeated(), with the definition:

```
function(e) warned <<- TRUE
```

Before the call involving this function, splitRepeated() intializes a local version of the variable warned:

```
warned <- FALSE
```

Now the R rule for non-local assignment guarantees that any call to the handler function will set `warned` in the environment of the call to `splitRepeated()`. It's a simple and convenient mechanism, and in this example the entire programming is done and used in `splitRepeated()`, so the intent is fairly clear, once the underlying R rule is understood. Both the *Mission* and the *Prime Directive* are reasonably satisfied.

Much more extensive examples of using the mechanism are possible, however, and some of these bother me more. One technique is to return a list of functions that all manipulate some variables in a common environment, not local to any of the individual functions. The classic example simulates deposits and withdrawals from a bank account. The account is returned as the value of an initial function call, say:

```
a <- makeAccount(....)
```

The object `a` is a list with functions called as `a$deposit()`, `a$withdraw()`, etc. These functions manipulate non-local objects created in the environment of the call to `makeAccount`. The mechanism here is similar to what a language such as Java would do via a class definition for the object `a` and methods invoked on that object. Fields in the Java object correspond to variables in the R environment. But unlike Java, the R mechanism has no formal definition of the fields and no "metadata", in our terminology, to let us examine the programming. The mechanism is convenient in some applications, but mistakes may not be caught quickly or clearly, so the *Prime Directive* should give us pause.

13.6   The Language

R implements the grammar of the S language, with a few extensions. This is a traditional grammar of the flavor of C and the many languages that have more or less followed in the style of C. In a typical interactive R session, the user supplies input text according to that grammar (aside from mistakes), and the R application then parses and evaluates accordingly. Why learn about the grammar? It defines what information can be included in the parsed expression, and therefore what range of expressions the R evaluator needs to treat. Often, you can provide more general expressions than you might expect, but when trying out something odd, keep in mind that parsing is just the first step. Expressions that follow the rules of the grammar but make no sense will generate errors when one tries to evaluate them; at least, we very much hope so. See the warning on page 471 for an example.

Expression	Rule	Class
Call	*expr* (*sublist*)	`"call"`
Binary	*expr op expr*	`"call"`
	expr $ *nameString*	
	expr @ *nameString*	
	nameString :: *nameString*	
	nameString ::: *nameString*	
Unary	*unaryOp expr*	`"call"`
Subset	*expr* [*sublist*]	`"call"`
	expr [[*sublist*]]	
Conditional	if(*expr*)	`"if"`
	if(*expr*) else *expr*	
Iteration	for(Name in *expr*) *expr*	`"for"`
	while(*expr*) *expr*	`"while"`
	repeat *expr*	`"repeat"`
Grouping	(*expr*)	`"("`
	{ *exprlist* }	`"{"`
Function	function(*formlist*) *expr*	`"function"`
Flow	break	`"break"`
	next	`"next"`
Token	*constNameString*	

Table 13.1: **The Language.** The rows summarize the syntactic rules for syntactic type *expr*—an expression according to the R parser. See the text for the meaning of the other syntactic types in the second column.

The essential computation of the R parser is to read sufficient input to find a complete *expression* in the grammar, to interpret that expression, and to return an R object representing it. The expression objects from the parse are usually called unevaluated expressions elsewhere in the book, to emphasize that they are produced and handled independently of evaluation, which happens when the expression object is passed to the R evaluator.

Understanding the grammar of the language then boils down to understanding what syntactic patterns are legal expressions. Table 13.1 describes the main rules for expressions. Each row of the table defines one of the alternative rules for a valid expression. The table is a definition of the grammatical alternatives, one per row, for expressing the form of the general expression, denoted by *expr*. In the usual style of such grammatical descriptions, the valid syntactic constructions are defined recursively. Thus, one form of legal *expr*, in the first row, is composed of any other legal expression, followed by a left parenthesis, a *sublist* and a right parenthesis. Then *sublist* is another grammatical form, in this case not shown in the table—see the descriptions below—that corresponds to the rule for an argument list in the call to a function. In other words, the first rule defines a standard function call in the S language, including the option of naming arguments.

The table follows both the actual grammar rules as written in the yacc software for R and also the corresponding table for the S language in *Programming with Data*, [5, section 3.2], indicating the closeness of the grammatical forms in S and R. The names used in the table for syntactic patterns follow those in the actual grammar.

The remaining syntactic types in the table are defined informally as follows.

sublist: A comma-separated list, each element being either an expression or a name followed by "=" followed by an expression. Notice that the arguments to the single- and double-square bracket operators have this syntactic definition also. Therefore named arguments are legal to the ` [ ` and ` [[ ` operators. They even work sometimes (but not in the primitive function as the example below shows), because the interpretation is being done by methods interpreting multiple index arguments.

constNameString, *nameString*: One of the terminal token types. In classical parsers such as R uses, a separate preliminary stage of the parse breaks the input text into *tokens*, sequences of characters forming one of the predefined low-level constructs in the language. The *constNameString* group of tokens are those that can stand alone as an expression, essentially numerical and logical constants, "NULL", syntactic names, and strings. Syntactic names include arbitrary strings enclosed in backticks. The *nameString* group of tokens includes only syntactic names and string constants.

op, *unaryOp*: More groups of token types. The *op* group includes the usual operators for arithmetic, comparisons and logical expressions, plus operators ` % `, ` ~ `, ` ? ` and user-defined binary operators specified as a pair of "%" characters enclosing an arbitrary sequence of characters.

Warning: parsing is only the first step.

For example, the rule for assignments allows an arbitrary expression on the left of the assignment. In practice, although assignment expressions in the S language are probably more general than in nearly any other language, not everything makes sense. Reading the grammar points out that checks for meaningless assignment expressions must be done during evaluation. The expression

```
f("yy")<-3
```

will generate an error because the form of the left-side is not interpretable as a replacement expression, but the error is not from the parser—try `quote(f("yy")<-3)` to convince yourself. Expressions that are syntactically valid but computationally meaningless are to be expected in any language that uses classical scientific notation. Good code will report them at evaluation time, preferably with a meaningful error.

More insidious problems arise when an expression that may appear meaningful is silently misinterpreted. Primitive functions present particular dangers here. Although the general grammar implies that all functions and some operators interpret a general argument list, primitive functions have no formal arguments. Apparent argument names provided in documentation are not honored if used; worse, the standard behavior is to ignore argument names rather than generating an error. For example, the `` `[` `` operator might appear from its documentation (and from the generic function corresponding to it) to have arguments `"i"` and `"j"` for the first and second subscript. In its primitive form, it does not and will happily ignore such names. Thus if x is a matrix, you might believe that

```
x[ j=1, i=2]
```

would extract the first column, second row. But in fact the primitive ignores the argument names and returns the first row, second column. Methods for these functions do have legitimate argument lists and can be used in the usual way, but be very careful when using `callNextMethod()` with explicit arguments.

13.7 Memory Management for R Objects

Memory management in R is automatic, in contrast to C or C++. Programmers do not need to allocate or delete storage explicitly (and are actively discouraged from doing so for most purposes); instead, evaluating function calls and assigning objects triggers allocation and occasional deallocation (via garbage collection). Once again, the dual themes of function calls on the one hand and, on the other, objects and object references are central to understanding what happens.

R's memory management has proven successful for a wide range of applications. Occasionally, particularly with very large objects, hard limitations or noticeable slowdown may obstruct programming. Understanding how it works can help anticipate or work around such problems. In this section we look briefly at some of the important techniques used, with emphasis on the aspects with implications for programming.

R objects come from three essential sources:

1. constants in the language (numbers, strings and a few specially named objects such as TRUE and Inf);

2. references, that is, objects obtained by name from an environment;

3. new objects produced by evaluating function calls.

All objects in fact are dynamically allocated at some time during the R session. Constants are allocated essentially in the parser. Objects assigned in an environment were either constructed from some computation or restored from previously saved objects (equivalent to a call to unserialize() as far as memory allocation is concerned). As a result, all the memory for objects eventually comes from the same mechanism, that by which a vector or other basic R object is created. This uniformity is important in practice because it allows the mechanism to be tuned and studied.

Programmers do not explicitly manage memory for R objects, which occasionally frustrates those who would like more control. In particular, objects cannot be deleted; the function rm() removes the assignment of an object in an environment, but does not delete the memory for the object. Unused dynamic storage is recovered by *garbage collection*, which usually takes place automatically and, from the user's view, unpredictably. It's possible to force garbage collection by calling the function gc(), but a substantial computation is required, so it's unlikely to be a good idea just for the sake of recovering storage for a few objects.

Garbage collection recovers storage from objects that do not have a current reference. Primarily, a reference is an assignment in an environment, the essential mechanism we have studied throughout the book. Essentially, the computation works through all the places that references can reside and arranges that the objects so referenced will survive deallocation. References reside in active environments and in a few special lists of objects such as those protected in evaluating a C routine (Section 11.3, page 422).

References in environments are created by assignments. The technique of replacement functions makes all these conceptually equivalent, by turning each replacement expression into an ordinary assignment of the value returned by the replacement function, as shown on page 466. So each assignment or replacement computes a new object and assigns that with the given name. The previously assigned object, if there was one, is not deleted but if nobody else refers to it, it's a candidate for recycling on the next garbage collection.

When replacement occurs in a loop, this simple model seems to lead to potentially large memory growth, in principle and sometimes in practice. For example, a new R programmer, totally innocent of vectorizing, might write a computation such as:

```
for(i in 2:length(x))
  x[[i]] <- (1 - eps) * x[[i]] + eps * x[[i-1]]
```

Aside from the large number of function calls involved, the description in the previous paragraph suggests we're about to allocate storage of the square of `length(x)`. Each pass through the loop reassigns x:

```
x <- `[[<-`(x, i, value = ....)
```

It seems that each such call will allocate a new object of the same length as x and leave the previously allocated version stranded until garbage collection.

Indeed, that situation is possible when the replacement function is an ordinary R function, but in this example the function `` `[[<-`() `` is a primitive that uses an extra field of information to keep allocations limited. Aside from saving a reference to the object in the environment, an assignment marks the object itself, using an internal C field `NAMED(x)`. This field has three values, defining the state of assignment of the object: 0 means that the object has not been assigned; 1 that there is one assignment of the object; 2 that there are multiple assignments of the object. Consider the computation on page 463:

```
> allObjects <- objects("package:base", all=TRUE)
> primitives <- sapply(allObjects,  ....
```

The assignment to `allObjects` takes the return value of the function call (which presumably has 0 in its `NAMED()` field) and assigns it, marking the object with 1 in the field. The same object will then be assigned in the environment of the call to sapply() as X, the first formal argument. To indicate the multiple references, the NAMED() field will be set to 2.

The distinction between single and multiple references allows C-level replacement functions to avoid extra copies. The typical code is:

```
if (NAMED(x) == 2)
    x = duplicate(x);
```

If the object is multiply assigned, it must be duplicated to protect the other references. If the local assignment is the only one, duplication is not needed, because this reference will now be to the modified object. In our hypothetical loop, it's likely that x will have multiple references on the first pass through the loop, causing a copy to be made. But the copy, after being assigned, will only have 1 in its NAMED() field. As a result, all subsequent replacements will take place without further duplication, allocating only $2n$ elements rather than $O(n^2)$.

Logic based on the NAMED() field is only available in C, and only useful if the object in question has not been automatically duplicated; therefore, the .Call() and .External() interfaces could use the mechanism, but not replacement functions written in R nor those (unlikely) using .C() or .Fortran(). This is a suitable thought on which to conclude. Such highly tuned replacement functions are attractive in making certain computations feasible in iterations on large objects (and so perhaps opening new computations for exploring such objects). Improving R for computations on large objects is an attractive extension of the system. But such computations need to be implemented very cautiously. The flexibility provided by not duplicating arguments can lead to really nasty bugs and untrustworthy software. The *Mission* and the *Prime Directive* both remain relevant.

Appendix A

Some Notes on the History of S

Why history? Mostly, because it's interesting, and puts a human face on the misleadingly abstract descriptions we all generate for our projects. These notes may suggest a little of the context and answer a few questions, such as "Why isn't "." an operator, as it is in other languages?"

The history of S has a definite starting date and place: May 5, 1976 at Bell Labs, Murray Hill, New Jersey. A group of five people began a series of informal meetings to consider designing a system for statistical computing, or possibly adopting an existing system. The system was to serve the needs of the statistics research group at Bell Labs (roughly twenty people). For the previous decade or more, the group had been using a largely Fortran-based collection of software that had evolved into an extensive library, including a graphics system called GR-Z and a variety of subroutines for numerical computations, simulation, and miscellaneous computations with data.

Figure A.1 on page 476 is a copy of what I believe was the first "graphic" at that first meeting. Coincidentally or otherwise, it also has two clues to the later evolution of S. The upper portion depicts the concept of an interface between a proposed user-level language and an "algorithm", which meant a Fortran-callable subroutine. Our research-oriented motivation mandated that the system incorporate extensibility at a fundamental level—not by any means standard for statistical systems of the time. The concept and the term "interface" have been with us ever since. The lower portion of the figure shows diagrammatically a hierarchical, list-like structure for data, the direct forerunner of lists with named components, structures with attributes

475

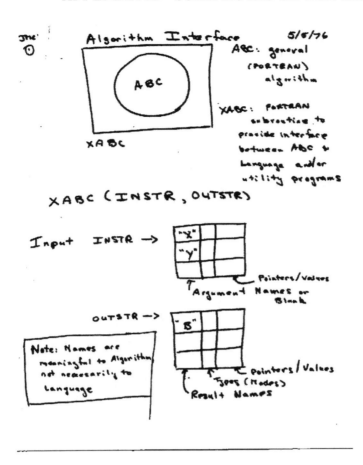

Figure A.1: First designs for a statistical system (May 5, 1976).

and eventually classes with slots.[1] The two portions of the sketch in fact lead to the themes of function calls and objects, in retrospect.

At the end of a month of meetings, the decision was to go ahead with the implementation of a system, at least experimentally. Of the five discussants, Rick Becker and John Chambers were the main implementers, with contributions at various times from a number of colleagues, and using the

---

[1]Interestingly, the Fortran code corresponding to such structures arose in a collaboration with a Bell Labs organization that later evolved into the AT&T area responsible for design and manufacture of computer chips and similar devices. It provides a good example of the Bell Labs philosophy that collaborations could actually enhance research rather than take time away from it.

existing Fortran library as an essential base. By the end of 1976, a preliminary version was available for local use. After being called "the system" for some months, and after a request for suggested names turned up none that the authors found acceptable, someone noted that all the suggestions contained the letter "S". So, partly with the precedent of the recently designed C language, we settled on that. (It took a few years to wean people from including the quotes around the name, perhaps a sign of embarrassment.)

The first version of S was implemented in a computer system that was very local, not to say weird. The withdrawal of Bell Labs from the Multics project at the end of the 1960s had left research with a main computer running a Honeywell operating system (originally from General Electric) quite different from the then-dominant IBM systems. As interest in S grew, portability was an increasing concern; specifically, the lack of portability and the huge implementation headache it presented. As it happened, early work on the UNIX operating system was going on in parallel, and facing similar issues of portability. Our rescue came with the development of a portable version of UNIX. We soon decided to make a UNIX version of S, which would then be defined to be portable, wherever UNIX was. (Numerical issues made it a little more complicated than that, but numerical analysts were concurrently developing modern models for floating-point computations, as discussed in Section 6.7, page 191.)

The initial UNIX implementation was Version 2 of S, but largely consistent with the first version. At this time, too, AT&T began licensing UNIX and S, with both university groups and third-party resellers in mind. The implications of licensing for S were crucial; now, we could begin to involve a wide group of participants including statistics groups at universities and research laboratories worldwide. These eventually included two statisticians at the University of Auckland who designed a system "not unlike S"—more on that shortly.

About ten years after the initial meetings, an essentially complete revision of S took place, incorporating ideas that at one point threatened to spawn a different, perhaps competing system. The experiences of users and ideas circulating around UNIX were additional influences. The new version, eventually labeled S3, featured dynamically generated, self-describing objects and a strong (though not strict) adherence to the ideas of "functional programming". Building on UNIX was reflected in saving objects as files, in the system() interface, and in the use of a number of tools. So the answer to why "." is not an operator is that, like UNIX, S allowed "." in names, and used an initial dot to partially hide system objects, such as .Options.

After the release of S3 and publication of *The New S Language* [1], the language remained largely backward compatible. A large-scale, ten-author effort on statistical models, accompanied by the first effort at merging the functional style of S with concepts of classes and methods, was released around 1992 and documented in *Statistical Models in S* [6]. The S3 classes and methods did not intrude deeply into the system, with the result that an implementation was grafted fairly easily on the existing software. By the same token, there was little formal support for classes and methods, and no metadata to define classes. From a technical view, the system used "instance-based methods", in that each object could have its own class attribute and therefore its own method dispatch pattern.

The next, and so far the last major design change in the language came with the S4 version, released around 1998 and documented in *Programming with Data* [5]. This introduced a new class and method system, the basis for the description in Chapters 9 and 10, although without removing the existing S3 software. By this time, use of S was sufficiently widespread that major removal of existing features was becoming difficult. The S4 version introduced as well some more specific new techniques, including connections, a C interface that could manipulate S objects (the .Call() interface), and some new object types and structures.

The other major event of the 1990s and beyond was, of course, R. In Auckland, New Zealand, Ross Ihaka and Robert Gentleman designed a system using a language largely compatible with S, but with a different evaluation model, including some features deriving from the Lisp/Scheme family of languages. The system was described in a 1996 paper [17], and soon drew wider interest. An important feature was that the new system joined the growing cadre of free or open-source software systems. As interest grew, the authors invited a new, self-managing group of volunteers to take over effective control of the system. R-core and the current approach to R were on the way.

Subsequently, R has grown and spread beyond anything the original authors of S are likely to have imagined. But that's another story. The AT&T, and subsequently Lucent, S software was purchased in 2004 by the Insightful corporation, and continues to evolve in the S-Plus system. Overall, data analysts now have a wealth of software available to them at least an order of magnitude more extensive and varied than was the case before, say, 1996. Equally gratifying to me is that the software facilities and their continued orientation towards research and towards implementing new techniques have provided researchers in many fields with a direct way to implement and share their ideas, to the benefit of the whole community.

Bibliography

[1] R. A. Becker, J. M. Chambers, and A. R. Wilks. *The New S Language.* Chapman & Hall, Boca Raton, FL, 1988.

[2] W. John Braun and Duncan J. Murdoch. *A First Course in Statistical Programming with R.* Cambridge University Press, Cambridge, 2007.

[3] Cynthia A. Brewer. *Designing Better Maps: A Guide for GIS Users.* ESRI Press, Redlands, CA, 2005.

[4] John M. Chambers. Data Management in S. Technical report, AT&T Bell Laboratories Statistics Research Report No. 99, 1991.

[5] John M. Chambers. *Programming with Data: A Guide to the S Language.* Springer, New York, 1998.

[6] John M. Chambers and Trevor Hastie, editors. *Statistical Models in S.* Chapman & Hall, Boca Raton, FL, 1992.

[7] John M. Chambers, David A. James, Diane Lambert, and Scott Vander Wiel. Monitoring networked applications using incremental quantiles. *Statistical Science*, 21:463–475, 2006.

[8] William S. Cleveland. *Elements of Graphing Data.* Hobart Press, Summit, NJ, 1985.

[9] William S. Cleveland. *Visualizing Data.* Hobart Press, Summit, NJ, 1993.

[10] D. Cook and D. F. Swayne. *Interactive and Dynamic Graphics for Data Analysis With R and GGobi.* Springer, New York, 2007.

[11] Michael J. Crawley. *Statistics: An Introduction Using R.* John Wiley & Sons, Hoboken, NJ, 2005.

[12] Peter Dalgaard. *Introductory Statistics With R*. Springer, New York, 2002.

[13] Editors of the American Heritage Dictionaries. *The American Heritage Dictionary of the English Language*. Houghton Mifflin, Boston, 4th edition, 2000.

[14] Brian S. Everitt and Torsten Hothorn. *A Handbook of Statistical Analyses Using R*. Chapman & Hall, Boca Raton, FL, 2006.

[15] Trevor Hastie, Robert Tibshirani, and Jerome Friedman. *The Elements of Statistical Learning*. Springer, New York, 2001.

[16] IEEE. IEEE Standard P1003.4 *(Real-time extensions to POSIX)*. Technical report, IEEE, New York, 1991.

[17] Ross Ihaka and Robert Gentleman. R: A language for data analysis and graphics. *Journal of Computational and Graphical Statistics*, 5:299–314, 1996.

[18] W. Kahan. Lecture Notes on the Status of IEEE Standard 754 for Binary Floating-Point Arithmetic. Technical report, Elect. Eng. & Computer Science University of California, Berkley, October 1997.

[19] Paul Murrell. *R Graphics*. Chapman & Hall, Boca Raton, FL, 2005.

[20] John North. *Stonehenge, Neolithic Man and the Cosmos*. Harper & Collins, New York, 1996.

[21] Deepayan Sarkar. *Lattice: Multivariate Data Visualization with R*. Springer, New York, 2008.

[22] G. W. Stewart. *Matrix Algorithms, Vol. I, II*. SIAM, 1998, 2001.

[23] W. N. Venables and B. D. Ripley. *Modern Applied Statistics with S*. Springer, New York, 4th edition, 2002.

[24] John Verzani. *Using R for Introductory Statistics*. Chapman & Hall, Boca Raton, FL, 2005.

[25] Larry Wall, Tom Christiansen, and Jon Orwant. *Programming Perl*. O'Reilly, Sebastopol, CA, 3rd edition, 2000.

Index

Index of **R** Functions and Documentation

Index of **R** Classes and Types

Errata and Notes for "Software for Data Analysis: Programming with R"

John M. Chambers

April 25, 2009

The following are the known errors and significant changes, as of the date above. (Glitches that just involve layout, like too much or too little white space, are omitted.) The column "Fixed" asserts that this error was (or will be) fixed in the corresponding printing. Since printings are not supposed to change the pagination of the book, errors requiring more extensive changes have sometimes not been fixed.

Many thanks to all the contributors of corrections, with special thanks to Dirk Eddelbuettel and Spencer Graves.

Chapter 1

Location		Fixed
page 1, section 1.1, line 3	"able", not "ale".	3?
pages 6 and 29	In describing licenses, it is "GNU General Public License", since the *G* in *GPL* stands for *General*.	3?

Chapter 2

Location		Fixed
page 26	The `fit <- mgcv::gam()` example is trickier than suggested. One needs to copy `mgcv::s` to the global environment, and then call it as `s(Age, k=4)`.	

Chapter 3

Location		Fixed
page 72	Replace the non-existent class name `"gpsPath"` with `"GPSTrack"`	3?
page 75	In the `recoverHandler()` listing, the call to `deparse()` should be `deparse(call)`.	3?

Chapter 4

Location		Fixed
page 79	In the last sentence of the first paragraph of section 4.1, "channel for their work $\cdots$"	3?
page 92	Second paragraph, third sentence, "your installed package".	3?
page 96	In the first bullet point, "the `DESCRIPTION()` file" should be "the `"DESCRIPTION"` file" .	3?
page 99	In the last alias: `\alias{Matrix-package}`	3?
page 106	First sentence of the `NAMESPACE` section: "$\cdots$ of your package's source".	3?

Chapter 5

Location		Fixed
page 113	Should always be `lmFit`, not `lmfit`	3?
page 114	After the `wRead` listing, "The function `wRead()` ⋯"	3?
page 126	While it's true that the two local assignment operators are equivalent, the grammar does limit the use of `` `=` ``, not allowing things like `if(x = 1)`	
pages 127-130	To be consistent, all instances of `getQ` should capitalize `Q`. Also, the definition in both cases should call `doQuantile()`, not `recompute()` when the `dataBuf` is not empty, and on page 129, `probs` should be `IQ$probs`. See the files `"IQclosure.R"` and `"IQreplace.R"` in the `Examples` directory of the `SoDA` package.	3?
page 133	Second paragraph, first sentence ends with an unwanted ";".	3?
page 133	The `swivel.com` web site changed its setup, invalidating our example. The example has been changed to use my own web site.	3?

Chapter 6

Location		Fixed
page 173	Before the first `evalq()` example, "The strict way to evaluate `diff(Time)` ⋯"	3?
page 180	The `SQL` `WHERE` clause should use =, not ==.	3?
page 209	Second paragraph, " ⋯ but only `ncol-1` otherwise."	3?
page 232	In the example, `seqn2 <- seq(along = g21)`	3?
page 234	Last paragraph, "(pseudo-)random", with the parentheses on the upper line.	3?

Chapter 7

Location		Fixed
page 239	After the bullet item: "the lattice package both ···"	3?
page 247	The example should subtract a small amount from the first element of the quantiles to avoid NA corresponding to min(resids).	3?
page 249	In the example, xy$X and xy$Y should be xy[, "X"] and xy[, "Y"].	3?
page 252	plotGPSTrack() should call arrowColors() to agree with the definition above.	3?
Pages 259-260	To be consistent with ColorBrewer, change all occurrences of *divergent scale* to *diverging scale*.	3?
page 273	**Positioning** ··· section, second paragraph: "But within a particular graphics object, ···"	3?
page 276	The plot is slightly incorrect, in not maintaining the aspect ratio of 1 for x and y distances (should be about 20% higher). The gridSegments.R example in version 1.0-4 and later of the SoDA package gets it nearly right.	3?

Chapter 8

Location		Fixed
page 291, top	"objects provide one mechanism."	3?
page 294, second line	"only used 7 of the bits"	3?
page 297, top	The function is readLines(), not readLInes().	3?
page 302	The definition of nameRegexp is not bullet-proof if the text in question could be a number starting wth ".", such as .1. This doesn't affect the example on the next page, but where relevant, computations should first check that the text does *not* match the pattern for a number.	
page 318, top	Should say "··· idiom of $$tref{$chunk}".	3?
page 320	Should always be scanText(), not scantext()	3?

Chapter 9

Location		Fixed
page 339	Second line: "transforms x"	3?
section 9.6 and page 353	Various comments in this section deprecate S4 classes that extend (contain) S3 classes, in particular asserting that S3 methods won't work. Starting with version 2.8.0 of R, support is provided for such extensions. The section will be rewritten to reflect this and give more encouragement for extending S3 classes. See ?Classes, ?S3Class and ?setOldClass.	3?
page 362	The definition of validTrackObject is missing braces and the first line, `x <- object@x; y <- object@y`	3?
page 365	After the paragraph "If you want to convert ···", add the sentence: "Note that the function is used here as a function, not an S3 method; therefore, S3 mechanisms such as nextMethod() must be eliminated or changed to S4 mechanisms."	

Chapter 10

Location		Fixed
pages 385-386 and 399	From version 2.8.0 on, the "..." argument can be used in some generic function signatures.	3?
page 392	Middle of the page, it's "more reliable", not "more more"	3?
page 399	Section on nonstandard generic functions: a more precise statement of the requirement is "a successful call eventually calls standardGeneric()"	3?
page 402, bottom	Note that the output of this example has been edited to remove printing. It will be more verbose if you run it.	
page 405	End of first paragraph: "in the SoDA package".	3?

Chapter 11

Location		Fixed
page 416, bottom (and 482)	The author's correct name is "Dirk Eddelbuettel".	3?
page 423	After the sentence "To turn character ⋯ mkChar()", add a footnote: "Readers who have followed the .C() version of this example in the previous section may now ask why that version works, since it casually assigns an arbitrary string in the output. Fortunately, the interface code for .C() arranges to call mkchar() on all strings before returning."	

Chapter 12

Location		Fixed
page 441	The code for the gbm package, including the C++ code, was all written by Greg Ridgeway.	3?

Chapter 13

Location		Fixed
page 456	For the regular expression see the correction for page 302	
page 469	Table 13.1, in the "Function" line, *expr*, not expr.	3?
page 470	Under *sublist*, last sentence: "because the interpretation ..."	3?